Law and Practice in the Age of Reform

MEDIEVAL CHURCH STUDIES

VOLUME 17

LAW AND PRACTICE IN THE AGE OF REFORM

The Legatine Work of Hugh of Die (1073–1106)

by

Kriston R. Rennie

BREPOLS

British Library Cataloguing in Publication Data

Rennie, Kriston R.
Law and practice in the age of reform : the legatine work of Hugh of Die (1073-1106). -- (Medieval church studies ; v. 17)
1. Hugh, of Die, 1040-1106. 2. Papal legates--France. 3. Catholic Church--France--Bishops. 4. Canon law--History--To 1500. 5. Ecclesiastical law--France--History--To 1500. 6. Church history--11th century.
I. Title II. Series
262.9'09021-dc22

ISBN-13: 9782503531908

D/2010/0095/115
ISBN: 978-2-503-53190-8

Printed in the USA on acid-free paper

To my mother and father

Contents

Acknowledgements

This book originally began as a Doctorate of Philosophy at the University of Southampton under Timothy Reuter, only to be completed at King's College London with Jinty Nelson. Its subject matter, which has developed significantly since its inception, would never have materialized without the former's intuition and generosity, nor would it have taken shape without the latter's critical enquiry and guidance. Since the examination of my dissertation to the present day, I have gathered even more debts, not all of them academic. The Pontifical Institute of Mediaeval Studies in Toronto awarded me a fellowship in 2006–07, providing an ideal base from which to write this book and exposing me to a vibrant academic life and intellectual community as well. I owe a great deal to my former colleagues and peers in Toronto, from whose friendship and ideas I continually benefit. Along those same lines of gratitude, my tenure at Goodenough College in London from 2003 to 2005 provided more than just subsidized shelter during the course of my PhD; it also helped in cementing some lifelong friendships.

On an individual basis, I wish to thank especially the constant encouragement of Kathleen Cushing, Joseph Goering, the anonymous reviewer(s) of this manuscript, and many others who have read, heard, commented on, and in some way contributed to the final development of this book. My deepest and most sincere gratitude, however, must go to my parents, whose unfettered support has never faltered over the years. To them this book is dedicated. No less deserving of such praise is my wife, Megan, who has been with me from the very beginning, which — without saying too much — says a great deal. In all, the patience, understanding, and inspiration of family members and friends have helped considerably in bringing this study to publication. In recalling my reasons for studying medieval history in the first place, and my continued resilience to pursue another profession, I am grateful to the institutions, libraries, communities, and individuals in Lethbridge, St Andrews, Ottawa, London, Toronto, Dunedin, and Brisbane for every piece of advice and wisdom that was ever given.

The arguments in this book have been presented, in various forms and stages of development, at the Institute of Historical Research in London in 2005; the International Congress of Medieval Studies in Kalamazoo, Michigan, in 2007; the International Medieval Congress at Leeds in 2008; the XIII International Congress of Medieval Canon Law in Esztergom, Hungary, in 2008; and to the Australia and New Zealand Association of Medieval and Early Modern Studies in Hobart, Tasmania, in 2008. Some arguments have also appeared in the *Journal of Medieval History, History, Revue d'histoire ecclésiastique, Annuarium historiae conciliorum, Revue de droit français et étranger*, the *Bulletin of Medieval Canon Law*, and *Zeitschrift der Savigny-Stiftung für Rechtsgeschichte, Kanonistische Abteilung.*

—Kriston R. Rennie
University of Queensland,
Brisbane, Australia
August 2010

Abbreviations

74T	*Diversorum patrum sententie sive Collectio in LXXIV titulos digesta*, ed. by John Gilchrist (Vatican City: Biblioteca Apostolica Vaticana, 1973). English translation: *The Collection in Seventy-four Titles: A Canon Law Manual of the Gregorian Reform*, ed. and trans. by John Gilchrist (Toronto: Pontifical Institute of Mediaeval Studies, 1980)
Acta pont. Rom.	*Acta pontificum Romanorum inedita*, ed. by J. Pflugk-Harttung, 3 vols (Tübingen: Fuess, 1880–88)
Amatus of Oloron	*Epistolae*, in *RHGF*, XIV (1806), 762–76
DA	*Deutsches Archiv für Erforschung des Mittelalters*
Ep. vag.	*The 'Epistolae vagantes' of Pope Gregory VII*, trans. by H. E. J. Cowdrey (Oxford: Clarendon Press, 1972)
GC	*Gallia Christiana*, 16 vols (Paris: Palmé, 1715–1865)
Hefele-Leclercq	Charles Joseph Hefele and H. Leclercq, *Histoire des conciles*, 12 vols (Paris: Letouzey, 1907–52)
Hinschius	*Decretales Pseudo-Isidorianae et capitula Angilramni*, ed. by P. Hinschius (Leipzig: Tauchnitz, 1863; repr. Aalen: Scientia, 1963)
Hugh of Die, PL, CLVII	*Epistolae et privilegia*, in PL, CLVII (1898), cols 507–28
Hugh of Die, *RHGF*, XIV	*Epistolae Hugonis Diensis episcopi*, in *RHGF*, XIV (1806), 776–96

Hugh of Flavigny	*Chronicon Hugonis monachi virdunensis et divionensis abbatis Flaviacensis*, ed. by G. H. Pertz, MGH, SS, 8 (1848), pp. 288–502
Ivo of Chartres, PL, CLXII	*Epistolae*, in *Sancti Ivonis Carnotensis Episcopi opera omnia*, PL, CLXII (1854), cols 1–287
JEH	*Journal of Ecclesiastical History*
JL	*Regesta pontificum Romanorum*, ed. by P. Jaffé, 2nd edn ed. by W. Wattenbach and others, 2 vols (Leipzig: Veit, 1885–88)
Labbe	*Sacrosancta concilia ad regiam editionem exacta*, ed. by Philippe Labbe, 16 vols (Paris: Societatis typographicae librorum ecclesiasticorum jussu regis constitutae, 1671–72), X (1671)
Mansi	*Sacrorum conciliorum nova et amplissima collectio*, ed. by J. D. Mansi, 31 vols (Florence: Apud Antonium Zatta, 1759–98)
MGH	Monumenta Germaniae Historica (Hannover: Hahn, 1826–)
Briefe	Die Briefe der deustchen Kaiserzeit
Libelli	Libelli de lite imperatorum et pontificum saeculis XI et XII conscripti
Schriften	Schriften der MGH
SRG	Scriptores rerum Germanicarum
SS	Scriptores
NCMH	*The New Cambridge Medieval History*, ed. by Paul Fouracre and others, 7 vols in 8 books (Cambridge: Cambridge University Press, 1995–2004)
PL	*Patrologia cursus completus [...] series Latina*, ed. by Jacques-Paul Migne, 221 vols (Paris: Garnier, 1844–1902)

RDC	*Revue de droit canonique*
Reg.	*Das Register Gregors VII*, ed. by Erich Caspar, MGH, Epistolae Selectae, 2, 2 vols (1920–23). English Translation: *The Register of Pope Gregory VII*, trans. by H. E. J. Cowdrey (Oxford: Clarendon Press, 2002)
RH	*Revue historique*
RHDFE	*Revue historique de droit français et étranger*
RHE	*Revue d'histoire ecclésiastique*
RHEF	*Revue d'histoire de l'église de France*
RHGF	*Recueil des historiens des Gaules et de la France*, ed. by M. Bouquet, 24 vols (Paris: Palmé, 1738–1904)
RQH	*Revue des questions historiques*
SG	*Studi Gregoriani*
Urban II, PL, CLI	*Beati Urbani II Pontificis Romani epistolae et privilegia*, PL, CLI (1844), cols 283–560
Urban II, *RHGF*, XIV	*Epistolae*, in *RHGF*, XIV (1806), 688–737
ZRG kan. Abt.	*Zeitschrift der Savigny-Stiftung für Rechtsgeschichte, Kanonistische Abteilung*

Chapter 1

INTRODUCTION

Over the course of his twelve-year pontificate, from 1073 to 1085, Pope Gregory VII sought to deliver the Roman Church from 'servile oppression or, rather, tyrannical servitude, and restore her to her original liberty'.[1] Transforming reforming objectives into practical realities was for him a matter of translating 'abstract principles into concrete governmental actions'.[2] In France,[3] as elsewhere in Christendom during the last quarter of the eleventh century, this ultimate objective was realized by countering clerical unchastity, marriage, and concubinage (nicolaitism), the buying and selling of ecclesiastical offices and prebends (simony), and lay interference and investiture — the three main and well-known tenets of church reform. But in no way were

[1] *Das Register Gregors VII*, ed. by Erich Caspar, MGH, Epistolae Selectae, 2, 2 vols (1920–23); trans. by H. E. J. Cowdrey, *The Register of Pope Gregory VII, 1073–1085* (Oxford: Clarendon Press, 2002) (hereafter *Reg.*), VIII. 12: 'ut in restauratione illius antiquitus sancte ecclesie omnes unanimiter consensum et pro posse adiutorium tribuentes eam de servili oppressione immo tyrranica servitute eripere et prisce libertati restituere'.

[2] Walter Ullmann, *The Growth of Papal Government in the Middle Ages* (London: Methuen, 1955), p. 262; cf. Karl Leyser, *Medieval Germany and its Neighbours, 900–1250* (London: Hambledon, 1982), pp. 155, 157.

[3] Determining the geographical limits of the kingdom of France in the mid-eleventh century is a complicated procedure. In the north, the diocese of Cambrai had always been part of the province of Reims (the kingdom of France) as well as politically of the kingdom of Germany. In the west, Brittany and Flanders are likewise considered within this scope; so too is the kingdom of Burgundy, which was politically a part of the empire, but to which region the see of Lyon and the see of Die belonged. The southern borders are separated from Spain by the ecclesiastical province of Narbonne, the regions of Aquitaine and Gascony, and the northern borders by the county of Champagne.

these developments efficiently or easily achieved; nor were they innovations of Gregory's pontificate. Developing and extending the existing papal machinery to enforce and uphold the papal programme in face of existing and steadfast opposition, Gregory sought to 'implement what he saw as the principal demands, both spiritual and moral, of the Christian religion in the age during which he lived'.[4]

One of the papacy's most efficient weapons for reaching these objectives was the effective use of papal legates. These agents of reform, or 'disciple officials' as Max Weber would have argued, were 'selected in terms of their official qualifications, status, or personal dependence'.[5] Doubtless, it was to these chosen few that a majority of church business was directed. And it was thanks to a few figures in particular that the reformers' programme of ecclesiastical renewal and liberty was implemented (in part) and disseminated successfully north of the Alps. In transferring leadership to these trusted and energetic agents of reform, commissioning them to specified regions while endowing them with full papal authority, the papacy greatly enhanced its opportunity for social contacts in the more distant provinces of Western Christendom.

Under Gregory VII, church reformers came to rely on papal legates more and more as instruments for relieving both administrative and legislative pressures. In this pursuit, there was hardly a greater instrument through which reforming principles could be diffused more readily, and where papal policy could be implemented more strongly, than the legatine council. In truth, this assembly provided the papal government with an 'arena for transforming papal theory into action'.[6] Empowered by the Pope to convene councils in the regions beyond Rome, the office of legation began to exercise a much larger role in church administration, developing as adjudicator in matters of litigation, while the holding of councils underwent 'important developments which were to stamp a new form of papal

[4] H. E. J. Cowdrey, *Pope Gregory VII* (Oxford: Clarendon Press, 1998), p. 508.

[5] I. S. Robinson, 'The Friendship Network of Gregory VII', *History*, 63 (1978), 1–22 (pp. 5–6); cf. Max Weber, *Economy and Society*, ed. by Guenther Roth and Claus Wittich, 2 vols (Berkeley and Los Angeles: University of California Press, 1978), II, 111–50; Reinhard Bendix, *Max Weber: An Intellectual Portrait* (Berkeley and Los Angeles: University of California Press, 1966), p. 295.

[6] Robert Somerville, 'Cardinal Stephan of St Grisogono: Some Remarks on Legates and Legatine Councils in the Eleventh Century', in *Law, Church and Society: Essays in Honor of Stephan Kuttner*, ed. by Kenneth Pennington and Robert Somerville (Philadelphia: University of Pennsylvania Press, 1977), pp. 157–66 (p. 157).

authority on the church'.[7] Eleventh-century legates, as Richard Southern wrote, were making 'lengthy perambulations over wide areas, taking up in their course whatever business came to hand. They held councils, heard disputes, pronounced judgement and remitted to Rome matters which could be brought to no conclusion on the spot.'[8] In the last quarter of the eleventh century, there was hardly any council, apart from those too insignificant to interest the papacy, which did not involve legates. The council arena and its presider, the legate, developed collaboratively as effective papal instruments, forever shaping both the governing of church law and its application in the field.

Without a forum in which to conduct legislative business, therefore, the legate's role would have served no greater purpose or threat than that of a papal letter or messenger. It was the council arena that created the opportunity, but more crucially the necessary legal platform for legates to implement reform policy and extend papal influence. One might even go so far as to suggest that councils were proof of the need for reform; they were assemblies motivated by the political, religious, and legal events of the time. And the legate's application of the law and reform in examining the numerous cases brought before him presents the inevitable outcome of his conciliar participation.

Yet while the dispatching of papal legates to areas beyond Rome was a 'venerable custom'[9] by the second half of the eleventh century, their administrative and representative function in provincial-like councils was not yet clearly delineated. In practice, the legatine office was still an *ad hoc* institution; the legate's role became more formalized and structured only through increasing experience and use. There was no other branch of the papal machinery that possessed the wherewithal, the authority, and the legal knowledge to root itself right in the midst of provincial politics. It was to the legatine office that Gregory VII entrusted a greater part of his reform initiative, and it was his influence in mobilizing, regulating, and supervising this office that has led modern historians to recognize it as distinctly 'Gregorian' in nature and function.

Struggling to administer the vast and distant regions of Christendom, to manage the innumerable ecclesiastical cases that were filtering into Rome from the provinces, and more generally in coming to terms with the inadequacies of his government, Gregory placed increasing confidence in what was for him the most

[7] Richard W. Southern, *The Making of the Middle Ages* (London: Hutchinson, 1953), p. 141.

[8] Southern, *Making of the Middle Ages*, p. 142.

[9] Somerville, 'Cardinal Stephan of St Grisogono', p. 157.

reliable administrative branch capable of conveying sound papal judgement. Legates of this period acted as itinerant courts and judges, instruments sent to the scene of a dispute for extending papal influence to the threshold (*ad limina*) of Western Christendom. They were in essence preservers of justice, 'empowered to bring action against those who violated church law, and at the same time as judges, commissioned to hear and decide cases in the pope's name and with the force of papal authority'.[10]

This book examines the legatine work of one such reforming figure — by far the most active, itinerant, and influential member of the church reform movement in France: Hugh (Hugo), Bishop of Die (1073–82), Archbishop of Lyon (1082–1106), and papal legate to Gregory VII (1075–85) and Urban II (1094–99). In reconstructing Hugh's legatine and conciliar activity in the regions of his jurisdiction (i.e., northern France and Burgundy), new light is shed on the many relevant and often confused issues surrounding eleventh-century legates, councils, and the law — three inextricable components of church administration and reform. Most significant is the fact that Hugh of Die's legatine work provides a rare and firsthand account of law in practice, offering a crucial context in which to assess the reformers' impact and success in France during the 1070s and 1080s. His councils at Anse (1075), Dijon (1076), Clermont (1076), Autun (1077), Poitiers (1078), Bordeaux (1079), Valence (1079), Toulouse (1079), Avignon (1080), Lyon (1080), Issoudun (1081), Saintes (1081), and Meaux (1082) epitomize his legatine activity; they represent the most time-consuming, active, and controversial aspects of his ecclesiastical career; they signify the arena where he wielded the greatest legal authority for inculcating religious, moral, and spiritual change, where he shared in part the pope's authority for the instruction of the faithful, and where he could carry out church reform most forcefully and effectively by his own standards, all the time tempered by the extant canon law.

In the wider context of eleventh-century ecclesiastical, social, and legal history, the following study examines Hugh of Die's role as an instrument of papal policy. As will be seen throughout, Hugh's efforts in promulgating and disseminating reform were shaped significantly by his council activity. The manner in which he conducted this business sheds light on every aspect of his work, revealing not only his personal interpretation and application of the law, but also his vigour in suppressing clerical marriage, the selling of church offices, lay investiture (to a lesser extent), and the gravity with which he conducted his duties as legate. New light is cast on Hugh's personality and achievements by looking at the nature and

[10] James A. Brundage, *Medieval Canon Law* (London: Longman, 1995), p. 42.

influence of his legatine and legal activity in France — qualities that can be appreciated best in light of the ferment of activity during Gregory's pontificate. The dialectical relationship between reform and law in eleventh-century France is a recurring theme throughout this investigation, illustrating in more demonstrable terms the flow of ecclesiastical business between the papal court in Rome and France and vice versa.

We begin our study, therefore, by examining Hugh's ecclesiastical career *c.* 1073–1106, providing the fullest possible account from available contemporary sources, concentrating primarily on the period of his first legation, from 1075 to 1085 (Chapter 2). Following this overture is a complete analysis of the legatine office under Gregory VII, documenting key historical and legal developments of this representative office in the 1070s and 1080s, focusing especially on matters of authority, power, and jurisdiction (Chapter 3). Attention is then given to some fine distinctions in the legatine application of the law (i.e., law and reform in theory and practice), as the reformers treated and understood it, revealing the idiosyncratic nature of legatine councils and the papacy's reliance on obedience and a uniform interpretation of the law (Chapter 4). Extending from this is an analysis on the legal education and training of Gregorian legates that ultimately shaped Hugh's legatine and conciliar methods (Chapter 5). In short, the first five chapters of this book examine how effective legates were for extending eleventh-century reform policy and legislation, and how developed the machinery of papal legation was under Gregory VII to suit the reformers' administrative and legal needs.

Chapter 6 examines Hugh of Die's application of reform in the regions of his assigned jurisdiction, seeking to clarify the hazy role that reforming legates played in transmitting and disseminating the extant law to France in the last quarter of the eleventh century. The papal reform initiative in France is re-evaluated in this regard, focusing on the reformers' approach towards countering a disobedient clergy, assessing also their legal impact in disseminating Gregorian policies among the French episcopate and lay elite in the late 1070s and early 1080s. Using Hugh of Die as an *exemplar*, the three reforming tenets of simony, nicolaitism, and lay investiture are given greatest attention, evaluating in three separate sections the obstacles that these abuses posed to the church in France, and the reformers at large. The laity's role in extending and promoting the reform movement precedes an analysis of dispute settlement and all other ecclesiastical business that fell within the purview of the 'Gregorian' legate.

Drawing extensively from Hugh of Die's thirteen legatine councils under Gregory VII, this legate's activities are set firmly within the overall social, political, and legal context of France in the late eleventh century. From the conciliar events described below comes a greater sense also of Hugh's relationship with various ecclesiastical and lay magnates throughout France, and most crucially with the pope in Rome, exhibiting firsthand his familiarity and use of the extant canon law — instruments through which church reform was being disseminated and implemented actively in the late eleventh century.

By examining more closely Gregory VII's use of the legatine office and Hugh of Die's energetic conciliar activity in France, the gap between the reformers' grand designs and their means of execution is narrowed significantly. In moving away from Gregory VII's 'radical actions' — such as his deposition and excommunication of King Henry IV of Germany in 1076 and 1080 — historians can now examine the 'contribution made by personalities to the reform movement, not merely on the papal side, but across the spectrum of reforms'.[11] The following book, assessing the localized, grassroots application of law and reform in France through Hugh of Die's conciliar activity, is one step in this direction. It will become clear to the reader that Gregory VII was not so much an innovator in reforming ideology. However, his efforts and ability to transform reform ideas into reality made him, at least with regards to the legatine office, an innovator in the field of papal institutions.

Why France?

Admittedly, each region of Christendom in the late eleventh century presented particular challenges to the reformers' aims, which in turn often demanded individual, local, or regional attention. Outside of Italy, the church in France was by far the largest and most accessible target for the reform movement. In no other country, as Friedrich Kempf contended, 'was the reform so energetically pushed as in France'.[12] Indeed, Gregory VII's concern with French affairs marks a central theme of his pontificate, making up nearly one-third of his entire letter collection. As Jean Gaudemet has calculated, 123 of the *Register*'s 390 letters and 35 of the 76 *Epistolae vagantes* show very plainly the importance that Gregory placed on

[11] John Gilchrist, *Canon Law in the Age of Reform, 11th–12th Centuries* (Aldershot: Ashgate, 1993), pp. xv–xvi.

[12] *Handbook of Church History*, ed. by Friedrich Kempf and others, III: *The Church in the Age of Feudalism*, trans. by Anselm Biggs (London: Burn and Oates, 1969), p. 378.

French affairs.[13] While the inclusion of these letters in the *Register* is no guarantee of their being dispatched or ever reaching their addressee, these records nevertheless illustrate the diversity and character of papal business to this region. Gregory's contact with French magnates was often for safeguarding the rights of St Peter and obedience to the precepts of the Roman Church; his concern with the obedience of the French episcopate, well documented in letters addressed to various churches and churchmen, shows his concern for the spiritual and moral welfare of the Christian faithful in France. From hindsight, these figures reflect the frequency with which the Pope was addressing, or often forced to address, that region.

Of course, the reformers' interest in France can be seen much earlier than Gregory VII's pontificate. The Peace and Truce of God councils of the late tenth and early eleventh century are often credited with shaping the spiritual and social character of this later reform movement. The decrees issued at the councils of Charroux (989) in the first instance, and at the later-held councils of Narbonne (990), Le Puy (990 and 994), Anse (994), Limoges (997), Poitiers (1000 and 1014), Elne-Toulouges (1027), and Bourges (1031), among others, are revealing for their devotion to defining proper clerical and lay behaviour.[14] Serving to protect church property, privileges, and persons, restricting also the patterns of legitimate warfare on the warring aristocratic social class (*bellatores*), these councils sought to establish a standard of personal and moral liberty — objectives that parallel very closely the reformers' ambitions in the second half of the eleventh century.

As H. E. J. Cowdrey has argued, these regional councils played a 'vital part by creating in France a milieu within which the reformed papacy came to be, on the whole, quietly accepted by the French church'.[15] Pope Leo IX's Council of Reims in 1049 offers an exceptional example in this regard, as it was at this meeting that the peace movement was first pronounced in the universal legal setting of a papal council. Significantly, it was also at this council that the main tenets of church reform were first promulgated in legislative terms. In issuing decrees against simony and nicolaitism, the Pope laid the foundations for successive reformers, defining in explicitly legal terms the boundaries of expected clerical and lay behaviour. These foundations surely influenced later figures like Gregory VII and Hugh of

[13] Jean Gaudemet, 'Grégoire VII et la France', *SG*, 13 (1989), 213–40 (p. 214).

[14] See Odette Pontal, *Les Conciles de la France capétienne jusqu'en 1215* (Paris: Cerf, 1995), pp. 119–42.

[15] H. E. J. Cowdrey, 'The Peace and Truce of God in the Eleventh Century', *Past and Present*, 46 (1970), 42–67 (p. 54).

Die, helping to define more clearly their primary reforming targets, while sharpening their legal methods for rooting out these rampant clerical and lay abuses.[16]

As these earlier councils attest, the clergy was not alone in its attempts at ecclesiastical renewal and liberty. The laity, as will be seen below in more detail, was an essential audience for the reception of reforming legislation in France. Furthermore, they assumed a vital role in disseminating and enforcing this legislation in the various principalities, duchies, and counties beyond the grasp of the king's political control. While in the ninth century the Carolingian emperors Charlemagne (r. 800–14) and Louis the Pious (r. 814–40) 'had been the effective masters of the church in west Francia',[17] successive kings of France struggled to assert their control as heads of a church. The division of royal rights among the lay elite in the tenth and eleventh centuries meant that 'most of the bishoprics were in the gift and under the suzerainty of the magnates'.[18] And episcopal appointments, not to mention the granting of cathedral churches, lands, and jurisdictions, were often the result of this vassalage.

But the history of the Capetian dynasty (987–1328) nevertheless saw many bishoprics placed directly under royal control, furthering the king's participation and role in the churches comprising his kingdom. 'Even at their weakest', as Elizabeth Hallam noted, 'the early Capetians still controlled more bishoprics and key monasteries than any other great lord in France.'[19] By the time that Philip I came to power in 1060, the king's ecclesiastical domain consisted of the episcopal sees of Chartres, Orléans, Paris, Meaux, Sens, Troyes, and Auxerre (all in the province of Sens); Beauvais, Senlis, Soissons, Noyon-Tournai, Laon, Reims, Châlons-sur-Marne, Thérouanne, and Amiens (in the province of Reims); Langres, Mâcon, and Châlon-sur-Saône (province of Lyon); and Le Puy (province of Bourges). Added to this group were the archbishoprics of Bourges and Tours acquired under Philip I, earning the King much criticism from the reformers for his attempt to assert royal influence.[20]

[16] Kathleen G. Cushing, *Reform and Papacy in the Eleventh Century: Spirituality and Social Change* (Manchester: Manchester University Press, 2005), p. 67.

[17] Elizabeth M. Hallam, *Capetian France, 987–1328* (London: Longman, 1980), p. 86.

[18] Robert Fawtier, *The Capetian Kings of France: Monarchy and Nation (987–1328)*, trans. by Lionel Butler and R. J. Adam (London: Macmillan, 1960), p. 71.

[19] Hallam, *Capetian France*, p. 86.

[20] See Alfons Becker, *Studien zum Investiturproblem in Frankreich: Papsttum, Königtum und Episkopat im Zeitalter der gregorianischen Kirchenreform (1049–1119)*, Schriften der Universität des Saarlandes (Saarbrücken: West-Ost, 1955), pp. 21–25.

For the clergy and laity alike, the lynchpin for successful reform in France, as elsewhere in Western Christendom, rested heavily on the notion of obedience (*obedientia*). For Gregory VII and his papal predecessors, this understanding was founded presumably on a spiritual and moral understanding of the Holy Scripture: 'To obey is better than sacrifice and to hearken than the fat of rams' (I Sam. 15. 22). Alternatively, disobedience (*disobedientia*) to the precepts of church law, righteousness, and justice (*iustitia*), was considered tantamount to heresy: 'For rebellion is as the sin of witchcraft, and stubbornness is as iniquity and idolatry' (I Sam. 15. 23).[21] This Old Testament passage is cited nineteen times in Gregory's letters, each time in reference to those men who refused to obey or assist in reforming the church according to the Pope's reforming principles.[22] Walter Ullmann interpreted it as 'the hallmark of the Christian and particularly of the Christian prince',[23] suggesting that an unquestioned obedience to the authority of the Roman Church and to its representative the pope represented a legalization of the faith. Any Christian who knowingly disobeyed the norms of living (*norma iustitiae*) therefore could not be considered a true, orthodox Catholic.[24] Thus for Gregory, *obedientia* was the fundamental theory upon which justice and righteousness was founded.

This meaning may also have borne some resemblance to the sixth-century monastic Rule of St Benedict, linking obedience to the first grade of humility, associating an individual's concern with the glory of eternal life with submission to a greater, divine hierarchy.[25] But in practice, Gregory sought obedience most

[21] See *The 'Epistolae vagantes' of Pope Gregory VII*, trans. by H. E. J. Cowdrey (Oxford: Clarendon Press, 1972) (hereafter *Ep. vag.*), letters 10 and 32 for the verbatim reference.

[22] See *Reg.*, II. 45 (1075), 66 (1075), 75 (1075); IV. 1 (1076), 2 (1076), 11 (1076), 23 (1077), 24 (1077); VI. 10 (1078), 11 (1078); twice in VII. 14a (1080), 16 (1080), 24 (1080); VIII. 15 (1080); IX. 20 (1082), 35 (1083); *Ep. vag.*, letters 10 and 33.

[23] Ullmann, *Growth of Papal Government*, p. 284.

[24] *Reg.*, II. 55a, sentence 26: 'Quod catholicus non habeatur, qui non concordat Romane ecclesie.'

[25] The Rule of St Benedict: 'Primus humilitatis gradus est obedientia sine mora. Haec convenit iis qui nihil sibi Christo carius existimant. Propter servitium sanctum quod professi sunt, seu propter metum gehennae, vel gloriam vitae aeternae, mox ut aliquid imperatum a majore fuerit, ac si divinitus imperetur, moram pati nesciunt in faciendo. De quibus Dominus dicit: In auditu auris obedivit mihi. Et item dicit doctoribus: Qui vos audit, audit me.' See *Reg.*, VII. 6; cf. H. E. J. Cowdrey, 'The Spirituality of Pope Gregory VII', in *The Mystical Tradition and the Carthusians*, ed. by James Hogg, Analecta cartusiana, 1 (Salzburg: Institut für Anglistik und Amerikanistik Universität Salzburg, 1995), pp. 1–22 (pp. 2, 19). See also Karl Josef Benz, 'Die

efficiently through friendship and alliance, and in his judicious approach to tempering the extant canon law. He 'established and maintained close contact with a potentially useful agent by means of letters, visits by papal legates, but above all — if possible — by a personal meeting in Rome'.[26] Methods such as these were used to increase fidelity to St Peter and to his successor(s).[27] In essence, Gregory was always searching for potential allies for his reform movement, and available lay or ecclesiastical members had to be assured that there was something in it for them before they would commit themselves entirely to supporting the reformers' objectives. The application and dissemination of reform and law was Gregory's foremost priority, actively soliciting obedience from members of the local clerical and lay elite — a measure inextricably aimed at extending social contacts beyond the papacy's more immediate control of Rome and the Campagna.

The ideology of eleventh-century church reform is not so much under scrutiny here as the rhetoric that it has produced. Its meaning — the idea of restoring ancient discipline — had become Gregory VII's flagship, often returning to and drawing on the moralizing and polemical writings of Pope Gregory the Great (590–604) for purposes of authority, custom, tradition, and defence.[28] What

Regula Benedictini in den Briefen Papst Gregors VII.', in *Itinera Domini: Gesammelte Aufsätze aus Liturgie und Mönchtum* (Münster: Aschendorff, 1988), pp. 263–79, especially p. 278. As the title of this article indicates, Benz examines the presence of Benedictine allusions in the correspondence of Gregory VII, finding ten letters with a total of nineteen allusions. These are *Reg.*, II. 12, to Bishop Burchard II of Halberstadt (26 October 1074) and VII. 5, to King Harold Hein of Denmark (15 October 1079) (likened to the Rule of St Benedict (RB), 72. 10); *Reg.*, VII. 5 (ibid.) and VII. 6, to King Alphonso VI of Léon-Castile (15 October 1079) (RB, 2. 30. 33); *Reg.*, III. 21, to Hammadid, the Emir of an-Nāsir, king of the province of Mauretania Sitifensis in Africa (later in 1076) (RB, 4. 9); *Ep. vag.*, 12, to all the abbots and superiors of religious houses in France (1075) (RB, 61. 14, and respectfully 70. 7); *Reg.*, VI. 1, to all the faithful clergy and laity in Germany (1 July 1078) (RB, 72. 9); *Reg.*, VI. 7, to Hugh of Die (25 November 1078) (RB, 27. 5. 8–9); *Ep. vag.*, 65, to King Sancho Ramirez of Aragon (1076–85) (RB, 4. 47); *Reg.* I. 33, to the monks of the monastery of S. Maria di Butrio (28 November 1073) (RB, 27. 5); *Reg.* I. 37, to Countess Adelaide of Turin (7 December 1073) (RB, Prologue 4 and 22).

[26] Robinson, 'Friendship Network', p. 2. On the idea of obedience as it relates to episcopal authority, see particularly I. S. Robinson, '*Periculoso Homo*: Pope Gregory VII and Episcopal Authority', *Viator*, 9 (1978), 103–31 (pp. 111–13).

[27] See *Reg.*, I. 19.

[28] Paul of Bernried, in his *Life of Gregory VII* (in *The Papal Reform of the Eleventh Century: Lives of Pope Leo IX and Pope Gregory VII*, trans. by I. S. Robinson (Manchester: Manchester University Press, 2004), pp. 262–364) begins his biography with the words 'Gregory VII, therefore, on whom the spirit of Gregory I truly rested', clearly suggesting some likeness between

Gregory VII actually knew about the state of that primitive church, however, is questionable; but his genuine intention to adhere closely to the canonical principles created and practised by his namesake leaves the impression that he considered himself to have possessed a clear picture of sixth-century spiritual and moral objectives. He continually asserted an ambivalent attitude in claiming 'to introduce nothing novel, nothing of our own devising', seeking 'only what the salvation of all men and their necessity duly demand'.[29] His theories, however, and those of his followers were anachronistic; as Karl Leyser noted, they 'challenged custom, tradition, and established practices with their own vision of the past and the argument of lasting truth'.[30]

Because of his close adherence to the traditions and customs established by his papal predecessors, Gregory's reception into the canon law of the twelfth and thirteenth centuries is scarcely evident.[31] This is due primarily to Gregory's citing of historical precedents — his ability and favour to improve on the decrees of the Church Fathers for the purposes of necessity or use — derived from the already established decretals (both genuine and false) and canons that comprised basic church legislation. The Pope's intentions were to conserve and strengthen the Christian notion of law (*ius*) and justice (*iustitia*) for the pragmatic purpose of achieving complete spiritual unity throughout the *societas Christiana*. Yet Gregory's efforts to transform the episcopate and to disseminate his decrees against simony, nicolaitism, and lay investiture, inevitably led to new developments for methods of application and implementation, but certainly not of old ideology. Where canons were going neglected, Gregory made it his business to 'transform what exists in order to make it prevail'.[32]

Gregory VII's aims and methods in France were thus directly related to his legal actions and attitudes; they arose from his greater personal, religious, moral, and legal convictions for the state of Christendom, the *societas Christiana*.[33] And

the two popes. It is, however, too vague to infer whether it was intended to define a quality of character or a similar approach to church policy or government.

[29] *Reg.*, V. 5: 'Et ideo nichil novi, nichil nostris adinventionibus superinducere conamur, sed illud solummodo querimus, quod et omnium salus postulat et necessitas.'

[30] Leyser, *Medieval Germany*, p. 154.

[31] See John T. Gilchrist, 'The Reception of Pope Gregory VII into the Canon Law (1073–1141)', *ZRG kan. Abt.*, 59 (1973), 35–82, and 'The Reception of Pope Gregory VII into the Canon Law (1073–1141), Part II', *ZRG kan. Abt.*, 66 (1980), 192–229.

[32] Leyser, *Medieval Germany*, p. 155.

[33] For practical purposes, the *societas Christiana* refers here to Western Europe. See Gerhart B. Ladner, 'The Concepts of "Ecclesia" and "Christianitas" and their Relation to the Idea of Papal

the roots of his conviction — the Pope's principal concerns not only in France, but also with the Church at large — were to some extent already firmly established by the first year of his pontificate, in 1073. A letter to Bishop Roclin of Chalon-sur-Saône in that year concerning the abuses inflicted on that church by King Philip I of France (r. 1060–1108) attests to the Pope's already hard stance against simoniacal abuses — an attitude well known and recognized by nearly everyone. The Pope's genuine concern for the *libertas* of churches in France, a kingdom that he recognized 'to have been the richer in wisdom and religion and strength, and very much the more zealous towards the Roman church',[34] reflects the genuine level and nature of his concern.

From the beginning it seemed that King Philip I would pose the greatest threat to Gregory's reform initiative in France, but this episode in Chalon proved to be the only case in a reign that otherwise exhibited restraint on the King's part, and very little serious conflict (see below, Chapter 6). Confiding in Duke William VIII of Aquitaine (sixth count of Poitou) — himself held in high esteem by the Pope for his love of St Peter — the Pope sought external pressure in remedying the King's iniquities: 'After manifold destructions of churches which it has pleased him [Philip] to ruin', wrote Gregory in 1074, 'he has so put aside the restraint of the royal dignity.'[35] Gregory called upon all French bishops to help initiate a change in Philip's 'evil customs upon the model of the good kings of France'.[36] But on the whole, Gregory's objectives in France were not slowed to any significant degree by monarchical conflict and resistance. The correspondence relative to France demonstrates that political questions played almost no role. The Pope's relationship with the French king, moreover, as well as that with the local and regional lay magnates of France, did not — as it had done in Germany — obstruct the papacy's ambitions for reform.[37]

Among the French clergy, however, simony and clerical unchastity were everywhere present. Lacking in papal and monarchical presence, and dominated by powerful political nobles in Aquitaine, Poitou, Normandy, Anjou, Brittany, Blois-Champagne, and Burgundy, France was especially prone to these abuses. A

"Plenitudo potestatis" from Gregory VII to Boniface VIII', *Miscellanea historiae pontificiae*, 18 (1954), 49–77 (p. 52).

[34] *Reg.*, I. 35: 'Quam rem de regno illo tanto profecto tulimus molestius, quanto et prudentia et religione et viribus noscitur fuisse pontentius et erga Romanam ecclesiam multo devotius.'

[35] *Reg.*, II. 18.

[36] *Reg.*, II. 18. See also *Reg.*, II. 5.

[37] Gaudemet, 'Grégoire VII et la France', pp. 216–17.

letter to the Breton bishops in 1074 reprimanding their incestuous unions, for example, called for the seriousness of this crime to be brought home by diligent preaching (*sedula predicatione*) in each his own diocese. The Pope wished to be notified of those who persisted in obstinacy, 'so that both the obedient may be released from their guilt by apostolic remission and the rebellious may be immediately bound by synodal judgement with the chains of anathema'.[38] Gregory hoped that setting an example of canonical rigour (*rigor canonicus*) would compel lesser men to amend their wicked crimes. But the Pope was also pragmatic; he recognized the need to counter these growing abuses from a legal standpoint, and devoted his entire pontificate to developing and extending the papal machinery to meeting these reforming objectives. Achieving these goals, in hindsight, turned out to be beyond the reach of Gregory's own lifetime; but the seeds of his efforts in France, embodied by his reform programme's legal objectives and the mobilization of like-minded and ambitious papal legates like Hugh of Die, were already firmly planted by the end of his life in 1085.

Historiography and Methodology

Despite their potential for providing a rich historical narrative, eleventh-century conciliar, legatine, and legal sources are scarcely straightforward or precise in their accounts. Any investigation into this period of eleventh-century church reform, moreover — whether from a legal, social, political, or ecclesiastical standpoint — is complicated further by the plethora of extant German, French, and English historiography. In short, understanding fully this period of church reform proves to be a most difficult and ambitious task. In his influential study on the Church in Western Europe (1988, translated into English in 1993), Gerd Tellenbach noted how any student of the High Middle Ages that sets out to tackle the many monographs and syntheses devoted to this subject is sure to experience a feeling of helplessness as much a result of the extensive literature as from the inadequately defined formula of reform.[39] Since the publication of Augustin Fliche's seminal multi-volume work *La Réforme Grégorienne* between 1924 and 1937,[40] the histor-

[38] *Reg.*, II. 1.

[39] Gerd Tellenbach, *The Church in Western Europe from the Tenth to the Early Twelfth Century*, trans. by Timothy Reuter (Cambridge: Cambridge University Press, 1993), pp. 157–58.

[40] Augustin Fliche, *La Réforme Grégorienne*, Spicilegium sacrum Lovaniense, 6, 9, 16, 3 vols (Paris: Bloud & Gay, 1924–37).

iographical trend has shifted over the last eighty-five years from considering the latter half of the eleventh century as homogenous or monolithic, to seeing it more clearly as a revolutionary and continuous period of change.[41]

In exploring beyond Gregory VII's personality, moreover, scholars have opened the floodgates for more probing research on the wider context of the social, economic, religious, and legal factors of reform. H. E. J. Cowdrey, in particular, has made a significant impact on this field with studies on the peripheral regions of Christendom, showing great interest in Gregory's treatment of the political, religious, and moral matters in areas like France, England, Ireland, Hungary, Bohemia, Poland, Russia, Scandinavia, among a few others.[42] With the notable exceptions of Jean Gaudemet's article on Gregory VII and France (1989),[43] however, and the inclusive studies of Elizabeth Hallam (1980) and Jean Dunbabin (1985), little modern research has been devoted to examining the presence and effect of Gregorian ideas on peripheral regions. The regional work of Elizabeth Magnou-Nortier on Narbonne and Toulouse, Jane Martindale on Aquitaine, Bernard Bachrach on Aquitaine and Anjou, and Constance Brittain Bouchard on the clergy and laity in Burgundy, have all contributed to broadening our knowledge of the period, but much work remains to be done on the local, grassroots application of reform.[44]

[41] The use of reforming terminology like *reformatio* and *reformare* occurs very seldom in Gregory's *Register*. When it does appear, however, it commonly refers to the renewal of the Church. For Gregory — best described in his letter to clergy and people of Aquileia in 1077 (*Reg.*, v. 5) — this meant a desire to renew and restore 'for the honour of God and the salvation of the whole of Christendom' whatever has been neglected and corrupted by evil custom. On the appearance and use of this renewal terminology in secondary literature, see Gerhart B. Ladner, 'Gregory the Great and Gregory VII: A Comparison of their Concepts of Renewal', *Viator*, 4 (1973), 3–31; and I. S. Robinson, 'Reform and the Church, 1073–1122', in *The New Cambridge Medieval History*, ed. by Paul Fouracre and others, 7 vols in 8 books (Cambridge: Cambridge University Press, 1995–2004) (hereafter *NCMH*), iv, pt i (2004), 268–334 (pp. 272–73).

[42] In addition to sections in his monograph on Gregory VII, see especially H. E. J. Cowdrey, 'The Gregorian Reform in the Anglo-Norman Lands and in Scandinavia', *SG*, 13 (1989), 321–52; and 'Pope Gregory VII and the Anglo-Norman Church and Kingdom', *SG*, 9 (1972), 79–114.

[43] Gaudemet, 'Grégoire VII et la France', pp. 213–40.

[44] I refer specifically to Bernard S. Bachrach, 'A Study in Feudal Politics: Relations between Fulk Nerra and William the Great, 995–1030', *Viator*, 7 (1976), 111–22, and 'Towards a Reappraisal of William the Great, Duke of Aquitaine (995–1030)', *Journal of Medieval History*, 5 (1979), 11–21; Constance Brittain Bouchard, 'The Geographical, Social and Ecclesiastical Origins of the Bishops of Auxerre and Sens in the Central Middle Ages', *Church History*, 46

Invaluable for setting the social, religious, and political context in which Hugh of Die was active in France, the above-mentioned works are complemented by some key studies in the field of medieval canon law. On this subject there exists a growing amount of secondary literature, beginning with the comprehensive summary of Western canonical collections by Paul Fournier and Gabriel Le Bras in 1931–32 (still widely consulted in the field), to the more modern work on eleventh-century (i.e., pre-Gratian) collections by John Gilchrist, Uta-Renate Blumenthal, Detlev Jasper, Bruce Brasington, Roger Reynolds, and Kathleen Cushing, to name but a few.[45] Of particular value to the present study is the work of Linda Fowler-Magerl, whose database of pre-Gratian canonical collections (*Clavis canonum*, 2005) has revolutionized the study of canon law, allowing for more precise comparisons of eleventh-century manuscripts relevant to this period of church reform.[46]

The recent work by Christof Rolker, moreover, is evidence that the study of medieval canon law as a whole is taking a new direction.[47] Still reliant upon the groundwork of our predecessors, historians are beginning to move away from the grand narratives first established in the late nineteenth and early twentieth century. In their place, individual canon law collections are now being examined for what they truly represent: bodies of legal texts compiled in a specific time period and geographical region, thereby reflecting regional and local customs and

(1977), 277–95, 'Laymen and Church Reform around the Year 1000: The Case of Otto-William, Count of Burgundy', *Journal of Medieval History*, 5 (1979), 1–10, 'The Origins of the French Nobility: A Reassessment', *American Historical Review*, 86 (1981), 501–32, *Sword, Miter, and Cloister: Nobility and the Church in Burgundy, 980–1198* (Ithaca: Cornell University Press, 1987), 'Burgundy and Provence, 879–1032', in *NCMH*, III (2000), 328–45, and 'The Kingdom of the Franks to 1108', in *NCMH*, IV, pt II (2004), 120–53; Elisabeth Magnou-Nortier, *L'Introduction de la réforme grégorienne a Toulouse (fin XIe–début XII siècle)* (Toulouse: Centre régional de documentation pédagogique, 1958) and *La Société laïque et l'église dans la province ecclésiastique de Narbonne (zone cispyrénéene) de la fin du VIIIe a la fin du XIe siècle* (Toulouse: Association des publications de l'Université de Toulouse-Le Mirail, 1974); Jane Martindale, 'Peace and War in Early Eleventh-Century Aquitaine', in *The Ideals and Practice of Medieval Knighthood*, ed. by C. Harper-Bill and R. Harvey (Woodbridge: Boydell, 1992), pp. 147–76, and '"His Special Friend"? The Settlement of Disputes and Political Power in the Kingdom of the French (Tenth to Mid-Twelfth Century)', *Transactions of the Royal Historical Society*, 5 (1995), 21–58.

[45] See the bibliography, below.

[46] Linda Fowler-Magerl, *Clavis Canonum: Selected Canon Law Collections Before 1140*, MGH, Hilfsmittel, 21 (2005).

[47] See the bibliography, below.

traditions, expressing also contemporary religious, social, and political concerns. Overall, the present state of scholarship is exactly as Martin Brett predicted in 1995: incredible zeal is now being directed towards enlarging 'our understanding of local study of canon law, both in the making of modest collections and the revision of larger ones', thereby showing their authors as 'a larger and better-read group than we have sometimes supposed'.[48]

In comparison to this expansive and burgeoning research in the fields of church reform and canon law, conciliar historians, on the other hand, are faced with a rather disparate historiography. Nowhere is this more apparent than when piecing together the course of conciliar events for the last quarter of the eleventh century, a period where some councils escape our notice altogether. Council collections like that compiled by the eighteenth-century scholar Johannes Dominicus Mansi (printed in Florence and Venice between 1759 and 1798), have produced errors of notation that at times omit all traces of original evidence; this is particularly disconcerting for the eleventh century when trying to identify the sources from which historians were drawing their material. There are certainly occasions where letters, *acta*, or charters can be traced accurately to a particular cartulary or chronicle, but for the majority of collections — including the eminent work of the Jesuit scholars Philippe Labbe, Gabriel Cossart (1671–72), and Étienne Baluze (1682–83)[49] — the original documentation has not always survived in its complete form.

That is to say that the origins of conciliar evidence cannot always be determined. It therefore becomes impossible in many cases to verify the authenticity of councils without sufficient manuscript evidence, and it is hardly necessary to point out that these above-mentioned seventeenth- and eighteenth-century editions do not meet modern critical standards. At the turn of the twentieth century, Jean Leclercq strongly criticized Mansi's thirty-one-volume work for being a mere reproduction of all anterior editions without any supplication, teeming with errors and false tables — in short, 'une oeuvre a refaire'.[50] Yet, despite all of these shortcomings, it remains to this day the most comprehensive, widely circulated,

[48] Martin Brett, 'Canon Law and Litigation: The Century before Gratian', in *Medieval Ecclesiastical Studies: In Honour of Dorothy M. Owen* (Woodbridge: Boydell, 1995), pp. 21–40 (p. 40).

[49] Philippe Labbe, *Sacrosancta concilia ad regiam editionem exacta*, 16 vols (Paris: Societatis typographicae librorum ecclesiasticorum jussu regis constitutae, 1661–72) (hereafter Labbe), and Étienne Baluze, *Miscellanea*, 5 vols (Paris: Per Bibliopolarum Societatem, 1678–1715).

[50] Charles Joseph Hefele and H. Leclercq, *Histoires des conciles*, 12 vols (Paris: Letouzey, 1907) (hereafter Hefele-Leclercq), I, 112.

and often-cited collection used by historians — there is simply no better, critical, or more modern edition.[51]

Indispensable for reconstructing Hugh of Die's ecclesiastical career *c.* 1073–1106, volume twenty of Mansi's *Sacrorum conciliorum* (printed in 1767) — documenting the years 1070–1109 — presents little more than a compendium of records from Hugh of Flavigny's *Chronicon*, the letters of Gregory VII and Hugh of Die, in addition to a handful of other contemporary sources.[52] For the thirteen legatine councils convened by Hugh of Die between 1075 and 1085, however, Mansi's work accounts for a total of twelve entries (with the exception of Valence, 1079) — thus offering a near-complete summary of Hugh's conciliar activity under Gregory VII. The few entries for Hugh's conciliar activity under Pope Urban II are also recorded in this edited collection.

Where conciliar evidence is lacking, however, other contemporary sources can be used to flesh out the details that have gone unnoticed. Fitting Hugh of Die's councils within the larger social and legal context in which they were initially convened helps to reconstruct his entire legatine career. By far the fullest accounts in this regard are Gregory VII's *Register* and *Epistolae vagantes*, offering at times detailed histories of individual legal cases, sometimes confirming ecclesiastical sentences issued at Hugh's legatine councils, while also providing some otherwise unknown background to disputed cases and settlements at both the regional and local level. In most cases, Gregory's letters are the only proof that a council ever took place.

[51] A series of *prospecti* intended to supersede Mansi's multi-volume edition were published by various authors: an anonymous author in 1867 (Paris) announced a new collection in four volumes; Abbot Jacques-Paul Migne also announced a collection in twenty-four volumes; V. Palmé announced a collection in 1870 under the direction of Henri Nolte; and, in 1900, another prospectus vowed to reproduce Mansi's collection by printing a supplement that would contain: 1) texts missing from the *Amplissima*, whether unpublished or figuring into a collection *extra-conciliaire*; 2) the *testimonia* missing from Mansi's collection; 3) notable variants to the published texts; 4) a redressing of the attributed errors; 5) mention of the errors and the gaps that have arisen from the notes of various editors; and 6) extended coverage and complete texts of synodal statutes up to the Council of Trent and, after 1564, a substantial overview.

[52] Remaining chronicle accounts are primarily found as excerpts in *Recueil des historiens des Gaules et de la France*, ed. by M. Bouquet, 24 vols (Paris: Palmé, 1738–1904) (hereafter *RHGF*). See the Chronicle of Tours, from the anonymous canon of the Church of Saint-Martin (*Ex chronico Turonensi*, in *RHGF*, XII (1877), 461–78); *La Chronique de Saint-Maixent*, ed. by Jean Verdon (Paris: Les Belles Lettres, 1979). More recently, Paul of Bernried's *Life of Pope Gregory VII*, *The Life of Pope Leo IX*, Bonizo of Sutri's *Liber ad amicum*, and Bruno of Segni's sermon concerning simoniacs, have all been translated into English by Ian Robinson (in *Papal Reform of the Eleventh Century*).

Yet Gregory's correspondence is a collection of outgoing papal communication, rendering the existing evidence naturally one-sided.[53] Filling this historiographical gap are Hugh of Die's letters, preserved in Volumes CXLVIII, CLI, CLVII, and CLXII of Migne's *Patrologia Latina*, and Volume XIV of Bouquet's *Recueil des historiens des Gaules et de la France* (1806). Both editions offer a scattering of letters from various contemporary sources. As a result, the subject matter deals with a number of legal and ecclesiastical affairs. The *notitia litteraria* of Migne's collection (Volume CLVII), taken verbatim from the *Histoire littéraire de la France*, notes the historical necessity for compiling a modern edition for Hugh's entire letter collection. Such a work, the author admitted, would serve to understand better what was happening in the eleventh-century Gallican Church.[54] This undertaking was no doubt Migne's intention, however incomplete were the results. Such a worthwhile endeavour is not attempted here, but a chronological list of documented letters is included in the appendix of this work (see Appendix 2). In total, Hugh of Die's correspondence amounts to sixty-two extant letters, the majority of which (forty-two to be precise) concerns his role as Archbishop of Lyon from 1082 to 1106.

The exact origins of Hugh of Die's letters remain somewhat confounded, however, appearing in the above-mentioned editions yet ostensibly copied from rarely cited eleventh-century sources. Four letters can be traced back to Archbishop Anselm of Canterbury's letter collection,[55] while eight epistles are attributed to the collection of Ivo of Chartres — the renowned canonist and bishop.[56] A further three letters are cited verbatim from Hugh of Flavigny's *Chronicon*, which is by far our largest contemporary source for the latter half of the eleventh century.[57] First appearing in the sources as a monk of Saint-Vanne, Verdun (in the

[53] Alexander Murray, 'Pope Gregory VII and his Letters', *Traditio*, 22 (1966), 149–201 (p. 149).

[54] *Patrologia cursus completus [...] Series Latina*, ed. by Jacques-Paul Migne, 221 vols (Paris: Garnier, 1844–1902) (hereafter PL), CLVII (1898), cols 499–500.

[55] See Anselm of Canterbury, *The Letters of Saint Anselm of Canterbury*, trans. by Walter Fröhlich, 3 vols (Kalamazoo: Cistercian, 1993), bk II, letter 11; bk III, letters 24 and 123; and bk IV, letter 18. Two other letters, bk III, 64 and 124, are from Hugh to Anselm.

[56] See Ivo of Chartres (Yves de Chartres), *Correspondance*, ed. by J. Leclercq, Les Classiques de l'histoire de France au Moyen Âge, 22, 2 vols (Paris: Les Belles Lettres, 1949), I, letters 24, 54, 55, 59, 60, 62, 65, and 68.

[57] Only one original, autograph manuscript survives; it can presently be viewed at the Staatsbibliothek in Berlin (Berlin, Deutsche Staatsbibliothek, MS Phillips 1870). Flavigny is

province of Trier),[58] Hugh of Flavigny fled to France at the age of twenty-one with his Gregorian abbot Rudolf (1075–99). Between 1085 and 1096, Hugh managed to associate himself with the high ecclesiastical circles of Hugh of Die (then archbishop of Lyon) and Abbot Hugh of Cluny. Hubert Dauphin suggests that the chronicler often travelled as companion to his abbot of Saint-Bénigne at Dijon, Jarento, which company gave him the opportunity to become well acquainted with both the Abbot of Cluny and the Archbishop of Lyon.[59]

While composing his *Chronicon* between *c.* 1090 and 1102, Hugh of Flavigny had numerous bodies of documents at his disposal ('fontes formales et materiales').[60] Whether using charters, necrologies, conciliar *acta*, or continuing on from the previously written histories of the bishops of Verdun, Hugh fully exploited the archives from the monasteries of Saint-Vanne and Saint-Bénigne. He also drew mainly upon Gregorian letter collections — that is, from propagandist collections favourable to the reform party. In the second book of his chronicle, dealing with the period from his own lifetime, a total of thirty-five Gregorian letters are cited verbatim. As Ian Robinson has pointed out, these 'are glossed and supported with canonical *auctoritates* in a sense far closer to their original polemical intention'.[61] Indeed, it is widely suggested that Hugh may have had at his disposal a copy of Gregory's papal *Register*, or at the very least a copy of

located near Semur, in the duchy of Burgundy (approx. 240 km north of Lyon), between Autun (to the north-west) and Dijon (to the south-east).

[58] For the most recent study on this figure, see Patrick Healy, *The Chronicle of Hugh of Flavigny* (Aldershot: Ashgate, 2006); Patrick Healy, 'Hugh of Flavigny and Canon Law as Polemic in the Investiture Contest', *ZRG, kan. Abt.*, 91 (2005), 17–58. For a study of Hugh's *alma mater*, see Hubert Dauphin, 'L'Abbaye Saint-Vanne de Verdun et la Querelle des Investitures', *SG*, 1 (1947), 237–61.

[59] Hubert Dauphin, *Le Bienheureux Richard, Abbé de Saint-Vanne de Verdun* (Paris: de Brouwer, 1946), pp. 20–21.

[60] Max Manitius, *Geschichte der lateinischen Literatur des Mittelalters*, 3 vols (Munich: Beck, 1911–31), noted Hugh's use of Idacius, Victor Vitensis, Jordanis, Gregory of Tours, Nennius, Sulpicius Severus, Paul the Deacon, Einhard, the *Annals of Fulda*, *Liber pontificalis*, the letters of Hincmar of Reims, the *Gesta episcoporum* of Metz, the *Annals of Prudent*, Anastasius from the chronicles of Theophanus, Flodoard of Reims, Richer of Saint-Remi, Rodulfus Glaber, and many other sources from letter collections such as Popes Nicholas II and Urban II, Henry IV, Countess Matilda of Tuscany, Empress Agnes, Archbishop Lanfranc of Canterbury, Bishop Anselm II of Lucca, and Archbishop Manasses I of Reims. For a more in-depth consideration of individual sources, see Healy, *Chronicle of Hugh of Flavigny*, pp. 100–37.

[61] I. S. Robinson, 'The Dissemination of Letters of Pope Gregory VII During the Investiture Contest', *JEH*, 34 (1983), 175–93 (p. 181).

the letter collection used by Bernold of Constance († 1100) in the appendix to his *Apologeticus* (*c.* 1075).[62]

One of the most valuable letter collections from which this chronicle potentially benefited was Hugh of Die's episcopal register.[63] Hugh of Flavigny certainly pays a great deal of attention to French episcopal affairs for the years 1075–80, exhibiting a knowledge that strongly suggests that his 'immediate source was probably not a copy of the papal Register but rather the personal episcopal register of the bishop of Die'.[64] Indeed, the first seven letters of Hugh's chronicle relate Hugh of Die's legatine activity in *Francia* as the 'common denominator'.[65] It is entirely possible that Hugh of Flavigny acquired such a register while remaining in Hugh of Die's entourage from 1085 to 1096 before becoming the abbot of Flavigny, but no complete version exists to validate such claims.

Similar to Mansi's work, this chronicle is not without criticism. G. H. Pertz, the modern editor of this chronicle, reproached Hugh of Flavigny's negligence in properly using the sources at his disposal, and in what he considered to be the poor care taken in their transcription.[66] Augustin Fliche, on the other hand, opposed this view, deeming Hugh's use of Gregory's letters in particular to be a mark of scrupulous scholarship.[67] Patrick Healy's recent work emphasizes Hugh of Flavigny's credibility as an historian by exploring the chronicler's 'careful attitude to his sources'.[68] Whatever the case, this chronicle remains — despite its occasional and recognizable inconsistencies — a reliable and dependable account for Hugh of Die's life and council activity.

As the following study makes evident, a complete rendering of Hugh of Die's legatine and conciliar activity *c.* 1075–1106 must consider all existing contemporary sources, carefully weighing their historical value and accuracy. For only by piecing together and contextualizing the complex narrative of conciliar events — including whenever possible back-histories for individual cases, council summonses, subscription lists, sentences issued and decrees promulgated — can

[62] Healy, *Chronicle of Hugh of Flavigny*, pp. 107–08.

[63] Healy, *Chronicle of Hugh of Flavigny*, pp. 104–07.

[64] Robinson, 'Dissemination of Letters', p. 182.

[65] Robinson, 'Dissemination of Letters', p. 182.

[66] *Chronicon Hugonis monachi virdunensis et eivionensis abbatis Flaviacensis*, ed. by G. H. Pertz, MGH, SS, 8 (1848) (hereafter Hugh of Flavigny), pp. 280–503 (p. 283).

[67] Fliche, *La Réforme Grégorienne*, I, 58–60.

[68] Healy, *Chronicle of Hugh of Flavigny*, p. 100.

real light be shed on the genuine efforts, objectives, and successes of Gregory VII's reform initiative in France. Indeed, in reconstructing French conciliar events for this period, Hugh of Die's role as an instrument of reform gains significantly in historical meaning and context, thereby offering a rich and full account of law and practice in the age of reform.

Chapter 2

Hugh of Die: Bishop, Archbishop, and Legate

It is tempting to view Hugh of Die's life and ecclesiastical career as one of zealous, if not ruthless, efficiency for the purpose of church reform. From 1073, his name begins to appear with increasing frequency in our two main sources for this period, Hugh of Flavigny's *Chronicon* and the letters of Pope Gregory VII. Any reconstruction or interpretation of this period relies heavily on these two sources, drawing primarily from Erich Caspar's critical edition of the papal *Register* (1920–23, based on Registrum Vaticanum 2), which account greatly informed Hugh of Flavigny's later narrative (writing *c.* 1090). Neither account, however, offers a detailed picture of Hugh's personal character, only glimpses into his ecclesiastical activity which are often recorded from an entirely papal perspective.

Our understanding of Hugh's life thus relies heavily upon his ecclesiastical career, defined more narrowly by his first legation under Gregory VII. The evidence for this period, although selective and scattered, enables a concise and full study of his conciliar activity. But gaps of significant proportion still remain in the historiography, especially when attempting to unravel the details of his childhood, education, character, and distinct role as the bishop of Die and archbishop of Lyon.[1]

Hugh as Bishop and Legate to Gregory VII

Returning to Rome following a council in Chalon-sur-Saône (1073), Cardinal-bishop and legate Gerald of Ostia assisted in electing a suitable replacement for

[1] For Hugh of Die's early life, see Wilhelm Lühe, *Hugo von Die und Lyon: Legat von Gallien* (Breslau: Jungfer, 1898), pp. 119–36.

the simoniacal bishop of Die, Lancelin (*symoniacus dictus episcopus*).[2] According to the Lotharingian chronicler Hugh of Flavigny, whose contemporary narrative account offers a summary of these events, Hugh of Die was instantaneously and miraculously hailed (*invenitur, rapitur, tenetur*) as Lancelin's successor. Upon entering the church where deliberation was taking place between the legate and cathedral canons, he was selected with the favour and grace of all those present, and his election was confirmed soon after by the clergy and people.[3] Drawing heavily from the contemporary Swabian chronicler Berthold of Reichenau — who noted how Hugh was 'made bishop not by human but by divine election'[4] — Pope Gregory VII's biographer, Paul of Bernried (writing from Germany *c.* 1128), later described the light that was said to have come down from heaven for this occasion, 'brighter than day and in the minds of all who were present there was no doubt that the Holy Spirit had arrived'.[5]

Of particular relevance to this study is the exegesis of personal connections and contact between Hugh of Die and Gregory VII. More specifically, we seek to identify the individual bond and its relevance established between pope and legate — a relationship evidenced early on in Gregory's pontificate, in the circumstances warranting Hugh's appointment to the bishopric of Die on 19 October 1073. This unanimous (*unanimiter*) election is recounted in the Pope's letter to Count William of Die, in which Gregory commends the recently elected bishop to the people of his church.[6] Arriving at Rome in December of that year, Hugh's official consecration did not take place until the following spring, 16 March 1074, after spending nearly four months at Gregory's court.[7] It was here at the Lateran Palace that the bishop-elect was 'imbued with divine dogma and strengthened in the

[2] Hugh of Flavigny, p. 410. Gerald of Ostia was returning to Rome via the ancient route of the Alps (by way of Die, Gap, Embrun, and Briançon), when the need of choosing a successor to the bishopric of Die called for his attention.

[3] Hugh of Flavigny, p. 411: 'Sublimatus est electus noster cum gaudio et cordis iubilo in pontificali solio, acclamatus est et confirmatus episcopus de Dei et Christi eius iudicio, de clericorum pene omnium testimonio, de plebis quae tunc affuit suffragio, de sacerdotum et bonorum virorum collegio.'

[4] Berthold of Reichenau, *Chronicon*, in *Die Chroniken Bertholds von Reichenau und Bernolds von Konstanz, 1054–1100*, ed. by Ian S. Robinson, MGH, SRG, 14 (2003), year 1078, p. 315; cf. Hugh of Flavigny, p. 410.

[5] Paul of Bernried, *Life of Pope Gregory VII*, chap. 58, pp. 302–03.

[6] *Reg.*, I. 69 and 85a; cf. Hugh of Flavigny, p. 411.

[7] Hugh of Flavigny, p. 412. Hugh of Die's consecration took place without the customary investiture from King Henry IV of Germany.

sanctions of the Church'.[8] And it was in Rome that Hugh became acquainted with his fellow bishop-elect Anselm II of Lucca — a relationship that Hugh of Flavigny took pains to describe in his *Chronicon*.

Scarcely distinguishable at the beginning of Gregory's pontificate, the reforming mentality of these two bishops-elect in Rome prior to consecration suggests Gregory's interest in shaping their legal and reforming mentalities, establishing new links in his communication and friendship networks. Hugh of Flavigny described them as equal in age and charity; their friendship is strengthened in this account as one incapable of change ('mutabilitatis nescia'), so much so that the prefect of Rome is said to have marvelled at their inseparability, calling the one bishop-elect day and the other light ('alterum horum diem, alterum vocaret lucem'): because the day is not without light, and the day accompanies light ('quod dies non sit sine luce et lucem dies comitetur'). So involved was their relationship over these months in Rome that it was surprising to see one without the other ('ut unum videri sine altero mirum videretur'). From this intimate description forms the picture of two personalities whose reforming mentality was closely aligned, and whose inclinations resembled those of the Pope.[9]

Following March 1074, however, their career paths diverged. Notwithstanding Hugh's departing Rome with a strong commitment to eliminating simony and nicolaitism,[10] the true foundation and extent of his ecclesiastical and legal knowledge is called into question. The evidence for Anselm of Lucca's life, on the other hand, leaves little doubt as to his accomplishments in the field of canonical reform and law. As Kathleen Cushing observed in her monograph on Anselm's canonistic work, he was a man clearly recognized for his 'knowledge and intellectual abilities, especially of the law; his tireless devotion to the cause of Pope Gregory VII; and his indisputable sanctity'.[11] One need look no further than his *Collectio canonum* (*c.* 1083) to weigh his influence on later canonistic thought and 'his consecration to the task of refashioning the law of reform'.[12]

[8] Hugh of Flavigny, p. 411; Healy, *Chronicle of Hugh of Flavigny*, p. 186; cf. Robinson, 'Friendship Network', p. 4.

[9] Hugh of Flavigny, p. 411.

[10] *Reg.*, I. 69: 'Nos enim inter cetera eum sollicite ammonuimus, ut contra symoniacam heresim totis erigeretur viribus et ecclesias sue parroechie non prius consecraret nec consecratas aliter divinum officium celebrare permitteret, nisi prius absolute a laicorum minibus, sicut canonicum est, suo iuri et episcopali eius providentie redderentur.'

[11] Kathleen G. Cushing, *Papacy and the Law in the Gregorian Revolution: The Canonistic Work of Anselm of Lucca* (Oxford: Oxford University Press, 1998), p. 1.

[12] Cushing, *Papacy and the Law*, p. 63.

Hugh of Die's ecclesiastical career followed a different trajectory, for he lent his services much less to the '"legal" justification of reform'[13] than to the application of the extant canon law.[14] Yet Hugh and Anselm were contemporaries and friends, and Gregory's initiative and personal interest appears to have motivated both men in the formative stages of their clerical vocations. It just so happens that Hugh of Die had more direct contact with the Pope: not only did Gregory consecrate him bishop and suggest his promotion to the archdiocese of Lyon in 1082, but in appointing him permanent legate to northern France and Burgundy in 1075, he maintained close contact with him throughout the course of his pontificate — both in person and through correspondence. Anselm too was commissioned as legate — to Lombardy in the early 1080s (see Appendix 3, below) — though evidence of his personal relationship with the Pope is comparatively scarce.

This silence in the sources, however, does not imply Gregory's favour for one figure over another. It could be argued that the more-established communications networks in Italy, in addition to the customary use of impermanent papal messengers and envoys closer to Rome, did not necessitate Anselm's activity as legate prior to the 1080s. As Gregory's 'deathbed testament' implies, in which he allegedly named Bishop Anselm II of Lucca, Cardinal-bishop Odo of Ostia, and Hugh of Die as possible successors to the apostolic see, the Pope considered both men as suitable and worthy successors to the papal throne.[15] This tribute is

[13] Cushing, *Papacy and the Law*, p. 111.

[14] For the fullest studies on Hugh's life and ecclesiastical career, see Hazel Goggin, 'Hugh Bishop of Die and Archbishop of Lyons (1073–1106): An Agent of Papal Reform in France' (unpublished doctoral dissertation, Trinity College, Dublin, 1995); Gilles Bollenot, 'Un Légat pontifical au 11ème siècle: Hugues évêque de Die (1073–1082) primat des Gaules (1082–1106)' (unpublished doctoral dissertation, Université de Lyon, 1973); Theodor Schieffer, *Die päpstlichen Legaten in Frankreich vom Vertrage von Meersen (870) bis zum Schisma von 1130*, Historische Studien, 263 (Berlin: Ebering, 1935), pp. 1–243; and Lühe, *Hugo von Die und Lyon*. Supplementary readings can be found in Cowdrey, *Pope Gregory VII*, pp. 355–74, and I. S. Robinson, *The Papacy 1073–1198: Continuity and Innovation* (Cambridge: Cambridge University Press, 1990), pp. 146–78, in addition to a series of dated articles by Abbé Rony: 'La Légation d'Hugues, archevêque de Lyon, sous le pontificat d'Urbain II (1088–1099)', *RQH*, 112 (1930), 124–46; 'La Politique française de Grégoire VII: Conflit entre le pape et son légat', *RQH*, 108 (1928), 5–34; 'Élection de Victor III: Conflit entre le nouveau pape et Hugues, archevêque de Lyon', *RHEF*, 14 (1928), 145–60; 'Hugues de Romans: Légat pontifical (1073–1106)', *RQH*, 107 (1927), 287–303.

[15] For evidence of Gregory's deathbed testament, see Hugh of Flavigny, p. 466; cf. *Briefsammlungen der Zeit Heinrichs IV.*, ed. by Carl Erdmann and Norbert Fickermann, MGH, Briefe, 5 (1977), no. 35, pp. 75–76. H. E. J. Cowdrey, 'Death-bed Testaments', in *Fälschungen im Mittelalter*, MGH, Schriften, 33, 6 vols (1988), IV, 703–24.

especially interesting in light of Hugh's treatment of certain canonical matters, which often challenged Gregory's conception of how canon law should be applied in the field.

As a whole, the foundation of Hugh's legal training remains a relatively unexplored field (see below, Chapter 5), resulting in part from the uncertain details of his birth, his family and childhood, and the extent and location of his education. A letter from Gregory VII to the monks of Saint-Barnard in Romans[16] (9 March 1075) suggests that Hugh was both a native of Romans and a son of the church of Vienne, in the kingdom of Burgundy.[17] Strengthening this hypothesis with an entry in his chronicle, Hugh of Flavigny tells us that Hugh of Die returned to Vienne *c.* 1080 to overcome an illness,[18] allegedly — as it is often interpreted — retiring to the seclusion, comfort, and safety of his family home.

Any remaining details along these lines are not supported by contemporary evidence. Only the *Gallia Christiana*, for instance, depicts Hugh of Die as *vir primae nobilitatis*, a man of first nobility — implying perhaps the noble status of his family — but fails entirely to cite any primary evidence, rendering the basis for such claims questionable. Seldom reliable for identifying original sources, serious doubt is cast on this material's value for historical enquiry and accuracy. Yet it is this record alone that mentions the beginning of Hugh's ecclesiastical career upon entry as a monk into the priory of Saint-Marcel, near Chalon-sur-Saône.[19] The origins of his family and parentage are not provided, but it appears that he had two siblings both actively pursuing the religious life.[20] His brother Guigo was a monk at the monastery of Chaise-Dieu (in Auvergne), and later went on to become abbot at the monastery of Île-Barbe (Lyon). The other sibling, whose associations to the religious life are not described, led a seemingly insignificant life in comparison to the achievements of his brothers.[21] Apart from these tenuous connections however, whose details at times rely too heavily on the *Gallia Christiana*, practically nothing is known of Hugh's early life until 1072, when his name first appears as a witness to an official *actum*.

[16] In the province of Vienne.

[17] *Reg.*, II. 59; cf. Bollenot, 'Un Légat pontifical', p. 57. Lühe, *Hugo von Die und Lyon*, p. 1, notes the imprecise nature of Hugh's birth, but calculates that it could not have been any later than 1043 for him to have achieved the office of bishop by the canonical age of thirty.

[18] Hugh of Flavigny, p. 412: 'posito domno Hugone apud Viennam pro corporis curatione'.

[19] *Gallia Christiana*, 16 vols (Paris: Palmé, 1715–1865) (hereafter *GC*), IV, col. 97.

[20] See Lühe, *Hugo von Die und Lyon*, pp. 4–5.

[21] Bollenot, 'Un Légat pontifical', p. 58.

In that year, Hugh was present at the election of Abbot of Saint-Rigaud (Saône-et-Loire, near Ligny-en-Brionnais).[22] His name appears in the charter as *praecentor et camerarius* (chamberlain) to the church of Lyon, whose role it was to monitor the expenditure of the cathedral's chapter while also policing activities within the cloister.[23] The duration of his time in this office is uncertain, but it would have provided Hugh — as a member of the Archbishop of Lyon's entourage[24]— with the occasion to expand existing networks, while developing new contacts. It is not unreasonable to suggest that during his time at Lyon, Hugh gained valuable experience and insight into both local and regional affairs of a political and ecclesiastical nature, an understanding that he was later able to apply to his legatine commissions, as well as for the effective execution of his clerical offices.

Existing sources, however, do not define the circumstances of Hugh's promotion to the office of bishop in 1073. This paucity of evidence is indeed unfortunate because it seems suspicious that Hugh just happened upon the deliberation in Die, especially as there is no explanation or obvious reason for his presence there.[25] It is far more likely that this occasion had been prearranged by the Pope,[26] or that he was even travelling in Gerald of Ostia's entourage. The latter argument gains especial favour when we consider Berthold of Reichenau's description of the event, paying careful attention in his chronicle to the intimacy of their relationship ('videns eum, non parum de adventu illius gavisus est; namque ipsi notus et amicissimus fuerat').[27] Given this contemporary evidence, there is reason enough to suspect that Hugh's promotion to the bishopric of Die was influenced directly by his close ties with the Cardinal-bishop.

The difficulty here lies in trying to comprehend how a relatively unknown *camerarius* from the cathedral of Lyon went on to become one of the reformers'

[22] *GC*, IV, *Instrumenta*, chap. 26, col. 282. For further mention of Hugh's association with this office, see Hugh of Flavigny, p. 410.

[23] Bernard Bligny, *L'Église et les ordres religieux dans le royaume de Bourgogne aux XIe et XIIe siècles* (Paris: Persée, 1960), p. 57.

[24] Archbishop Gebuin of Lyon (1077–82).

[25] Hugh of Flavigny (p. 410, ll. 26–27) mentions a possible sojourn to Rome ('ibat enim Romae ad sanctum Petrum'), which would explain Hugh of Die's presence at Die, ancient city of Dea Augusta, and old capital of la Cité des Voconces.

[26] Based on the uncertainty of this date, it is impossible to postulate on whether Hugh's election was the brainchild of Pope Alexander II or Pope Gregory VII.

[27] Berthold of Reichenau, *Chronicon*, year 1078, p. 316, ll. 2–3.

greatest and most energetic weapons in France. Gregory was fastidious in choosing his representatives, and the language of contemporary sources in describing Hugh's election to Die stresses the spiritual distinction of his promotion. His convenient election at Die in 1073, and the significance of his being consecrated by Gregory in Rome in 1074, might suggest that the reformers had targeted him at an early stage — a protégé of papal government. While such an interpretation is admittedly tenuous, the slightest possibility of this connection might show that Hugh's later promotion to the legatine office in 1075 was an entirely strategic manoeuvre, a pre-emptive and conscious move on the papacy's behalf.

The measures effecting Hugh of Die's rise through the ecclesiastical ranks are thus quickly brought to light. And from this string of expedient promotions — although the evidence is not so precise as to admit it — the potential motivational or manipulative impact of Gregory's personal charisma is revealed. Given this consideration, it is plausible to suggest that Gregory's persuasive character, in addition to his intimate and developing relationship with Hugh, played an important role in shaping the latter's indivisible loyalty to the reform movement from *c.* 1073 onwards. Indeed, as will be seen throughout this study, it was Gregory's increasing ability to govern the office of legation, in addition to his ability to influence others, which created the opportunity for reform in this province of Western Christendom.

Determining exactly when these two figures came into direct contact, however, proves exceedingly difficult on account of the insufficient evidence. It is entirely possible that Hugh of Die was in attendance at Gregory's Lenten (Roman) synods in 1074, 1076, 1078, and 1082, for instance, but there is no conclusive evidence such as a subscription list to back up this claim. Our most reliable source — and indeed our fullest source for this investigation — is the existing correspondence, which serves to alleviate any lingering doubts of unfamiliarity. Taking into account the nine books of Gregory's papal *Register* (390 letters), his *Epistolae vagantes* (76 letters), and Hugh of Die's correspondence (62 letters), there exist a total of fifteen letters between Gregory and Hugh. The language and subject matter of these missives is more than enough to suggest a close acquaintance, not to mention their exhibiting a uniform mentality towards eradicating rampant church abuses in France. All fifteen letters, it must be said, deal exclusively with matters of legation.

The first reference to Hugh of Die's legatine status is found in the record for Gregory's 1076 Lenten synod.[28] A letter to Archbishop Manasses I of Reims one

[28] *Reg.*, III. 10a.

year earlier (4 March 1075), however, mentioning the dispatch of an un-named legate to 'Gallia',[29] hints at Hugh's appointment likely taking place sometime in the spring of 1075.[30] The territorial jurisdiction of his legation is defined only as 'Gallia', but we know his activity (including his jurisdiction and authority) to have often extended beyond the borders of northern France and Burgundy, into the more accurately defined regions of Narbonne, Gascony, and Spain — those territories assigned to his fellow legate, Bishop Amatus of Oloron (later Archbishop of Bordeaux from 1089 to 1101).[31] At the time of Hugh of Die's legatine appointment, he was commissioned to the regions of France and Burgundy, with the exception of the diocese of Cambrai (which fell under the ecclesiastical province of Reims) and any territory west of the river Rhine, which fell under King Henry IV of Germany's imperial control.

The first example of Hugh's legatine activity can be seen in the sources at Anse in 1075, an ecclesiastical assembly marking his first of thirteen legatine councils as Gregory VII's legate in France. Having adopted his reforming mentality while residing at the papal court in Rome *c.* 1074, and from previous experience in church councils and other unknown ecclesiastical business, Hugh was here presented with his first opportunity to unleash Gregory VII's reforming agenda. To the modern historian, this council represents a landmark for Hugh's church reform efforts in France, marking the beginning of an intensive series of councils spanning his entire legatine career. However, this transition was not immediate, nor were its effects felt rapidly. 'Only gradually', as Cowdrey aptly noted, did Hugh 'emerge as having distinctive functions.'[32] Any relevant legal training that Hugh acquired through his religious education, his time spent as chamberlain to the cathedral church of Lyon, or during his first two years as Bishop of Die, now came into play as he first set foot on the council (thus legal) floor. Hugh's gradual, perhaps even cautious, approach in this arena is indicative of his inexperience in convening ecclesiastical meetings of such importance. With increasing experience, however, comes competence and confidence, though the evidence for his first council at Anse is certainly not overflowing with insight into the difficulties posed by this novel encounter.

[29] Hugh of Flavigny, p. 412.

[30] See Schieffer, *Die päpstlichen Legaten*, p. 92.

[31] *Ep. vag.*, 21. See also Max Fazy, 'Notice sur Amat, evêque d'Oloron, archevêque de Bordeaux et légat du Saint-Siège', *Bulletin de la faculté des lettres*, 34 (1908), 77–142 (p. 84).

[32] Cowdrey, *Pope Gregory VII*, p. 358.

The proceedings at Anse are mentioned only briefly in Hugh of Flavigny's *Chronicon*, indeed confirming the events, but quickly overtaken by the account for Hugh of Die's third council at Clermont in 1076.[33] Lacking any narrative account, it is important to ask whether the location of Anse can offer any insight into the council's relevance.[34] Located in the diocese of Lyon, approximately twenty-five kilometres north-west of the city of Lyon (on the Sâone River), Anse at first glance appears to have held no significant ecclesiastical or political standing. Historically, however, because of its proximity to the Burgundian monastery of Cluny, and perhaps also on account of its nearness to Lyon, Anse maintained a history of provincial council proceedings dating back to the late tenth century.[35] The councils of 994 and 1025, in particular, acted as more than just peace assemblies benefiting the privileges and possessions of Cluny. In 1070, Archbishop Humbert of Lyon held a council there with Bishops Hugh of Besançon, Agano of Autun, and Achard of Chalon-sur-Saône, where the latter bishop donated the cloister of Saint-Laurent to the monastery of Île-Barbe (Lyon), a dependent of Cluny. But despite this prestigious association with the Burgundian reform monastery, and the history of councils in this region, Hugh of Flavigny ostensibly considered the council of secondary importance. Either his methods were not so systematic as to record a more detailed entry of the council's outcome or, more likely, he did not have any judgement to record in his chronicle.

The reasons for holding a council at Anse, therefore, are not expressly given. One might assume that it convened to discuss questions of ecclesiastical discipline, but even the nature of this discussion escapes mention. And other than Hugh of Flavigny's brief chronicle entry, the only other reference to this council comes from Hugh of Die's letter to Archbishop Ralph I of Tours (1075). The contents of this letter, however, serve only a general purpose, but its context offers the first clear indication that Hugh was carrying out reform in this region of France. Ralph of Tours had not been invited to Anse, but the reasons for gathering there were clearly defined for him as repairing (*ad reparandum*) the

[33] Hugh of Flavigny, p. 413.

[34] The traditional meeting place for ecclesiastical councils at Anse was the church of Saint-Bernard. See H. E. J. Cowdrey, 'Cardinal Peter of Albano's Legatine Journey to Cluny', *Journal of Theological Studies*, 24 (1973), 481–91.

[35] *Sacrorum conciliorum nova et amplissima collectio*, ed. by Johannes D. Mansi, 31 volumes (Florence: Apud Antonium Zatta, 1759–98) (hereafter cited as Mansi), XIX, col. 99.

state of the Holy Church.[36] As for the council participants, they are only vaguely described as necessary ecclesiastics (*necessarii ecclesiastici*). Indeed, any evidence that exists for Anse reveals very little by way of relevant conclusions.

Yet despite this exiguous record, there may be reason to think that the Council of Anse was more eventful than the existing evidence admits. The record for Gregory's 1076 Lenten synod reveals a series of sentences that could potentially have originated at the Council of Anse in 1075. Sentences had clearly been passed against Bishop Herman of Vienne, 'justly deposed for simony, acts of perjury and sacrilege, and apostasy'; Bishop Stephen of Le Puy, 'simoniac and homicide'; Bishop Berengar of Agde (in the province of Narbonne), 'because he has held communion with the bishop of Narbonne and has performed episcopal functions on his behalf'; Desiderius and the clerks of the church of Romans (Saint-Barnard, in the diocese of Vienne), for having driven from that church the regular clerks and holding communion with excommunicates; Abbot Berald of Saint-Gilles, likewise; Count Raymond IV of Saint-Gilles, 'on account of consanguinity'; Count Godfrey of Forcalquier, for similar reasons; Humbert of Beaujeu 'on account of harassments of the church of Lyons'; and Archbishop Pontius II of Grenoble for reasons not mentioned.[37]

It is entirely possible that Hugh brought these matters from Anse (1075) to Rome for further disciplinary action. Some uncertainty arises, however, in trying to determine whether these cases were judged at Anse or independently of this council, especially in light of the fact that the council is loosely dated. Indeed, questions remain as to whether the above-mentioned sentences were in any way connected with Hugh. The chronology of Hugh of Flavigny's chronicle, as well as the existing council evidence, shows that this council took place sometime late in 1075, while Gregory's Lenten synod convened on 14 February 1076. Between these dates was Hugh's second council in Dijon on 2 January. With this in mind, it proves increasingly difficult to link the cases of the Lenten synod specifically to either Dijon or Anse. Indeed, the exiguous records of both councils provide little insight into their actual outcome. Confounding the matter further is the possibility that the records of the Lenten synod drew on accumulated sentences of both councils.

[36] Hugh of Die, *Epistolae et privilegia*, in PL, CLVII (1898), 507–28 (hereafter cited as Hugh of Die, PL, CLVII) (letter 2, col. 508).

[37] *Reg.*, III. 10a.

The vague language of Gregory's 1076 letter does not alleviate this concern. By this papal account, Hugh is nowhere mentioned in connection with these sentences, neither as a participant nor a presiding judge over the council(s). It is plausible to suggest Hugh's familiarity with some of these men due to their proximity with his bishopric in Die, or on account of his former position as chamberlain in the cathedral at Lyon. But not all of the accused fell under his territorial jurisdiction as legate. The bishops of Le Puy (Velay, in the ecclesiastical province of Bourges) and Agde (in Narbonne), for example, resided in regions beyond his legatine jurisdiction of Gallia. The only direct reference to Hugh's participation, in truth, comes from the last sentence of Gregory's council summary, which confirms 'the things that the bishop of Die has done in the diocese of Die about tithes and small tithes and churches, and the remaining things that he has decided in our legateship'.[38] In this case, however, the collection of tithes proves nothing more than one of the many tasks commissioned to legates in this period, commonly carried out in the provinces on the Pope's behalf.

Whatever the case, following 1075/76, Hugh of Die's legatine role takes on new historical perspective, meaning, and context. As a direct result, his contemporaneous role as the Bishop of Die fades quietly into the background. There is, very simply stated, no further extant evidence from which to contextualize Hugh's episcopal duties. Ostensibly favouring his legatine and conciliar activity under Gregory VII, the contemporary evidence for Hugh's clerical vocation begins to proliferate only with the next stage in his ecclesiastical development, to a period in history that coincides with the final years of Gregory's pontificate.

Hugh as Archbishop and Legate to Urban II

After serving nine years in the office of bishop, Hugh was promoted to the see of Lyon in 1082 following the death of Archbishop Gebuin.[39] As legate, Hugh was entreated by the Pope to take up the matter of replacing the deceased archbishop, but was instructed that he might assume the position himself if no other suitable candidate could be found.[40] The ideal figure, according to Gregory, was to be a

[38] *Reg.*, III. 10a: 'Et ea, que Diensis episcopus in episcopatu Diensi de decimis et primitiis et ecclesiis fecit, et cetera, que in legatione nostra statuit, nos quoque confirmamus.'

[39] Hugh of Flavigny, p. 460; cf. *La Chronique de Saint-Maixent*, p. 147.

[40] *Reg.*, IX. 18. See also John Gilchrist, 'Canon Law Aspects of the Eleventh-Century Reform Programme', *JEH*, 13 (1962), 21–38 (p. 31).

soldier of Christ and a defender of righteousness, 'for which he should desire not only to work but also to undergo death in the flesh'.[41] Although this letter does not specify whether Hugh was Gregory's preferred choice to fill the see, it was not long before he had assumed the title of archbishop and, along with it, the role of primate over the ecclesiastical provinces of Lyon, Sens, Tours, and Rouen — a privilege first assigned to that see in 1079, and one reconfirmed by Popes Urban II in 1095 and Paschal II in 1116.[42]

The length of Hugh's Lyonnais office is noted at twenty-three years, eight months, and seven days, placing his official consecration to the see of Lyon on 31 January or 1 February 1083.[43] It was then that he began his long and fairly stagnant career as an archbishop, until his death at Susa (near Turin) in 1106. While existing sources fail to render a complete picture of Hugh's activity *c.* 1082–1106, forty-two of his sixty-two known letters pertain to his tenure as the archbishop of Lyon — a significantly large number (see Appendix 2). Dealing primarily with matters of regional and local interest, the majority of these records exist in the form of donation charters, confirming the rights and privileges of various churches and monasteries, in addition to a handful of missives concerning matters of ecclesiastical succession and dispute settlement.

The dearth of evidence *c.* 1085–93 is particularly inhibiting, though some explanation can be posited. Driven from Rome to Salerno in the throes of King Henry IV's military campaigns, Gregory VII could not have foreseen his death on 25 May 1085 impeding the reforming initiative in France once exuded by Hugh of Die. Indeed, in 1085 there was no way for the ailing pope to have anticipated that his final 'deathbed testament' would give rise to what Cowdrey has called 'one of the most obscure subjects in the history of the medieval papacy'[44] — that is, the contested election of Abbot Desiderius of Montecassino as Pope Victor III (1086–87). Not only was the Roman see vacant for nearly two years following Gregory's death, with the imperial (i.e., German and anti-papal) factions growing ever stronger in Rome, but Hugh of Die's mounting and public opposition to

[41] *Reg.*, IX. 18.

[42] See *Reg.*, VI. 34–35; *Beati Urbani II Pontificis Romani epistolae et privilegia*, PL, CLI (1844), cols 283–560 (hereafter Urban II, PL, CLI) (letter 165, col. 438); Paschal II, *Epistolae*, in PL, CLXIII (1854), cols 31–470 (letter 461, col. 399); Mansi, XX, col. 1079. See also Peter R. McKeon, 'Gregory VII and the Primacy of Archbishop Gebuin of Lyons', *Church History*, 38 (1969), 3–8.

[43] *GC*, IV, col. 98.

[44] H. E. J. Cowdrey, *The Age of Abbot Desiderius: Montecassino, the Papacy, and the Normans in the Eleventh and Early Twelfth Centuries* (Oxford: Clarendon Press, 1983), p. 177.

Desiderius' election resulted in his own excommunication *c.* 1087 at the Council of Benevento.[45]

Owing in large part to the obscurity of Victor III's pontificate and the interim vacancy following Gregory VII's death in May 1085, surprisingly little is known about French reforming activity in the late 1080s and early 1090s. That Hugh of Die's legation expired with Gregory's death only adds to the obscurity of this period, calling into question his legal ability, intensity, and opportunity for reform and conciliar activity.[46]

The truth is that few contemporary accounts ever comment on the state of the church in France during this period. Coinciding with the end of Gregory's pontificate, moreover, is a noticeable decline in narrative evidence, namely the loss of his papal *Register* — that crucial epistolary source for the years 1073 to 1085. Without this source, examining the movements and impact of reforming luminaries like Hugh of Die is a challenging task. In many ways Gregory's death ushers in a new phase in historical methodology, removing from the equation the outgoing correspondence of the papal chancery, leaving only a few remaining sources from which to reconstruct the historical narrative of this period. Of particular significance to this period is Hugh of Die's correspondence with Countess Matilda of Tuscany (1046–1115) — which exists in two long-winded letters — the contemporary Chronicle of Montecassino, and extant conciliar *acta* — key sources that, when considered contemporaneously, offer a more complete picture of Hugh's ecclesiastical activity and reforming initiative north of the Alps *c.* 1085–93.

The earliest signs of this ecclesiastical activity are evidenced *c.* 1088 in a dispute settlement between Archbishop Hugh of Besançon and the abbot and monks from the monastery of Saint-Bénigne at Dijon. Acting as 'servant of the

[45] For a record of this council, see Mansi, XX, cols 639–42; cf. PL, CXLIV, col. 964: 'Itaque donec parvitatem nostram electioni factae, atque a se approbatae repugnare conspexerant, ipsi modis omnibus insistebant ne onus pro utilitate Ecclesiae nobis impositum abjiceremus. Ubi vero nos tandem cedere perviderunt, conceptam diu flammam clibanus exsaturatus evomuit. Quapropter cernentes sibi fratrum omnium unanimitatem constanter obluctari, ab eorum et nostra sunt continuo communione sejuncti'; Peter the Deacon, *Chronicle of Montecassino*, ed. by Hartmut Hoffman, MGH, SS, 34 (1980), p. 454. Richard of Saint-Victor (at Marseille) regained all privileges under Urban II, on 20 February 1089 (see *Regesta pontificum Romanorum*, ed. by P. Jaffé, 2nd edn ed. by W. Wattenbach and others, 2 vols (Leipzig: Veit, 1885–88) (hereafter JL), 5392). Shortly thereafter, he was reinstated as legate to southern France and Spain (JL, 5424).

[46] On this subject see Christopher Cheney, 'The Deaths of Popes and the Expiry of Legations in Twelfth-Century England', *RDC*, 28 (1978), 84–96.

church of Lyons' (Lugdunensis Ecclesiae servus), Hugh of Die ordered the Archbishop to return to Saint-Bénigne the church of Sainte-Marie of Salins, whose property had been in dispute since Gregory VII's pontificate.[47] According to contemporary evidence, Hugh of Besançon's predecessor, Archbishop Hugh II of Montfauçon († 28 September 1085), had previously been summoned to the Council of Meaux in 1082 to present more clearly his claims against the Abbot of Saint-Bénigne. When Hugh II failed to attend the council — which was presided over by Gregory's legates in France Hugh of Die and Amatus of Oloron — without providing so much as a canonical excuse for his absence, the legates ruled in the Abbot's favour, thinking prematurely that the issue had been settled conclusively.

Even Urban II's newly invested interest in the case, in addition to Hugh of Die's correspondence with the Archbishop of Besançon, was not immediately effective to ensuring the church's rightful return to the Abbot of Saint-Bénigne. In fact, one of the very last accounts for Hugh of Die's life — a letter dated 1106 (the year of his death) — reveals that the dispute had yet to be resolved fully.[48] In a third attempt, this time under the direction of Pope Paschal II (1099–1118), Hugh declared that the clerks of Besançon and Abbot Jarento of Saint-Bénigne had come to Lyon in order to settle the dispute. And it is only from this later account that the more explicit details concerning the dispute's nature and history first are brought to light.

After hearing the complaints of both parties Hugh of Die decided that a civil arrangement as opposed to a judicial sentence would suit the occasion.[49] He instructed the monks of Dijon to remit to him all the complaints that they could formulate against the clerks of Besançon on the subject of the church of Salins, which the clerks claimed to hold by perpetual right.[50] Acting this time without the

[47] Hugh of Die, letter 10, PL, CLVII, col. 516; see also *Chartes et documents de Saint-Bénigne de Dijon*, ed. by Maurice Chaume and Georges Chevrier, 2 vols (Dijon: Société des Annales de Bourgogne, 1943), II, 147–48, no. 370.

[48] Hugh of Die, letter 28, PL, CLVII, cols 526–27.

[49] Hugh of Die, letter 28, PL, CLVII, col. 526.

[50] These complaints conceded to the monks of Dijon permission to build a chapel at Salins of seven columns in length (not counting the apse) and four columns in width, as well as a cemetery around the chapel (itself seven columns in length), specifically designed for the burial of the monks. The clerks also conceded to the monks one-tenth of their vineyard until the nearest Pentecost (2 June 1107). As recompense Abbot Jarento and his monks promised rightfully to obey the church of Besançon.

apostolic authority afforded by his former legatine status under Gregory VII, Hugh of Die appears to have arranged the whole concession as the archbishop of Lyon, threatening anyone who might ignore his final settlement.

In total, the dispute over the church at Salins lasted over twenty years. Not only was the resolution drawn out but three separate reforming popes (Gregory VII, Urban II, and Paschal II) appointed Hugh of Die to act as intermediary between the archbishop and clerks of Besançon and the abbot and monastery of Saint-Bénigne. This persistence demonstrates the papacy's tenacity for disputes warranting repeated complaints to Rome. It also shows the continuity of Hugh of Die's activity in certain ecclesiastical matters and the papacy's reliance and occasional dependency on his diplomatic skill and local legal, social, and political knowledge. It is for this reason, drawing particular attention here to his determination and relentlessness in reaching a desired settlement, that ecclesiastical cases such as this often were delegated to his discretion by successive popes.

But what does this dispute reveal about Hugh of Die's relations with Pope Urban II? Like his reforming predecessor Gregory VII, Urban II came to rely on Hugh's intimate knowledge of French ecclesiastical and political affairs. Existing correspondence between these two figures shows no signs of conflict or personal discord, which stands in sharp contrast to the hostility exhibited by Hugh towards Pope Victor III.[51] Elected as Pope Urban II in 1088, Cardinal-bishop Odo of Ostia was one of three names put forward in Gregory VII's final testament (mentioned above). Hugh of Die's first letter to Countess Matilda shows an existing bond of loyalty with Odo as both men considered Desiderius's election as cunning and un-canonical. Present at the Council of Capua in 1086, the Cardinal-bishop initially opposed Abbot Desiderius's accepting the papal throne through means of lay support and bribery. At the very least, this opposition reveals a like-mindedness between the two men with regard to reforming principles and a parallelled determination for implementing and upholding the reform movement initiated by Gregory VII and his predecessors.

It must be remembered, however, that this favourable relationship followed a rather turbulent period in Hugh of Die's ecclesiastical career. As an outspoken and energetic opponent to Desiderius's election, Hugh earned for himself the sentence of excommunication at the Council of Benevento on 29 August 1087 (mentioned above), together with his alleged co-conspirators Abbot Richard

[51] See Hugh of Die, *Epistolae Hugonis Diensis episcopi*, in *RHGF*, XIV (1806), 776–96 (hereafter Hugh of Die, *RHGF*, XIV), letter 18, 793–94.

of Saint-Victor (at Marseille) and Archbishop Peter of Aix-en-Provence.[52] But while this ecclesiastical sentence should have exacted Hugh's complete removal from the Roman Church — consisting of a loss of ecclesiastical status in celebrating the Eucharist and in performing his spiritual duties as the archbishop of Lyon — it made little apparent difference to his governing this metropolitan office.

Writing to Countess Matilda of Tuscany *c.* 1087, Hugh provides a lengthy testimony outlining his opposition to Abbot Desiderius's recent election as Pope Victor III. Though criticized as 'distorted and tendentious',[53] this first letter to Matilda offers a rare glimpse into the Archbishop's personal character and charisma. The Archbishop's pleas to the Countess are particularly unique in this regard for interpreting personal opinion, thought, and motivation — personal characteristics seldom identified in the remaining sixty letters of his extant correspondence. It is clear from this first letter to Matilda that Hugh intended a violent prosecution against the injustices of papal succession, which essentially amounted to little more than a polemical account of reforming opinion and mentality. The use of language in this correspondence reveals the extent to which Hugh was willing to advance in order to prevent the election from ever being recognized.

Yet regardless of his articulated complaints, Hugh's pleas to the Countess went ignored, presumably because the letter — written before Desiderius's consecration as Pope Victor III in May 1087 — was received too late to be of any significance. This tempered action is interesting to note as it calls into question Hugh's motivation in seeking the Countess' intervention in the first place. Intervention was presumably expected, especially considering Gregory VII's exhibited respect for Matilda as a chief reforming associate, an influential and authoritative lay figure. That the Countess was 'totally committed to Gregory in purpose and activity'[54] is not disputed. Her political circle and the breadth of her comital power in the regions under her rule were 'well organized to provide both propagandist and military support'.[55] But could her petitioned intervention truly have thwarted

[52] For connections between Peter of Aix-en-Provence and Abbot Richard of Saint-Victor, Marseille, see M.-H. Laurent, 'Chanoines et réforme à Aix-en-Provence au XIe siècle', *SG*, 4 (1952), 171–90.

[53] Cowdrey, *Abbot Desiderius*, p. 198.

[54] Cowdrey, *Abbot Desiderius*, p. 307.

[55] Cowdrey, *Abbot Desiderius*, p. 307; see also Uta-Renate Blumenthal, *The Investiture Controversy: Church and Monarchy from the Ninth to the Twelfth Century* (Philadelphia: University of Pennsylvania Press, 1988), pp. 106–34.

Desiderius's succession? Hugh certainly thought so — this much is evident from his dispatching of letters and further exemplified by the invested language of his correspondence.

The Archbishop's association with Matilda is nonetheless open to interpretation. Whether Hugh of Die had established a relationship with the Countess during Gregory's lifetime — through letters or in person at Rome — must also be considered in this context. There is no existing evidence prior to 1086–87 that suggests an intimate acquaintance between these two figures, though it is plausible to suggest their contact through the one common and likely medium of Gregory VII and his papal court. Their coinciding presence at the Roman synods of 1074 and 1075, for instance, is testimony of their being in Rome at the same time, thereby greatly enhancing the opportunity for their meeting.

Furthermore, the endearing language of Hugh's letters to Matilda seems to parallel Gregory's rhetoric in his earlier correspondence with the Countess. Hugh's second letter (written *c.* 1088) offers a most intimate glimpse of his reverence for the Countess, which, it might even be argued, was little more than an extension of Gregory's friendship network. In this 1088 letter, for example, Hugh complimented Matilda's fervent charity (*fervens charitas*), her prudence for the Holy Spirit, her benign devotion to God, but perhaps most importantly her piety, which Hugh regarded along the same lines as Gregory VII and Anselm II of Lucca.[56] Given such considerations, which seem to imply a deeper familiarity or personal connection, it is not unreasonable to suggest that Hugh had even come to expect Matilda's support.

Indeed, Hugh's letters to Matilda exhibit a reliance on the diplomatic use of her lay rule; to seek her advice and support in the matter of Desiderius's election was to recognize her authority extending across the governed lands of southern Italy. Perhaps Hugh's primary motivation in seeking Matilda's support was that, since Gregory's death in 1085, the Countess had proved herself to be an 'active leader of the Gregorian party who sought to vindicate his cause at Rome itself and elsewhere in Italy'.[57] For Hugh, the Countess had replaced Gregory as the strongest advocate for church reform, showing herself to be a worthy protector of the Roman Church in the crucial interim period of papal rule from 1085 to 1087. With no better equivalent to reform partisanship, Hugh was compelled to send his pleas, which would normally have been directed to the papal curia in Rome,

[56] Hugh of Die, letter 9, PL, CLVII, col. 514.

[57] Cowdrey, *Pope Gregory VII*, p. 302.

to the next best candidate — to this staunch political and influential Gregorian supporter in Italy.

It seems likely from Hugh's second letter to the Countess that he was seeking out a trusted ally. His concern lay not with the deteriorated state of the papal throne, which had incidentally been settled with Abbot Desiderius's death on 16 September 1087, but more so with reconciling his own participatory role and recognized authority within the Roman Church. In a pleading tone Hugh explained to the Countess how, upon visiting Cluny (in the region of Mâcon, in Burgundy) sometime in 1087, he was confronted with letters instructing the monks of that monastery to abstain from taking communion from either him or Abbot Richard of Saint-Victor.[58] Denying the authenticity and credibility of the evidence presented to him, however, Hugh argued that these letters — purportedly written by the newly elected Odo of Ostia as Pope Urban II — were filled with lies and stood contrary to apostolic authority.

It is worth mentioning here that Hugh never used the term *excommunicatio* in his writing, implying perhaps a refusal to acknowledge the sentence imposed by the short-lived pontiff, or even that this excommunication charge never manifested into a legal sentence. That Hugh felt it necessary to relate the details of this episode to Matilda, however, tends to suggest his feeling slighted by the accusation — charges that he evidently felt warranted some clarification or justification. Perhaps of greatest significance here is the fact that news of Hugh's excommunication was circulating among the ecclesiastical and monastic circles of Italy and Burgundy, the consequences of which he experienced for the first time (in person) at Cluny in 1087.

Yet, in truth, very few sources ever mention the details warranting Hugh of Die's excommunication. Offering the fullest account, the contemporary Chronicle of Montecassino accuses the Archbishop of creating a schism (*schismata*) in the Roman Church and of allowing pride and personal ambition for the apostolic see to impede a rightful papal election.[59] By citing Ambrose of Milan to the effect that 'he who breaks from the Roman Church must truly be considered a heretic', the author of the chronicle attempts to provide further accuracy to the legal consequences of Hugh's obstinacy (*pertinacius*) and crime of scandal (*scandalorum scelere*). Paying little attention to the sequence of events precipitating their separation from the Roman Church, the chronicle's summary of Victor III's 1087

[58] Hugh of Die, letter 9, PL, CLVII, col. 515.

[59] Peter the Deacon, *Chronicle of Montecassino*, p. 454.

Beneventan council nevertheless serves to confirm this action while going further to accuse Hugh and Richard of the crimes of idolatry, ambition, and disobedience.

From this biased account the objective of excommunication appears rather straightforward: Hugh was accused of plotting against the newly elected pope and, as a direct result of his public opposition, Victor III sought to exclude him from the *societas Christiana* — that body of universal Christian faithful. According to eleventh-century canon law, those who continued to associate with an excommunicate, whether or not they were conscious of the individual's sentence, risked falling victim to the same fate. Yet in practice the sentence of excommunication could do little more than exclude the individual from participating within the Christian society — no quantitative methods exist for measuring the degree of alienation. If in Hugh of Die's case his suffragans, subjects, and members of his church at Lyon ceased to communicate with him, not only would he endure the prohibition of social contact but his ability to govern would also be severely limited. Spiritual exclusion is likely what Victor III had in mind upon issuing the sentence, striving to eliminate Hugh's participation in the Roman Church — a position to which he had grown accustomed as legate to Pope Gregory VII from 1075 to 1085.

Given such consideration there is no reason to suspect that Hugh's excommunication was not issued in accordance with contemporary legal standards, though questions can be raised on the legal circumstances warranting this judgement. One can assume that the procedure for judging the accused was of little significance, especially with the primary presider and judge in this case being the pope. Hugh of Die and Richard of Saint-Victor were subject directly to papal judgement with absolutely no recourse to the law or legal right of appeal. This outright exertion of papal supremacy in matters of litigation presumably made for a swift and decisive case, leaving little room for the testimony of witnesses or the gathering of judges. Hugh's letters to Countess Matilda of Tuscany exemplify this evident frustration as one inflicted by an unjust sentence with no obvious method or line of defence. Referring to the excommunication sentence as false and unfounded accusations, Hugh neither questions nor challenges the legality of the charge but rather ignores it through prolonged silence and the obstinate continuance of his ecclesiastical duties.

Strengthening this argument further is the extant conciliar evidence *c.* 1090–94, which again evinces a continuous and seemingly undisturbed activity in Hugh of Die's dispensing of ecclesiastical duties and justice in select regions of France. In 1090, for example, Urban II issued a bull (addressed to both Hugh of Die and Bishop Hugh of Grenoble) restoring the monastery of Chartreuse to the disciples of Bruno, founder of the Carthusian order.[60] The two Hughs were employed to render through Seguin, the Abbot of Chaise-Dieu, the mountain of Chartreuse on which the monastery was erected. Hugh of Die's name appears in the confirmation list of this restitution to the provost Landuin (dated 17 September 1090).[61] Also in 1090, Hugh can be seen extending his archiepiscopal authority to Anjou, intervening in a long-standing dispute over the domain of Champigny between the monks of Saint-Serge (Angers) and Saint-Aubin.

In March 1093, to take another example, a provost from Trier by the name of Poppo (brother to the palatine-count Henry) was raised to the bishopric of Metz.[62] This election followed the death of Bishop Herman of Metz on 4 May 1090, which had left a vacant see for nearly three years. Hugh of Flavigny notes how the metropolitan bishop Wibert of Trier was considered 'contaminated' (*contaminatus* — a likely reference to the crime of simony), prompting Hugh of Die himself to perform Poppo's consecration together with his suffragan bishops of Mâcon and Langres. A similar event took place in the following year (1094) after a prelate of Verdun by the name of Richerius came to Lyon seeking absolution from lingering charges of simony. In Hugh's presence, this prelate purged himself of simony and was subsequently consecrated bishop of that see. Once again, Hugh performed the ceremony, this time in the deaconery of the church of Holy Stephen on Easter Sunday (9 April).

Notwithstanding this archiepiscopal activity, however, the present study is interested more in the details for Hugh of Die's legation under Pope Urban II (1088–99), a promotion known to us through the letters of Bishop Ivo of Chartres. Offering his congratulations to Hugh shortly after this reinstatement took place, Ivo's letters bring to light Hugh's apparent hesitation in accepting the ecclesiastical office forthright.[63] The most debilitating factor was arguably

[60] *Chartarum viennensis diocesis ineditarum*, in *Collection de cartulaires dauphinois*, ed. by Ulysse Chevalier, 10 vols (Paris: Picard, 1912–69), I, 211–316 (no. 2507). See also nos 2506, 2508–09; cf. *Acta pontificum Romanorum inedita*, ed. by J. Pflugk-Harttung, 3 vols (Tübingen: Fuess, 1880–88) (hereafter *Acta pont. Rom.*), II, 148.

[61] *Acta pont. Rom.*, II, 148.

[62] Hugh of Flavigny, p. 473; cf. *GC*, IV, col. 101: 'absque regione dono sola electione praeponentes eum aecclesiae'.

[63] Ivo of Chartres, *Epistolae*, in *Sancti Ivonis Carnotensis Episcopi opera omnia*, PL, CLXII (1854), cols 1–287 (hereafter Ivo of Chartres, PL, CLXII) (letter 24, cols 35–36): 'Sed hanc meam laetitiam postea pertubavit quod mihi dictum est te in tanta pertubatione humerum (tuum v.c.) hunc oneri nolle supponere'. See Ivo of Chartres, *Correspondance*, I, letters 24, 54, 55, 59, 60, 62, 65, and 68.

the physical consideration of his advanced age; by 1094 Hugh would have been approximately sixty-four years old, and the toils and labours associated with legatine activity — including the more practical considerations of travel — were undoubtedly both physically and mentally strenuous. The numerous tribulations encountered under his first legation (1075–85) to Gregory VII are testimony to this fact (see below). Hugh had likewise grown accustomed to, what may have been for him, the serene and static life of an archbishop.

Challenging these suspicions in his correspondence, Ivo of Chartres questions the insecurity, uncertainty, and reluctance that befell Hugh. There is also a sense in this letter of Hugh's waning confidence in adequately or properly (*commode*) carrying out the duties expected of the legatine office. Citing biblical analogies while stressing the depleted state of French affairs in need of Hugh's expertise attention, Ivo attempted to persuade his friend to again lend his hand in ploughing the fields of the Lord, to assist in plucking out any thorns, and to continue planting seeds and reaping the harvest.[64] From this favourable petition, there is no denying Ivo's opinion on Hugh's usefulness to the Roman Church. It was also a matter of principle not to ignore Urban II's expressed, and perhaps more immediate, wishes. Writing to the Pope in either 1091 or 1092, Ivo was determined to have a legate sent to France, though no preferential candidate was advanced by name.[65] From the congratulatory remarks issued in 1094, however, one can assume that Hugh of Die was heralded as Ivo's most obvious and favourable choice, and that the Bishop of Chartres clearly regarded the legate as a confidante and like-minded reforming ally.

As legate to Urban II, however, Hugh of Die convened only two councils. The first, held at Autun on 16 October 1094, culminated in his excommunicating King Philip I of France for repudiating his first wife, Bertha of Holland, and subsequently marrying Bertrada of Montfort, wife to Count Fulk IV of Anjou.[66] The second, at Portus Ansillae in 1099, effectively confirmed the foundation of

[64] Ivo of Chartres, letter 24, PL, CLXII, col. 36: 'Non haec quasi ignoranti scribo, sed persuasum esse vellem tuae paternitati, ut iterum manum ad aratrum mitteres, et de agro Domini spinas, quas posses, evelleres, et semina quaeque messem latura superseminare non differes.'

[65] Ivo of Chartres, letter 12, PL, CLXII, col. 25: 'Suggero etiam paternitati vestrae ut partibus nostris ordinetis aliquem legatum, virum bonum testimonii, qui non sua quaerat sed quae Jesu Christi.'

[66] Mansi, XX, col. 799: 'Phillipus Rex Francorum juvenili furore percitus Bertam uxorem legitimam repudiavit, et Bertradam uxorem Fulconis comitis Andegavensis cognatam suam sibi matrimonio junxit.'

a new monastery (*novum monasterium*) by Robert of Moslesme, giving rise to the Cistercian order.[67] Despite the narrative surrounding these two separate events, Hugh of Die's second legation was comparatively inactive to his first tenure under Gregory VII. In context, the itinerant nature of Urban II's pontificate, best exemplified by his papal councils convened in France *c.* 1095–96, would surely have rendered legatine activity in this region as superfluous — there was no need to represent the Pope when he himself was present.[68] This means, of course, that the waning of Hugh's legatine conciliar activity during this period does not reflect a personal lack of reforming incentive or enthusiasm; rather, it confirms that a study on law and practice benefits from a more concentrated appraisal of Gregory VII's pontificate, a period for which the extant sources offer a fuller representation of Hugh's legatine career and activity.

First addressed as *sanctae Romanae Ecclesiae legatus* (legate of the Holy Roman Church) in 1094, Urban II did not delay in setting Hugh to work.[69] That Hugh had already accepted the legatine office is clear from the transmission of this letter (dated 16 March), which suggests that the appointment took place during the last few months of 1093.[70] Whatever the case, contemporary narrative accounts from this point onward begin to show Hugh of Die exercising his legatine role, the jurisdiction of which is nowhere explicitly defined. It is tempting to assume his being commissioned to Gallia for a second time (i.e., imperial Burgundy or that area west of the Rhine), though this is an assumption based entirely on his previous work in these regions as legate to Gregory VII. The lack of substantial evidence, it must be said, is characteristic for this period of late eleventh-century church history, meaning once again that a majority of speculation derives from extant conciliar sources and papal correspondence.

The motives for Hugh of Die's appointment to the legatine office are explained best in the context of France's political climate. In the early 1090s, Urban

[67] Mansi, XX, cols 973–76.

[68] See Alfons Becker, *Papst Urban II (1088–1099)*, MGH, Schriften, 19. 1 (1964), pp. 213–26.

[69] Urban II, 116, PL, CLI, col. 389: 'Sollicitudinis nostrae vices, et agendorum consiliorum providentiam strenuitati tuae pure simpliciterque commisimus. Sed pro conservando pace et negotio facilius peragendo, utilius aestimavimus confratris nostril Remensis archiepiscopi consilium conciscere, quia in eius manu familiarius causa Regis versatur' (JL, 5523).

[70] Augustin Fliche, *Le Règne de Philippe Ier, roi de France (1060–1108)* (Paris: Société française d'imprimerie et de librairie, 1912), p. 363; Rony, 'La Légation d'Hugues', p. 126; Becker, *Papst Urban II*, pp. 195 and 210.

II had sought to gain a foothold in French political affairs by dealing resolutely with the Archbishops of Reims and Sens, whose sees were influential jurisdictions in the regions of the royal domain. The relationship between the church in France and King Philip I escalated when in 1092 the King separated from his wife Bertha, subsequently imprisoning her in a château at Montreuil-sur-Mer in Picardy, taking as his new wife Bertrada, wife to Count Fulk IV 'le Réchin' of Anjou.[71] Few members of the French episcopacy dared interfere in this iniquitous case, the only exception being Bishop Ivo of Chartres — the most outspoken opponent to this marriage. In reproaching Archbishop Rainald of Reims and his suffragans for their negligence in permitting such a scandal to take place, Urban realized his need for a willing and obedient agent of reform in this Christian province, if not for maintaining stability and enforcing papal wishes north of the Alps.

Urban II was beginning to experience firsthand the insolence of the French episcopate, a problem skilfully mediated by Gregory VII. In addition to his apathetic stance in reproving the French king, Rainald of Reims was acting contrary to papal will by refusing to consecrate the bishop-elect of Arras, a man by the name of Lambert. Having recently removed the see of Arras (in the *regnum Francorum*) from the see of Cambrai (politically part of the German kingdom), making it independent and attached only to the ecclesiastical province of Reims, Urban placed the see directly under the Archbishop's care. Yet even following Lambert's election to the see of Arras on 10 July 1093, Rainald mounted resistance to papal orders, refusing to perform consecration, which action ultimately forced the bishop-elect to receive his consecration from Urban at Rome on 19 February 1094 — details of which are provided in Hugh of Die's notification letter to Count Robert of Flanders.[72]

The removal of Arras from the German Empire might be treated as a victory for King Philip I of France. It was under the King's counsel that the inhabitants of Arras elected Lambert of Guines to that see, successfully gaining papal assent and giving rise to a principle manifestation of favourable politic between the King and Urban II.[73] The *gesta* from the abbey of Saint-Bertin (Flanders) described the

[71] For a detailed account of these affairs, see the Chronicle of Saint-Martin at Tours, *RHGF*, XII, 465, and Clarius, *Chronicon Sancti Petri Vivi Senonensis (Chronique de Saint-Pierre-le-Vif de Sens)*, ed. by Robert-Henri Bautier and Monique Gilles (Paris: Éditions du Centre national de la recherche scientifique, 1979), 1092; cf. Fliche, *Le Règne de Philippe*, pp. 40–77.

[72] Hugh of Die, letter 12, PL, CLVII, col. 517.

[73] See *Gesta episcoporum Cameracensium*, ed. by Ludwig Bethmann, in MGH, SS, 7 (1846), pp. 100–01.

division of these two churches of Cambrai and Arras, depicting Lambert's consecration as an act of hostility against the German king.[74] Here, the Pope acted for a *rapprochement* with the French king while 'augmenting the power of the King at the detriment of the Emperor'.[75] Forced to take these political conditions into consideration, Urban's incentive for promoting Hugh to the legatine office in 1094 is thus more clearly delineated. These more immediate and necessary motivations are clarified further by looking at the primary targets against which Hugh of Die set his legislative and administrative weapons in the 1090s.

Three cases in particular serve to illustrate Hugh of Die's gradual re-introduction into his legatine responsibilities. The first concerns the anathema issued against Count Fulk of Anjou for, amongst other charges, the capture and imprisonment in battle of his brother Geoffrey. A short history of this anathema is given in a charter dated 1094, which ultimately serves to absolve the Count of his prior actions.[76] According to this record, Geoffrey's incarceration at the hands of his brother dated back to 9 April 1068, shortly before Fulk usurped the comital title on 19 June of that year.[77] This legal record also reveals the Count's prior excommunication at the hands of Cardinal Stephen, legate to the Roman see under Pope Alexander II, for various injuries (*pro multitudo injuria*) caused to the church of Tours and the abbot from the monastery of Saint-Martin at Tours.

As for the imprisonment of Fulk's brother, Hugh of Die made counsel to have him freed. But in an unexpected turn of events, Godfrey is said to have refused his release on account of his unhealthy mental state (*desipientem*) — a likely result of his twenty-six- year imprisonment — which made him incapable of governing his states. The Count was later advised that if his brother might regain his senses, he should attempt to make concord with him and return what was rightfully his.

This 1094 charter represents only one complaint in a long line of Angevin comital governing. In 1081, to take another example, Pope Gregory VII had com-

[74] *Simonis gesta abbatum S. Bertini Sithiensium*, ed. by O. Holder-Egger, MGH, SS, 13 (1881), p. 651: 'sed propter discidium quod tunc erat inter apostolicum sacerdotium et orientale imperium, ad diminuendam orientalis regis dignitatem ab apostolico Urbano secundo plebi Atrebatensi indulto privilegio confirmatum est proprio uti pontifice'.

[75] Fliche, *Le Règne de Philippe*, p. 427.

[76] Hugh of Die, letter 13, PL, CLVII, col. 518: 'ut eum a vinculo anathematis, quo diutino tempore innodatus erat pro captione fratris sui Gaufridi, quem in bello publico ceperat, absolveremus'.

[77] Olivier Guillot, *Le Comte D'Anjou et son entourage au XIe siècle*, 2 vols (Paris: Picard, 1972), I, 114.

plained of Fulk's affair with a woman of close-blood relation, comparing the union to the sinful imagery of Adam.[78] Another letter, written by Gregory shortly thereafter, reveals that the Count was first excommunicated sometime in 1082/83 for unjustly driving Archbishop Ralph I of Tours from his see.[79] A copy of this letter, dispatched to the abbots, clerks, and laity in the archdiocese of Tours and the diocese of Angers, in addition to Abbot B. of Saint-Martin and the canons of that monastery, informs us that Fulk had remained excommunicate for a period of over ten years. Not until his arrival at the monastery of Saint-Florence on 24 June 1094 did Hugh of Die absolve the Count with the unanimous vote and praise of all religious men present.[80]

In a second case from 1094, Hugh of Die intervened in a dispute between Archbishops Guido of Vienne and Hugh of Grenoble,[81] and was advised by the Pope to consult the Archbishop of Reims in this matter as one whom he considered *familiarius causa regis*. The nature of the dispute is not clearly given; that it involved a complaint over rights to a here-unspecified property seems a plausible suggestion. With this letter, Urban warned the Archbishop of Vienne to cease interfering with papal instruction, threatening to concede nothing to him or his church if these authoritative wishes continued disobeyed.[82] Hugh of Die's role in this mater was as intermediary, transmitting and enforcing the Pope's desire to quell the seemingly longstanding abuse vexing the church of Grenoble.

A third case exhibiting Hugh's legatine activity comes from 23 May 1095, after his meeting face-to-face with the King of France at Mozac, in the Auvergne.[83] This

[78] See *Reg.*, IX, 23.

[79] See *Reg.*, IX, 24.

[80] Among the credible witnesses and consenters to this event were Archbishop Aldebertus of Bourges, Bishop Hoel of Le Mans, Abbots William of Saint-Florence, Bernard of Saints Sergius and Bacchos, Balderic of Bourgueil, and Godfrey of Vendôme.

[81] See Urban II, letter 116, PL, CLI, col. 389 (JL, 5523).

[82] Urban II, letter 117, PL, CLI, col. 390: 'Si quas vero nostrae auctoritatis litteras Viennensis archiepiscopus opposuerit, nihil causae tuae officere arbitreris. Nos enim nihil ipsi, aut Ecclesiae Viennensi concessimus, nisi quod juste hactenus possedisse cognoscitur, sua enim cuique volumes jura servari.'

[83] *Recueil des actes de Philippe Ier, roi de France (1059–1108)*, ed. by M. Prou, Chartes et diplômes relatifs à l'histoire de France (Paris: Imprimerie nationale, 1908), no. 135, p. 343: 'Actum est autem hoc publice Mauziaci, anno dominice incarnationis millesimo nonagesimo quinto, regni vero nostri XXX septimo, indictione III presente et confirmante sedis apostolice legato Hugone, archiepiscopo Lugdunensi, et subscribente, presentibus etiam episcopis aliquibus et multis nobilibus, quos huic donationi subscribere eamque confirmare jussimus.'

rapprochement between Philip I and this legate is verified by a charter confirming through Bishop Durannus of Clermont and Archbishop Aldebert of Bourges the monastery at Mozac to the abbey of Cluny. This donation, held at the behest of Count Robert of Auvergne and his son William, was approved by Hugh of Die as legate of the apostolic see, in addition to Duke Odo of Burgundy, Count Bishops Ademar of Le Puy, Agano of Autun, and Ademar of Limoges. This affair was regional in scope to the central governing of the King's court, but the presence of both legate and the Duke of Burgundy, as Augustin Fliche noted, suggests 'une importance particulière'.[84]

It is entirely possible that the question of Philip's marriage to Bertrada of Montfort was discussed at Mozac. It is just as likely that the King attempted to persuade Hugh into professing his consent for the illicit union, a feat already accomplished among some of the French episcopate. A letter from Ivo of Chartres to the King's chancellor (*dapifer*) Guy might reflect Hugh of Die's most likely response, which fell in line with Ivo's way of thinking. The Bishop makes it clear that Philip was trying to make peace with the apostolic see but maintained to do so while still keeping his second wife. Ivo stated his incredulity that such an appeasement between the King and the Pope could ever be reached without the total repudiation of Bertrada, for 'if we sin wilfully after that we have received the knowledge of the truth, there remaineth no more sacrifice for sins' (Hebrews, x. 26).[85]

Other than these few cases, no further evidence exists for Hugh of Die's second legation. As noted above, all remaining sources for this period document his ecclesiastical role as the archbishop of Lyon. And similar to his role as the bishop of Die from 1073–82, it is almost impossible to distinguish between Hugh the legate and Hugh the archbishop. In 1095, for example, Hugh implored Bishop Lambert of Arras's intervention in settling a dispute between the Bishop of Amiens and an archdeacon named Fulk.[86] Lambert was asked to gather the appropriate men in his presence in order to convince the Bishop of Amiens, from whom the complaints were being made, that justice was being served. If, as Hugh's letter informs us, they were not willing to meet, then the Archbishop of Reims (the metropolitan concerned) would be brought into the matter.

[84] Fliche, *Le Règne de Philippe*, p. 101.

[85] Ivo of Chartres, letter 47, PL, CLXII, col. 59.

[86] Hugh of Die, letter 16, PL, CLVII, cols 519–20.

It is of some interest here that Hugh of Die's letter to the Bishop of Arras lacks the titular designation of *apostolicae sedis legatus*. The reasons for this titular absence are difficult to explain, especially given the circumstances necessitating Hugh's interference in the first place. His position as primate of Lyon did not extend to the geographical regions under discussion, nor is there any reference to his having received prior instructions from the Pope on how to settle this matter. In the absence of these common and expected attributes, it is difficult to assess Hugh's role and purpose in this particular case. A matter implicating the Bishops of Arras and Amiens, not to mention the Archbishop of Reims, would surely have benefited from his juristic authority as legate, as external interference in any other legal capacity was scarcely ever appreciated or well received.

Unable to distinguish fully between Hugh's role as legate and archbishop, however, by no means implies a complete absence of evidence. In piecing together the various donation charters in Hugh's correspondence, exploiting to the full the extant letters and charters for Urban II's pontificate, a partial reconstruction of the years 1094–1106 is possible. In one of the few cases calling explicitly on his archdiocesan role, for example, Hugh of Die donated the church of Saint-Desiderius (in Brixia) to the monastery of Cluny in 1094.[87] He likewise conceded to the abbot of that monastery (Hugh) the chapel of Riottier, with the church of Saint-Paul's (situated just beneath its walls) and its appendages, under the annual payment of five *solidarii*.

But in truth, Hugh of Die's ecclesiastical activity for the remainder of his life is piecemeal at best; he is an enigma in the history of the church in France. While Pope Urban II made his extensive voyage throughout France *c.*1095–96,[88] Hugh of Die can be seen lurking in the background, though in what legal or representative capacity remains uncertain. His presence is first recorded at Cluny in November 1095, evidenced from a charter confirming the rights of that abbey.[89]

[87] Hugh of Die, letter 14, PL, CLVII, cols 518–19.

[88] René Crozet, 'Le Voyage d'Urbain II et ses négociations avec le clergé de France (1095–1096)', *RH*, 179 (1937), 308–09.

[89] 'Notitia de consecratione altaris Cluniacensis', in *RHGF*, XIV, 101: 'Anno incarnationis Dominicae MXCV, indict. III, octavo kal. novembris, domnus et venerabilis Urbanus Papa II sacra vitaltare primum et majus novi nostri monasterii, in honorem Dei, in memoriam beatorum apostolorum Petri et Pauli. Sacravit etiam per se et altare secundum missae matutunalis. Lugdunensis autem archiepiscopus Hugh, Pisanus archiepiscopus Dabertus, episcopus Signanus Bruno, eodem die in ipso monasterio, jubente Papa inter sacrando missasque agendo, post alia salutis hortamenta, coram episcopis et cardinalibus multorumque personis, huiuscemodi sermonem habuit ad populum.'

After allegedly failing to attend Urban II's Council of Clermont in 1095, however, Hugh was suspended *ab officio*.[90] As penance, he undertook a pilgrimage to Saint-Jacques of Compostella in north-western Spain — the details of which are carefully recorded by Hugh of Flavigny[91] — before rejoining the Pope's train early the following year. On 10 March 1096, Urban arrived at Marmoutier (in Tours) to dedicate a new church. A record for this dedication confirms Hugh's presence there, assisting the Pope in this and perhaps other matters, such as the consecration of a cemetery.[92]

From 16 to 22 March, Hugh attended the Pope's council at Tours (8–12 July).[93] A few months later, he was among those in attendance at the papal council of Nîmes.[94] Also in that year, and together with his suffragan bishops of Autun and Chalon-sur-Saône, Hugh arrived in Mâcon to elect Archdeacon Berardus to that see.[95] But the most prominent aspect of this meeting, according to Hugh of Flavigny, happened to be the chronicler's very own promotion from monk at Saint-Bénigne (Dijon) to the abbacy of Flavigny, at the age of thirty-two. Bishop Agano of Autun, who had for a long time complained of the desolation that occupied that monastery, played a role in securing Hugh's election.[96] Writing after the election, Hugh of Die entrusted the Bishop of Autun with the abbot-elect's

[90] Bernold of Constance, *Chronicon*, in *Die Chroniken Bertholds von Reichenau und Bernolds von Konstanz*, ed. by Robinson, year 1095, pp. 519–20: 'Domnus autem Hugo Lugdunensis archiepiscopus ad eandem sinodum vocatus, ab officio suspenditur, eo quod ipse non venerit nec legatum cum canonica excusatione illus pro se dixerit.'

[91] Hugh of Flavigny, p. 474. See also Rony, 'La Légation d'Hugues', pp. 145–46.

[92] 'Dedicatio ecclesiae majoris Monasterii', in *RHGF*, XIV, 99–100: 'Cui dedicationi Turonensis archiepiscopus Aurelianensis Rodolfus interfuit, qui propriis suis manibus pignora sanctorum, quorum nomina subscirbuntur, sub Dominico altari, jubente Papa, collocavit, et una cum archiepiscopo Lugdunensi et primate Hugone ab infirmorum capella, pridie a Brunone Signiensi episcopo jussu Papae dedicata, reliquias sanctorum quae inibi pernoctaverant, humeris propriis in majorem basilicam deportavit, et una cum domino Rangerio supradicto alphabetum latinum, illo graecum faciente, et fecit, basilicae ipsius parietibus, jubente Papa, crucis vexillum ex oleo imposuit, atque altare de crucifixo jussu Papae mox sacravit.'

[93] Hefele-Leclercq, V, 446; see also *Cartulaire de Cormery (791–1505)*, ed. by M. L'abbé J.-J. Bourassé (Paris: Dumoulin, 1861), no. XLIV (1096), pp. 88–90; cf. Pontal, *Les Conciles*, p. 234.

[94] See Mansi, XX, cols 931–42; cf. Pontal, *Les Conciles*, pp. 234–37.

[95] Hugh of Flavigny, p. 475: 'congregatis ad exequias Matisconensis episcopi domno Lugdunensi archiepiscopo, Eduensi quoque et Cabilonensi episcopis, electus archidiaconus Lugdunensis Berardus consecratur in episcopum Matisconensem'.

[96] Dauphin, *Le Bienheureux Richard*, pp. 8–9.

consecration, which took place on 23 November 1096.[97] Committing the abbot-elect to Agano's care, Hugh noted the affection that he held for the newly elected, revealing the more intimate relationship that existed between this legate and the chronicler. That Hugh of Die played a vital role in furthering the chronicler's ecclesiastical career is almost certain, receiving in return the fullest account of his own life. Hugh remained abbot of this monastery until his forced resignation in 1100, shortly before he discontinued writing his Verdun chronicle.[98]

With cases such as these, the local and regional focus of Hugh of Die's ecclesiastical activity *c.* 1097–1106 is transparent. In 1097 at the abbey of Saint-Remi at Reims, for instance, Hugh sought to resolve a dispute between that monastery and Archbishop Manasses II over the recent appointment of Abbot Robert. Hugh spent no less than three days at Saint-Remi trying to resolve this dispute before relinquishing the matter to Urban II for further consideration. Also in 1097, the Pope reproached the Archbishop of Aix for refusing to recognize the primacy of Narbonne, a matter that Hugh was instructed to settle in person — it remains unclear as to whether he was successful in his aim. In 1098, Hugh of Die was involved in reconciling Abbot Odilo of Saint-Gilles (diocese of Nîmes) with the abbey of Cluny.[99]

But after *c.* 1098/99, only a few letters attest to Hugh of Die's ecclesiastical activity, after which period little else is known. One is a letter (dated 1103) to the Bishops of Autun, Langres, and Chalon-sur-Saône, seeking their counsel in a dispute between the Bishop of Mâcon and the Cluniac monks;[100] another is a donation charter that saw the church of Saint-Germain given to the abbey of Cluny (dated 1106);[101] yet another source concerns a dispute settlement between the monks of Saint-Bénigne at Dijon and the clerks of Besancon over the church of Salins (dated 1106);[102] and a final record, also dated 1106, explains a recent settlement that was reached between the Archbishop of Besançon and the Abbot of Saint-Bénigne at Dijon.[103]

[97] Hugh of Die, letter 15, *RHGF*, XIV, 792.

[98] *The Cartulary of Flavigny, 717–1113*, ed. by Constance Brittain Bouchard (Cambridge, MA: Medieval Academy of America, 1991), p. 148.

[99] JL, 5719, 5720, 5721; *Acta pont. Rom.*, I, 66, no. 70; *Bullaire de l'Abbaye de Saint-Gilles*, ed. by M. l'Abbé Goiffon (Nimes: Jouve, 1882), no. 18, pp. 36–37.

[100] Hugh of Die, letter 27, *RHGF*, XIV, 796.

[101] Hugh of Die, letter 27, PL, CLVII, cols 525–26.

[102] Hugh of Die, letter 28, PL, CLVII, cols 526–27.

[103] Hugh of Die, letter 27, *RHGF*, XIV, 796–97.

In addition to these few prescriptive records, further evidence of Hugh's life can be gleaned from the writings of Anselm of Canterbury, who stayed at Lyon while exiled from England between 1097 and 1100 under King William II and again between 1100 and 1103 under King Henry I.[104] Informative for understanding Anselm's presence at Lyon during the early twelfth century as a member of Hugh of Die's entourage, these letters offer the only account of Hugh's death at Susa in 1106, in a letter written to Anselm by Abbot Hugh of Cluny.[105] Were it not for these few narrative accounts, in fact, very little would be known about the final years of Hugh's life and ecclesiastical career.

By far the most noticeable and perplexing aspect of this period is the decline in Hugh of Die's conciliar role, despite the council activity in France remaining sufficiently constant; church councils were held at Compiègne (1095–96), Rouen (1096), Saint-Pé (1096), Saintes (1096 and sometime again in 1097–98), Reims (1097, 1103, and 1105), Bordeaux (1098), Saint-Omer (1099), Étampes (1099), Soissons (1100), Anse (1100), Valence (1100), Poitiers (1100, 1104, and 1106), Troyes (1104), Beaugency (1104), Paris (1104), Nantes (1105), and Lisieux (1106).[106] It is well worth noting too that three of these councils were convened by Amatus of Oloron — the Archbishop of Bordeaux and former legatine colleague to Hugh under Gregory VII.

As to why Hugh practically disappears from the sources in the midst of ongoing church reform and conciliar activity, no sufficient historical explanation can be given. In view, there is a sense that the fragmented evidence is preventing us from seeing the full thrust of his ecclesiastical perambulations and contributions. Whatever the case, by far the most complete record for Hugh's council activity is that under Gregory VII. Before turning to this fuller representation of law and practice in the 1070s and 1080s, however, we must first examine in more detail Gregory's treatment, understanding, and use of the legatine office under his command. There is little doubt, as will be argued throughout this study, that this ecclesiastical office played a determining role in shaping the application and reception of law and reform in the field.

[104] See Anselm of Canterbury, *Letters*, II, 86–89, letter 176; *Eadmeri monachi Cantuariensis vita Sancti Anselmi archiepiscopi Cantuariensis (The Life of St Anselm, Archbishop of Canterbury by Eadmer)*, trans. by Richard W. Southern, 2 vols (London: Nelson, 1962), II, 116–17, letter 39, and, II, 130, letter 52.

[105] For this account, see Anselm of Canterbury, *Letters*, letter 409, III, 176–77.

[106] See Pontal, *Les Conciles*, pp. 237–49.

Chapter 3

The Legatine Office under Gregory VII

Writing to the faithful of Narbonne, Gascony, and Spain (*regnum* or *terram Hyspaniae*),[1] Pope Gregory VII noted how 'the Roman Church from the very earliest days of its foundation has had the custom of dispatching its legates to all regions which are distinguished by the name of the Christian religion'. 'Thus', he continued, 'matters which the governor and ruler of the Roman Church cannot manage to deal with by his own presence he can entrust on his behalf to legates, and through them proclaim the precepts of salvation and integrity of life to all the churches established throughout the world; and he can diligently instruct them by apostolic doctrine in all matters which belong to our holy religion.'[2] A quick glance at this 1077 mandate draws attention to two important factors: the papacy's difficulty in satisfactorily administering the provinces, and Gregory's resolve to correct this administrative, institutional, and legal inadequacy. Where potential difficulties existed, and where reform was not being upheld or implemented, Gregory turned increasingly to his most active representative body of papal legates. Acting on papal authority, and on behalf of whatever belongs to the well-being of the Roman Church, legates in the last quarter of the eleventh century were commissioned in matters of reform and law, to care for the salvation (*salus*) and general welfare (*communis*) of the Lord's flock.[3]

[1] Referring in this book to the north-eastern Christian region of modern Spain.

[2] *Ep. vag.*, 21 (1077). For other examples, see *Reg.*, II. 40 and V. 2; cf. Albert Grosse, *Der Romanus Legatus nach der Auffassung Gregors VII* (Halle: Kaemmerer, 1901), p. 8.

[3] *Reg.*, V. 2.

At least this was Gregory's understanding of the legatine institution under his control, an office whose validity and use rested firmly upon their ability to 'uproot and destroy, build and plant' (Jer. 1. 10).[4] But this model, which had undergone many changes since Gregory's election to the papal throne in 1073, and indeed in its transformation from the Roman office of envoy to a full-fledged institution by the twelfth century, was being adapted continually to transform the religious and moral objectives of his reforming policy into more practical realities.

In adapting and extending the papal machinery to focus on a need for justice (*iustitia*),[5] the legate's role thus became incorporated gradually into the extant machinery and personnel of the papal government. Richard Southern saw it as nothing more than a 'practical question of adapting old machinery to new, or at least much extended, uses'.[6] But it is difficult to view the eleventh-century legatine office in such systematic, and indeed simple, working terms. It is not entirely clear how Gregory's government went about implementing and disseminating reform and law to the distant regions of Christendom, particularly to regions like France where episcopal obedience and monarchical support was often weak or lacking.

Individual figures like Hugh of Die were crucial to establishing and maintaining social contacts in distant regions, assuming a role in the reformers' grand scheme. But who exactly were these men in whom Gregory placed so much faith and responsibility? What figures shaped his reforming network in Western Christendom? And with what authority and power were they commissioned? By far the most active agents of reform were Bishops Hugh of Die and Amatus of Oloron in France and Spain, Anselm of Lucca in Lombardy, and Altmann of Passau in Germany. But Gregory also depended at times on other, less permanent legations, whose mandates were of a specific nature and subject to more immediate expiration. This type of legate is classified in modern terminology as a legatine 'assistant', commissioned on the Pope's behalf alongside a more per-

[4] The Old Testament reads: 'Ecce constitui te hodie super gentes et super regna ut evellas et destruas et disperdas et dissipes et aedifices et plantes.' This is frequently referred to as the 'Injunction of Jeremiah', interpreted by medieval popes to have been implemented through the use of legates. See *Reg.*, II. 68 and VI. 12, for similar uses of this citation in the context of legates. On Gregory's concept of legation, see Richard Antone Schmutz, 'The Foundations of Medieval Papal Representation' (unpublished doctoral dissertation, University of Southern California, 1966), pp. 171–88.

[5] A term understood by the reformers to mean the administration of church law and the maintenance of strictly Gregorian principles.

[6] Southern, *Making of the Middle Ages*, p. 145.

manent or established representative.[7] Gregory's letters show the monk Teuzo and the Roman subdeacon Hubert to be the most frequently consulted men in this category. Although the Pope often, though not consistently, referred to both men with the commonplace legatine terminology (i.e., *legatus*), their status and jurisdiction was presumably conditional (i.e., temporary) and not nearly as commanding as the position held by his primary legates in France, Hugh and Amatus. Teuzo's role, for instance, often resembled that of papal messenger, acting as the necessary intermediary in keeping the Pope informed on the various legatine activities being carried out in France.

The papal *Register* also refers to Gregory's use of Abbot Hugh of Cluny, Hugh Candidus (Cardinal-priest of San Clemente), Subdeacons Rainbald and Roger, Cardinal-bishop Gerald of Ostia, the Roman clerks Albert, John Minutus, and Peter, Abbot Bernard of Saint-Victor (at Marseille), Cardinal-bishop Peter of Albano, the Cardinal-priest (and later abbot) Richard of Saint-Victor (at Marseille), and Prince Gisulf of Salerno (the only lay member), under the same conditions (see Appendix 3). These men and their legations have for the most part only ever been noted briefly in the few doctoral dissertations on medieval representation.[8] Gregory's dispatch of men from this sub-category definitely served immediate purposes, but they remain of secondary importance to the following analysis on law and practice in the late eleventh century.

Most appointments made to the office immediately after Gregory's election were continuations from the pontificate of his predecessor, Alexander II. Cardinal-bishop Gerald of Ostia, Cardinal-priest Hugh Candidus, Subdeacon Rainbald, the Roman subdeacon Hubert, and a Roman clerk by the name of Albert, were all reaffirmed in their legatine status soon after 1073.[9] Their duties consisted primarily of continuing in whatever matters had been committed to them by the previous pope. Extant evidence gives the impression that, while the objectives of their legatine missions might suggest a reforming initiative of sorts, their presence and activity throughout the remainder of Gregory's pontificate is overshadowed by the increasing conciliar enterprise of Bishops Hugh of Die and Amatus of Oloron. This is not to suggest that legates in France prior to 1075 (the year that Hugh came to the legatine office) were any less efficient in their objectives, but as Gregory gradually formalized his reforming policies, the wants and

[7] On 'legatine assistants', see Schmutz, 'Foundations', pp. 219–33.

[8] Particularly Grosse, *Der Romanus Legatus*; Schmutz, 'Foundations', p. 159 and passim; and Goggin, 'Hugh Bishop of Die', pp. 165–213; cf. Cowdrey, *Pope Gregory VII*, pp. 355–75.

[9] See *Reg.*, I. 6 and 8 respectively.

needs of the legatine office invariably underwent significant developments to accommodate these changes. This was one reason for his unprecedented introduction, promotion, and use of ultramontane (*ultramontanus*) legates in the regions of France, Germany, Lombardy, and Spain.

The selective commissioning of legatine assistants, and the more permanent appointments of Hugh of Die, Amatus of Oloron, Anselm of Lucca, and Altmann of Passau, reflect an evident distinction in representative function, particularly in reference to matters of authority, power, jurisdiction, and communication. This distinction is evidenced also in the 'obvious contrast between the German and French legations of this period'.[10] The arrangement that existed in France for appointing permanent native legates was not entirely suitable for Germany in the first part of Gregory's pontificate. The political crisis between the Pope and King Henry IV on the issue of investiture, not to mention Gregory's increasing distrust of the German episcopate to disseminate his reform policy and exhibit reform partisanship, were factors preventing him from dispatching permanent legations to that region.[11]

Attempting to secure papal obedience in Germany, Gregory did entrust short-term legations to Cardinal-bishop Hubert of Palestrina in 1074–75[12] (in collaboration with Cardinal-bishop Gerald of Ostia), and to Abbot Bernard of Saint-Victor (at Marseille) and Cardinal-deacon Bernard in 1077–78 (see Appendix 3).[13] It was not until the early 1080s, however, with the appointments of Altmann of Passau to Germany and Anselm II of Lucca to Lombardy, that Gregory dispatched trusted native legations to these regions where effective communication was becoming increasingly difficult. As Ian Robinson accurately noted, 'the Gregorian institution of the permanent legation originated in Gregory's special relationship with his French legates and the problems presented by the Investiture Contest necessitated its use in the imperial territories'.[14] But it was primarily in late eleventh-century France that 'permanent legation was used to most dramatic effect; for here the legates' reforming activities were unimpeded by civil war or by a powerful monarchy enjoying the support of the episcopate'.[15]

[10] Robinson, *Papacy*, p. 152.

[11] On the evident complications facing the papacy's use of legates in Germany, see *Reg.*, IV. 23 and VII. 3; and *Ep. vag.*, 31.

[12] *Reg.*, II. 25, 29–30, 51; III. 10; *Ep. vag.*, 14.

[13] *Reg.*, IV. 23–24; V. 7, 16; VI. 15, 16, 20; *Ep. vag.*, 17.

[14] Robinson, *Papacy*, p. 152.

[15] Robinson, *Papacy*, p. 152.

Given the papacy's trust in this office for implementing reform and the law, it is somewhat surprising to find so little modern discussion on the legatine office under Gregory VII. In one of the few studies exploring this topic in the High Middle Ages (1993), Robinson noted how the years 1073–1198 'witnessed the development of the papal legation as one of the most important instruments of papal government — the connecting link between the papal curia and the churches and secular rulers of western Christendom'. This development, he goes on to argue, 'was an innovation of the reform papacy',[16] and one which gave birth to 'the institution of permanent legation'.[17] But was this a period of continuous development? And what role did eleventh-century reformers play in further shaping this office to suit their administrative and legal needs? Existing scholarship in this field has yet to provide a suitable answer, suggesting very strongly that the eleventh century represents an in-betwixt period in the development of papal administration, especially in terms of jurisprudence and court legislation.

That Gregory VII relied heavily on the legatine office is evident early on in his pontificate. A letter to Cardinal-bishop Gerald of Ostia illustrates his concern that legates report back to Rome whatever decisions were made in distant regions. 'It has always been customary and extremely necessary', wrote Gregory in July 1073, 'that whenever a legate of the apostolic see has celebrated a council in a distant land, he should return without delay [to Rome] to announce all that he has done'.[18] This was a requirement for all legates, no matter what their status; as papal representatives, they were expected to uphold and fulfil certain existing regulations. And Gregory was well aware of the great extent to which his reform policy was spread 'through letters and legates' (per litteras et legatos).[19] The Pope claimed to be constructing no new device for eliminating an unchaste clergy, preferring rather to align himself safely with the methods employed by the diligence of his predecessors.

Thus from early on it seems that Gregory VII recognized the administrative inefficiencies of his own position and set out to govern more effectively the peripheral regions of Christendom. Establishing a willing and capable body for carrying out Gregory's judicial programme, however, was only a gradual process. The Pope's greatest challenge rested with developing, extending, and coercing this

[16] Robinson, *Papacy*, p. 146.

[17] Robinson, *Papacy*, p. 152.

[18] *Reg.*, I. 16.

[19] *Reg.*, II. 66.

army, in addition to conferring upon its members sufficient legal power as defined by the precedents of previous popes and the extant canon law.[20] By 1073, the reformers' assertion of judicial rights over the entire church 'enabled the reformed papacy to gather to the Curia a large number of cases and disputes that previously would have stayed in the country of origin'.[21] No other office or institution of the Roman Church could rival that of the legate in terms of influence and authority in matters directly affecting the Holy See. This raises obvious questions concerning the origins, development, and practical implementation of this authority, especially as the reformers understood it.

Adhering closely to some legal framework, Gregory's juristic ideology also helped shape the legatine office under his command. It is entirely plausible to suggest that the reform movement institutionalized this office in canon law.[22] For it was in the 1050s under Pope Leo IX that the 'old practices of authorizing papal legates'[23] were being increasingly revised. And Gregory, as subdeacon and later archdeacon in Rome, was 'one of the first to exercise the enhanced authority of a legate of the reform papacy'.[24] Sent on legatine missions to France (1054 and 1056) and Germany (1054–55 and 1057),[25] his deposing of six simoniac bishops at a council in Chalon-sur-Saône in 1056, for instance, is evidence of how quickly this enhanced authority was being applied in the field. The significance of legations in terms of exercising papal authority, and in gaining legal experience, might even be viewed as a prerequisite to the papal throne, especially considering that fifteen of the nineteen popes elected between 1073 and 1198 were active as legates — a significantly large number.

Given that papal leadership could never extend beyond the geographical constraints and the political concerns of the time, the office of legation in the latter half of the eleventh century developed as a vehicle of reform for the papacy's efforts to bind the Roman Church in political, judicial, and institutional terms. As Robert C. Figueira noted, legates 'provided a means by which information and resources were transmitted to the center of power, decisions were executed,

[20] Richard W. Southern, *Western Society and the Church in the Middle Ages* (Harmondsworth: Penguin, 1970), p. 19.

[21] Gilchrist, 'Gregory VII and the Juristic Sources', p. 4.

[22] John W. Perrin, 'Legatus, the Lawyers and the Terminology of Power in Roman Law', *Studia Gratiana*, 11 (1967), 461–90 (p. 464).

[23] Cushing, *Papacy and the Law*, p. 18.

[24] Robinson, *Papacy*, p. 146.

[25] See Cowdrey, *Pope Gregory VII*, pp. 32–36.

commissioned jurisdiction was applied, and physical resources were transferred outward from that center'.[26] The legate's reception by the lay and ecclesiastical men in the regions to which he was sent, moreover, was crucial for disseminating papal decisions and decrees to the provinces. Ideally, whatever was first pronounced in Rome was to be transmitted to the various provinces through diocesan or provincial synods, and through instruction at local monasteries and churches. Yet for some, Rome often appeared beyond the grasp of those in need of her assistance, and thus sometimes incapable of enforcing its decrees and punishments upon an abusive episcopate. Since the beginning of his pontificate, Gregory increasingly became aware of his duty to 'proclaim salvation, to promote virtue, and to instruct the world in sound doctrine'.[27] This much is evident from his aforementioned letter to all the faithful of Narbonne, Gascony, and Spain which plainly outlined Amatus of Oloron's expected role for eradicating and utterly rooting out whatever errors he might find in these regions, while simultaneously planting the 'seed-beds of virtues'.[28]

The office of legation thus fell within Gregory's ordering of the Roman Church. It was a flexible and developing instrument of papal government. But the function and role of this ecclesiastical office, although never defined during the initial years of his pontificate, became with experience and time increasingly delineated. By 1077, the transition from the existing machinery appears to have reached a watershed; in that year, Gregory did not hesitate to bestow upon his legate, the Cardinal-deacon Gregory, a similar role to his own in Roman councils: 'to avail to correct things that need correction, establish those that need to be established, and bring back to the pattern of canonical and apostolic discipline issues and concerns of ecclesiastical liberty and righteousness that have been for long and in many respects neglected, and through the aid of divine grace effectively to confirm them'.[29] For practical purposes, however, conferring this responsibility upon his legates extended only as far as the rigour of canons (*rigor canonicus*) would permit. For amongst the methods of supervising his legates, none could be stronger than the rigour of canons and the restraint of discretion, with the latter being almost impossible to clearly define in practical terms.

[26] Robert C. Figueira, 'Papal Reserved Powers and the Limitations on Legatine Authority', in *Popes, Teachers, and Canon Law in the Middle Ages*, ed. by James Ross Sweeney and Stanley Chodorow (Ithaca: Cornell University Press, 1989), pp. 191–211 (p. 191).

[27] Cowdrey, *Pope Gregory VII*, p. 592.

[28] *Ep. vag.*, 21.

[29] *Reg.*, IV. 26.

Terminology

At the beginning of Gregory VII's pontificate in 1073, the office of *legatus* did not possess a distinctive reforming characteristic or function. The titular designation itself was still being used alongside others to denote much older, representative offices like the Carolingian *missus* or *nuncius*, and the Latin terminology in the existing sources rarely serves to differentiate the nature of the authority attached to the legatine title. It was largely the accomplishment of later thirteenth-century decretalists in separating and classifying the coexisting offices that appear to the historian as sometimes fulfilling similar administrative functions.[30] Even by the reign of Pope Alexander III (1159–81), the varying ranks of papal envoys and agents adorned by the title *legatus* had yet to adopt a truly specific or defined role.[31] The fact that different moulds of the same office existed during Gregory's pontificate forces us to consider how the eleventh-century legate fits into the existent papal machinery of reform. It also raises the significant question as to whether legates can truly be labelled 'Gregorian'?

Over the last forty years especially, scholars have debated this question. And it seems to me that, on the whole, eleventh-century legates are still being misrepresented according to later canonistic (i.e., thirteenth-century decretalist) categories. The main problem with such a classification, in addition to being anachronistic, is that reforming legates had yet to embody specific legal and administrative functions like their twelfth- and thirteenth-century counterparts. This enchanced role was only just beginning to take shape in the second half of the eleventh century — it was still in embryonic form. Under Gregory VII in particular, legates were being used 'on an unprecedented scale to implement its decrees and to promote its conception of the papal primacy throughout Christendom'.[32] And no pope was as explicit as Gregory in transforming legates into legal instruments of reform, creating a natural precursor to the later decretalist office.

The need to bolster the legal function of the legatine office can be seen, in part, as a measure for securing papal obedience, further serving to establish and maintain reforming allies in the far regions of Western Christendom. With Henry IV controlling the trans-alpine passages in Lombardy, for example, Gregory

[30] See Jane E. Sayers, *Papal Judges Delegate in the Province of Canterbury, 1198–1254* (Oxford: Oxford University Press, 1971), p. 26.

[31] See especially Marcel Pacaut, 'Les Légats d'Alexandre III (1159–1181)', *RHE*, 50 (1955), 821–38 (p. 838).

[32] Robinson, *Papacy*, p. 146.

was in greater need of papal representation to his northerly provinces. Despite the short-term nature of their legations to Germany *c.* 1074–75 and *c.* 1077–78, Cardinal-bishops Gerald of Ostia and Hubert of Palestrina, and Cardinal-deacon Bernard and Abbot Bernard of Saint-Victor (Marseille), were all commissioned (as mentioned above) in an official legatine capacity, offering some proof that steps were being taken to secure the reformers position in Germany. Similar measures were taken in England, illustrating in this instance the papacy's conciliatory approach to King William I (Duke of Normandy) on matters affecting the Roman Church. The Roman subdeacon Humbert, the Roman deacon Albert, Cardinal-priest John Minutus of S. Maria in Trastavere, and Cardinal-priest Peter of S. Grisogono and librarian of the Holy Roman Church[33] were entrusted with legatine missions to this westerly Christian province from as early as 1073 (see Appendix 3).

Paradoxically, the papacy's growing or renewed interest in these distant regions coincides with Gregory's concentrated and committed activity in Rome. This pope did not travel extensively like his predecessors Leo IX (1049–54), Nicholas II (1058–61), and Alexander II (1061–73), or indeed like his successor Urban II (1088–99), thereby increasing his need for the greater extension of papal influence. These political realities do not completely alter our modern-day definition of *legatus*, but they suggest a variation in the reformers' use of legates in reaching the same objectives. Under Gregory, legates were being commissioned more actively to fill any noticeable holes in the papacy's ability to administer and rule. The legate was, as Robinson dubbed him, the crucial 'connecting link' between the Curia in Rome and the provinces.

In classifying legates of this period, it is necessary to adhere to the institutional realities of the time, as opposed to imposing upon this machinery of legation later twelfth- and thirteenth-century categories.[34] There is great merit in identifying all the elements of this ecclesiastical office before evaluating its structure and purpose. But as previous canonical scholars have shown, the tendency to clarify matters with respect to these objectives has made very little progress. The reasons for this are linked to the historiographical precedents set by German scholars in the late nineteenth and early twentieth centuries. A cursory glance at the study of the legatine institution at that time reveals a tendency by German syntheses to

[33] See *Reg.*, I. 8, 70; III. 10a; IV. 10, 17; V. 19, 22; VI. 7; VII. 1, 16, 23, 25–26; *Ep. vag.*, 23, 34.

[34] For this argument, see Schmutz, 'Foundations', and Richard Antone Schmutz, 'Medieval Papal Representatives: Legates, Nuncios, and Judges-Delegate', *Studia Gratiana*, 15 (1972), 441–63.

document the legations of individual popes in regions such as Spain, Portugal, France, Germany, England, and Scandinavia.[35] The majority of such research, unfortunately, has rarely exceeded the level of doctoral work, yet the trend for documenting legations where a previous historian had left off soon became an established standard. Some of this doctoral work is of lasting and great importance, but the majority is not. The work of Theodor Schieffer (1935), for instance, still remains our fullest study on the topic of papal legation in France, with very little modern scholarship contributing to this field for the eleventh century.[36] This phenomenon in no way discredits the historical approach or accuracy with which the majority of this previous research was undertaken, but it allows room for reconsideration, particularly when it comes to contextualizing the legate's practical, legal, and administrative role.

But how was this historiographical trend first established, and why has the eleventh century remained a neglected period in the history of medieval papal legation? The biggest fault, it seems to me, lies foremost with the scanty contemporary evidence. The simple fact is that the legatine office during the eleventh century — its basic framework and structure — had yet to be assimilated into the working machinery of Gregory's papal government. This reality has led to much modern historical focus being devoted solely to the legatine institution following Gratian's *Decretum*, *c.* 1140, particularly because a later look at this subject offers much more in the way of primary evidence, not to mention providing a more structured and formalized view of this ecclesiastical institution.

Later thirteenth-century decretalists Hostiensis (Henry of Susa), Bernard of Parma, and Johannes Teutonicus attempted to categorize papal legates of their own period by comparing their legal background against the earlier Roman offices of proconsul, praetorian prefect, senator, and *praeses*.[37] Their objective was to legitimize the legal maxims and significance of papal legates in their own time

[35] I refer here to the work of Otto Frommel, Albert Grosse and Erich Caspar, Otto Schumann, Johannes Bachmann, Otto Engelmann, Ina Friedlaender, Werner Ohnsorge, Gerhard Säbekow, Gerhard Dunken, and Wilhelm Janssen, among a few others.

[36] The most recent additions for this period of reform can be found in book chapters whose primary goals rarely challenge the existing views. I refer specifically to the work of Ian Robinson, *Papacy*, and H. E. J. Cowdrey, *Pope Gregory VII*. The most recent study on the legatine office is Stefan Weiss, *Die Urkunden der päpstlichen Legaten von Leo IX. bis Coelestin III. (1049–1198)* (Cologne: Böhlau, 1995).

[37] For a look at legation and the Roman law offices, see Robert C. Figueira, 'The Canon Law of Medieval Papal Legation' (unpublished doctoral dissertation, Cornell University, 1980), pp. 135–55.

as founded on the jurisdiction of classical Roman law (*Corpus iuris civilis*).[38] Figueira, in particular, has shown the place of civil law in the development of the legatine institution and canon law in the later twelfth and thirteenth centuries, making it clear that — unlike these later decretalist models — the institution in place during Gregory's lifetime was not rooted in the same legal tradition. Parallels can be drawn between the classifications of the legatine institution in the thirteenth century with the earlier Roman *legatus* or the Carolingian *nuncius*, but the role played by reforming legates seems not to fit into either category.[39] The development of the legatine office during the second half of the eleventh century helped shape the later decretalist view, but the latter's reliance on a greater body of Roman law stresses the impermanent and *ad hoc* nature of the legatine office prevalent during the reform period, which did not have such a *corpus* at its disposal. This condition adds to the argument that Gregory was developing this office more to suit the administrative and legal needs of his papacy.

Recognizing the dangers of imposing anachronistic terminology upon the eleventh-century institution reminds us that permanent legates under Gregory VII were of a new breed, acting under a different set of loose rules than their predecessors. They were not what later decretalists would call *legatus a latere*, nor were they merely *legatus natus* or *legatus missus* (*nuncius apostolicus*).[40] The nature of the legatine office under Gregory VII demonstrates an agglomeration of characteristics which appear separately in many of these later models, depicting the reforming legate as a far cry from the earlier Roman office of *nuncius* or *missus*, but embodying a new role as one chosen from his native region, referring to that area most familiar to him. The role of the papal plenipotentiary sent from the Curia, and the less important envoy with limited powers and duties, were both well-recognized offices in the period 1073–1198. The native legate of the eleventh-century reform movement, on the other hand, was a 'forerunner' to the later thirteenth-century invention of *legatus natus*, but 'of a type unknown to the later

[38] Robert C. Figueira, 'Decretalists, Medieval Papal Legation, and the Roman Law of Offices and Jurisdiction', *Res publica litterarum*, 9 (1986), 119–25.

[39] For the distinction between a medieval papal legate and *nuncius*, see Schmutz, 'Foundations', pp. 87–98, and Schmutz, 'Medieval Papal Representatives', pp. 441–63.

[40] This system was first classified in the thirteenth century by Pope Gregory IX (*Corpus iuris canonici*, 2 vols, ed. by E. Friedberg (Leipzig: Edelmann, 1878–81; repr. Graz: Akademische Druck- und Verlagsanstalt, 1959), IX. I. 30). See Rudolf Hiestand, 'Les Légats pontificaux en France du milieu du XIe à la fin du XIIe siècle', in *L'Église de France et la papauté (X^e^–XIIIe siècle)* (Bonn: Bouvier, 1993), pp. 54–80 (p. 56); cf. Robert C. Figueira, 'The Classification of Medieval Papal Legates in the *Liber Extra*', *Archivum historiae pontificiae*, 21 (1983), 211–28.

Middle Ages, created by the needs of the reform papacy and transformed by the changing circumstances of the twelfth century into less powerful but still influential papal representatives'.[41] He was, in this sense, both a standing legate and a permanent legate. But his role — that is, how far his authority extended — had yet to be defined fully, by the process of interaction with the clergy within his assigned jurisdiction, at times by the legate himself, and by the Pope, whose efforts to extend the office for his reforming objectives often led to elements of confusion or conflict.

Authority

Pope Gregory VII employed legates to distant regions bearing his authority in both legal and jurisdictional matters. Each member of the legatine office was hand-picked and commissioned with some measure of papal authority, which in theory at least translated into complete access and full legal recourse within the area of appointed jurisdiction. Canon law still and always bound the legate to act fully within the framework of canonical rigour (*rigor canonicus*) and restraint of discretion (*discretionis temperantiam*) — the true meaning of which is scarcely expounded in contemporary evidence. And whatever limitations this framework might have imposed depend entirely on the meaning of discretion. According to the fourth sentence of Gregory's *Dictatus papae* (*c.* 1075), to take a contemporary example, legates were able to exercise their functions from a higher authoritative platform than ever before, thus making them entirely capable of — but not necessarily willing — to undermine episcopal authority. It was this episcopal rank that bore the brunt of the reformers' attack, but it remains questionable whether it was ever Gregory's intention to intervene in the clerical order to any disruptive or debilitating degree. The fact of the matter is that while the Pope may truly have been employing his legates as instruments of restoration, they were more often than not perceived by the accused rather as instruments of aggression.[42]

The various reasons for dispatching legates might better serve to clarify this point. A glance at Gregory's *Register* shows the Pope using his representatives to settle matters that he himself was unable to conclude in person. Concerned about the state of the Polish church in 1075, Gregory sent two un-named legates to that region because the number of bishops there was so few, and their jurisdictions so

[41] Robinson, *Papacy*, p. 149.

[42] Schieffer, *Die päpstlichen Legaten*, pp. 100–01.

large, that the pastoral office was not being upheld satisfactorily (see Appendix 3).[43] Also in 1075, Abbots Gepizo of Saint-Bonifazio and Maurus of Saint-Saba of Rome were sent to the March of Fermo in Italy because Gregory's presence there was not possible.[44] The election in 1077 of an archdeacon to Aquileia could not proceed without first securing legatine approval;[45] likewise, in the same year, legatine intervention was called for in the election of a bishop to the Norman see of Dol, and in 1079 for the promotion of an elect to the archbishopric of Arles.[46] The collection of papal revenues (Peter's Pence) was the reason for sending Prince Gisulf of Salerno and the Cardinal-bishop Peter of Albano ('legati nostrae apostolicae sedis') to selected regions of France in 1084,[47] illustrating just how varied Gregory's use of legates could be.

The common denominator in all of these cases was the papal expectation for the Christian population to receive its representatives 'with due reverence and charity' (cum veneratione et caritate), yielding to them 'faithful obedience and collaboration' in 'all respects that either the business of their legation or the necessity of weariness shall require'.[48] Furthermore, legates were to be heard as if it were the Pope himself speaking, putting into effect whatever might be owed to the Pope if he were present, because according to the Gospel (as often cited by Gregory): 'He who hears you hears me, and he who despises you despises me' (Luke 10. 16).[49] Clearly, the representative role of the legate during Gregory's pontificate was not in question. It was the extent of their authority, and their application of reform and law, that led to deeper conflict and misunderstanding among the episcopate.

Gregory's own concept for the authority of his legates was founded upon the supervisory roles of apostolic vicar, *apocrisiarius*, and *legatus ad causam*.[50] Borrowing much from the terminology of these older offices, Gregory saw the

[43] *Reg.*, II. 73.

[44] *Reg.*, II. 40. For further details of their mission, see *Reg.*, II. 41, 46, and 48; cf. Fliche, *La Réforme Grégorienne*, II, 211–12; Schmutz, 'Foundations', pp. 194–97; Uta-Renate Blumenthal, 'The Papacy, 1024–1122', in *NCMH*, IV, pt II (2004), 8–37 (p. 25).

[45] *Reg.*, V. 5.

[46] *Reg.*, IV. 17 and VI. 21 respectively.

[47] *Reg.*, VIII. 23.

[48] *Reg.*, II. 40.

[49] This biblical reference is used five times in Gregory's *Register*: I. 17, 22; II. 40, 73; and III. 10.

[50] See Schmutz, 'Foundations', pp. 116–58.

primary functions of legatine authority as surrounding their role as personal representatives acting on the Pope's behalf, the conferring of the papal *vices*, and the empowerment of instructive legislation and code of conduct for judging cases, both minor (*causae minimae*) and major (*causae maiores*).[51] Apostolic vicars, like the later legatine office, were appointed *vice nostra*, but unlike the later office, they could not handle these *causae maiores*. Significantly, apostolic vicars and *apocrisiarii* lacked procuratorial powers — that is, the ability and authority to represent the principal directly. *Apocrisiarii*, however, were bound and subordinated much more closely to the papal office, establishing an obvious precedent for the expected obedience and subservience of the legate to his pope in the eleventh and later centuries.

The fundamental distinction between these offices surrounds the judicial limitations imposed on apostolic vicars, and the later freedom and authority bestowed upon legates during Gregory's pontificate. Perhaps most significantly imitated from the earlier offices was the increasingly defined concept of jurisdiction, which was to some extent applied to regulate and control legatine authority (discussed below). It was, moreover, the office of *legatus ad causam* that 'absorbed the other roles and developed into the medieval papal legate'.[52] It was this particular office that possessed the flexibility to adapt and expand to every legal situation. When compared to the eleventh-century legate, however, the *legatus ad causam* did not rival the latter in terms of autonomy (i.e., freedom of movement) or authority.

Earlier concepts of authority and power were undoubtedly used in shaping the reforming legate; their titles were also sometimes used interchangeably, making it easier to recognize the eleventh-century model of *legatus* as founded on the earlier representative offices. One particular case found in Hugh of Die's letters helps to illustrate this point. Writing to Archbishop Ralph I of Tours in 1075, inviting him to an upcoming council at Anse, in Burgundy, Hugh entitled himself uncharacteristically '*apocrisiarius* of the Holy Roman Church' (sanctae Romanae Ecclesiae apocrisiarius).[53] This reference, it should be noted, appears just once in Hugh's correspondence. That it was used in Hugh's first known letter as legate might possibly reflect his own misunderstandings about the true nature of the office to which he had recently been promoted. It is far more likely, however, that

[51] Hiestand, 'Les Légats Pontificaux', p. 72.

[52] Schumutz, 'Foundations', p. 138.

[53] Hugh of Die, letter 1, PL, CLVII, col. 507.

there was a prevailing tendency to associate with the older, more established and traditional models of papal representation, paying little regard to titular designations, and having very little practical reason to do so. It is well worth asking if the legate himself would have benefited in any great legal or administrative capacity from using one title or another.

The Pope's frequent use of *noster vicarius* (our vicar) when referring to Hugh of Die — particularly in cases to which he was being commissioned — shows little concern for differentiating between the older and newer representative offices. The preceding reputation of certain legates often called for little need to describe to the receiving party exactly who they were, what office they occupied, the purpose of their mission, and what office they ultimately represented — matters of great interest to local powers and authorities. While these discrepancies contribute little to solving the problem of classification, they suggest that perhaps the best method for understanding the authority of a reforming legate is to look more carefully at the Pope's own account.

Gregory's definition of the office under his care is portrayed best in a letter to Manasses I of Reims, reproving the Archbishop for considering Hugh of Die in a lesser category of papal representatives because he had not been sent directly from Rome. The Pope assured Manasses of the plenipotentiary powers assigned to 'anyone of whatever nationality [*gens*] on whom the Roman pontiff enjoins' a legation.[54] While the Archbishop tried his hardest to avoid the excommunication charge issued against him by this legate at the Autun council (1077), his argument that only one sent from Rome (*legatus Romanus*) should be received as a true papal agent carried little canonical backing.[55] Manasses's view on this matter, moreover, does not accurately reflect the general eleventh-century perception of legatine status, especially since his motives in expressing such a claim were entirely for his own benefit in attempting to escape ecclesiastical punishment. But in spite of Manasses's obvious bias, there remains a sense that his understanding of the legatine institution was not so willing to accept the authority of a non-Roman legate, particularly one who came from the insignificant Burgundian see of Die, and thus regarded as much inferior to his own metropolitan see of Reims.

That Gregory ever recognized two separate categories of papal legates is questionable. From his rebuke of Manasses, it seems plausible to suggest that Gregory made little distinction between *legatus* and *legatus Romanus*; both titles

[54] *Reg.*, VI. 2; cf. Otto Meyer, 'Reims und Rom unter Gregor VII', *ZRG, kan. Abt.*, 28 (1939), 418–52 (pp. 431–32).

[55] Manasses I of Reims, in *RHGF*, XIV, 611.

held the same duty and authority. Both were papal appointees and subject to designated mandates and jurisdiction. Gregory was quick to dismiss the Archbishop's claims that only those 'born at Rome, or educated from childhood in the Roman church, or promoted to some office within it'[56] were worthy of the legatine office.

That Manasses challenged Hugh's authority, based solely on this condition, rather seems to imply an unsuccessful stratagem for repudiating legatine authority. Certainly, the practice of dispatching legates from their native lands was not customary, and it was obviously met with some uncertainty by those who were directly affected. If indeed there was any significant difference between these two titles, it impacted very little on the way that Gregory set out to customize this office. Any apparent discrepancies did not arise from the different applications of a title (there were numerous synonyms for *legatus*, for example),[57] but were tied up in the more theoretical constructs of mandate (*mandata*) and jurisdiction (*iurisdictio*).

In defending the authority of his legates from beyond the Alps, Gregory outlined more clearly his understanding on the origins of papal representation. Harking back to the Councils of Nicaea (325) and Ephesus (431),[58] and drawing further on an example from the pontificate of Gregory I, Gregory VII set out to confirm the traditional papal use of dispatching men to act entirely on his behalf. In his letter to Manasses, the Pope described to the Archbishop with much

[56] *Reg.*, VI. 2: 'Sed quia premittendo "Romanis" continuo subiungitis "non ultramontanis", ostenditis vos tantum eos velle Romanos habere legatos, qui vel Rome nati vel in Romana ecclesia a parvulo edocati vel in eadem sint aliqua dignitati promoti.'

[57] The letters addressed to Hugh of Die alone reveal the infrequent use of titles such as *nostrus legatus* (*Reg.*, V. 20; VI. 40; VII. 17, 20; VIII. 18; IX. 16, 23), *legatus apostolicae sedis* (*Reg.*, IX. 24), *nostrus vicarius* (*Reg.*, IV. 16; VI. 21, 27, 28; VII. 18); and *nostrus confratus*, which appears many times in reference to Hugh as Bishop of Die, suggesting that any clarification of his legatine status is entirely unnecessary. All letters addressed directly to Hugh prefer the use of clerical titles, addressing him as either Bishop of Die or Archbishop of Lyon. Hugh of Die's own letters indicate the adoption of the title *legatus sedis apostolicae* or *Romanae Ecclesiae legatus* (*RHGF*, letter 10, XIV, 787; Hugh of Die, letter 2, PL, CLVII, col. 507; letter 3, col. 508; letter 4, cols 508–09; letter 11, col. 516; letter 12, col. 517; letter 13, col. 517; letter 17, col. 520; letter 19, col. 522; letter 22, col. 523; letter 28, col. 526; or the once-used 'apocrisarius sanctae Romanae Ecclesiae' (ibid., letter 1, col. 507). The majority of Hugh's letters written while he was the archbishop of Lyon are addressed as 'Hugo, sanctae Lugdunensis Ecclesiae servus', or sometimes combined with, or interchanged with his legatine title (commonplace with his second term under Pope Urban II).

[58] *Reg.*, VI. 2.

enthusiasm how it had not only been the custom of popes (namely Silvester I and Celestine I in the above-mentioned cases) to dispatch bishops for these matters, but also monks[59] who by the authority granted to them by papal mandate held the same weight and privilege in distant regions. Likewise, in another letter to the Archbishop dated January 1080, Gregory was again keen to remind Manasses how 'in the greatest and foremost councils, namely Nicaea and Chalcedon [451] and many others, a legate has presided and has provided a sure and final settlement of this kind'.[60] Returning once again to the precedents of previous popes in defending his own interests, and claiming characteristically that he was introducing nothing novel, Gregory attempted to reinforce the authority of papal legates in all ecclesiastical matters. Yet despite this informed defence against Manasses's claims, there remained some prevailing ideas among the episcopate about the nature and role of the reforming legate.

The Pope's conscious efforts to develop and extend the legatine office during his pontificate were thus influenced by the immediate need for reform. The sphere of influence in which papal legates were operating during the last quarter of the eleventh century was increasing in scope, as long as the Pope's supervisory methods did not interfere or impede the legate's authority and momentum to any great extent. The administrative and legal ability to meet this need, it might be argued, was made even stronger by Gregory's *Dictatus papae*. An underlying theme of this account — which has some canonical precedent in select church councils, the writings of Ambrose, Popes Gelasius, Gregory I, and Nicholas I, the Pseudo-Isidorian Decretals, and Peter Damian[61] — reflects the papal response to improving the state of the Roman Church to suit the needs of the papacy and political realities of the time. The *Dictatus papae* gave to Gregory and his successors the sole authority 'according to the necessity of time to impose new laws',[62] and to permit a number of other previously unaccustomed measures such as the right to form new dioceses, divide rich bishoprics, depose emperors,[63] and transfer

[59] Gregory was here referring to a monk by the name of Hilary who was sent to parts of Africa.

[60] *Reg.*, VII. 12.

[61] See Cushing, *Papacy and the Law*, Table 4, pp. 216–22.

[62] *Reg.*, II. 55a, sentence 7: 'Quod illi soli licet pro temporis necessitate novas leges condere, novas plebes congregare, de canonica abbatiam facere et e contra, divitem episcopatum dividere et inopes unire.'

[63] *Reg.*, II. 55a, sentence 12: 'Quod illi liceat imperatores deponere.'

bishops from see to see.[64] Gregory's ability to introduce and develop new legal methods for implementing reform moved him one step closer to creating a separate class of legates that were arguably 'Gregorian' in function and purpose.

Indeed, the *Dictatus papae* is perhaps proof that Gregory's thinking was both 'exploratory' and 'developing',[65] in effect increasing the legate's capacity to govern and administer. These twenty-seven sentences on papal authority, as Cowdrey believes, are of the utmost importance for 'illustrating a stage in the development of Gregory's mind'.[66] In this sense, the Pope's intentions in delegating apostolic authority to his legates can be seen as enhancing their juristic authority. The mere construction of this list implies that Gregory was attempting to found or modify prerogatives of papal authority and representation. The papacy's need to specify and document the legate's precedence in distant regions, thereby providing them with the greatest jurisdiction they had ever known, might be viewed in terms of the papacy's need for more direct representation. It might also suggest more clearly his conscious attempt to create a distinctive class of legates.

This makes sense in light of Gregory's campaign to promote reform in regions beyond Italy, and the necessity of creating a willing body of reformers to implement his reforming policy in distant provinces. The fact that these sentences remained relatively unused during Gregory's pontificate raises the question of their overall importance. But as Linda Fowler-Magerl noted, 'the influence on Deusdedit is apparent',[67] thereby suggesting their influence in Rome and Tuscany in the early 1080s. Hubert Mordek discovered a close parallel to the *Dictatus papae* in the *Proprie auctoritates apostolice sedis*, which further suggests the former's influence in Italy, where it has been found in four separate manuscripts (MSS Avranches, Bibliothèque municipale, 146; Pistoia, Archivo Capitolare del Duomo, C. 135; and Venice, Biblioteca Nacionale Marciana, lat. IV. 48; Montecassino, Archivio e Biblioteca dell'Abbazia, 216).[68] Although Anselm II

[64] *Reg.*, II. 55a, sentence 13: 'Quod illi liceat de sede ad sedem necessitate cogente episcopos transmutare.'

[65] Cowdrey, *Pope Gregory VII*, p. 502.

[66] Cowdrey, *Pope Gregory VII*, p. 504.

[67] Fowler-Magerl, *Clavis canonum*, p. 159.

[68] Hubert Mordek, '*Proprie auctoritates apostolice sedis*: Ein zweiter *Dictatus papae* Gregors VII.?', *DA*, 28 (1972), 105–32 (pp. 114–16). See also Friedrich Kempf, 'Ein zweiter *Dictatus Papae*? Ein Beitrag zum Depositionsanspruch Gregors VII.', *Archivum historiae pontificiae*, 13 (1975), 119–39; Myron Wojtowytsch, '*Proprie auctoritates apostolice sedis*: Bemerkungen zu einer bisher unbeachteten Überlieferung', *DA*, 40 (1984), 612–21.

of Lucca appears to have incorporated many of the *Dictatus papae*'s concepts in his *Collectio canonum* (*c.* 1083), there exist many thematic, legal, and moral discrepancies.[69]

Establishing legatine authority, therefore, was not solely aimed at bolstering legatine privileges, nor can it be interpreted simply as an assertion of papal supremacy. As Stephan Kuttner observed, Gregorian canonists were participants in a much larger quest 'for a consistent body of canonical rules, for a common law (*ius commune*) of the Church'.[70] For eleventh-century reformers, the compilation of such a *corpus* would enhance and solidify the authority of church tradition and custom, creating a consolidated theocratic principle of government derived at least initially from Petrine authority.[71] This establishment of papal supremacy held many practical implications. When papal jurisprudence was ever contradicted, for example, or when legislative cases could not be settled in distant regions by the common means of letters, legates, or councils, responsibility rested on the pope and his backing of canon law to make the necessary amendments. Yet by the second half of the eleventh century, a system of church law was already in place, shaping not only Gregory's reforming policies, but also the manner in which they could be implemented directly by the members of his reforming party.

One crucial forum in which reform and law was being implemented, of course, was the legatine council. By Gregory VII's pontificate, their legal and administrative functions were already somewhat formalized by the extant canon law and past experience but nowhere explicitly defined as a set of procedural *ordines*. Existing criteria for universal, ecumenical, provincial, or diocesan councils — best reflected in the ninth-century Decretals of Pseudo-Isidore (*Ordo de celebrando concilio*) and the first book of Burchard of Worms's *Liber decretorum* (*De synodo celebranda*, *c.* 1012) — do not always contribute to our understanding for the last quarter of the eleventh century.[72] Whether legatine councils of this period can be treated separately from other contemporary councils is a question worth

[69] Cushing, *Papacy and the Law*, p. 108.

[70] Stephan Kuttner, '*Liber canonicus*: A Note on the *Dictatus papae* c. 17', *SG*, 2 (1947), 387–401 (p. 396).

[71] For this topic see particularly Gilchrist, 'Reception of Pope Gregory VII', pp. 35–82.

[72] See Hefele-Leclercq, I, 4–8. For some more recent definitions, see *Dictionnaire du droit canonique*, 7 vols (Paris: Letouzey et Ané, 1935–65), III, cols 1268–1301; *Lexikon des Mittelalters*, 9 vols (Munich: Deutscher Taschenbuch, 2003), V, cols 1429–31; and the *New Catholic Encyclopedia*, 19 vols (Washington, DC: Catholic University of America Press, 1967–95), IV, 371–79.

considering in this light, for other than obvious distinctions of representative authority and jurisdiction (encompassing juristic notions of *plenitudo potestatis* and *pars sollicitudinis*), the course of events for conciliar proceedings presumably followed closely their local, diocesan, or provincial counterpart. This seems most evident from a liturgical perspective, examples of which can be found in the tenth-century *Pontificale Romano-Germanicum* and *Pontificale Romanum XII saeculi*.[73]

Only one account helps distinguish the ceremony of legatine councils under Gregory VII, exemplifying the separate status attached to councils of this genre. A letter from Pope Urban II (1096) reveals that the canons of St Martin, Tours, were excommunicated at the Council of Issoudun (1081) for not having received Bishop Amatus of Oloron in procession.[74] Urban eventually revoked this sentence after determining (fifteen years later no less!) that the canons maintained a special privilege obligating them only to receive in procession the Pope, the King of France, and the Archbishop of Tours. There is no mention as to whether his co-presider Hugh of Die was given the same treatment, but the silence of the source (*ex silentio*) — that is, the absence of his name next to that of Amatus — seems to imply his exclusion.

What this episode best reflects is the expected reception of legates in France as the Pope's alter ego. While there is no corroborating evidence into the exact procedural details of legatine councils *c.* 1081, the canons of St Martin certainly paid the price for not receiving Amatus in procession. This account further suggests a demonstration of papal subordination, obligating members of a council to follow what one can only assume was an existing set of *ordines*. In light of the excommunication charge, one might also assume that legates under Gregory VII were regarded seriously as if it were the Pope himself visiting. The fact that this charge remained until 1096 is perhaps proof that the excommunication charge was not an expression of anger, jealousy, or hubris on Amatus's part. Although

[73] C. Vogel and R. Elze, *Le pontificale romano-germanique du dixième siècle*, 3 vols (Vatican City: Biblioteca Apostolica Vaticana, 1963), I, 275–91; Michel Andrieu, *Le pontifical Romain au moyen-âge*, 4 vols (Vatican City: Biblioteca Apostolica Vaticana, 1938–41), I, 255–60. Further evidence of conciliar *ordines*, not just in the Romano-German Pontifical, can be found in *Die Konzilsordines des Früh- und Hochmittelalters*, ed. by Herbert Schneider, MGH, Ordines de celebrando concilio (1996). For discussion of their origin and use in Rome, see Roger E. Reynolds, 'The Liturgy of Rome in the Eleventh Century: Past Research and Future Opportunities', in *Scientia veritatis: Festschrift für Hubert Mordek zum 65. Geburstag*, ed. by O. Munsch and T. Zotz (Ostfildern: Thorbecke, 2004), pp. 227–39 (pp. 232–33).

[74] Pope Urban II, *Epistolae*, in *RHGF*, XIV (1806), 688–737 (hereafter Urban II, *RHGF*, XIV) (letter 49, pp. 719–20).

considered of local interest, this event clearly has wider implications for the status of legates — at least with regard to how Gregory wished to define it *c.* 1081. Their elevated rank among the papal machinery, as chief weaponry for upholding and maintaining justice, was thus directly influenced by their reception in the territories where they were most active in a legal setting.

The bishop's right of appeal to Rome only enhanced this legal capacity, often creating for the legate an increase in provincial legislative matters. Following the transmission to Rome of complaints from distant ecclesiastical provinces, the Pope had to choose whether to handle the case(s) directly or to delegate matters to one or more of his representatives. Legatine authority was thus at its highest in the council arena: bishops could not be condemned outside of this forum, representing, as it did, jurisdictional prevalence in what mimics the modern-day courtroom. Outside of this jurisdiction, the weight of accusations was less meaningful, and to condemn a prelate externally was not considered a catholic practice.[75] The number and quality of judges also played a large part in being able to issue a canonical sentence. An accused bishop possessed the right to twelve judges of his own choosing, and a sentence could not be passed until these twelve men had assembled in council setting and the case was heard and considered rationally. Only then, after careful consideration, oath-taking, and testimony, could it be passed on to the authority of the Roman see.[76]

Jurisdiction

Like the Roman offices of proconsul or urban prefect, the legate's authority derived a large part from the area in which he was able to operate and exercise his powers. The eleventh-century legate was given a geographical territory in which he possessed to an almost unaccountable degree the authority of the pope. The Roman origins of this geographical/legal concept fall into three distinguishable categories: ordinary jurisdiction (*iurisdictio ordinaria*), mandated jurisdiction

[75] Pseudo-Isidore, *Decreta Leonis papae*, in *Decretales Pseudo-Isidorianae et capitula Angilramni*, ed. by P. Hinschius (Leipzig: Tauchnitz, 1863; repr. Aalen: Scientia, 1963) (hereafter cited as Hinschius), ep. 5. I, p. 622. Cf. *Diversorum patrum sententie sive Collectio in LXXIV titulos digesta*, ed. by John Gilchrist (Vatican City: Biblioteca Apostolica Vaticana, 1973), and the English translation: *The Collection in Seventy-four Titles: A Canon Law Manual of the Gregorian Reform*, ed. and trans. by John Gilchrist (Toronto: Pontifical Institute of Mediaeval Studies, 1980) (hereafter cited as 74T), chap. 90.

[76] Pseudo-Zephyrinus, in Hinschius, ep. 1. V–VI, pp. 131–32; cf. 74T, chap. 97.

(*iurisdictio mandata*), and delegated jurisdiction (*iurisdictio delegatus*).[77] But in the eleventh century, churchmen did not possess such clear-cut, thirteenth-century categories. The authority of the reforming legate was not completely defined by a set of technical legal criteria; the eleventh-century legatine concept of *iurisdictio* came to be understood more by the reason of legation, in addition to the papal and legatine interpretation and application of the powers assigned to and inherent in that office.

Legatine jurisdiction, therefore, was not easily categorized, especially when it had to be superimposed on the impermanent and fragmented boundaries of ecclesiastical and political provinces. The Latin terminology, originally based on Roman jurisprudence and administration, is not always conducive to clarifying matters either. Take, for example, that non-descriptive area commissioned to Hugh of Die in 1075, whose jurisdiction does not at first represent distinct geographical boundaries like that given to his colleague Amatus of Oloron. For Hugh, the expressions *Gallia* and *in partibus Galliarum* can be taken to mean a combination of political, ecclesiastical, urban, regional, and geographical boundaries. It was, in one sense, a floating jurisdiction, which seems to represent a larger and less-defined area of jurisdiction. With this appointment, it might be argued that Hugh of Die's appointment enabled him to work in those areas like imperial Burgundy that did not belong politically to the kingdom of France. In contrast, legates dispatched with more specific boundaries would never have possessed the same jurisdictional freedom (*libera administratio*).[78]

The concept of legatine jurisdiction is itself an extension of papal jurisdiction, a smaller unit representing the larger Roman Church. In other words, the jurisdiction assigned to a legate represented a branch of the Roman Church — an obvious extension of papal influence and government in distant regions. From the theoretical view of centralization, the pope oversaw the *societas Christiana*, the metropolitan archbishops their ecclesiastical provinces, the bishops their dioceses, and the priests their parishes. Increasingly during Gregory's pontificate, however,

[77] Figueira, 'Decretalists', pp. 125–26; cf. Gabriel Le Bras, 'Le Droit Romain au service de la domination pontificale', *RHDFE*, 27 (1949), 377–98 (p. 390).

[78] See Robert C. Figueira, 'The Medieval Papal Legate and his Province: Geographical Limits of Jurisdiction', *Apollinaris*, 61 (1988), 817–60 (p. 856), Figueira, 'Canon Law', p. 159, and more recently, Figueira's 'The Medieval Papal Legate and his Province: Geographical Limits of Jurisdiction', in *Plenitude of Power: The Doctrines and Exercise of Authority in the Middle Ages; Essays in Memory of Robert Louis Benson*, ed. by Robert C. Figueira (Aldershot: Ashgate, 2006), pp. 73–105.

it was the permanent legate who regulated entire regions, taking precedence over all bishops in conciliar setting, no matter what their rank or privilege. As the pope's direct and active representative, legatine jurisdiction might be viewed best as papal jurisdiction removed from Rome, or even as a share of that larger jurisdiction (*plenitudo potestatis*).

In terms of centralizing papal government and controlling the peripheral regions of Christendom, it is easy to see why Gregory VII sought a firm jurisdictional control over the episcopate. It was after all this clerical group upon which the reformers set their fiercest sights, targeting them as leading instigators, offenders, aggressors, and potential converts to the reform movement. The Pope's use of legates as a means to achieve this aim for both the success of reform and the preservation of the faith are evident in the sources. By granting his legates more authority, Gregory was defining more clearly their jurisdictional roles, drawing sharper lines between the Pope and his bishops, threatening entirely the rights of metropolitan bishops, and further shaping the established ecclesiastical hierarchy. It is doubtful whether this was Gregory's genuine intention, resulting rather from his increased measures to implement reform in the provinces with greater efficiency and success.

The region governed by the eleventh-century legate was thus an agglomeration of ordinary, mandated, and delegated jurisdiction. More accurately defined, ordinary jurisdiction is derived from merely holding an ecclesiastical office, modelled on the customs and privileges assigned to bishops in their diocese, or priests in their parish. In this sense, ordinary jurisdiction was attached to the legatine title, bestowed upon the legate at the time of his appointment. By contrast, mandated and delegated jurisdiction in this case does not derive from the holding of an office, but designates the authority granted from the commissioning of the office. Legates under Gregory VII, clearly exercising greater authority than the local bishops (including the metropolitan archbishops and primates), assumed an enhanced jurisdiction that gained significance and importance from both the holding and commission of their particular office. The true scope of a legate's jurisdiction is understood by his authority to judge and conclude papal matters independently.

A papal letter written to the disobedient clerks of Romans in 1077, for example, confers enough authority upon Hugh of Die to act entirely on the Pope's behalf (*in nostram vicem*).[79] With regard to a controversy between Archbishop Warmund of Vienne and the clergy of Romans, Gregory instructed the disobedient clerics

[79] *Reg.*, IV. 16; cf. Schmutz, 'Foundations', p. 175.

of Romans to appear before the Bishop of Die (here called *vicarius*), to whom the Pope had committed his *vices* in other matters. They were further instructed to accept the legate's judgement on their behaviour, and to show due humility to him and to the Archbishop of Vienne, who were authorized to impose severe penalties on the clerics if they remained disobedient. In terms of authority, this example presents a clear transition from the earlier offices of apostolic vicar, *apocrisiarius*, and *legatus ad causam*, where papal representation did not yet exist on such a powerful and permanent level.

It was the legate's ability to judge *causae maiores*, when commissioned by the pope to do so, that truly set his office apart from any previously delegated papal institution. It is difficult, however, to assign a precise date when this privilege was first documented as conferred on a legate. Canon law did not permit a legate to engage in matters of criminal or capital punishment; naturally, such matters were reserved for the secular court. But the mandated jurisdiction assigned to reforming legates did permit them to rule freely within their designated territories — albeit under supervision. Their role in the promotion of clerics was never clarified, but Hugh's involvement in episcopal and abbatial elections, as well as in the translation of bishoprics, reflects his elevated status.[80] This authority was multifaceted, encompassing ordinary power, powers that were delegated for specific cases, and the transferring of mandated jurisdiction.[81] It was the later decretalist interpretation of these powers that formalized the legatine role in canon law, as well as distinctively categorizing the functions of offices like judge-delegate.

This hazy understanding of jurisdiction in the latter half of the eleventh century often gives the false impression that reforming legates possessed authority by the mere virtue of their office. This was, of course, far from being the case. The distinguishing factor between the eleventh-century legate and other contemporary representational offices surrounds the general mandate given to a legate upon first being dispatched. Reference has already been made to Amatus of Oloron's appointment to southern France and northern Spain; Hugh of Die was likewise appointed jurisdiction in parts of Gaul, albeit in less specific terms. Wherever a legate might travel, wherever he might hold a council or issue a sentence or decree, he did not require a legally binding or instructional letter to be read aloud in the assembly. He did not, in more simple terms, need a piece of

[80] Texts on episcopal translation and restitution are found in Burchard's *Decretum*, in PL, CXL (1880), cols 537–1057 (cols 616–18); cf. 74T, chaps 186–90.

[81] Figueira, 'Canon Law', pp. 161–62.

parchment warranting or proving his authority and power. This attachment was associated most commonly with the medieval papal nuncio from Gregory's time up to the modern period, distinguishing more clearly the level of autonomy and authority granted to legates within their jurisdiction. But it is primarily the close and participatory aspect of the reforming legate's relationship with the pope that diminished any necessity of this mandate. The greatest difference between the two coexisting offices rested in the legate's ability to exercise his powers independently (as mentioned), as the pope empowered him to do.[82]

The less-formalized attributes of the reforming legate are understood best in comparison with the office of judge-delegate, whose role came to be defined more clearly under Pope Gregory IX (1227–41).[83] With an increasing legal caseload for the papacy and legates alike, the office of judge-delegate came to assume the role of relief assistance, developing to lighten the papal burden and — following the pontificate of Pope Paschal II (1099–1118) — to operate as an 'expedient for ascertaining local knowledge'.[84] Thus the mandate given to a judge-delegate is explained best in terms of litigation, resembling the credence given to the papal nuncio and offering, in more legal terminology, the 'necessary phrases to create the judge's competence'.[85] One cannot help but relate this later office to the similar role exhibited by Gregory's legatine assistants. The authority of a judge-delegate, however, unlike the eleventh-century reforming legate, depended more on mandated and other delegated jurisdiction for the representational transferring of papal authority.

Reforming legates were thus subject directly to papal review, and they were expected to remain in constant communication with Rome. By the very nature of their office, their jurisdiction, and their relationship with the pope, the legate held a large share in the papal burden of responsibility. This portion, it might be argued, far exceeded that assigned to a regular bishop. But the distinction between the authority assumed by the pope, and that assigned to his representative, rested on a similar concept of 'fullness of power' (*plenitudo potestatis*) and the delegation of that power for administrative purposes. Like the episcopal office in the eleventh century, it is commonly held that legates of this period shared only in the ecclesiastical responsibility (*in partem sollicitudinis*) for the salvation of souls, but

[82] Schmutz, 'Medieval Papal Representatives', p. 459.

[83] Robert Somerville and Bruce Brasington, *Prefaces to Canon Law Books in Latin Christianity: Selected Translations, 500–1245* (New Haven: Yale University Press, 1998), p. 226.

[84] Sayers, *Papal Judges*, p. 9.

[85] Schmutz, 'Medieval Papal Representatives', p. 462.

never arguably in the fullness of power. To carry out the work of this centralized monarchy effectively required the careful balancing of the pope's *plenitudo potestatis* with the bishop's *pars sollicitudinis*. Later decretalists like Pope Innocent III believed this power to be signified by the papal *pallium*, referring to jurisdictional rather than sacramental powers.[86]

Under Gregory VII, the *sollicitudo* in parts of France was clearly committed to Hugh of Die.[87] That Hugh believed this privilege to extend to episcopal elections is evident from his later correspondence with Bishop Ivo of Chartres, in a matter concerning the consecration of the Bishop of Orléans in 1097. Citing a fifth-century decretal from Pope Leo I to Bishop Anastasius of Thessalonica, Hugh interpreted this source as justifying his right of consultation in elections within his jurisdiction.[88] Ivo replied by clarifying that Leo's grant to Anastasius was a personal privilege, and not as Hugh understood it a general rule. Citing another letter by Pope Leo, Ivo showed how Anastasius was acting under the authority of papal legate and not as the bishop of Thessalonica.[89] Following this line of thought, Ivo clearly believed that the legate's *pars sollicitudinis* did not extend to the sphere of episcopal elections, thus finding it unnecessary to seek Hugh's approval in the matter. The genuine issue at stake, rather, concerned Hugh of Die's legatine authority *c.* 1097.

Hugh's personal knowledge of legal authority and responsibility, on the other hand, suggests an alternative and opposing understanding. For this reason alone, his attempt to exercise greater powers might be interpreted best as an exercise of the greater procuratorial powers available to him. By that stage of his ecclesiastical

[86] Robert L. Benson, *The Bishop-Elect: A Study in Medieval Ecclesiastical Office* (Princeton: Princeton University Press, 1968), pp. 172–73.

[87] *Reg.*, VII. 1.

[88] Pope Leo I, *Sancti Leonis Magni Romani pontificis opera omnia*, PL, LIV (1881), col. 1261; Dionysius Exiguus, *Collectio prima Decretorum pontificum romanorum*, in PL, LXVII (1863), cols 229–316 (col. 293): 'Vices enim nostras ita tuae credidimus charitati, ut in partem sis vocatus sollicitudinis, non in plenitudinem potestatis.' Extended in Pseudo-Isidore: Pseudo-Vigilius, in Hinschius, ep. 7, p. 712; Ivo of Chartres, *Correspondance*, I, 234–36, letter 59: 'Quod vero scripsistis propter officium legationis vobis injunctae prius ad notitiam vestram hoc fuisse referendum, ut tunc eum demum consecraremus, cum quod vobis bene placeret agnosceremus, quoniam sic praeceperit papa Leo Anastasio Thessalonicensi episcopo, legato suo, personale hoc intelligimus fuisse privilegium, non generale decretum, maxime cum, secundum eumdem Leonem,. legationis officium pars sit apostolicae sollicitudinis, non plenitudo potestatis'; cf. Robinson, 'Church and Papacy' (p. 282).

[89] Ivo of Chartres, *Epistolae*, letter 60, cols 70–75.

legatine career, Hugh had good reason to suspect that his role in elections was of great importance, in spite of not having any existing legal mandate to back up this claim.

As to whether legates ever received the fullness of power directly from the pope, one example can be offered that relates to the deposition and excommunication of Archbishop Manasses I of Reims.[90] Harking back to the fifth-century Leonine theory stated above, Manasses accused Hugh of stepping beyond the boundaries of his authority in judging a bishop. Citing directly from the Pseudo-Isidorian Decretals, Manasses contended that Hugh's *vices* extended to a portion of solicitude, but not in the plenitude of power.[91] Unlike the rebuke received nearly twenty years later from Bishop Ivo of Chartres, Manasses's claims presumably rested also upon his elevated status as metropolitan bishop, whose prestigious office should have been protected (according to him) by tradition and custom, and therefore not subject to accusation. But this claim also rested on his familiarity with, and obedience to, canon law, well illustrated in this long-winded and defensive letter to Hugh of Die, and a similar letter of equal length issued to the Pope.[92] Yet while this example reflects one of the numerous uncertainties prevalent in the eleventh-century struggle to consolidate canon law in the midst of reform, it provides only a narrow episcopal view.

Gregory's view was not seemingly as strict or formalized. Referring to the privileges that could be granted to his representatives, the Pope declared how these could be altered 'in respect of matter, person, or time' (pro persona pro tempore pro loco), providing an extensive remit.[93] As long as these concessions did

[90] Robinson, 'Church and Papacy', p. 282.

[91] Manasses I of Reims, in *Briefsammlungen der Zeit Heinrichs IV*, pp. 178–82 (no. 107, p. 181).

[92] See n. 91, above, and *RHGF*, XIV, 781–86, respectively. In defending the reasons why he would not attend Hugh's Lyonnais council in 1080, Manasses referred back to a sentence of Justinian law (mentioned only in passing). This one example does not provide enough evidence, however, to suggest Manasses's mastery of this law, or the availability of its edition. It seems more likely that the Archbishop was using a copy of the Pseudo-Isidorian Decretals. His later reference in this same letter to the decretals of Euvaristus (100–09), Eutychian (275–83), Leo I, and Gregory I, strengthens this suspicion.

[93] *Reg.*, VI. 2. Bernold of Constance considered the pope's *plenitudo potestatis* in jurisdictional terms. For 'just as a king divides his kingdom among dukes, counts, and judges, and yet does not diminish his royal power, so too the pope divides his "care" among all bishops without diminishing his "universal and principal power"'. See his *Apologeticus*, no. 23, in *Libelli de lite imperatorum et pontificum saeculis XI. et XII. conscripti*, ed. by Ernst Dümmler, Friedrich Thaner, and Ernst

not violate the authority of the holy fathers, which Gregory clearly believed was not the case, they could only 'have regard to the benefit of the holy church'. In other words, the pope could grant his legate or bishop a share in the fullness of power if it was for the greater good of the Church, effectively to serve the reformers' more immediate needs and interests.[94]

There is then a distinctive similarity between the theoretical constructs of *pars sollicitudinis* and legatine jurisdiction. Similar to bishops, legates were given a share in the responsibility of the whole, referring to the care with which they must represent the Roman Church in their respective parish, diocese, province, or larger jurisdiction. Each share (*pars*) was specific to the designated person, and to infringe on this space was worthy of rebuke. In 1079, the Roman subdeacon Hubert was chastised by the Pope for his interference in the *sollicitudo* of Hugh of Die, suggesting very clearly that the terminology in this case represented a principle much more concrete than abstract. According to Gregory, the responsibility for ecclesiastical matters in the region of France had been committed previously to Hugh alone, deeming Hubert's business there as undesirable, unnecessary, and utterly inappropriate.

What these terms suggest with some certainty is 'the participatory and derivative aspects of legatine jurisdiction, and thus implicitly connote a type of representation far more direct than could be provided by the compartmentalized bilaterality and intermediate mechanisms of classical Roman representation, whether in stipulation or procuration'.[95] In more simple and less-legal language, the eleventh-century legate now had more independent control of his office and jurisdiction than ever before, this being a time when methods of papal supervision were limited, and the means to control and regulate this representative office were still being tested and structured. The participatory aspect of legatine jurisdiction suggests the Pope's more personal connection and care in selecting legates first-hand — an evident development from the office of *nuncius*, whose representational status did not surpass the boundaries of procuratorial power.

Sackur, MGH, Libelli, 2, (1892), 87–88: 'Unde liquido demonstratur, quod quilibet episcopus nec super gregem sibi commissum tantam potestatem habeat, quantum presul apostolicus, qui licet curam suam in singulos episcopos diviserit, nullomodo tamen se ipsum sua unversali et principali potestate privavit, sicut nec rex suam regalem potentiam diminuit, licet regnum suum in diversos duces, comites sive iudices diviserit'; cf. Figueira's translation in 'Canon Law', p. 202.

[94] *Reg.*, VI. 2.

[95] Benson, *Bishop-Elect*, p. 92.

Thus the legatine role in caring for the salvation of souls is not under question. For the bishop, this share of responsibility was inherent in the episcopal office, in his symbolic marriage to the Church. For the legate, the burden of responsibility carried more weight because of his larger jurisdiction, and hence the greater judicial, spiritual, and moral authority, all of which could only have increased his share in the overall responsibility. It is the legate's role in exercising the fullness of power that remains suspect. The distinction between these two roles was clarified in the twelfth and thirteenth centuries as the legate's function became more consolidated in canon law. Bernard of Clairvaux addressed the issue in 1135, marking the fullness of power as a unique privilege given specifically to the apostolic see.[96] By that stage, the papal concept of *plenitudo potestatis* began to appear more frequently in the papal chancery.[97] Under Pope Alexander III — and not before — the *plenitudo potestatis* was eventually presented in papal letters as the authority given by the pope to his legate.[98] It was not effectively until the appearance of the twelfth-century cardinal-legate that this representation of supreme papal authority came to be seen in practice, and it would appear that the eleventh-century papal reform played a decisive role in this later development. But even then, the legate's fullness of power was only ever understood 'within the limits of the definition of that power'.[99]

There is nonetheless a noticeable growth in legatine authority from the eleventh to the later twelfth century. But does this evident shift make it more possible to identify the true extent of the authority embodied by the reforming legate under Gregory VII, without falling into anachronism? One questionable method for assessing this level of competence has been to compare it with our understanding of papal powers, using the decretalist view of specialized 'papal reserved powers'[100] upon the earlier models of legatine authority. In other words, we can compare the powers of administration (*potestas administrationis*) possessed by the pope to those of his legates. While the dangers of applying later views are evident, a comparison of this sort might serve to understand the roots of decretalist thought, some of which was presumably influenced by the administration of the legatine office under Gregory's pontificate. Determining the origins

[96] Bernard of Clairvaux, *Opera omnia*, PL, CLXXXII (1879), letter 131, cols 286–87.

[97] Ladner, 'Concepts of "Ecclesia"', p. 63.

[98] Robinson, *Papacy*, p. 92.

[99] Ladner, 'Concepts of "Ecclesia"', p. 63.

[100] See Figueira, 'Papal Reserved Powers', pp. 194–211, especially pp. 205–11.

of this later thought, however — i.e., which of Gregory's letters (if any) the decretalists were citing — must be left to the experienced canonist. And the extent to which the eleventh-century legatine institution influenced and shaped the later representative offices of *legatus natus*, *legatus a latere*, *legatus missus*, and *iudex delegatus* has already been suggested.

There were numerous powers possessed only by the pope, setting him apart from his subordinates. This supreme *imperium* no doubt rested with the spiritual authority on which the papacy was founded, but also on the pope's autonomous claim to the fullness of power. Yet even a cursory glance at Hugh of Die's legatine activity shows him exercising many of these later defined papal reserved powers, stressing further the *ad hoc* nature of the papal institution in the eleventh century. A summary of thirteenth-century decretalist views according to Johannes Teutonicus, Hostiensis, and Bernard of Parma shows that the pope held the authority to decide *causae maiorae* and questions of faith, to judge, depose, restore, and transfer bishops, and to receive their renunciations and exempt them from metropolitan authority. He also had the power to convoke councils, transfer bishops, divide or unite a cathedral church, dispense in cases of affinity and consanguinity, absolve incendiaries and counterfeiters, dispense bigamists, interpret a canon, restore a heretic, determine penance in violent crimes, etc.[101]

By comparison, the reforming legate held the authority to decide *causae maiorae* and *minimae*, questions of faith, to judge and depose bishops, but not to restore or transfer them or their bishoprics.[102] Legates and bishops certainly held the power to convoke a council with papal permission, but their function in matters of absolution or dispensation is not entirely certain. Altogether, of the twenty-two papal reserved powers estimated by the decretalists, a total of five can be said with some certainty to have been performed regularly by legates during the eleventh century. Certainly, this represents only a small fraction, but when exercised effectively and in concert, these rights and privileges proved powerful instruments in disseminating Gregory's reform policy to various regions. In effect, these comparatively few powers provided the legate with many legal, religious, and moral weapons.

[101] Figueira, 'Canon Law', pp. 493–503.

[102] The thirteenth sentence of Gregory's *Dictatus papae* reinforced the Pope's privileged authority in translating bishops: 'Quod illi liceat de sede ad sedem necessitate cogente episcopos' (*Reg.*, II. 55a).

Conclusion

While the office of legation was by no means a novel concept, the way in which it was managed during Gregory's pontificate proved innovative. The Pope had found reliable means to enforce papal conformity by dispatching trusted ecclesiastics to carry out the necessary, unfinished, and often drawn-out business that filtered into Rome. Under Gregory, the effectiveness and strength of the legatine office reached a high point.[103] What made his administering of the papal machinery more effective than his predecessors was to hand-pick men with a commanding familiarity in provincial regions; figures like Hugh of Die, who were familiar not only with the local and regional church personnel, but figures who knew the language, customs, and tradition; men with zealous and rigorous personalities who shared Gregory's ideal for a celibate clergy and a church free from bribery and lay influence. His choices for a reforming party came not from the high secular clergy, as was customary, but from the native regions to which most, like Bishops Hugh of Die, Amatus of Oloron, and Altmann of Passau, were from sees of minor importance. (The see of Lucca, admittedly, was a key site on the Via Francigena — that 'main route from Canterbury to Rome in the tenth and following centuries'[104] — and therefore does not fit as neatly into such a classification.) From this ordering of men and machinery, the legatine office developed with very few established rules or guidelines. There was clearly yet to be, as there was to be with the later decretalists, a code of practice or *ordines* on which legates could model their legal approach.

In spite of this observation, as Gilchrist convincingly argued, a careful reading of Gregory's *Register* 'leaves the impression that Gregory had no policy, no consistent treatment of issues that came before him, and no administration sufficiently developed to enable him to preserve his energies for the "great affairs" that involved him and his circle'.[105] While Gilchrist's conclusions draw from his study of the Pope's economic policy, the same claims can be made with our present study. The Pope's use of the office of legation, like his economic policy, was certainly 'elementary and fragmented precisely because it depended on the

[103] Schieffer, *Die päpstlichen Legaten*, p. 88; cf. Robinson 'Reform and the Church', p. 327.

[104] See Linda Fowler-Magerl, 'The Collection and Transmission of Canon Law along the Northern Section of the Via Francigena in the Eleventh and Twelfth Centuries', in *Bishops, Texts and the Use of Canon Law around 1100: Essays in Honour of Martin Brett*, ed. by Bruce C. Brasington and Kathleen G. Cushing (Aldershot: Ashgate, 2008), pp. 129–40.

[105] John Gilchrist, 'Eleventh and Early Twelfth Century Canonical Collections and the Economic Policy of Gregory VII', *SG*, 9 (1972), 377–417 (p. 377).

sort of law found in the canonical collections at large'.[106] That law lacked cohesion, and its primitiveness produced inevitable conflict and contradiction. Hugh of Die's treatment of specific cases, and Gregory's response to these decisions — sometimes confirming, sometimes revising, and sometimes reproving (see below, Chapter 4) — testifies to these inevitabilities, making us wonder whether Gregory was acting *sui iuris* or *secundum auctoritates*.

But it goes without saying that legatine authority in the eleventh century was far from infinite; it was most limited in jurisprudential matters. In the thirteenth century, these constraints were imposed most easily on legates through a process of classification — tantamount to being typecast — a construction used by the pope to safeguard the methods of supervision. This measure was to ensure that all legates remained 'subject to papal supervision (to varying extents) and to the pope's ultimate review'.[107] Only under special instructions from the pope (*mandata*) could legates ever expect to administrate without restraint. But no matter how competent and successful a legate might appear he could never entirely avoid papal supervision, at least not while operating legally within the boundaries of canon law. Ideally, the eleventh-century legatine office embodied an active and omnipresent institution of papal will and justice set up to extend papal influence to the borders of Christendom. But this construct was purely theoretical; Gregory's use of legates and their own conduct while on legation was at times a very different story.

Given these complex institutional, administrative, and legal considerations, Hugh of Die must be viewed not merely as a legate bearing papal authority but also as a confrontational field reformer, commissioned with a specific mandate by the pope. He was a priest, a bishop, and an archbishop. Hugh was an instrument of reform, a willing advocate for restoration, a wilful and methodical extender of papal influence, and the Roman Church's most obvious and immediate response to simony, nicolaitism, and lay investiture in France. But most of all, Hugh, like his counterparts in the legatine field, was a judge and arbitrator whose 'education, knowledge, and mastery of the processes and procedures of the law opened new paths to influence status'.[108] How he went about cleaning up these abuses — as

[106] Gilchrist, 'Eleventh and Early Twelfth Century Canonical Collections', p. 379.

[107] See Robert C. Figueira, '*Legatus apostolice sedis*: The Pope's "Alter Ego" According to Thirteenth-Century Canon Law', *Studi medievali*, 27 (1986), 527–74 (p. 539).

[108] Charles Duggan, 'Papal Judges Delegate and the Making of the "New Law" in the Twelfth Century', in *Lordship, Status, and Process in Twelfth-Century Europe*, ed. by Thomas N. Bisson (Philadelphia: University of Pennsylvania Press, 1995), p. 195.

illustrated in the following chapter — was at times entirely of his own volition and discretion, sometimes overstepping the boundaries of his jurisdiction and thus earning a papal warning.

Yet whatever might be said about the extent and nature of Hugh's authority and jurisdiction, there remains little doubt that the legatine office under Gregory VII was transformed to become wholly 'Gregorian' in the way it worked. Such a development cannot fail to take into account this office's later and inevitable modifications under successive papal administrations, exhibiting continuity in the legal and administrative function of this ecclesiastical office. In directing this branch of papal government to meet their immediate needs and interests, individual popes certainly left their mark on the legatine office, and none more so than Gregory VII.

Chapter 4

LAW AND REFORM: THEORY AND PRACTICE

Inaugurated as Bishop of Die in 1073 with the Pope's utmost confidence and support, Hugh's familiarity with the reformers' agenda is not in question. Digesting in person the early teachings of Gregory's 1074 Lent synod, at which he was present, proved influential and instructional for his undertaking of the legatine office later in 1075.[1] The decrees from this Roman council, which exist in full as twenty-six *capitula*, are representative of the reformers' objectives for combating simony, nicolaitism, and lay investiture.[2] Offering one of the most detailed accounts for a universal synod during Gregory's pontificate (with the exception of his 1078 November synod),[3] the potential influence of this legislation in shaping Hugh of Die's legal mentality is manifest. The council arena provided Gregory with an opportunity for persuading newly recruited members of his reforming party as well as those summoned to attend his Roman councils,

[1] Mansi, XX, cols 401–31. See also Gregory's letters to Archbishops Siegfried of Mainz and Werner of Magdeburg, and Bishop Otto of Constance (*Ep. vag.*, 6–8); cf. Uta-Renate Blumenthal, *Gregor VII. Papst zwischen Canossa und Kirchenreform* (Darmstadt: Primus, 2001), pp. 150–59.

[2] See especially Mansi, XII, *capitula* 6, 'De primo statuto, id est de simoniacis' (cols 408–10); 7, 'De secundo statuto, id est de emptoribus ecclesiarum' (col. 410); 8, 'Quod et sacra scriptura damnet venditores spiritualium officiorum' (cols 410–11); 9–10, 'Item quod emptores eorum damnet, et quod mediatores hujus negotii damnet' (cols 411–13); 11, 'De tertio statuto dictae decretalis epistolae, id est, ut incontinentes altari nullatenus minstrent' (cols 413–15); 12, 'De anathemate eorum qui defendunt incontinentiam sacerdotum per Sozomeni cap. ex tripartita historia depromptum' (col. 415); 13, 'Quod non sacrorum ministries, sed laicis permissum est, ut unusquisque suam habeat uxorem' (cols 415–17); 17, 'De quarto statuto praedictae decretalis epistolae, ne populus officia clericorum recipiat, quos apostolica statuta contemnere videat' (cols 422–23).

[3] For this record see *Reg.*, VI. 5b.

offering a prime occasion for moral, religious, and legal instruction. It is plausible to suggest that much of Hugh's reforming zeal and enthusiasm stems from his exposure at this Roman council, from viewing firsthand the implementation of Gregory's reforming policies in a legal setting, all the while learning and adopting his own methods for the application and interpretation of that law for future recourse in the council arena.

The preliminary responsibilities assigned to Hugh's episcopal office fit with this 1074 Roman legislation. 'For amongst other things', as Gregory wrote in his papal *Register*, Hugh was urged 'to raise himself up with all his powers against the simoniac heresy, and that he should not consecrate the churches of his diocese, nor should he allow those which have been consecrated otherwise to celebrate divine service, unless they are first released from the hands of the laity and, as is canonically correct, restored to their own right and to his episcopal oversight'.[4] Indeed, from the very beginning of Hugh's legatine career, anyone opposed to his implementing the commands of the Roman Church, by apostolic authority, could render themselves subject to anathema.

As noted above (see Chapter 2), it proves difficult to distinguish between Hugh of Die's episcopal and legatine duties: his vocation as the bishop of Die, from 1073 until his translation to the archdiocese of Lyon in 1082, fades into the background of his legation under Gregory VII. To be sure, details of episcopal careers are often lacking for this period, making Hugh's case little more than a casualty of time. The papal polemic against clerical marriage, simony, and lay investiture is also to blame, consuming Hugh's entire ecclesiastical career while narrowing further any distinction between his role as bishop and legate. The letter to Count William of Die noted above shows the business of both offices as being relatively similar in purpose. In fact, only three pieces of evidence ever directly mention Hugh's activity as the bishop of Die.[5] The first two refer to his role in witnessing a donation charter, one in 1074[6] and the other in 1076.[7] The third case

[4] *Reg.*, I. 69.

[5] Lühe, *Hugo von Die und Lyon*, pp. 3–13, provides the fullest account for Hugh's activity as bishop.

[6] *Chartarum viennensis diocesis ineditarum*, no. 123, p. 30. This donation was made by Count Guigo's *ministralis*, Gerard Roux (Rufus) to the monks of Cornillio: 'dedit monachis Curnillionis viginti quatuor festaria frumenti ad mensuram ville de Orbes, quod frumentum accipiebat in oreo comitis qum segetes excutiebantur; in parrochia ubi Sancti Laurentii, in loco qui dicitur Portils,. dedit vineas quas ibi habebat'.

[7] Archbishop Leodegar of Vienne donated the church of St Ferreolus to the church of Saint-Julien. See *Cartulaire de Brioude*, ed. by M. Henry Doniol (Clermont: Thibaud, 1863), no. 238,

can be viewed in the wider context of Gregory's economic reorganization of the Roman see.

Seeking revenues generated by monasteries and cathedral chapters in France, Gregory issued an encyclical letter in 1075 appealing for the renewal of payment and taxes owed to the Roman see. Referring to the tradition of paying an annual tax established under his predecessors Nicholas II and Alexander II (clearly modelled on the idea of the English Peter's Pence and the *census* collected from Norway and Sweden), Gregory reprimanded the abbots and superiors of religious houses in France for their carelessness (*neglegentia*) and obstinacy (*induratus*) in paying their dues. The task of collecting these taxes and enforcing payments was given to Bishop Hugh of Die, who had up to this point 'faithfully performed all the duties [...] laid upon him'.[8]

There are nonetheless some lingering doubts surrounding the nature of these episcopal duties that, following 1075, could have been carried out just as legitimately under Hugh's legatine title. It was common for legates to undertake matters of tax collection in addition to numerous other less significant but altogether necessary ecclesiastical trivialities.[9] Their role as representative administrators of the Roman Church demanded competency at all levels, despite the council arena being by far the most active environment for the assertion of legatine authority and jurisdiction. It was essentially the legate's role in juristic surroundings, moreover, that could earn for him a reputation as an intransigent reformer. Hugh of Die's legatine career is a prime example of one such reformer whose character has been typecast too carelessly or hastily by these criteria. The reasons for this treatment are exemplified best through the antagonism of his ecclesiastical activity, first evidenced in his early years as the bishop of Die.

For despite the Pope's initial encouragement, Hugh of Die was issued a papal warning in January 1075 for the severity with which he was exercising his ecclesiastical office.[10] With this letter, Gregory advised his bishop to be more cautious when dealing with his subjects, hinting at the Pope's recognition of Hugh's

pp. 247–50. D. B. Zema, 'Economic Reorganization of the Roman See during the Gregorian Reform', *SG*, 1 (1947), 137–68 (pp. 164–66).

[8] *Ep. vag.*, 12.

[9] Robert C. Figueira, 'Subdelegation by Papal Legates in Thirteenth-Century Canon Law: Powers and Limitations', in *In iure veritas: Studies in Canon Law in Memory of Schafer Williams*, ed. by Steven B. Bowman and Blanche E. Cody (Cincinnati: University of Cincinnati, College of Law, 1991), pp. 56–79 (p. 56).

[10] *Reg.*, II. 43 (Rome, 5 January 1075).

sometimes-excessive behaviour in handling ecclesiastical matters, suggesting his preference for the strictness of canon law over pastoral mildness. Gregory professed how much more pleasing it would be if Hugh were 'censured for mercy' rather than 'incur the hatred' of his church for excessive severity ('pro nimia severitate'). Exactly what Gregory knew of these machinations is indeed suspect, as is the source and reliability of the information that prompted him into immediate action. Gregory called for sympathy with the actions of this inexperienced bishop, urging him — as Hugh of Flavigny attests — not to abuse the power granted to him for the correction of vice and suppression of evil, but to teach goodness and holiness and to be himself an example.[11]

Gregory's confidence that his young bishop would correct the troubles of his Burgundian see is apparent in this account, yet mention was nonetheless given to the constraints of apostolic command binding each subordinate to the apostolic see. This careful reference to the limitations of church law is worth noting, especially considering the possibility that the cautionary letter issued to Hugh in 1075 resulted from his breach of these legal limits or his more literal application of the extant law — two likely scenarios.

Whatever actions truly encouraged this account (the details of which remain unknown), Gregory's personal interest in Hugh's conduct was manifested at an early stage of his ecclesiastical career, heightening the Pope's sensibilities towards his bishop's legal inclinations. The Pope alludes in this letter to the unnecessary troubles caused to both the Roman Church and the accused by hasty judgement. While Gregory's warning presumably affected the administration of his episcopal see, Hugh's promotion to the legatine office followed soon after this letter's transmission, suggesting that the Pope regarded Hugh's zeal as only a minor infraction. This sequence of events is perhaps also indicative of the favour given to Hugh's treatment of ecclesiastical business, willing to overlook slight deviations from the Pope's display of discretion.

That the Pope regarded Hugh as more than a disposable instrument for reform seems a safe assertion: the legate's experience with papal reform policies prior to 1075, and his familiarity with the areas and people within his later legatine jurisdiction, are all beyond reasonable question. What remains to be determined is this legate's application and understanding of reform and law in the context of late eleventh-century France. As the following examples illustrate, Hugh of Die's legatine employment of discretion and canonical rigour can be seen testing and

[11] Hugh of Flavigny, p. 412: 'Plurimum illi inculcans, potestate data non abuti, quo minus depravata corrigeret, dampnanda recideret, sancta et honesta doceret, et docenda faceret.'

somewhat haphazardly shaping Gregory VII's reform initiative in France. His application of the law was simultaneously extending and defining the boundaries and limitations for legatine authority in the last quarter of the eleventh century. The relationship between the Pope and his legate was at times of secondary concern to enforcing reform ideology by the most efficient means possible. Through a process of trial and error in- and outside the council arena, Hugh's own legatine authority developed alongside the papacy's ability to extend its influence to the borders of Western Christendom, often stepping beyond the parameters of what Gregory considered lawful and fair. Acting in the name of equity (*aequitas*) and justice (*iustitia*), Gregory was at times forced to trump the legalistic views of his legates, which administrative action brings to light some fine distinctions in the contemporary treatment and understanding of law and practice in the age of reform.

Shortly following his 1078 Lent (Roman) synod, to take a more definitive example, Gregory VII deemed it necessary to issue an official revision of sentences passed by Hugh of Die upon French bishops (9 March 1078), challenging and reversing a total of six judgements passed at the legate's Autun (September 1077 — four cases) and Poitiers (January 1078 — two cases) councils. Gregory's complaint lay exclusively with the manner in which these conciliar sentences were reached, reflecting his concern that Hugh's adjudicating methods were following too closely the rigour of the canons (*rigor canonicus*) rather than the more papal-desired restraint of discretion (*discretionis temperantiam*).[12]

The most important case, and the first to be addressed in this memorandum, concerned the sentence issued against Archbishop Manasses I of Reims (1069–80) for his absence from successive councils at Autun (1077) and Poitiers (1078).[13] After more careful investigation, Gregory concluded that the charge brought forth by his legate Hugh of Die 'seemed not to have been passed with the weightiness and accustomed mildness of the Roman Church',[14] and henceforth restored Manasses to his rank and office. The subtlety of this explanation and the ambiguity of its' meaning can be interpreted as antagonistic towards Hugh of Die's council (thus legal) methods. The Pope's genuine concern, however, rested

[12] *Reg.*, V. 17.

[13] See Robinson, 'Friendship Network', pp. 15–18.

[14] *Reg.*, V. 17: 'quia sententia super eum data non Romane ecclesie gravitate et solita mansuetudine videbatur'.

in knowing whether his representative had in any way violated canon law. As long as the Pope and his legate were operating within the existing framework of church discipline, their objectives for enforcing reform policy should in theory scarcely have been distinguished. Any noticeable difference in their methodological approach should not have restricted Hugh's power to depose Manasses, unless by the Roman Church's 'gravitas et solita mansuetudo' Gregory was referring to an evident misunderstanding or contradiction in this law.[15] This seems to me the most plausible case, rendering Hugh's deposition of the Archbishop as unjustifiable, thereby warranting a papal revision of his sentence.

Although Gregory's revision might seem like a direct challenge to the power of the legatine court, his intervention was warranted by the precepts of papal authority. Legates were still ultimately required to answer to the Pope in cases that issued anathema and, as a result, the sentences of excommunication and deposition passed by Hugh had to be lifted because (in the words of John Gilchrist) they 'had not been given by Rome'.[16] In matters of appeal, and reinforced by the twentieth sentence of his *Dictatus papae* (issued *c.* 1075),[17] Gregory was responsible for protecting those members of the Roman Church who had sought her protection. Following his first suspension at the Council of Autun in 1077, Manasses had launched an appeal that was not officially settled until his final excommunication at Lyon in 1080. Before the Pope had become convinced of his guilt, however, this appeal — ignored entirely by Hugh of Die — enabled the Archbishop to reclaim his office on a legal technicality. One can only assume that the seriousness of this case and Hugh's relaxing of canon law — not to mention Manasses's repeated complaints made directly to the Roman see — had backed Gregory into a tight corner. From this perspective, it was not Hugh's authority that was being questioned, or for that matter his conciliar methods, but rather his personal conception of canonical rigour: that is to say, his application of law for reforming purposes.

The five remaining cases discussed in Gregory's 1078 memorandum were resolved more easily. Archbishop Hugh of Besançon was restored to his episcopal office (after failing to attend the Autun council) on the condition that he purge himself of the charges 'before our legate' (coram legato nostro), with his suffragans or neighbouring bishops.[18] This settlement was proposed after Gregory discovered

[15] *Reg.*, V. 17.

[16] Gilchrist, 'Canon Law Aspects', p. 28.

[17] *Reg.*, II. 55a: 'Quod nullus audeat condemnare apostolicam sedem apellantem.'

[18] These were the Bishops of Belley, Avenches, and Basel.

that the council summons had been withheld purposely from the Archbishop by his own clerks, and thus never shown to him. Exercising fully his canonical rights, Hugh had appealed the case and thus managed to sidestep any pleas of extenuating circumstances. It appears that Hugh of Die, however, was not entirely unjust in his initial sentencing; he was following closely the canonical procedure which demanded the Archbishop's presence to the summoned council, or at the very least, his sending of representatives or a legitimate excuse in his absence. Unfortunately for the legate, however, the factors explaining the Archbishop's absence from Autun — as Gregory was impelled to conclude by condition of law — could not justify papal confirmation of the suspension charge.

Archbishop Richerius of Sens, suspended at Poitiers (1078) for his failure to attend, was likewise restored to his office. In return, he promised (*in manu nostra*) to explain to Hugh of Die either personally or through his messenger why he had not attended the council. He also promised that 'in matters of ecclesiastical business he would, as best he might, faithfully and humbly secure for himself counsel and aid, and compose his mind'. The Archbishop's assurance appears to have meant a great deal to Gregory, enough so that Richerius' reinstatement seems to have been granted almost immediately and without dispute. In fact, the relative ease with which this settlement was reached implies that Richerius had made his promise directly to the Pope in Rome (explaining the meaning of *in manu nostra*), escaping Hugh's judgement through an appeal to the papal court.

Archbishop Richard of Bourges, who had left his church 'in a spirit of anger and not by synodal judgement', could not be condemned for any wrongdoing. Gregory was inclined to return to him his staff and ring — taken from him at the Council of Autun — in exchange for his promise to clear himself of any charges before Hugh of Die. The exact nature of the charges facing him are unknown, but one might speculate that Hugh played a role in inciting or provoking the Archbishop's anger at the Council of Autun, which meeting he appears to have attended dutifully. Of course, there is no definitive proof to implicate Hugh in this regard, but his ability to aggravate those whom he considered indolent towards the goal of reform should not be overlooked or underestimated.

Bishop Gosfred of Chartres (1077–89), who had 'not been summoned and had been condemned in absence' at the Council of Autun, was restored to his episcopal office on the condition that Hugh of Die take another look at his case. Because canon law forbid judgement to be passed against those who had not been summoned, the charge facing Gosfred had to be reversed by the Pope. This having been said, the truth of Gosfred's excommunication, and his subsequent reinstatement by the Pope in 1078, does not entirely agree with the evidence found in Gregory's *Register*. Writing to Hugh shortly after the Autun council (*post* September 1077), the Pope admitted to having just found out about the Bishop's excommunication — which he himself considered pleasing news — and was more than willing to confirm the sentence because Gosfred appears to have improperly intruded there.[19] Gregory was concerned about Hugh's delay in transmitting this news to Rome, hinting that the source of his briefing originated from an appeal made by Gosfred directly to Rome. At some point between the Autun council in September 1077 and Gregory's Lent synod in 1078, Gosfred had managed to clear himself of any suspicion regarding the manner of his ascension to the see of Chartres. Gregory eventually recognized him as bishop of that see, where he remained for another twelve years — not, however, without further conflict with Hugh of Die.[20]

And lastly, Gregory's memorandum served to clear Archbishop Ralph I of Tours of any lingering charges. Resulting from the absence of legal accusers, '(even the bishops who had accused him defaulting from the accusation), and because his case had been reconsidered and settled by our predecessor of blessed memory Alexander [1061–73]', the Pope decided that this case could not be considered further 'without a known accusation' (sine certa accusatione).[21] Gregory expressed his desire that a legate be sent to Tours, assembling all the suffragan bishops,[22] clergy, and people, in order to find any truth in the accusations. If Ralph could be found innocent of the charges, the accusations brought against him were to be silenced forever. If, on the other hand, testimony could be given against him to prove his guilt sufficiently and satisfactorily, he was to be 'punished by a canonical sentence' (canonica sententia feriatur). Either way, the sentence issued against the Archbishop by Hugh of Die was ultimately rejected on account of insufficient evidence.

Of particular interest here is the frequency with which Gregory VII issued such warnings, taking into consideration their desired and ultimate effect on the reforming initiative of papal legates north of the Alps. Writing to Bishops Hugh of Die and Amatus of Oloron shortly after their Council of Saintes (8 January 1081), Gregory expressed his incredulity at hearing the news that had recently come to his attention: 'that your religious selves have suspended all the Norman

[19] *Reg.*, v. 11 (Rome, late 1077).

[20] Papal intervention likewise followed Hugh of Die's Issoudun council (March 1081), which saw the excommunication and deposition of Bishop Gosfred of Chartres (see *Reg.*, ix. 15).

[21] *Reg.*, v. 17.

[22] Bishops of Le Mans, Rennes, Angers (Anjou), Nantes, Corseul, Vannes, and Dol.

pontiffs [...] who were summoned to the council'. Although their suspensions were canonically merited, Gregory was quick to excuse the Norman bishops and abbots ('omnes Normannorum pontifices') for their failure to attend, which, he argued, had resulted 'not out of disobedience but out of fear of the King of France, in other words because they could not come safely'.[23] As is common with most legal matters, however, there is more to this case than the evidence admits.

For his decision to reinstate the bishops, Gregory provided an uncharacteristically thorough explanation to his legates — an explanation best interpreted in view of his efforts to maintain and build on his alliance with the English king and duke of Normandy William I (*c.* 1028–87). Although William did not, as the Pope discerned, 'conduct himself as scrupulously [*non ita religiose*]' as the Church desired, he nonetheless exhibited 'peace and righteousness among his subjects' and did not 'destroy or sell the churches of God'.[24] In this letter, Gregory proceeds to educate his legates on how the King 'shows himself a great deal worthier of approval and more to be honoured than other kings'. This one episode stands in contrast to Gregory's treatment of the King *c.* 1079, the year in which he sought fealty from William unsuccessfully and for a second time, holding him under the suspicion also of preventing Archbishop Lanfranc of Canterbury from visiting the apostolic see.[25] Yet regardless of these past relations, William was not to be ranked among Gregory's adversaries, such as the recalcitrant King Henry IV of Germany (r. 1056–1106) and the sometimes meddling and disobedient King Philip I of France. He did not go out of his way to thwart the Roman decrees; rather, he was described as helpful because he 'compels even by an oath priests to abandon the wives and laymen the tithes that they are holding'.[26] Indeed Gregory undoubtedly hoped to win William to his cause with temperance and mercy (a worthy endeavour in light of the Guibertine schism that was already underway), attempting

[23] *Reg.*, IX. 5.

[24] *Reg.*, IX. 5: 'quod ecclesias Dei non destruit neque vendit et pacem iustitiamque in subditis suis moderari procurat'.

[25] For Gregory's less-conciliatory treatment of the King, see *Reg.*, VI. 30 and VII. 1. Writing to the Roman subdeacon Hubert, who was active as his legate in England, the Pope exclaimed how no king, not even a pagan one, 'has presumed to attempt against the apostolic see what this man has not been ashamed to do — namely, that any of whatever insolent and shameless cast of mind should debar bishops and archbishops from the threshold of the apostles'.

[26] *Reg.*, IX. 5: 'presbyteros uxores, laicos decimas, quas detinebant, etiam iuramento dimittere compulit'.

to secure for himself and his church a powerful lay ally along the lines of the Normans of southern Italy.[27]

The measures taken to secure William's assistance are particularly interesting to note. Exonerating the Norman pontiffs for their absence, Gregory ultimately called on his legates for a milder and more prudent treatment of the situation — exhibiting a tone in his correspondence that we might rightly call a papal warning. Citing Popes Leo I (440–61) and Gregory the Great (590–604), the Pope provided justification for showing more tolerance and treating more mildly this king whom he hoped could be readily 'won for God and stimulated to a perpetual love of blessed Peter by the charm of gentleness and by a display of reason than by severity or the rigour of righteousness'.[28] 'In this matter', continued Gregory, 'let your prudence take notice of how it seems to us.' In a display of mercy that risked compromising Hugh's legatine incentive, Gregory did not deem it inappropriate that the King's power 'should be treated more mildly or that from regard for his integrity the negligences of his subjects and those whom he loves shall be to some degree tolerated'.[29]

Letters of reinstatement were issued soon after to all the suspended, and the presiding legates were further advised not to 'vex the aforesaid king in such matters' without first obtaining the Pope's consent ('prefatum regem in talibus ulterius sine assensu nostro non exasperet').[30] The nature and tone of this warning — whether or not it was Gregory's intention — imposed upon the office of legation a stricter framework within which they could exercise legal authority. By reversing the decisions of his representatives, the Pope was limiting their jurisdictional freedom of operation while seemingly tightening the methods of his supervision. But the Pope's greatest concern, it seems, was with reconciling the matter as quickly as possible to avoid causing offence to William. For this reason alone it seems unlikely that he was actively trying to change the working parameters of the papal-legatine relationship. Gregory presumably wanted his legates to consider the matter from his cautious (i.e., less legalistic), and more

[27] Robert Guiscard and his sons, Prince Richard of Capua and Roger of Apulia.

[28] *Reg.*, IX. 5; cf. Pope Leo I, *Opera omnia*, chap. 6, letter 12, cols 651–53; and Pope Gregory I, *Registrum epistularum*, ed. by Dag Norberg, Corpus Christianorum Series Latina, 140 (Turnhout: Brepols, 1982), VI. 42, pp. 414–15.

[29] Pope Gregory I, *Registrum epistularum*, VI. 42, pp. 414–15: 'Unde non indignum debet existimari potestatem illius mitius esse tractandam atque respectu probitatis ipsius subditorum et eorum, quod diligit, negligentias ex parte fore portandas.'

[30] *Reg.*, IX, 6.

political (i.e., more juristic), point of view. Such a presumption or expectation, it must be said, could not have been implicit.

While the political motivations underlying Gregory's treatment of this case are thus generally understood, it proves more difficult to interpret the Pope's apprehension over legatine action. Steering away from the more strictly enforced decrees of his 1074/75 and 1078 Roman synods,[31] Gregory in this case adhered to considered thought, restraint of righteousness, and canonical rigour. This flexible application of the law, in turn, presumably informed the legal expectations of his legates. The Pope's approach in regulating his legates strengthens the argument that Gregory alone knew the limitations of Christian tolerance and canon law, and that Hugh — whether or not he was aware of it — was frequently crossing the phantom boundaries. Regardless of the ultimate papal decision on this matter, Hugh had not to our knowledge violated the precepts of canon law by suspending the Norman bishops and abbots. But a personal belief that his actions (and those of his colleague, Amatus) were in line with church discipline carried little authority, especially when such views might contradict the juristic views held by the Pope.

Gregory's ambivalent attitude might equally suggest the fine line between what was considered canonically right and wrong. There were of course collections of canons on which legal authority was based in the late 1070s and early 1080s — such as the ninth-century Pseudo-Isidorian Decretals, Burchard of Worms's *Liber decretorum* (*c.* 1012), or possibly even the *Diversorum patrum sententie* (*c.* 1075), etc. (see below, Chapter 5) — but individual cases called for different circumstances. Such legal and administrative inconsistencies must surely have complicated the agent-principal relationship, not to mention calling into question the true extent of legatine authority as it existed in the last quarter of the eleventh century. In warning his legates to seek papal consent on select matters, Gregory was effectively inhibiting their legal ability, arguably slowing down the legislative process, and likely causing his agents to second-guess their own reforming initiative and confidence in the council arena. The effects of this self-doubting — brought on by the Pope's questioning — were potentially hazardous to the reformers' success, and ultimately for establishing the representative legal authority of legates in the various provinces. If legatine sentences were being reversed continually, their legal authority risked being undermined completely.

[31] See *Reg.*, II. 52a; *Reg.*, VI. 5b; and Hugh of Flavigny, p. 419.

Although the majority of cases tend to come from Gregory's disciplining disobedient prelates and members of the clergy for their lackadaisical attitude towards implementing reform, papal warnings were a recurring theme throughout his pontificate. The frequency of this papal communication in the *Register* — as both a legal and administrative method for safeguarding the reformers' interests in distant regions — implies an expected conformity to law in practice, especially as the reformers treated and understood it. It is Gregory's experience with the extant law, in particular, in addition to his treatment of individual cases, which helps to explain his juridical approach for servicing the reformers' more immediate needs and objectives.[32]

That Gregory was actively denouncing the methods of his legates is a theory worth reconsidering in this light. From the three cases presented above, it becomes increasingly evident that papal warnings of this nature cannot be treated as strictly isolated or personal attacks. There exist a handful of occasions where Gregory deemed it necessary to intervene in the enacted legal decisions of legatine councils, or the manner in which decisions were being carried out in the provinces. The regularity of such warnings in the papal correspondence diminishes their impact somewhat, suggesting that the communication directed towards Hugh of Die was perhaps little more than a common measure of papal supervision.

Take, for example, that case in which Gregory reproved Abbot Richard of Marseille (1082?) for his excommunicating the monks of Moissac on account of their taking over the church of Saint-Sernin.[33] Commanding him to release the monks from their bond of excommunication — satisfied of their withdrawal from the church at Abbot Hugh of Cluny's insistence — Gregory advised Richard not to 'exercise authority intemperately or rashly', for fear that such action against 'men of good report' (honestas personas auctoritatis) would detract from its force.[34] The course of events leading up to this initial sentencing are nowhere documented, but there is a sense that Richard's actions fell in line with the rigour of the canons; it was, on the other hand, a failure to communicate with the papacy

[32] On the legal impact of Gregory VII's pontificate, see especially the work of John Gilchrist, 'Gregory VII and the Juristic Sources of his Ideology', *Studia Gratiana*, 12 (1967), 3–37; John Gilchrist, , 'Reception of Pope Gregory VII', pp. 35–82, and 'Reception of Pope Gregory VII, Part II', pp. 192–229.

[33] See Blumenthal, *Gregor VII.*, pp. 218–19; cf. *Cartulaire de Saint-Sernin de Toulouse*, ed. by C. Douais (Paris: Picard, 1887), no. 290, pp. 204–05.

[34] *Ep. vag.*, 50.

in Rome that led to his eventual reprieve, reminding us very much of an episode involving Hugh of Die following his 1081 Issoudun council (18 March).[35]

Obstructing the business of legation was a similarly punishable offence, and one that in Gregory's mind was considered just as worthy of papal rebuke. Encountering opposition in transferring authority onto his legates, the Pope seemed genuinely repelled by the insolence of Archbishop Liemar of Bremen who, in December 1074, hindered Cardinal-bishops Hubert of Palestrina and Gerald of Ostia from holding a council in Germany. Calling on the endowed commission and authority assigned to legates for correcting 'whatever needed correction and of making good whatever needed making good in matters of religion',[36] Gregory essentially reproved Liemar for rendering his (i.e., the reformers') desired outcome impossible.

In October of that same year (1074), Gregory again deplored the reception given to his aforementioned legates in the kingdom of Germany. Not having been welcomed with the due honour owed to them (according to Gregory), Hubert and Gerald were unable to do 'what the Christian religion required and still requires'[37] — the exact details of which remain unknown. Addressing Bishop Burchard II of Halberstadt, as one offering sincere affection for the Roman Church ('sanctam Romanam ecclesiam sincero affectu diligere'), Gregory emphasized the necessity for adhering to the 'truth and the liberty of the authority which was represented in them'. It was better for legates to please God than men, even if this meant their being cast aside or given scant hearing in the region to which they had been commissioned.

The reception of legates was little improved by 1077, when Gregory called upon his legates Cardinal-deacon Bernard and Abbot Bernard of Marseille to secure his safe passage through Germany.[38] The ongoing kingship dispute between

[35] In his efforts to extract the council information from his legate following the Council of Issoudun (1081), Gregory reminded Hugh to carefully commit to writing and immediately send to Rome whatever has been done in councils (for this account, see *Reg.*, IX. 15). This 'custom' was intended to keep the papacy abreast of all ecclesiastical matters in distant regions, as well as providing an effective balance of supervision over the activity of individual legates. Cowdrey, *Pope Gregory VII*, pp. 595–96, notes the lack of any specific instructions for Hugh to this effect until this point. Evidence that Gregory considered it an established custom can be inferred from his instructions to Cardinal-bishop Gerald of Ostia in July 1073 (*Reg.*, I. 16).

[36] *Reg.*, II. 28: 'corrigenda essent corrigerent, que religioni addenda adderent'.

[37] *Reg.*, II. 12.

[38] See *Reg.*, IV. 23–24.

Henry IV and Rudolf of Swabia, in addition to present dangers in Lombardy, made it impossible for Gregory to cross north of the Alps by his own volition. Recognizing the kings' unwillingness to cooperate, fearful also of their hunger for more power and land, and taking precautions against their expected contravention of apostolic orders, the Pope commissioned his legates with the authority to excommunicate either king, if necessary. A warning issued simultaneously to the faithful in Germany, however, did not prevent the Abbot of Marseille from being imprisoned for six months by Count Ulrich of Lenzburg — a diplomatic disaster ostensibly beyond Gregory's control in Rome.[39] To remedy the situation, which impinged greatly on the flow of communications between the papal court in Rome and Germany, Gregory was resigned to dispatch letters to Archbishop Udo of Trier, a trusted ally in the reformers' attempts to pacify this northern region.[40]

Clearly, papal rebuke was not reserved solely for acting members of the legatine office. Confirming the authority bestowed upon his legates, Gregory reminded the Corsicans in 1077 of their obligations to obey his chosen representative, Bishop Landulf of Pisa. Committed with the 'power to act on our behalf in spiritual matters, so that he may receive the land on behalf of blessed Peter and as our representative, and may rule it with all zeal and diligence, and may concern himself with all matters and causes belonging to blessed Peter and through him to ourself',[41] Gregory clarified his expectations for this office. Troubled both by legitimizing and confirming the authority bestowed upon his legates, the Pope at times struggled to ensure the right conduct of ecclesiastical and legal business in the areas to which they were commissioned. In view of his efforts to centralize the administration of the Roman Church, it is not at all surprising to find cases where unfamiliar (i.e., foreign) ecclesiastics were regarded with disdain and mistrust in the provinces.

Taking such cases into consideration, only a limited number of examples ever refer to Gregory's concern with specified legal conditions. The motives for his interfering in the decisions of his legates were influenced quite often by more local political and ecclesiastical considerations. One particular incident involving Cardinal-bishop Gerald of Ostia shows just how influential these factors were in Gregory's treatment and tempering of the extant law. Writing from Rome in July

[39] *Reg.*, V. 7. See Cowdrey, *Register*, p. 252 n. 4.

[40] See *Reg.*, V. 7, 16.

[41] *Reg.*, V. 4.

1073, Gregory rebuked Gerald for his deposing the so-called Archbishop of Auch, William (1068–96) — the reason being that the legal conditions of this case were conflicting.[42] Here it seems that two separate and isolated views developed on the legal nature of William's deposition, a sentence that was entirely justified for his communicating with an excommunicated person. 'Constrained by great difficulty', and moreover because he was 'experiencing no small concern about all these things', Gregory was forced to reinstate the Archbishop, provided that he offer a more thorough explanation of his actions in person to Rome. Working against Gerald in order to achieve his desired conciliar outcome, Gregory's intentions do not contravene those of his legates.

Citing from this same letter, in fact, Gregory demonstrates the leniency and professional courtesy that he was prepared to extend to his legates. Even after the accused, a so-called Bishop Pontius of Tarbes (1073–*c.* 1080), had made the lengthy journey to Rome, Gregory 'returned no answers to his complaints', the motivating reason being his regard for the authority of his legate Gerald. The Pope's desire for equity (*aequitas*) bound him to judge each case fairly because 'in comparable cases comparable rights are to be upheld' (quia in paribus causis paria iura tenenda sunt).[43] And as long as some legal proof could be found to support the accusation and charge of his legates, there was little cause for papal interference. A flexible and open-minded attitude, as this one case suggests, was Gregory's favoured approach to settling legal cases. As long as some acknowledgment was given to his authoritative role in the matter, there was little reason for the development of discordant views with his legates.

With Gregory VII's continual and consistent adherence to considered thought, restraint of righteousness, and canonical rigour comes a sense of his legal expectations, and those expected of his legates. In no way were his representatives to express partisan interests ('nullomodo partibus faveatis') in their promotion of righteousness ('iustitia'). Such affiliations were subject to the taint of mistrust ('exobete immunes'), which was an unspeakable action in Gregory's mind. A neutral position was always the best, as witnesses in a case whose judgement would in no way be persuaded by promises or threats ('nullis promissionibus aut terroribus cessimus').[44] Of course, this theoretical concept represents a model interpretation of legatine conduct, and one that was seldom exercised on account of the unpredictability of individual legal cases and the flexibility and

[42] *Reg.*, I. 16.

[43] *Reg.*, I. 16.

[44] *Ep. vag.*, 31.

interpretation of the extant canon law. Given this more practical consideration, one might go so far as to say that discordant interpretations of the law were perhaps inevitable — characteristics of governing that directly influenced the ways in which law was applied in the last quarter of the eleventh century.

Resulting from these expectations, the parameters of canonical right and wrong behaviour became delineated more clearly. The cases examined above show Hugh of Die as being at times too strict but rarely too lax in jurisprudential matters. For this the Pope was obligated to correct him, not for the sake of humiliation or defeat, but to keep him in line with the reforming measures to which his ecclesiastical career was devoted. Not once can we legitimately claim that Hugh of Die outright challenged this obedience; neither did he ever contest the supremacy of the Pope or undermine Gregory's spiritual, moral, or legal authority. Differences of opinion only surfaced when the law itself came under question, where its application in the council arena risked compromising the reformers' political, social, moral, religious, and legal position. Such considerations invariably draw on the legal training and knowledge of reforming legates like Hugh of Die, whose legalistic application of the extant law Gregory was carefully scrutinizing.[45]

From this perspective, the papal warnings issued against Hugh of Die suggest a necessary means of control, authorization, and supervision, for the effective and centralized administration of the Roman Church. The *ad hoc* developments of the legatine office under Gregory VII were gradual, as obscure in this period as the body of canon law on which its authority was based, often transforming in authority and influence to fit the needs of the papacy. At the beginning of his pontificate, Gregory's concept of how this office could be utilized best for disseminating reform principles to distant regions is still not entirely clear (see above, Chapter 3). What is certain is that he did not aim to create any new device but rather adhered to the methods employed by the diligence of his predecessors.[46] In one sense, the true capability of permanent legates such as Hugh of Die and Amatus of Oloron was registered through their canonistic behaviour, which, in Gregory's view, on occasion warranted papal intervention. One might even argue that, before the councils of Autun (1077) and Poitiers (1078), Gregory had not fully considered the immediate impact of his legates deviating from the path of canon law. If the Pope failed to control legatine activity, if legatine actions were

[45] See Kriston R. Rennie, '*Imbutus divinis dogmatibus*: Some Remarks on the Legal Training of Gregorian Legates', *RHDFE*, 85 (2007), 303–13.

[46] *Reg.*, II. 66.

not properly supervised, or if their exercising of canon law was either too strict or too loose, his role in governing the church risked coming under threat and criticism from his opponents.

Offering revisions to cases that he considered were judged too hastily or unfairly, Gregory set limits to legatine authority, defining legal parameters within which legates could operate. It remains to be seen, however, whether that was ever his genuine intention. Likely regarded as 'mere tactical directives',[47] papal warnings of the kind issued to Hugh of Die and his colleague Amatus of Oloron were not intended as debilitating or counterproductive measures. Disarming the legate's ability and enthusiasm for disseminating reforming principles would have proved a futile gesture. The opposite effect was desired: to delineate more sharply the approved methods for carrying out papal business to the borders of Christendom. It is not out of the question to suggest that Hugh benefited greatly from Gregory's supervision, incorporating the criticism for better productivity, legal cognisance, and competency. Aligning the Pope's ideology with that of his legates was presumably the intended objective, creating — as it were — a mobilized and efficient machinery for the reformers' needs and interests. The lynchpin for success, moreover, was a uniform understanding, appreciation, and application of the extant canon law — a seemingly difficult target to reach considering the diverse backgrounds of each reformer, whose familiarity with canonical texts and collections are only assumed and seldom identifiable.

The evidence for Hugh of Die's Autun (1077) and Poitiers (1078) councils, in particular, show him conforming to his own interpretation of canon law — that is, his personal understanding of how it should be applied in the council arena. Where he remained confident in the abuses brought against the Roman Church by French prelates, he was sure to exercise a formidable level of discipline and punishment. The council arena was for him a place of supreme, apostolic judgement: a travelling tribunal at which he was the head. The cases heard at Autun were judged according to what Hugh himself considered as the strictest censure of canon law; he, as much as Gregory, perceived the episcopate as being the 'head and cause' (caput et causa)[48] of an impure clergy, as the disobedient rank among the ecclesiastical order who must be freed from 'servile oppression' (servilis oppressio) and 'tyrannical servitude' (tyrannica servitudo) in order to 'restore her to her original liberty' (pristinam libertam restituere).[49]

[47] Benson, *Bishop-Elect*, p. 223.

[48] *Reg.*, II. 45.

[49] *Reg.*, VIII. 12.

One last consideration for Gregory's memorandum is his genuine concern for equity (*aequitas*). Hugh of Die's decision to postpone judgement on selected cases at his Autun and Poitiers councils might likewise suggest that his energetic reforming personality was qualified by a similar concern with equity. If cases originated over the course of the council, and were thus unknown to him beforehand, it was far more diplomatic for him to pass them on to Gregory's consideration rather than risk making a judgement that might counter papal authority or will. When the legate was called upon to act beyond this agenda, circumstances such as distance, the practical impossibility of consultation with the Pope in Rome, made it inevitable that Hugh's own skills and judgement would come into play. For this exchange or interplay between the centre in Rome and local interests — what Richard Southern referred to as the 'flow of business'[50] — no mechanism was better suited to serve the Pope's interests than the legate; he was an administrative and legal instrument capable of bridging the gap between the Curia and the provinces.

Taking into account his early ecclesiastical career as bishop and legate, Hugh of Die's tireless devotion to reform is almost indistinguishable from Gregory's, though some methodological distinctions exist in their reaching of legal objectives. By no means a jurist or canonist to the extent of the twelfth-century lawyer popes, Gregory's treatment of individual cases discloses his juristic ideology and temperament. This treatment of the law often stood in contrast to the legalist approach favoured by his legate, Hugh of Die — though not always in complete opposition. The roots of Hugh's legalistic knowledge were more likely to have shaped these discordant views, helping to explain the possible impetus for, and consequences of, legal disparity between the Pope and his representatives in distant Christian provinces. Given such personal and legal considerations, it is worth examining now in greater detail the legal education, experience, and expectation that shaped Hugh of Die's legal and conciliar activity, before turning to the narrative of this conciliar activity itself.

[50] Southern, *Making of the Middle Ages*, p. 146.

Chapter 5

LEGATINE EDUCATION AND TRAINING

In addition to exposure at Roman synods, eleventh-century reformers drew their juristic authority from a select few canonical sources, favouring — as contemporary records attest — the ninth-century Pseudo-Isidorian Decretals, Burchard of Worms's *Liber decretorum* (*c.* 1012), the anonymous *Diversorum patrum sententie* (*c.* 1075), and Anselm II of Lucca's *Collectio canonum* (*c.* 1083). Exactly where, when, and how one might become versed with these formal sources is a matter of great interest to the present study. Similarly relevant are practical considerations of textual availability, circulation, and ease-of-use and consultation. For the reforming legate, whose increasing experience in the legatine office could bolster his legal competency, existing knowledge of these and other canonical collections provided the essential basis and framework for the application of law in practice. The greatest challenge to the historian lies with identifying the legal texts and collections on which the reformers were most dependent.

This is primarily because few allusions can be found to formal sources in Gregory's writings, or in the writings of Hugh of Die for that matter. Of the sixty-two surviving letters for Hugh's ecclesiastical career *c.* 1073–1106 (see Appendix 2), for instance, no reference is made to existing or contemporary canonical collections, rubrics, *tituli*, *incipits*, *explicits*, or *capitulationes*.[1] While Gregory drew mostly from the patristic teachings of his namesake Gregory I (590–604),[2] and the canonistic teachings of his papal predecessors, Hugh of Die likewise modelled his background on some established precedent and authority. The theoretical and practical nature of that authority is nearly impossible to distinguish. An extensive

[1] These epistles are found in PL, CLVII, and *RHGF*, XIV, some of which are cited verbatim from Hugh of Flavigny's narrative account.

[2] Gregory I provided forty-seven texts for the 74T, of which forty figure into Gregory's *Register*.

knowledge of reforming law, litigation, and procedure was presumably mandatory for someone of his ecclesiastical rank and stature, with some formal education and legal training undoubtedly coming prior to his promotion to the legatine office in 1075. Although the extent of his legal knowledge can only be estimated and not authenticated, there is little reason to doubt Hugh's legal and procedural competence, especially in light of the circumstances that led to his fast-tracked rise through the ecclesiastical ranks.[3] In the absence of such evidence, however, closer attention must be given to Hugh's possible contact with canonistic materials and reforming legislation, assessing his contribution to their dissemination north of the Alps. In this way, some light can be shed on the possible background of his legal knowledge and understanding, which in turn will help establish (to a degree) the basis and legitimacy of his conciliar enactments.

Relatively few connections to canonical sources and authorities can be made. A document known as the *Obituarium Lugdunensis ecclesiae*, for example, offers a possible link between Hugh of Die and Burchard's *Liber decretorum*.[4] Among

[3] Hugh of Flavigny, p. 411: 'Qui demum reversus, papae inter cetera electionem Diensis aecclesiae innotuit, et electum ipsum quam maxime paternitati ipsius commendavit. Non multo post ipse qui commendabatur advenit, et quia solam clericatus tonsuram habebat — detestabatur enim symoniacorum ordinations — in mense Decembrio per manum eius usque ad presbiteratus gradum promotus est, cum hoc aliqui calumpniarentur Romanorum, et promerent morem sanctae Romanae ecclesiae, neminem licet electum antistem a papa ordinandum nisi in eadem deserviret aecclesia. Quod tamen in ipso domnus autentica potestate sua fecit; complacuerat enim sibi in illo anima eius. In quadragesima vero, sabbato in presbiterum, et sequenti dominica ad missas in episcopum consecratus est. Sic post octonos consecrationis dies affatim inbutus divinis dogmatibus, et ubertim roboratus aecclesiasticis sanctionibus, benedictione percepta dimissus est ad regendos filios, quibus pastor et rector ordinatus est.'

[4] *Obituarium Lugdunensis ecclesiae*, ed. by M.-C. Guigue (Lyon: Scheuring, 1867), pp. 129–30: 'Dedit de libris Historiam integram et aliam in quatuor libris, Augustinum de verbis Domini super Johannem, de octo questionibus, de cura pro mortuis, de adulterannis conjugiis, de continencia, de baptismo contra Donatistas, de anima et ratione, de fide et operibus, de pastoribus, de ovibus, de bono conjugali, de bono viduitatis; librum Sancti Ambrosii de Virginibus; librum beati Gregorii Nazanzeni; librum beati Ambrosii de officiis; librum de patriarchis; Cypriani librum; ultimam partem moralium Gregorii; librum Didimi de Spiritu Sancto; epistolam Theophili Alexandrini; epistolam Sancti Ieronimi; epistolam Sancti Augustini ad Dardanum de presencia Dei; epistolam Cornelii pape ad Sanctum Cyprianum; sermonem Sancti Augustini adversum Judeos; epistolam Sancti Augustini ad Consencium de vera corporis resurrectione; epistolam Sancti Augustini ad Volusianum; epistolam Volusiani ad Sanctum Augustinum; epistolam Augustini ad Volusianum; epistolam Hilarii ad Augustinum; epistolam Augustini ad Hylarium; epistolam Augustini ad Paulinum, episcopum; epistolam Augustini adversus epistolam Juliani; epistolam Alipii et Augustini, episcoporum, ad Maximum medicum; epistolam Sancti Augustini ad Syxtum, presbiterum; epistolam beati Ieronimi ad Eustochium, de virginitate servanda; Originem super

the contents of this library — which exists in the form of a record taken by the cathedral canons at Lyon upon his death in 1106 — Hugh possessed a donation copy of Burchard's multi-volume work.[5] Taking into consideration the absence of direct references to this material in his personal letters, however, no prescribed method exists for establishing the collection's use while he was active as legate, bishop, or archbishop. The same can be said for the selected works of Anselm of Canterbury (*c.* 1033–1109), Gregory the Great, the numerous epistles from early Church Fathers like Ambrose (*c.* 340–97), Jerome (*c.* 347–420), and Augustine (354–430), or the philosophical works of Boethius (*c.* 480–524) and Macrobius (fourth–fifth century), all of whose works appear listed in no apparent order alongside Burchard's *Decretum*. Obvious pitfalls exist in trying to ascertain when these and other sources were first collected, which texts were inherited at Lyon, and which ones might be claimed as Hugh's personal acquisitions. The absence of detailed information poses further questions: titles are often omitted from this record, rendering speculative any conclusions on the merit or prestige that might come from possessing such works. Neither does the existence of certain manuscripts or codices equate to Hugh's familiarity with their materials. Merely possessing a collection does not signify a learned man, nor does it prove with any conviction that such materials were ever read or put to use in any theological, moral, or legal arena.

Exodum; quinque benedictionales; textum unum; librum Mathei cum epistola Ieronimi, de prodigo filio; librum Amselmi, Cantuariensis archiepiscopi, de veritate, de libertate, de casu dyaboli, de incarnatione Verbi, Cur Deus homo, de contemptu virginali et de originali peccato, de precessione Spiritus Sancti, epistolam de azimo et fermentato; Vitam beati Gregorii; Regulam beati Benedicti; librum Sancti Martini de confessione peccatorum; epistolas Sancti Pauli; epistolas Gregorii; duas missales; textum grecum et epistolarium grecum; librum Boecii; librum hymnorum et Cantica canticorum; librum Bruchardi; librum Macrobii; librum Oracii; duo psalteria greca,; Vitam Sancti Nicecii; Moralia Job. Rexit autem hanc ecclesiam annis viginti tribus, mensibus octo, diebus septem. Apud Sanctum Hyreneum canonicos regulariter viventes instituit, quibus terras, que quondam juris ejusdem sancti fuerant, multo pretio a laicis redemptas in communes usus eorum contradidit, eosque sub sua tuitione reservavit, et sub protectione suorum successorum, in presencia quamplurium probabilium virorum, in eternum fore mandavit, atque ut hoc firmius teneretur omnibus hujus sue constitucionis violatoribus anathematis gladium intemptavit'.

[5] For some recent work on Burchard, see Greta Austin, *Shaping Church Law Around the Year 1000: The 'Decretum' of Burchard of Worms* (Aldershot: Ashgate, 2009); cf. Hartmut Hoffmann and Rudolf Pokorny, *Das Decret des Bischofs Burchard von Worms*, MGH, Hilfsmittel, 12 (1991); *Bischof Burchard von Worms, 1000–1025*, ed. by Wilfried Hartmann (Mainz: Selbstverlag der Gesellschaft für Mittelrheinische Kirchengeschichte, 2000). For a look at the manuscript evidence and its influence on reform, see F. Pelster, 'Das Dekret Buchards von Worms in einer Redaktion aus dem Beginn der gregorianischen Reform', *SG*, 1 (1947), 321–51.

Given these uncertainties, hypothetical enquiry is of some value in this consideration. Peter Damian's († 1072) use of the *Decretum*, for example, is often taken as proof that it was circulating throughout Italy before 1050 as a 'practical hand-book in the hands of the reformers'.[6] Detlev Jasper has shown the *Decretum*'s influence in the contemporary and later canonistic writings of Anselm II of Lucca's *Collectio canonum*, Cardinal Deusdedit's *Collectio canonum* (1087), Bonizo of Sutri's *Liber de vita christiana* (*c.* 1089–95),[7] Cardinal-presbyter Gregory of San Grisogono (Polycarpus, *Collectio canoum*, *c.* 1104–13),[8] and Ivo of Chartres. And as Peter Landau has shown, even Gratian consulted Burchard for his *Concordia discordantium canonum* (*c.* 1140).[9] Overall, the *Decretum*'s lasting influence corroborates its usefulness to bishops in the first instance, but also as a tool for educating priests and clerics — a work accessible to a wide audience throughout the eleventh and twelfth centuries.[10] As Greta Austin has recently argued, moreover, the *Decretum* was by no means a collection 'eclipsed' by later papal reforming collections, as once thought.[11] Quite the contrary: the *Decretum* 'formed the nucleus of the later *Panormia*';[12]

[6] J. Joseph Ryan, *Saint Peter Damiani and his Canonical Sources: A Preliminary Study in the Antecedents of the Gregorian Reform* (Toronto: Pontifical Institute of Mediaeval Studies, 1956), pp. 13, 161.

[7] Detlev Jasper, 'Burchards Dekret in der Sicht der Gregorianer', in *Bischof Burchard von Worms*, ed. by Hartmann, pp. 167–98 (pp. 184–92); cf., pp. 109–10.

[8] Jasper, "Burchards Dekret in der Sicht der Gregorianer', pp. 195–97.

[9] Peter Landau, 'Burchard de Worms et Gratien: À propos des sources immédiates de Gratien', *RDC*, 48 (1998), 233–45; Peter Landau, 'Vorgratianische Kanonessammlungen bei Dekretisten und in frühen Dekretalen-Sammlungen', in *Proceedings of the Eighth International Congress of Medieval Canon Law, San Diego, 1988*, ed. by Stanley Chodorow (Vatican City: Biblioteca Apostolica Vaticana, 1992), pp. 94–116; Peter Landau, 'Neue Forschungen zu vorgratianischen Kanonessammlungen und den Quellen des gratianischen Dekrets', *Ius Commune*, 11 (1984), 1–29, especially p. 18; Rudolf Weigand, 'Mittelalterliche Texte: Gregor I., Burchard und Gratian', *ZRG kan. Abt.*, 84 (1998), 330–44, especially pp. 332–44; Jean Gaudemet, 'Regards sur l'histoire du droit canonique antérieurement au Décret de Gratien', *Studia et documenta historiae et iuris*, 51 (1985), 73–130.

[10] See Paul Fournier, 'Les Collections canoniques romaines de l'époque de Grégoire VII', *Mémoires de l'Institut national de France: Académie des inscriptions et belles-lettres*, 41 (1920), 271–397 (repr. in *Mélanges de droit canonique*, ed. by Theo Kölzer, 2 vols (Aalen: Scientia, 1983), II, 425–550).

[11] Austin, *Shaping Church Law*, p. 27; cf. Paul Fournier, 'Le Décret de Burchard de Worms: Ses caractères, son influence', *RHE*, 12 (1911), 670–94 (p. 689) (repr. in *Mélanges de droit canonique*, ed. by Kölzer, I, 393–448).

[12] Austin, *Shaping Church Law*, p. 29.

it continued to be consulted, copied, and received by compilers well into the twelfth century.[13]

In France, the *Decretum* was used for 'ecclesiastical administration, synods, pastoral care, teaching or secular business',[14] and other day-to-day matters. The fact remains, however, that Hugh of Die evinces no use of Burchard's collection, despite its likely appearance in Burgundy *c.* 1050.[15] From the last quarter of the eleventh century, moreover, the *Decretum* begins forming the nucleus of numerous southern French (and other) canon law collections, thus implying its value and circulation in and around this region. With increasing copies circulating in France, Italy, and Germany throughout the second half of the eleventh century, the possibility of Hugh's access to, and knowledge of, the *Decretum* is certainly improved. Still missing, however, is any direct connection or explicit reference in the extant sources.

Drawing almost exclusively on sources of Christian authority — adhering closely to the decrees of his papal predecessors and the seven ecumenical councils[16] — Gregory's knowledge of canon law is far more explicit than his legates.[17] Relying rather on scriptural and patristic authority, and consequently paying very little attention to those early Church Fathers who were not popes — all the while claiming to protect and serve the well-being of the Roman Church in the interests of justice and righteousness — Gregory's application of the extant law was directed towards slightly different ends. Heavily influenced by existing political and ecclesiastical conditions, and founded on a seemingly genuine concern for equity (*aequitas*), the Pope drew on these familiar ancient and canonical traditions and privileges as 'the basis and also the limitations of papal authority [...] within the Christian church'.[18]

[13] See *The Collection in Seventy-four Titles*, ed. and trans. by Gilchrist, p. 11.

[14] *The Collection in Seventy-four Titles*, ed. and trans. by Gilchrist, p. 83.

[15] See Lotte Kéry, *Canonical Collections of the Early Middle Ages (ca.400–1140): A Bibliographical Guide to the Manuscripts and Literature* (Washington, DC: Catholic University of America Press, 1999), pp. 134–48, especially p. 146.

[16] Nicaea (325), Constantinople (381), Ephesus (431), Chalcedon (451), Constantinople II (553) and III (680–81), and Nicaea II (787). For Gregory's reliance on the material sources, see Ronald Knox, 'Finding the Law: Developments in Canon Law during the Gregorian Reform', *SG*, 9 (1972), 421–66 (p. 426); cf. Jasper, 'Burchards Dekret in der Sicht der Gregorianer', pp. 174–79.

[17] On the reception of law under Gregory VII, see the quantitative research by John Gilchrist (see the bibliography, below).

[18] Cowdrey, *Pope Gregory VII*, p. 520.

Thus, it would seem, the nature of Gregory's 'authority' was recognized only by tradition. Reluctant 'to introduce anything novel or of his own devising' (nichil novi, nichil nostris adinventionibus superinducere conamur),[19] he sought only to restore the customs and privileges of the Roman Church, or so he claimed. Paradoxically, the foundation of legal authority developed during his pontificate to include texts originally derived from the Pseudo-Isidorian Decretals.[20] Notably absent, however, is any direct use of Burchard's *Decretum*, despite the latter's implicit reliance on patristic writings and conciliar *acta* as a basis for legal authority.[21] That Gregory was citing from select earlier materials, however, gives us some idea as to the reformers' general thrust in what it was that they were attempting to legitimize. And the later transmission of these ninth-century decretals (both genuine and false) into collections like the *Diversorum patrum sententie* (= 74T) helps define the reformers' primary legal concerns, as they expanded their legal foundation to include a wider range of authoritative legal texts which could benefit the *utilitas Romanae ecclesiae*.

In light of the canonical sources employed by Gregory VII, our interest lies in knowing the collections favoured by his legates. Of particular appeal is the legatine knowledge of the 74T — compiled by an anonymous author *c.* 1075 and extant in more than twenty manuscripts.[22] In considering the transmission, dissemination, and potential use of this collection by reformers like Hugh of Die, very few conclusions have been reached on account of the contradictory and scanty evidence. The French historians Paul Fournier and Gabriel Le Bras went so far as to suggest the 74T's appearance in France as early as the pontificate of Leo IX (1049–54), arguing for its commission and use by Archdeacon Hildebrand (later

[19] See *Reg.*, V. 5.

[20] For a recent historiographical look at the position and function of research on Pseudo-Isidore, see Horst Fuhrmann, 'Stand, Aufgaben und Perspektiven der Pseudoisidorforschung', in *Fortschritt durch Fälschungen? Ursprung, Gestalt und Wirkungen der pseudoisidorischen Fälschungen*, ed. by Wilfried Hartmann and Gerhard Schmitz (Hannover: Hahn, 2002), pp. 227–62, in addition to his section on the forgeries ('The Pseudo-Isidorian Forgeries') in Detlev Jasper and Horst Fuhrmann, *Papal Letters in the Early Middle Ages* (Washington, DC: Catholic University of America Press, 2001), pp. 137–95.

[21] See Greta Austin, 'Authority and the Canons in Burchard's *Decretum* and Ivo's *Decretum*', in *Readers, Texts and Compilers in the Earlier Middle Ages: Studies in Medieval Canon Law in Honour of Linda Fowler-Magerl*, ed. by Martin Brett and Kathleen G. Cushing (Aldershot: Ashgate, 2009), pp. 35–58.

[22] See Kéry, *Canonical Collections*, pp. 206–07; Uta-Renate Blumenthal, 'Codex Guarnerius 203: A Manuscript of the *Collection in 74 Titles*', *Bulletin of Medieval Canon Law*, 5 (1975), 11–33; Gérard Fransen, 'Autour de la collection en 74 titres', *RDC*, 25 (1975), 61–73.

Gregory VII).[23] Since the publication of their two-volume book on the history of canonical collections (1931–32), historians such as J. Haller and Anton Michel have tried to establish the collection's authorship to Humbert of Silva Candida (*ante* 1061), but the date of its appearance has varied. Offering a current view on this collection, Linda Fowler-Magerl argues for the collection's provenance in Lotharingia, possibly at Cologne, where it was eventually 'brought to Rome to support of the interests of monasteries'.[24] It was then, as she argues in a more recent study (2005), amended at a Beneventan scriptorium (possibly even Montecassino),[25] and prepared with the intention of sending it north of the Alps (*in Gallias*) with reforming legates like Hugh of Die.[26]

Indeed, Hugh of Die's familiarity with the 74T is a theory worth floating, not least because its composition date coincides with his rise to the legatine office in that same year. The legate's presence at the Roman synods of 1074, 1076, and 1078 all presents likely opportunities for his gaining access to a copy.[27] Difficulties nevertheless continue to obscure our understanding the 74T's circulation under Gregory VII, particularly because a majority of the eighteen Italian and French manuscripts known to contain the 74T belong to the post-Gregorian era of the late eleventh and early twelfth century (1085–1140) — suggesting that they were circulating too late to be of any real significance to Hugh's first legation.[28] Jasper

[23] Hildebrand's request for Peter Damian to compile a collection of legal texts pertaining to the authority of the Roman See is cited as evidence: 'Hoc tu subtiliter, ut et alia multa perpendens, frequenter a me charitate, quae superat omnia, ut Romanorum pontificum decreta, vel gesta percurrens, quidquid apostolicae sedis auctoritati specialiter competere videretur, hinc inde curiosus exscerperem, atque in parvi voluminis unionem novae compilationis arte conflarem' (*Opusculum quintam*, PL, CXLV (1853), col. 89); cf. Paul Fournier, 'Le Premier manuel canonique de la réforme du XI siècle', *Mélanges d'archéologie et d'histoire de l'école française de Rome*, 14 (1894), 147–223 (pp. 191–202). See Horst Fuhrmann, 'Über den Reformgeist der 74-Titel Sammlung (*Diversorum patrum sententiae*)', in *Festchrift für Hermann Heimpel zum 70. Geburtstag* (Göttingen: Vandenhoeck & Ruprecht, 1972), II, 1101–20 (p. 1102).

[24] Linda Fowler-Magerl, 'The Relationship between Seemingly Unspectacular Pre-Gratian Collections in the Manuscripts Paris, Bibliothèque Nationale, Lat. 3858C and Florence, Biblioteca Medicea Laurenziana, Ashburnham 1554', in *Scientia veritatis*, ed. by Münsch and Zotz, pp. 244–45.

[25] Fowler-Magerl, 'Fine Distinctions', p. 165.

[26] Fowler-Magerl, *Clavis canonum*, p. 117.

[27] For evidence of Hugh's presence at these councils, see Hugh of Flavigny, p. 411, *Reg.*, III. 10a and *Reg.*, V. 22 respectively.

[28] The collections of Gebhard of Salzburg (1081), Manegold of Lautenbach (1081–85), Bernold of Constance (1054–1100), the Anonymous of Hersfeld (1090–1093), and the

has shown the collection's first use in 1073/74 by the canonist Bernold of Constance (with a transcription of canon 307 on folio 193 of the MS Sankt Gallen, Stiftsbibliothek, 676), and again *c.* 1076 in his libellus *De fontibus iuris ecclesiastici*, and certainly before 1077 in his *De damnatione scismaticorum* and *Apologeticus*.[29] Anselm II of Lucca used some 136 *capitula* in his *Collectio canonum*, though there it was considered 'as little more than a guidebook or compendium of canonical texts, to be altered, re-ordered and, especially, re-directed towards different ends'.[30]

Just as relevant for determining the 74T's use by reformers is the collection's transmission to regions beyond Rome. Hugh of Die's role in the movement of canonical texts is of particular interest here, as three manuscripts from the 74T's Swabian appendix refer to its dissemination by legates *in Gallias* ('a legatis ipsius sedis apostolice in Gallias pro ecclesiasticarum dispositione causarum deportate')[31] — loosely interpreted as meaning imperial Burgundy or that region west of the Rhine. Drawing on this Swabian inscription commonly attributed to the authorship of Bernold of Constance, Anton Michel posited the idea that the collection was first carried to Germany in 1077 by Gregory's legates, Cardinal-deacon Bernard and Abbot Bernard of Saint-Victor in Marseille.[32] Johanne Autenrieth

Collection of Letters in Munich Clm 14596 (1080–1100), are the most contemporary accounts for incorporating parts of the 74T. Fournier, 'Le Premier manuel', pp. 150–54, was first to identify the manuscripts borrowing directly from the 74T as Vatican City, Biblioteca Apostolica Vaticana, Cod. Vat. lat., 4160 and 4977; Rome, Biblioteca Vallicelliana, F. 54; Rome, Biblioteca Casanatense, B.V.17; Montecassino, Archivio della Badia, 522; Florence, Biblioteca Medicea Laurenziana, Pluteus XVI, Cod. 15; the Stuttgart manuscript from the Württembergische Landesbibliothek, *jur. et polit.*, 107; Engelberg, Stiftsbibliothek, 52; Vienna, Österreichische Nationalbibliothek, 2206 and 2153; British Museum, 22286; Real Biblioteca de San Lorenzo de el Escorial, L. III. 19 and Z. III. 19; and Munich, Bayerische Staatsbibliothek 22289.

[29] Bernold of Constance, *Apologeticus*, pp. 58–88, and *De damnatione scismaticorum*, in MGH, Libelli, 2, pp. 26–58; Fowler-Magerl, *Clavis canonum*, p. 110; Jasper, 'Burchards Dekret in der Sicht der Gregorianer', p. 178; *The Collection in Seventy-four Titles*, ed. and trans. by Gilchrist, p. 44.

[30] Cushing, *Papacy and the Law*, pp. 80, 82 — on the 'dispersion and disposition' of 74T in Anselm's *Collectio canonum*, see her Table 3, pp. 213–15.

[31] This notation is found in Engelberg, Stiftsbibliothek, MS 52; Stuttgart, Württembergische Landesbibliothek, MS HB. VI. 107; and Munich, Bayerische Staatsbibliothek, Clm 9515.

[32] Anton Michel, *Die Sentenzen des Kardinals Humbert, das erste Rechtsbuch der papstlichen Reform*, MGH, Schriften, 7 (1943), pp. 136–41. For their collaborative commissioning, see *Reg.*, IV. 23–24; V. 7, 16.

agrees with this dating,[33] while J. Haller sees it happening one year earlier (*c.* 1076) through the legatine commissioning of Bishop Altmann of Passau and Patriarch Sigehard of Aquileia.[34] One recent theory posits the 74T's transmission as early as 1074, with the assistance of Gerald of Ostia and Hubert of Palestrina.[35]

Far more certain is the 74T's appearance *c.* 1079 in regional canon law collections like the *Collectio Burdegalensis* — likely compiled at Bordeaux shortly after Hugh of Die's council there in October 1079. Extant in only two manuscripts (Würzburg, Universitäts-Bibliothek, MS M. p. j. q. 2, fols 2^{v}–95^{r}, and Bordeaux, Bibliothèque municipale, MS 11, fols 147^{r}–171^{v}), this collection also contains a list of conciliar canons from Hugh of Die's 1078 Poitiers council (existing as ten rubrics). Considered as an abbreviated form of Burchard of Worms's *Liber decretorum* interpolated with various chapters from the 74T, this Bordeaux collection closely resembles the contemporary *Collectio Tarraconensis*,[36] though the latter collection alone contains a copy of Gregory's *Dictatus papae* (*c.* 1075) and is dated slightly later on account of its *terminus post quem* — a decree on the election of pontiffs from Gregory's 1080 Lent synod.[37] While it is unlikely that both collections were compiled at a Poitevin scriptorium,[38] Hugh of Die remains

[33] Johanne Autenrieth, 'Bernold von Konstanz und die erweiterte 74-Titelsammlung', *DA*, 14 (1958), 375–94.

[34] J. Haller, 'Pseudoisidors erstes Auftreten im deutschen Investiturstreit', *SG*, 2 (1947), 91–101 (pp. 91–96).

[35] Healy, *The Chronicle of Hugh of Flavigny*, p. 191. For evidence of their legatine activity to these regions, see *Reg.*, I. 42.

[36] A Poitevin collection of canon law compiled *c.* 1080 and extant in three manuscripts: Paris, Bibliothèque nationale de France (BnF), lat. 5517, fols 46^{v}–141^{r}; Tarragona, Biblioteca Pública (Provincial), 26; and Milan, Biblioteca Ambrosiana, D. 59 sup.

[37] *Reg.*, VII. 14a: (6) 'Item de electione pontificum: Quotiens defuncto pastore alicuius ecclesie alius est ei canonice subrogandus, instantia visitatoris episcopi, qui ei ab apostolica vel metropolitana sede directus est, clerus et populus remota omni seculari ambitione timore atque gratia apostolice sedis vel metropolitani sui consensu pastorem sibi secundum Deum eligat. Quod si corruptus aliquo vitio aliter agere presumpserit, electionis perperam facte omni fructu carebit et de cetero nullam electionis potestatem habebit, electionis vero potestas omnis in deliberatione sedis apostolice sive metropolitani sui consistat. Si enim his, ad quem consecratio pertinet, non rite consecrando teste beato Leone gratiam benedictionis amittit, consequenter is, qui ad pravam electionem declinaverit, eligendi potestate privatur.'

[38] See Kriston R. Rennie, 'The *Collectio Burdegalensis*: A Poitevin Collection?', in *Proceedings of the Thirteenth International Congress of Medieval Canon Law, Esztergom, Hungary, 3–9 August 2008* (Vatican City: Biblioteca Apostolica Vaticana, forthcoming).

the best candidate for the transmission of the 74T and other canonical texts to France in the late 1070s.

Indeed, Hugh of Die's legatine perambulations *c.* 1078–79 coincide nicely with the arrival in west-central France of distinctively Gregorian legislation. The most recognizable pieces finding their way from Rome to north of the Alps in this period are Gregory's *Dictatus papae*,[39] *In die resurrectionis* (concerning the reading of psalms), *Licet nova consuetudo* (which defines the dates for the ember fasts and ecclesiastical consecrations),[40] Berengar of Tours's Eucharistic oath taken sometime in 1079,[41] and decrees one and three through thirteen of Gregory's 1080 November synod.[42] Among the most widely circulated and influential

[39] This connection is posited by Fowler-Magerl in her *Clavis canonum*, pp. 117, 133, and 'Fine Distinctions', pp. 165–66.

[40] See Uta-Renate Blumenthal, 'Poitevin Manuscripts, the Abbey of Saint-Ruf, and Ecclesiastical Reform in the Eleventh Century', in *Readers, Texts and Compilers*, ed. by Brett and Cushing, pp. 87–100; cf. Uta-Renate Blumenthal and Detlev Jasper, '*Licet nova consuetudo* — Gregor VII. und die Liturgie', in *Bishops, Texts and the Use of Canon Law around 1100: Essays in Honour of Martin Brett*, ed. by Bruce C. Brasington and Kathleen G. Cushing (Aldershot: Ashgate, 2008), pp. 45–68.

[41] Berengar of Tours's oath is documented in the record for Gregory VII's Lent synod of 1079 (*Reg.*, VI. 17a): 'Ego Beringarius corde credo et ore confiteor panem et vinum, que ponuntur in altari, per mysterium sacre orationis et verba nostri Redemptoris substantialiter converti in veram et propriam ac vivificatricem carnem et sanguinem Iesu Chrisi domini nostri et post consecrationem esse verum Christi corpus, quod natum est de virgine et quod pro salute mundi oblatum in cruce pependit et quod sedet ad dexteram Patris, et verum sanguinem Christi, qui de latere eius effusus est, non tantum per signum et virtutem sacramenti, sed in propriete nature et veritate substantie. Sicut in hoc brevi continentur et ego legi et vos intelligitis, sic credo nec contra hanc fidem ulterius docebo. Sic me Deus adiuvet et hec sacra evangelia. Tunc domnus papa precepit Berengario ex auctoritate Omnipontentis et sanctorum apostolorum Petri et Pauli, ut de corpore et sanguine Domini nunquam ulterius cum aliquo disputare vel aliquem docere presumeret, excepto causa reducendi ad hanc fidem eos, qui per eius doctrinam ab ea recesserant.'

[42] For a record of the full decrees, see *Reg.*, VI. 5b. The relevant rubrics are given as follows: (1) 'De Teutonicis contradicendis, ne predia ecclesiastica a regibus data sive ab invitis episcopis detineant'; (3) 'Ut contradicentur, ne aliquis accipiat investituram ecclesiarum de manu laicorum'; (4) 'Et ne prebende vel officia ecclesiastica vedantur'; (5) 'De symoniacis'; (6) 'De falsis ordinationibus' and 'Qualiter vera penitentia detur'; (7) 'De decimis a laicis iniuste detentis'; (8) 'De abstinentia sabbati'; (9) 'Ut nullus abbas decimas et primitias sine auctoritate Romani pontificis seu episcopi consensu, in cuius diocesi habitat, detineat'; (10) 'Ut nullus episcopus gravamen seu servile servitium ex usu abbatibus imponant'; (11) 'De sancti Petri hereditate occultata'; (12) 'Ut episcopi, qui consenserint fornicationem vel incestum in suis parroechiis, a suo officio suspendatur'; (13) 'Ut, qui certam partem in sollemni missa volunt habere, aliquid procurent offerre'.

legislation, however, and indeed the reason why scholars often associate the city of Poitiers as a centre of canonical activity in the eleventh century, are the ten decrees from Hugh of Die's 1078 Poitiers council. This particular legatine council, in fact, is measured almost exclusively by the ten decrees pronounced during the council proceedings — canons that were copied into no fewer than five French and Italian canon law collections of the late eleventh century.[43] It is for this reason that Gabriel Le Bras considered Poitiers one of the most important and influential regional meetings for the eleventh century.[44] That these ten decrees were transmitted through a council of this sort is evidence too that reforming ideology was being implemented actively in the provinces, and that Hugh of Die's role in council affairs was succeeding to some extent in disseminating reform to the French localities.

The dissemination of these ten canons, moreover, signifies the full weight of Gregory's reforming initiative in France.[45] Well known to scholars of this period, the legislation deals with the three main tenets of reform, first promulgated at Pope Leo IX's Reims council in 1049.[46] Their polemic, similar to the canons of Gregory's 1074 and 1075 Lent synods, attacks the abuses of lay investiture (1), simony (2–4), and nicolaitism (9), with the remaining canons directed at the right conduct of religious men (5–8, 10). Especially relevant by comparison is their adherence to the Roman decrees issued at Gregory's November synod held later that year,[47] similarities which imply their circulation to French prelates before 1078, the most likely occasion being Hugh of Die's 1077 Autun council.

Indeed, in addition to the growing number of legal cases considered in council setting, the Council of Autun represents Hugh of Die's first attempt at promulgating and enforcing reform decrees in France. The proclamations emanating

[43] These are the *Collectio Burdegalensis*, the *Collectio Tarraconensis* (versions I and II); the *Collectio XIII librorum*, and the *Collectio VII librorum*.

[44] Gabriel Le Bras, 'L'Activité canonique à Poitiers pendant la réforme grégorienne (1049–1099)', in *Mélanges offerts à René Crozet*, ed. by Pierre Gallais and Yves-Jean Riou (Poitiers: Société d'études médiévales, 1966), pp. 237–39 (p. 238).

[45] Cowdrey, *Pope Gregory VII*, p. 363. For analysis of these canons, see J.-C. Tillier, 'Les Conciles provinciaux de la province ecclésiastique de Bordeaux au temps de la réforme grégorienne (1073–1100)', *Bulletin philologique et historique du comité des travaux historiques et scientifiques*, 2 (1968), 561–81 (p. 566).

[46] Mansi, XIX, cols 735–41.

[47] See *Reg.*, VI. 5b; Hugh of Flavigny, p. 419. Among the thirty-three *capitula* are Gregory's concerns for simony (1, 9, 13), lay investiture (8), and nicolaitism (11, 12).

from this council, however, do not survive in the form of conciliar canons. Rather, they can be inferred only from Gregory's letter to Hugh (12 May 1077) directing him on the election of Gerard II to the see of Cambrai.[48] The first principle prohibited regular canons from becoming monks. The second is described best in the context of the letter, where Hugh was entreated to 'ensure by clear and resounding proclamation that, by henceforth upholding canonical and apostolic authority when promoting bishops, none of the metropolitans nor any of the bishops should dare to lay a hand in order to consecrate him upon anyone who shall have received the gift of the episcopate from a lay person, unless he wishes also himself to forfeit the honour of his own dignity and office'.[49]

A letter from Archbishop Manasses of Reims to Gregory confirms that Hugh did indeed carry out this declaration.[50] Referring to the consecration of Bishop Ralph of Amiens *contra auctoritatem et canones* by two of his own suffragan bishops, Helinand of Laon and Theobald of Soissons, Manasses attempted to exculpate himself by denying knowledge of what he recognized as a blatant violation of Gregory's 1074 and 1075 Roman decrees. It is his familiarity with these earlier reform decrees, and his acknowledgement of their circulation, that confirms Hugh's efforts in promulgating them at this legatine council.

Because of their value to contemporary reformers, as well as to the subject of this present study, the ten Poitevin canons (existing only as rubrics) are included below:

> (1) The holy council decrees that no bishop, abbot, priest, or clerk is to receive the gift (*donum*) of any bishopric, abbey or benefice from the hand of the king or the count or any laymen. The bishop is to receive these from his metropolitan, the abbot, the priest, and other inferior persons from his bishop. If the laity, in contempt of canon law, should presume to remain by force in possession of churches they shall be excommunicated; let there be in those churches no divine office, let no one pray (*oro*) there, or light candles, or be buried there; baptism only in time of need should be given but not penance or eucharistic communion.[51]

[48] See *Reg.*, IV. 22.

[49] *Reg.*, IV. 22.

[50] See Manasses I of Reims, in *RHGF*, XIV, 611.

[51] Mansi, XX, col. 498: 'Decrevit sancta synodus ut nullus episcopus, abbas, presbyter, vel quaelibet persona de clero accipiat de manu regis vel comitis, vel cuiuslibet laicae personae donum episcopatus, vel abbatiae, vel ecclesiae, vel aliquarum ecclesiasticarum rerum. Sed episcopus a suo

(2) That nobody shall hold an episcopal see, abbacy, archdeaconry, prebend or other ecclesiastical honours, neither should they keep prelacies in two churches, only in one, and neither having been bought. And whoever has paid for an ecclesiastical benefice shall be summarily deposed.[52]

(3) That no priest or layman shall claim a benefice by law of inheritance.[53]

(4) That no bishop shall receive payment for administering the sacraments, or for blessing churches, or any other blessing.[54]

(5) That no abbot or monk may impose a penance unless he has received this charge from his own (*proprius*) bishop.[55]

(6) That abbots, monks, and canons must not buy a church or in any way claim it for themselves without the consent of the bishop of the diocese. They may keep the revenues and benefices of the churches which they already hold peacefully. The priest shall be responsible to the bishop for the care of souls and for the services of Christians.[56]

(7) That abbots who are deacons — and who are not priests — should be ordained priests or lose their prelacies. Also those who have arch-diaconates should become deacons, all those who have arch-presbyterites should become priests, or lose their honours. That if, having held back some just reason, they

metropolitano, abbas, presbyter, &caeterae inferiores personae a proprio episcopo, Si vero laici, decretis canonicis resistentes, ecclesias violenter tenere praesumpserint, ipsi excommunicentur; in ecclesis vero illis nullum divinum officium fiat, nullus ibi oret, lumen non ponatur, mortuus non sepeliatur, tantum baptismi gratia ibi non negetur, infirmis remedio poenitentiae & communionis non subveniatur.'

[52] Mansi, XX, col. 498: 'Ut nemo episcopatum, abbatiam, archdiaconatum, archipresbyteratum, praebendam vel alios ecclesiasticos honores, vel in duabus ecclesiis praelationes exerceat nisi in una tantum: & neutrum horum quisquam per pecuniam acquirat. Et quicumque tali modo iam adquisisse comprobantur, omni remota occasione deponantur.'

[53] Mansi, XX, col. 498: 'Ut nullus de clero, sive de populo, ecclesiastica bona iure consanguinitatis requirat sibi habenda.'

[54] Mansi, XX, col. 498: 'Ut nullus episcopus pro sacris ordinibus, vel pro ecclesiarum benedictionibus, vel quibuslibet aliis benedictionibus munus accipiat.'

[55] Mansi, XX, col. 498: 'Ut nullas abbas, monachus, vel quilibet alius poenitentias injungat, nisi quibus proprius episcopus hanc curam dederit.'

[56] Mansi, XX, col. 498: 'Ut abbates, monachi, canonici ecclesias, quas nunquam habuerunt, non emant, nec alio modo sibi vindicent, nisi consentiente episcopo, in cuius fuerint diocese. In illis vero, quas hactenus absque calumnia habuerunt, redditus beneficiaque obtineant. Presbyter tamen de cura animarum, & de Christianitatis ministerio episcopo respondeat.'

might not be able to be priest or deacon, they should lose their prelacies (*praelationes*).[57]

(8) That sons of priests and illegitimate children in general may not be admitted to orders except by becoming monks or regular canons. They should under no circumstances hold prelacies (*praelationes*); neither should they keep servants, unless they are freed by their lords.[58]

(9) That no deacon, priest, or subdeacon should have a concubine or a woman living in his house in circumstances which might give rise to suspicion; anyone assisting at the Mass of a simoniac or unchaste priest shall be excommunicated.[59]

(10) Priests bearing arms or practising usury shall be excommunicated.[60]

As the only list of decrees issued at any of Hugh of Die's thirteen legatine councils, these Poitevin canons present the first and only example during Hugh's career where *acta* survive as council evidence. Their impact, as scholars like Fowler-Magerl and Blumenthal convincingly assert, is measured by their transmission to numerous extant collections attributed to Poitiers in the late 1070s and early 1080s. Four of the ten canons (3, 7–8, and 10) issued at this 1078 council eventually found their way into Pope Gregory IX's *Corpus iuris canonici* (1234/35) and remained as part of church discipline until the first part of the twentieth century (1917), reflecting this assembly's importance for the shaping of canon law in later centuries.[61] In this case, Hugh of Die's role in the council

[57] Mansi, XX, col. 498: 'Ut abbates diaconi, qui presbyteri non sunt, presbyteri fiant aut praelationes amittant. Qui archdiaconatus tenent, diaconi fiant: qui archipresbyteratus, presbyteri fiant, aut honores amittant. Quod si aliqua justa causa prohibente presbyteri aut diaconi esse non potuerint, praelationes amittant.'

[58] Mansi, XX, col. 498: 'Ut filii presbyterorum & caeteri ex fornicatione nati ad sacros gradus non provehantur, nisi aut monachi fiant, aut in congregatione canonica regulariter viventes. Praelationes vero nullatenus habeant; sed neque servi, nisi a dominis suis libertate donentur.'

[59] Mansi, XX, col. 498: 'Ut nullus diaconus, presbyter, vel subdiaconus concubinam habeat; sed nec aliam foeminam, unde mala suspicio habeatur, in una domo secum teneat, & quicumque huiusmodi sacerdotis, sive per pecuniam ordinati, missam scienter audierint, excommunicationi subjacere debeant.'

[60] Mansi, XX, col. 498: 'Clerici arma portantes, & usurarii excommunicentur.'

[61] Gregory IX, *Corpus iuris canonici*, X 1.15.1: 'Ut abates et decani et praepositi, qui presbyteri non sunt, presbyteri fiant, aut praelationes amittant; qui archidiaconatus tenent, diaconi fiant, qui vero archipresbyteratus, presbyteri, aut amittant honorem. Quod si aliqua iusta causa prohibente presbyteri aut diaconi esse non potuerint, praelationes amittant' = Poitiers 1078, canon 7; X 1.17.1: 135: 'Ut filii presbyterorum et ceteri ex fornicatione nati ad sacros ordines non promo-

arena served firsthand in transforming the extant church law and shaping it for posterity. That a papal legate was actively pronouncing reforming policies in the council arena is a seemingly customary practice for this period, though the evidence is admittedly scarce. The reception of this legislation into west-central France, on the other hand, is instructive for measuring the reformers' influence on the surrounding region of Poitiers, and within the ecclesiastical province of Aquitaine at large.

Exhibiting a measure of prestige and authority within his principality, Duke William VIII of Aquitaine played a prominent role in further disseminating the 1078 Poitevin legislation. According to Bishop Ernaldus of Le Mans, whose account verifies the decrees as products of this council, the ten canons were brought to Saint-Hilaire-le-Grand at the Duke's request.[62] Assuring their careful notation in order to seek clarification from his monastery — which had, until the middle of the eleventh century, belonged to the counts of Poitou[63] — William's interest arguably secured their reception into local canonical collections.

veantur, nisi aut monachi fiant, vel in congregatione canonica regulariter viventes. Praelationem vero nullatenus habeant. Sed neque servi, nisi a dominis suis libertate donentur' = Poitiers 1078, canon 8; X 3.1.1: 449: 'Clerici arma portantes et usurarii excommunicentur' = Poitiers 1078, canon 10; X 3.5.1: 465: 'Ut nullus de clero sive de populo ecclesiastica bona iure consanguinitatis sibi requirat habenda'= Poitiers 1078, canon 3; cf. Le Bras, 'L'Activité canonique', p. 238.

[62] Mansi, XX, col. 499: 'Ernaldus Cenomanensis episcopus, et Guandalbertus Fulconi decano salutem. Abbas majoris monasterii, et monachi eius conquesti sunt de me apud Lugdunensem primatem, et caeteros primores Pictavensis concilii, quod eorum oratoriam capellam apud Sablolium aedificare prohibemus. At illi rationem ostendentes, quod id fieri non deberet, rogaverunt, ut eis aedificandi licentiam tribuerem. Quorum auctoritati non obedire inreligiosum ducens, quod petebant benigne concessi. Mandamus itaque tibi et ex nostra auctoritate jubemus, ut cum domno Hilberto S. Martini monacho, per quem episcopalem aquam et altare et crucem ferream misimus, Sablolium usque pergas, et in loco quem ostenderit aquam spargas, et crucem figas. Vale.' This account, which is also found in Baluze's *Miscellanea*, IV, 565, fails to cite its original source. Confirming further these canons as products of Hugh of Die's 1078 Poitiers council is a letter from William to the canons of Saint-Hilaire (Mansi, XX, col. 500): 'Si autem aliquis ex istis, scilicet ex clericorum filiis, vel caeteris spuriis, antequam edictum Domini papae Gregorii VII. quod de illis promulgatum est in concilio Pictavensi a Domino Hugone Diensium episcopo, et sedit apostolicae legato esset recitatum, factus est in illa canonicus sicut ille utique permisit, ut ita permaneat, permittimus.'

[63] On the secular, religious, and reforming characteristics attributed to the dukes of Aquitaine, see Martindale, '"His Special Friend"?', p. 36; Jean Dunbabin, *France in the Making, 843–1180* (Oxford: Oxford University Press, 1985), pp. 62, 118, 175; A. Fliche and V. Martin, *Histoire de l'Église*, 21 vols (Paris: Bloud & Gay, 1945–62), VII (1948), 297–302; A. Debord, *La Société laïque dans les pays de la Charente, X^e–XIIe s.* (Paris: Picard, 1984), pp. 180–82. For a firsthand account of his participation and cooperation with the reformers, see *Reg.*, II. 24.

Thanks in part to the Duke's assistance (however directly), the 1078 Poitevin canons exist in a handful of contemporary canonical collections as well. Of particular significance is their transmission *c.* 1079–80 in the *Collectio Tarraconensis* (fols 46v–141r of BnF, MS lat. 5517) and the *Collectio Burdegalensis*.[64] Because of a reference in the latter collection to the Poitiers canons as 'Decretum generale quod decrevit sancta sinodus in Pictaviensi concilio' (fol. 156v of Bordeaux MS 11), Fowler-Magerl suggests the possibility of their being earlier products of Gregory's reforming legislation in Rome.[65] Such a connection, which seems to me very convincing, helps quantify our understanding of Hugh of Die's legal and administrative role in the council arena: through his assistance, Roman legislation was being disseminated actively in and around Poitiers, with the 1078 canons eventually finding their way into local canonical collections.

In view of such legislative impact, Hugh of Die's conciliar activity 1075–78 bears witness to his gradual development as an effective instrument of justice (*iustitia*) and law (*ius*), helping to extend reform and law to a larger audience north of the Alps. As Hugh became more accustomed to his role in the *ad hoc* legatine office, his competence, skill, efficiency, and enthusiasm in the council arena, not to mention his growing familiarity and confidence with canon law, were making advancements on all fronts. His first five councils at Anse (1075), Dijon (1076), Clermont (1076), Autun (1077), and Poitiers (1078) were landmarks for the dissemination of reforming principles and the transmission of ideas through ecclesiastical and lay circles alike. The councils of Autun (1077) and Poitiers (1078), in particular, offer clear examples of Hugh's ability to ensure the desired papal and legal outcome. From these councils develops a sense also of Hugh's legal efficiency and knowledge, especially as each meeting grew progressively diverse in terms of the cases discussed, and influential in terms of the participants, outcomes, and decrees promulgated.

What remains largely unknown, however, is the extent to which the reformers relied on select canonical materials to inform their legal outlook and practice. Despite its evident transmission to south-western France in this period, and its appearance in regional canon law collections like *Burdegalensis* and *Tarraconensis*, the 74T's use by reforming legates like Hugh of Die is largely circumstantial.

[64] For a fuller analysis of this Bordeaux collection, including a summary of its contents and *capitula*, see Kriston R. Rennie, 'The *Collectio Burdegalensis* and the Transmission of Canonical Texts to Bordeaux *c.*1079', in *ZRG kan. Abt.*, 94 (2008), 1–20, and Joseph Tardif, 'Une Collection canonique poitevine', *RHDFE*, 21 (1897), 149–216.

[65] Fowler-Magerl, *Clavis canonum*, p. 130.

As Christof Rolker has recently argued, it is no longer accurate to label the 74T as 'le premier manuel canonique', as Fournier first proposed in 1894. Rather, it was a collection 'mainly concerned with monastic liberties, and above all with the authority of papal privileges conferred on monasteries'.[66] That is to say that the 74T was of little possible use beyond monastic quarters, despite its being copied into contemporary 'reforming' collections like Anselm of Lucca's *Collectio canonum*, the *Collection in Three Books*, the *Collection in Four Books*, the *Collection in Seventeen Books*, the *Collection in Thirteen Books*, and the *Panormia*, among others.[67]

In giving further consideration to the 74T's composition, moreover, Hugh of Die's consultation with this collection for purposes of procedure or authority seems far less likely. Only a relatively small portion of the collection's seventy-four titles actually deals with matters of litigation (Chapters 44–110).[68] And it is particularly this field, comprising for instance the procedure for judging cases, which would have been of significant relevance to the papal legate in the council arena. That said, the anonymous author evidently placed some importance on the procedures that go into making up a council, including relevant *capitula* on the character and credibility of the accuser (whose testimony was the key factor in bringing the case to attention, as well as seeing it through to its final judgement), the jurisdiction of each case within the concerned ecclesiastical province, the gathering of judges and testimony of witnesses, among many other aspects (Chapters 89–90, 98). Significant too is the fact that the 74T's longest title (15) deals with the issue of simony — the primary target of reformers in France (see below, Chapter 6).

Thus any direct connection between the 74T and its use by papal legates is purely speculative, though our inability to procure evidence in this regard does not eliminate the possibility that it was being used in the reforming circles of France. Surely an argument *ex silentio* does not imply that it is lacking in value? The evidence of its appearance in contemporary regional French canon law collections like the *Collectio Tarraconensis* and *Collectio Burdegalensis* provides proof of its circulation to west-central France in the late 1070s — exactly which

[66] Christof Rolker, 'The *Collection in Seventy-four Titles*: A Monastic Canon Law Collection from Eleventh-Century France', in *Readers, Texts and Compilers*, ed. by Brett and Cushing, p. 72.

[67] See Fowler-Magerl's *Clavis canonum*.

[68] Fowler-Magerl's *Clavis canonum*, p. 116. The majority of this collection deals with liturgical instructions on issues of marriage, baptism, heresy, etc.; on this point, see Knox, 'Finding the Law', pp. 444–45.

version was used by the compiler of each collection has not yet been determined. The difficulty falls to making the relevant connections. Certainly, some prior instruction or consultation with a consolidated body of canon law was necessary before a legate could exercise the responsibility of his jurisdiction. It would have proved counterproductive for Gregory to commission men to this office who were not proficient to some degree in legal matters.

References to canon law can certainly be inferred from many of the conciliar judgements passed by Hugh of Die at French councils, expressing in the first instance this legate's knowledge of Gregory's 1074/75 Roman decrees — issued at his Autun (1077) and Poitiers (1078) councils. But without sufficient manuscript evidence it is impossible to locate exactly which source or recension was being consulted. Was Hugh citing from Burchard's *Decretum*, the 74T, or some other contemporary or ancient legal text? Did he, perhaps, have access to this legal material through a regional canon law collection like those described above? Having such evidence might allow us to determine more readily the possible canonical sources, narrative histories, or other contemporary sources at Hugh's disposal while he was chamberlain at Lyon, before his rise to the legatine office in 1075.

In the absence of this information, the true foundation and framework for Hugh's legal knowledge remains speculative and incomplete. It is impossible to verify whether Hugh preferred one collection to another or whether he merely borrowed from whatever collection was most accessible and familiar to him. It is, however, entirely plausible to conclude that Hugh gained a considerable knowledge of reforming law directly from Rome, as well as from his own personal experience in the council arena and through personal contact with Gregory VII. How he applied this legal knowledge for the treatment of certain canonical matters within his jurisdiction, as witnessed in the previous chapter, at times risked compromising the reformers' position, bringing his actions to bear against Gregory's more immediate needs and interests, and those set out by the reformers. Competent and familiar with certain undisclosed legal texts, there is a sense that Hugh's legal knowledge was the root and cause of his unwillingness to deviate from the rule of canon law. That he maintained this uncompromising disposition throughout the course of his legation seems especially true in light of the following evidence for his application of reform and law in the late 1070s and early 1080s.

Chapter 6

TOWARDS REFORM IN FRANCE

There is no better way to conclude this study on law and practice than to compare Gregory VII's reforming objectives in France with the strict council methods of his legate Hugh of Die. Such a methodology throws light on the many obstacles facing church reformers in the late 1070s and early 1080s, while revealing the numerous reasons that called for an increased conciliar, legislative, and legatine agenda during Gregory's pontificate. By examining the issues of simony, nicolaitism, and lay investiture in France, necessary consideration is given in this final chapter to the laity's role in the reform movement. Of greatest interest to the present study, however, is Hugh of Die's contribution to, and overall success in, rooting out these abuses, and the legal and conciliar manner by which these objectives were reached.

The Problem of Simony

Writing from Italy in the late 1090s, Bishop Bruno of Segni described the world as he perceived it in the middle of the eleventh century: 'plunged in evil; holiness had disappeared; righteousness had perished and truth had been buried. Iniquity reigned; avarice held dominion', and, he continued, 'Simon Magus possessed the Church'.[1] While this description no doubt served some greater polemical purpose, Bruno's depiction was not far from the truth. Simony was one of the most widespread abuses affecting the Church in this period, and although the problem was

[1] Bruno of Segni, 'The Sermon of the Venerable Bishop Bruno concerning Simoniacs', in *Papal Reform of the Eleventh Century*, ed. and trans. by Robinson, chap. 1, p. 377.

political, social, and theological, it was 'treated almost exclusively within a juristic framework'.[2]

During Gregory VII's pontificate, Christian subjects found guilty of simony were seen as transgressing though ignorance, 'resisting the Holy Spirit from presumptuous obstinacy', casting aside divine laws and despising apostolic decrees.[3] Originally derived from the Acts of the Apostles (8. 9, 18–21),[4] simony's theoretical meaning was broadened by early church thinkers like Augustine and Ambrose of Milan (citing Acts 20. 35), with its original notion transformed even more under the moralizing of Pope Gregory the Great (590–604) who declared it to be a heresy.[5] Augustine stressed the importance of rising through the ecclesiastical ranks from the minor to major orders, while Gregory I lamented over the diminishing devotion and discipline caused by those who continually ignored the clerical hierarchy, in effect turning the sacred into profane.[6] Anyone knowingly taking part in this crime, as Gregory saw it, 'shares in the guilt of the man from whom this singular crime took its origin'.[7]

This ideology, particularly influenced by the thinking of Gregory I, is echoed in later canon law. But the eleventh- and twelfth-century concepts of simony changed very little from their sixth-century theoretical models. Citing from the decretals of Pope Celestine I (422–32), Leo I (440–61), and Gregory I, for

[2] John T. Gilchrist, '"Simoniaca Haeresis" and the Problem of Orders from Leo IX to Gratian', in *Proceedings of the Second International Congress of Medieval Canon Law* (Vatican City: S. Congregatio de seminariis et studiorum universitatibus, 1965), pp. 209–36 (p. 210).

[3] *Reg.*, II. 45.

[4] The Vulgate reads: 'Vir autem quidam nomine Simon qui ante fuerat in civitate magus seducens gentem Samariae dicens esse se aliquem magnem [...] cum vidisset autem Simon quia per inpositionem manus apostolorum daretur Spiritus Sanctus obtulit eis pecuniam dicens date et mihi hanc potestatem ut cuicumque inposuero manus accipiat Spiritum Sanctum Petrus autem dixit ad eum pecunia tua tecum sit in perditionem quoniam donum Dei existimasti pecunia possideri non est tibi pars neque sors in sermone isto cor enim tuum non est rectum coram Deo.'

[5] Timothy Reuter, 'Gifts and Simony', in *Medieval Transformations: Texts, Power, and Gifts in Context*, ed. by Esther Cohen and Mayke B. De Jong (Leiden: Brill, 2001), pp. 157–68 (p. 161); cf. Gilchrist, 'Simoniaca Haeresis', p. 215. For a look at the development in canon law which treated simony as a heresy, see also Jean Leclercq, 'Simoniaca Heresis', *SG*, 1 (1947), 523–30.

[6] Pope Gregory I, *Reg.*, IX. 213 (*Registrum epistularum*, ed. by Norberg, p. 771), from John the Deacon, *Life of Gregory* (PL, LXXV, cols 126–27); cf. 74T, chaps 125–27, p. 137.

[7] *Reg.*, XII. 9 (*Registrum epistularum*, ed. by Norberg, pp. 980–82).

example, the eleventh-century *Diversorum patrum sententie* (74T) stresses the dangers in considering the office of bishop as an object of desire and ambition. A grievous concern for the papacy was that laymen were promoting bishops as soon as an office became vacant — a practical reflection of what was regularly occuring. Even if they were deemed of 'blameless merit' (inculpatum meritum), it was still (in theory) necessary to 'rise first through the various offices of the ecclesiastical order'.[8] By contemporary canon law standards, bishops were chosen by the clergy and people (*clerus et populus*), with the consecration of the provincial bishops and the consent of the metropolitan.[9] 'If anyone desires the episcopate', as Pope Symmachus (498–514) noted to his brother Caesarius in a sixth-century decretal, 'he should not seek powerful men as his supporters by giving them bribes, nor should he by any kind of fear force the clergy or citizens to register their vote on his behalf or entice them to do so by any kind of rewards.'[10] The thwarting of canonical elections, but also the impudence of those promoted to the episcopate in simoniacal fashion, therefore, posed the largest threat to church order. Such men elected by the laity were viewed as ignorant, inexperienced, and devoid of religious life; they were regarded as lacking humility and the necessary training and education to fulfil the purposes traditionally valued by the episcopal office.

By the eleventh century, simony had come to adopt a notion of impurity, embodying temporal elements of gift exchange, reciprocity, money, inheritance, and manipulation — characteristics prevalent in the social and political relations between the clergy and laity. It was from these assertions of aristocratic status that the Church was attempting to free itself. Yet simony inspired a much different passion among the community than nicolaitism (discussed in more detail below). Its growth was very much connected to lay involvement in taking tithes from the parochial church, meddling in often-patrimonial appointments, presenting the opportunity for men of 'low birth or bad character to enter the church'.[11] Similar

[8] *Reg.*, IX. 218 (*Registrum epistularum*, ed. by Norberg, pp. 781–82), from John the Deacon, *Life of Gregory*, III. 2 (PL, LXXV, col. 130); cf. 74T, chap. 129.

[9] Pope Celestine I, letter 4, chap. 5 (PL, L), cols 434–35, from Pseudo-Isidore, in Hinschius, ep. 2. V, p. 560, and letter 5, chap. 2, col. 436, from Pseudo-Isidore, in Hinschius, ep. 3. II, p. 561; Pope Leo I, *Opera omnia*, chap. 1, letter 167, col. 1203, from Pseudo-Isidore, in Hinschius, ep. 70. I, p. 616; cf. 74T, chaps 113–14, 117.

[10] Pope Symmachus, *Epistolae et decreta*, in PL, LXII (1863), cols 49–80 (chap. 6, letter 6, col. 55), from Pseudo-Isidore, in Hinschius, ep. 1. V, p. 657; cf. 74T, chap. 123.

[11] R. I. Moore, 'Family, Community and Cult on the Eve of the Gregorian Reform', *Transactions of the Royal Historical Society*, 30 (1980), 49–69 (p. 67).

to the potential dangers that nicolaitism posed in creating episcopal dynasties, simony risked promoting men to ecclesiastical offices without any regard for their education, competence, skill, or even their religious devotion. This fear of pollution was interwoven with a fear of manipulation, where men could aspire to high ecclesiastical standing by non-spiritual means of money or inheritance. Even by the sixth century, simony was considered not only in terms of a cash transaction, but also included performing services in the hope of gaining office, and granting or receiving office with an expectation of delivered services.

The rhetoric against simony can be seen most sharply in Humbert of Silva Candida's *Adversus simoniacos* (written *c.* 1050), after which period the problem of simony became especially acute.[12] That is not to say, however, that a concern for simony was nonexistent in France prior to the mid-eleventh century. The Council of Poitiers in 1014, for example, convened and presided over by Duke William V of Aquitaine, shows a strong lay concern for those who had obtained their office falsely through simony. The Council of Bourges in 1031 decreed that 'no gift was to be accepted by the bishop or his ministers in return for holy orders' (canon 3), and that 'laymen should not place priests in the churches expect through the bishop' (canon 22)[13] And as Cushing noted, 'in the aftermath of the synod of Sutri in 1046, simony quickly became one of the chief preoccupations of the papacy'.[14] Pope Leo IX promulgated decrees against the abuse in 1049 at the papal councils of Rome, Reims, and Mainz;[15] Nicholas II condemned the abuse at his 1059 Roman synod,[16] as did Alexander II at his Roman council in 1063.[17] In France, moreover, legates were attacking the abuse of simony actively, as exemplified by the councils of Narbonne in 1054, Lyon in 1055, Toulouse in 1056, Tours in 1060, among others.[18]

[12] Humbert of Silva-Candida, *Humberti cardinalis libri* III. *adversus simoniacos*, ed. by F. Thaner, in *Libelli de lite imperatorum et pontificum saeculis* XI. *et* XII. *conscripti*, ed. by Ernst Dümmler, Lothar von Heinemann, and Friedrich Thaner, MGH, Libelli, 1 (1891), pp. 95–253.

[13] Mansi, XIX, cols 501–02: 'Ut de sacris ordinibus munus ab episcopo, vel ab eius ministris, non accipiatur' (canon 3) and 'Ut laici presbyteros in ecclesiis, nisi in manu episcopi, non ponant' (canon 22).

[14] Cushing, *Reform and the Papacy*, p. 98.

[15] See Mansi, XIX, cols 721–26 (Rome); cols 741–42 (Reims); and cols 749–50 (Mainz).

[16] Mansi, XIX, cols 897–98.

[17] Mansi, XIX, cols 1023–26.

[18] Mansi, XIX, cols 837–38 (Lyon); cols 843–44 (Narbonne); cols 847–53 (Toulouse); and cols 926–28 (Tours). See Pontal, *Les Conciles de la France*, pp. 166–72.

Similar to his papal predecessors, Gregory VII's campaign to counter simony attacked every level of the ecclesiastical hierarchy. The extant evidence in the papal *Register*, however, taking into account our interest in the legatine work of Hugh of Die, narrows our focus significantly to the highest clerical grades. Those offenders, whether publicly or secretly known, were seen as undermining religion, hurling stones and arrows against the Lord and striking the immovable rock of the Holy Roman Church.[19] This wider view of Gregory's moral attitude is offered in a letter to Count Robert I of Flanders (1076), which clearly describes those ecclesiastics who had obtained their office illicitly as 'thieves and robbers' (fures et latrones). 'Whoever is made bishop according to the holy canons', Gregory continued, 'enters by the door, that is, by Christ. For the saying of Holy Scripture that "Evil priests are a people's ruin" is borne out in our own time more clearly than daylight.'[20] Those who were regarded as simoniacs, those guilty of not upholding righteousness (*iustitia*), were not to be considered as bishops 'but as enemies of Christ. As they have no concern to obey the apostolic see, by the same token you should pay them no obedience'.[21] For 'not to resist such men to the uttermost', as Gregory VII interpreted the writings of Gregory the Great, was nothing short of denying the Christian faith.[22]

By the latter half of the eleventh century, the most common punishment for simony was deposition, but mere rumours of one's association with the abuse could often lead to a greater moral and social disgrace.[23] While one's office could be regained generally through purging, often followed by a renewed consecration into office (a process much more complicated than suggested here), the social

[19] *Reg.*, I. 11: 'lapides et sagittas latenter contra Dominum iactaverunt, iam nunc ad subvertendam religionem et immobilem sancta Romane ecclesie'.

[20] This is not a biblical reference, but comes from the writings of Pope Gregory I, *Reg.* IX. 219, in *Registrum epistularum*, ed. by Norberg: 'Nam cum scriptum sit: Ut prius quis probetur, et sic ministret, multo amplius ante probandus est, qui populi intercessor assumitur, ne fiant causa ruinae populi sacerdotes mali' (p. 787). This reference appears only one other time in Gregory VII's *Register*, in a letter (1083) to Bishops Gerard II of Cambrai, Radbod of Noyon, Rorico of Amiens, and those princes and rulers of churches serving under Count Robert I of Flanders (*Reg.*, IX. 35). It is no coincidence that Gregory used this saying in addressing Robert in 1076, and again in reference to him in 1083. Gregory clearly trusted the 'good report' about the Count, and believed the complaint made known to him by Archdeacon Arnulf of Thérouanne, and unidentified Abbot 'M.', and especially the deacon (and Flemish clerk) Ingelrannus, as pitiful.

[21] *Reg.*, IV. 11.

[22] *Reg.*, I. 11.

[23] See *Reg.*, II. 61–62.

implications that brought about the accusations might present a larger, lingering, or defamatory threat in the surrounding community. A bishop accused by his cathedral canons of purchasing his office, for instance, would not find his return to office a welcome one. A conciliar injunction from Gregory's 1075 Lent synod broadcast that 'those who have been promoted by the simoniac heresy, that is, with the intervention of money, to any rank or office of holy orders may no longer exercise any ministry in holy church'. If they were not deposed immediately, they at least had to forfeit their acquisitions (i.e., their churches) 'so that no one for the future may be allowed to sell or buy them'.[24]

It is important here to note Gregory's distinction between lay providers and ecclesiastical ordainers. This is done more easily by comparing the decrees prohibiting simony that were — similar to those issued against nicolaitism — not enforced consistently or widely until Gregory's 1078 Lent synod. Two decrees, numbers 4 and 5, reveal the Church's marked attitude:

> (4) If anyone shall sell prebends, archdeaconries, provostships, or any ecclesiastical offices, or provide to them otherwise than the decrees of the holy fathers prescribe, let him be suspended from office. For it is proper that, as he has freely received a bishopric, so he should freely distribute the members of that bishopric;[25]

and

> (5) Ordinations which take place through the intervention of a price or of pleas or of service to some person done for this intention, or which take place not by common consent of clergy and people according to canonical enactments, and have not been approved by those to whom consecration belongs, we have adjudged to be void, since those ordained in such a way do not enter through the door, that is, through Christ, but, as the Truth himself bears witness, are thieves and robbers.[26]

[24] *Ep. vag.*, 6–7: 'ut hi qui per symoniacam heresim, hoc est interuentu precii, ad aliquem sacrorum ordinum gradum vel officium promoti sunt, nullum in sancta ecclesia ulterius locum ministrandi habeant'.

[25] *Reg.*, VI. 5b: 'Si quis prebendas archidiaconatus prepposituras vel aliqua officia ecclesiastica vendiderit vel aliter, quam statuta sanctorum patrum precipiunt, ordinaverit, ab officio suspendatur. Dignum enim est, ut, sicut gratis episcopatum accepit, ita membra eiusdem episcopatus gratis distribuat.'

[26] *Reg.*, VI. 5b: 'Ordinationes, que interveniente pretio vel precibus vel obsequio alicui persone ea intentione impenso vel que non communi consensu cleri et populi secundum canonicas sanc-

Clearly, the fourth decree is aimed against the episcopate, emphasizing the gift of the bishopric as being given and received freely (*gratis*), and the necessity for offices under the bishop's care to be transferred under the same conditions; any failure to do so could result in suspension from office (*ab officio*). Lay elite, on the other hand, are targeted more suitably by this council's fifth decree. Here, Gregory introduced the impurity associated with money, and the concept of purchase or exchange, which are both clear allusions to the secular and temporal world. The sale of an ecclesiastical office committed without the assent of the clergy was judged to be void. Finding it difficult to invoke punishments extending beyond the ecclesiastical realm, which is not to say that excommunications were avoided altogether, Gregory's most threatening measure against lay providers who committed simony was to cancel their transaction outright in an attempt to eliminate their participation in spiritual matters.

The dissemination of these general Roman decrees to France was not immediate or far-reaching. Gregory's letters, for instance, more commonly function as instruction to the faithful for the simultaneous expulsion of simony and nicolaitism, with a seemingly greater concern being placed on the latter abuse. And, with the exception of Bishop Josfred of Paris being commissioned by the Pope to lead a general campaign in the French church against both abuses in March 1077, these directions were directed more commonly at Italian or German figures like Patriarch Sigehard of Aquileia, Archbishop Anno of Cologne, Henry IV, and others.[27]

The papacy's attempt to counter simony is nevertheless prevalent in the existing records for the late eleventh century. The abuse had become so well-recognized by the last quarter of the eleventh century that it scarcely required reference to its biblical originator Simon Magus, whose name appears only four times in Gregory's *Register* — all in cases referring to individual sees involving Bishops Jaromir of Prague, Godfrey of Milan, the legatine activity of a Cluniac monk in Spain (Robert), and the denunciation of Henry IV and Guibert of Ravenna to the bishops of southern Italy.[28] A quick glance at Erich Caspar's index of the *Register* reveals the Pope's repeated use of synonymous language associated

tiones fiunt et ab his, ad quos consecratio pertinet, non comprobantur, irritas esse diiudicamus, quoniam, qui taliter ordinantur, non per ostiam id est per Christum intrant, sed, up ipsa veritas testatur, fures sunt et latrines.'

[27] See *Reg.*, IV. 20; II. 62; II. 67; and III. 3 respectively. See also *Reg.*, V. 18 for Gregory's call to Bishop Huzmann of Speyer.

[28] See *Reg.*, I. 17; I. 27; VIII. 2; VIII. 5, respectively.

with the abuse, with one of the most preferred expressions being *symoniacus heresis*.[29] A look at Hugh of Die's activity in France from 1077 onwards, moreover, provides a better indication of Gregory's genuine concern for the moral and spiritual condition of the Church resulting from this abuse; it also offers some insight into the Pope's attitude for using all the means available to him for enforcing decrees against simony throughout the *societas Christiana*.

Similar to countering nicolaitism (discussed below), the most comprehensive attack on simony in France did not come until Hugh of Die's Poitiers council in January 1078, although papal instructions must have come much earlier. The legate's contribution in promulgating these decrees marks one of the few successes where the papacy achieved the desired dissemination of its reforming objectives to a large French audience, both lay and ecclesiastical.[30] Indeed, the numerous punishments handed out by Hugh of Die in council setting often surrounded his attempt to extirpate simony — an estimated eleven cases from thirteen councils. Whatever Hugh's personal understanding of the abuse might have been, his methods to eradicate it through extensive judgements at his legatine councils are manifest in the extant evidence. Admittedly, however, the extent of his moral and spiritual objection took time to develop.

Take for example Hugh of Die's second legatine council, convened at Dijon in 1076.[31] The only details for its proceedings are found in Hugh of Flavigny's *Chronicon*, where it is recorded incorrectly as Hugh of Die's third council (*tertium*).[32] Like the documentation for Anse in 1075, there is little substantive evidence indicating the council's outcome, with the exception of the following account: 'Persequebatur symoniacos, adversus quos ei iugis pugna, conflictus

[29] See *Reg.*, p. 706. *Symoniacus* (appears 7 times), *symoniaci* (9 times), *symoniacus et invasor* (4 times), and *simoniaca heresis* (21 times) were among the most frequently used terms in Gregory's *Register*.

[30] The decrees that offer the best comparison to Gregory's Lent synod are taken from Mansi, XX, col. 498: (2) That nobody shall hold an episcopal see, abbacy, archdeaconry, prebend or other ecclesiastical honours in two churches, and whoever has paid for an ecclesiastical benefice shall be summarily deposed; (3) That no priest or layman shall claim a benefice by law of inheritance; (4) That no bishop shall receive presents for administering the sacraments or any other blessing; (6) That abbots, monks and canons must not buy a church or in any way claim it for themselves without the consent of the bishop of the diocese. They may, in fact, keep the revenues and benefices of the churches which they already hold up to that point. The priest shall be responsible to the bishop for the care of souls and for the services of Christians.

[31] The Dijon council can be dated accurately by Hugh of Die's invitation to Archbishop Ralph I of Tours: letter 2, PL, CLVII, cols 507–08.

[32] Hugh of Flavigny, p. 413.

fuit perpetuus, quos etiam prout potuit ab aecclesia eliminavit, et orthodoxos substituit.' This council was likely held to suspend, depose, or excommunicate those simoniacs who were persecuting the Roman Church. In fact, Hugh of Flavigny's brief description seems to tie up well with the list of *acta* from Gregory's 1076 Lenten synod, strongly suggesting that the excommunication sentences were associated more closely with the Council of Dijon. There may also be reason enough to suspect that Hugh's efforts to promote Gregory's reform principles were already well underway. It was not until the Council in Autun (1077), however, and more specifically at Poitiers (1078), that these principles were described in the form of decrees issued.

The dangers that simony posed to both the lay and ecclesiastical society in the kingdom of France, therefore, made a late entry in Gregory's reforming agenda. The missing evidence for Gregory's 1074 and 1075 synods, and our inability to assess fully the impact of reforming principles on the years leading up to 1077–78, not to mention the papacy's struggle to disseminate simoniacal decrees to a larger audience in that region, makes some sense of the scanty evidence found in Gregory's letters. The dispatching of papal letters and summoning bishops to Rome for Lenten and November synods was not an entirely effective means in uniting both clerical and lay members for quelling the abuse. It would seem that the ecclesiastical and laymen in France needed constant reminders, but their familiarity with Gregory's objectives depended on who was attending the legatine and Roman councils, and who was assisting or resisting them at home. Churchmen that did not fit into this category were unlikely to have been instilled with the principles of reform. Hugh of Die's success in promulgating reform principles at his 1078 Poitevin council is proof that the papal machinery for advocating reform up to this point was perhaps not as sufficiently developed or satisfactorily extended as Gregory would have liked.

Only one case truly discloses the enthusiasm and zeal with which simoniacs were being pursued in France prior to this date. At the Council of Clermont in 1076, Hugh excommunicated Étienne de Polignac for invading the see of Le Puy ('Podiensis sedis invasor')[33] — vacant since 1073. Recognized as the Bishop of Clermont for over twenty years (1052–73), Étienne had allegedly abandoned his cathedral with the assistance of his kinsman, Viscount Guillaume de Polignac, for personal or convenient reasons.[34] There is some question as to whether he was

[33] Hugh of Flavigny, p. 413; see also Mansi, XX, col. 481.

[34] *GC*, II, cols 261–62; cf. P. R. Gaussin, *L'Abbaye de la Chaise-Dieu (1043–1518)* (Paris: Cujas, 1962), pp. 84, 125.

perhaps driven from the see of Clermont by Guillaume, a man that Hugh of Flavigny describes only as 'symoniacus et invasor'.[35] Yet Étienne's translation also raises immediate suspicion of political and regional manipulation for profitable purposes, such as the acquisition of new lands or revenues. Whatever the truth of this matter, his challenge to the churches of Clermont and Le Puy draws attention to his disobedience.

After promising Gregory that he would renounce his simoniacal claim to the see of Le Puy, Étienne made no noticeable efforts to that effect, forcing Gregory to issue anathema against him at his 1075 Roman synod.[36] Meanwhile, ever since the news of this unlawful occupation had reached his ears in Rome, Gregory was active in trying to replace him with a bishop-elect of the same name.[37] But Étienne appears to have gained enough support and influence in that region to maintain his position, which he presumably hoped to square with the Pope. The record for Gregory's 1076 Lenten synod confirmed Étienne as one excommunicated 'by our legates' (a legatis nostris)[38] for charges of simony, as well as mentioning a far more mystifying and altogether unexplained allegation of homicide.[39] (Only the simoniacal sentence, however, was ever reconfirmed — in a papal letter issued the following year).[40] The reference made in 1076 to 'a legatis nostris', moreover, implies that Étienne's excommunication came at the hands of Hugh of Die and perhaps even the Roman subdeacon Hubert.

A papal letter issued to the canons of Le Puy in March 1077 expresses more clearly Étienne's wrongful occupation of that see, and his vexing it with tyrannical oppression ('tyrannica oppressione affligere').[41] But it is Hugh of Flavigny's account alone that provides us with some insight into the Clermont proceedings that warranted the Bishop's final excommunication. According to the chronicler, Étienne had made a sworn agreement (*pactio*) with Hugh of Die at some point over the course of the council, before the altar of Saint Mary, and 'over the body of St Peter, concerning the liberation of this church'.[42] This agreement forbid

[35] Hugh of Flavigny, p. 413.

[36] *GC*, II, cols 261–62.

[37] *Reg.*, I. 80.

[38] *Reg.*, III. 10a.

[39] See also Hugh of Flavigny, p. 417; Mansi, XX, col. 482. The charge of murder, mentioned in the record for Gregory's 1076 Lenten synod, is nowhere discussed.

[40] *Reg.*, IV. 19.

[41] *Reg.*, IV. 18.

[42] *Reg.*, IV. 18; cf. Hugh of Flavigny, p. 417; Mansi, XX, col. 481.

Étienne to serve the faithful, entrusting that he would comply and obey the apostolic decree to abandon his episcopal duties at Le Puy. No less than fifteen days had passed since the agreement was made, however, when Étienne returned to Le Puy with a small entourage of companions to regain his see forcefully. His excommunication — his 'separation from the bosom of the holy church' — followed shortly thereafter.[43]

The news of Étienne's excommunication was relayed soon after to a much wider audience ('universis Galliarum episcopis et cunctis ordinibus sub eis constitutis'), suggesting the lengths to which Gregory was prepared to go to ensure that the see of Le Puy would no longer be weighed down with oppression.[44] Despite Étienne's alleged oath not only to give up this church, but also to 'assist the election and establishment of a shepherd in it [...] he did not cease to oppress this church and to wear out its sons by a twofold attrition — that is to say, bodily and spiritual'.[45] For his persistent disregard of expressed papal wishes, Gregory was again forced to confirm Étienne's excommunication and, referring to the crime of simony, pronounced anathema on all those 'who henceforth give him counsel that he should persist in this heresy'. It was forbidden, as this papal letter stressed, for anyone to offer any amount of money to the church, to the altar of Saint Mary or to the hands of the priest, so that the church could be 'freed from so godless an oppression'.[46]

As this patchy evidence suggests, the papacy encountered great difficulty in expelling Étienne from Le Puy. The regional support of his kinsman ostensibly enabled him to hold the office indefinitely, but the papacy's difficulty in finding and installing a suitable successor also played some part in delaying the process. Étienne's case was never fully resolved at Clermont and required further review at the Council of Autun later the following year (September 1077). In a letter written to Hugh of Die in May 1077, Gregory expressed his desire to bring this case to a conclusion, instructing his legate to deal diligently (*diligenter*) with this and other matters in order to relieve the papacy's 'concern and long toil'

[43] *Reg.*, IV. 18.

[44] *Reg.*, IV. 19. The canons of Le Puy were instructed to select a new bishop in Hugh of Die's presence ('coram predicto Diense episcopo'), suggesting the importance of the legate's role in episcopal elections, acting on the Pope's behalf in confirming and perhaps even ordaining the bishop-elect.

[45] *Reg.*, IV. 19.

[46] *Reg.*, IV. 19.

(sollicitudo et longa fatigatio).[47] The tone of Gregory's letter to Hugh hints at the nuisance that this case was causing to the Curia. By that stage of the negotiations, the papacy had been toiling with this case for nearly four years (1073–77), and yet they were still ill-prepared to bring it to an end at Hugh's Council of Clermont. If the matter was indeed as serious as the papal letters suggest, why then had it not been settled more immediately? Why had the papacy tolerated Étienne's unlawful occupation of a see?

One potential reason for Gregory's prolonged leniency is that the see of Le Puy 'was exempt from metropolitan authority and directly subject to the apostolic see'[48] — a condition granted in 1051 by Gregory's predecessor Pope Leo IX, just before Étienne became Bishop of Clermont.[49] This certainly helps explain the Pope's extended concern for the provincial affairs of Bourges (as metropolitan), but it does not completely excuse Étienne's prolonged control over his diocese. At the height of Gregory's pontificate (*c.* 1077–78), similar charges of simony would have faced much quicker sentencing. Yet Gregory's hardening reform policy in the first years of his pontificate demonstrates a certain hesitation from the time in which his reform principles were first issued in Roman synods to their application in France. It was not until the Council of Autun in 1077 that Gregory's decrees against simony were circulated more widely through his use of letters and legates.

Indeed, the most controversial simoniacal case to emerge under Gregory VII's pontificate concerned Archbishop Manasses I of Reims (1069–80). It was at Hugh of Die's Autun council that the infamous and prolonged dispute between legate and archbishop came to light, demonstrating to a new degree Gregory VII's concern for the church in France. According to Hugh of Flavigny's *Chronicon*, it was at this council that charges of simony were first brought against the Archbishop by some of his clerics at Reims. Among the accusers were Manasses of Châtillon, the provost and archbishop of Reims from 1096 to 1106, and Bruno, chancellor and master of the cathedral school of Reims and future founder of the Carthusian order,[50] who accused the Archbishop of plotting against them,

[47] *Reg.*, IV. 22.

[48] Cowdrey, *Register*, p. 84 n. 1.

[49] *GC*, II, col. 698.

[50] Hugh of Die, letter 8, in *Gregorii VII Romani pontificis Epistolae et diplomata pontificia*, PL, CXLVIII (1844), col. 745; see Manasses's letter to Hugh of Die, *RHGF*, XIV, 783; cf. John R. Williams, 'Archbishop Manasses I of Rheims and Pope Gregory VII', *American Historical Review*, 54 (1949), 804–24 (p. 810).

violating their homes, selling their prebends, and stealing their goods.[51] The matter is not dealt with here in any more detail, but evolved in succeeding councils, eventually coming to a head at Hugh's Lyonnais council in 1080.[52]

Urged by Gregory to attend this later council — to 'answer, to make legal satisfaction, and to be cleared canonically, with regard to all charges'[53] — Manasses failed to attend after being summoned for a third and final time, for which absence he was deposed by Hugh. The reasons for his non-attendance, however, were imaginative to say the least. He defended his case at length in a letter to Hugh in which he wrote that the

> apostolic lord [Gregory] made me promise that if I was called to a council in Gaul either by a messenger or by letters of the apostolic see, I should not fail to come, unless I might be obstructed with a canonical excuse. But this he did not add that, if the call to the council was countermanded, I should abandon the journey. Wherefore, when recently informed by you about the council at Troyes, in which reminder the name of the abbot of Cluny was equally included, I made my way to that place without delay with my abbots and clerks and holders of my church; because, as I said before, I heard no mention from the apostolic lord that the promise already spoken was countermanded; and because I accepted that the abbot of Cluny, who ought to judge me, would be present; and because in this countermand made by you, my understanding was that you had no problem which would mean that the meeting could not take place, nor did I receive any letter to the effect that you or the said abbot had equal parts in countermanding the councils. Therefore I went there and although you would not come I nevertheless fulfilled the part in the council which related to me.[54]

Not only did Manasses exonerate himself, but he also produced extenuating reasons why it had not been necessary for him to attend the Lyonnais council.[55] In a direct challenge to the authority of papal legation and the apostolic canons, he asserted that he was only required to face Abbot Hugh of Cluny, 'who by the order of the apostolic lord ought to judge him'.[56] He refused to attend a council held outside of Gaul — referring here to the kingdom of Burgundy — and one that was beyond the reach and influence of the French king — Lyon was politically a part of the empire. Alternatively, Manasses proposed some possible

[51] Hugh of Flavigny, p. 415; Mansi, XX, col. 484.

[52] See *Reg.*, VII. 20; cf. Manasses, *RHGF*, XIV, 781–86.

[53] *Reg.*, VI. 2.

[54] Manasses, *RHGF*, XIV, 782.

[55] Williams, 'Archbishop Manasses I of Rheims', p. 817.

[56] Manasses, *RHGF*, XIV, 782.

opportunities and favourable dates for Hugh to hold a council in Soissons, Senlis, or Compiègne, deeming these locations more suitable because they fell under the King's political influence in the kingdom of France.[57] The charter evidence places these three sees, which all incidentally lay within the ecclesiastical province of Reims (Belgica Secunda), under the joint patronage of Manasses and King Philip I of France, helping to explain better his recommendation that a council convene there instead of imperial Burgundy. Manasses was known to have had many enemies, and because no French national church existed at this time, he proposed meeting in regions that might possess a 'collective will'[58] among the episcopate in supporting his defence against the papacy.

It seems evident that Manasses considered himself to be above and beyond the authority of all papal representatives, no doubt in relation to his status as metropolitan of Reims. He did not feel the least bit compelled to answer charges against him presented by anyone other than Gregory or a 'Roman legate' (legatus Romanus). 'Roman', as Manasses understood it, was someone 'not from beyond the mountains' (non ultramontanis), but 'only those born in Rome, or educated from childhood in the Roman Church, or promoted to some office within it'.[59] In the Archbishop's view, Hugh of Cluny fit this description more suitably, prompting him to refer continually to the Abbot as the only man qualified to judge him;[60] Hugh of Die, as Manasses emphasized on more than one occasion, did not belong to this esteemed category. Gregory was offended that Manasses would dare elevate himself to such an exalted position, thereby threatening to diminish the rights of the apostolic see, or even rendering them invalid and illicit. The Pope's greatest concern in this matter rested firmly upon Manasses's obduracy for the authority of the legatine office, not to mention his swelling pride. These were the key issues impelling the papacy's opposition: Manasses's outlook was 'too narrowly provincial and selfish', and Gregory held the great responsibility of ensuring that ecclesiastical offices were 'honestly and justly administered'.[61]

[57] Manasses, *RHGF*, XIV, 786.

[58] Tellenbach, *The Church in Western Europe*, p. 211.

[59] *Reg.*, VI. 2: 'Rome nati vel in Romana ecclesia a parvulo edocati vel in eadem sint aliqua dignitate promoti.'

[60] Manasses, *RHGF*, XIV, 785: 'Quando domnus abbas Cluniacensis, qui nos post domnum Apostolicum judicare debet, abest, canonica excusatio est.'

[61] Williams, 'Archbishop Manasses I of Rheims', p. 823.

The Archbishop also hid behind what he considered legitimate canonical reasons of personal safety. 'By reason of a divided kingdom' (timore videlicet dissidentis regni),[62] he justified his inability to cross the territory between Reims and Lyon on account of the turbulence caused in that region by the Count of Nevers and the bishops of Auxerre, which according to him prevented anyone in the kingdom of France from safely crossing.[63] But Gregory found little sympathy in this excuse. He contended that Manasses should have been able to 'pass through all the dangers of this journey', if indeed there were any, 'with the most safe and secure of guides, namely the archbishop of Lyons and the bishop of Langres'.[64] This letter expresses more explicitly Gregory's frustration with Manasses's persistent disobedience to the Roman Church. Even prior to Hugh's Lyonnais council (1080), the Archbishop's unwillingness to attend to council summonses was beginning to wear on Gregory's patience, implying perhaps the Pope's growing reluctance to treat Manasses as a partner for reform. The fact that he continually hid behind the rules of canon law surely aggravated and weakened Gregory's tolerance even further.

But whether Gregory liked it or not, Manasses found sufficient protection in the authority of canon law. This comes as little surprise when we consider the origins of the Pseudo-Isidorian (False) Decretals — compiled in Reims between 847 and 852, and first cited by Archbishop Hincmar of Reims in 852 and/or 857.[65] The convenience of this body of legal texts in the cathedral library — perhaps even gaining access to the contemporary 74T — suggests that it was both available and familiar to Manasses. In addition to excusing his absence, the Archbishop stuck to these and other canonical precepts in an attempt to avoid his accusers.[66] He argued that sheep could not accuse their shepherds — that is, inferiors cannot make accusations against their superiors;[67] that a presbyter could in no way 'presume to make any accusation against a bishop, a deacon against a presbyter, a subdeacon against a deacon, an acolyte against a subdeacon,

[62] *Reg.*, VII. 12.

[63] Manasses, *RHGF*, XIV, 782.

[64] *Reg.*, VII. 12.

[65] See Jasper and Fuhrmann, *Papal Letters*, p. 174; Horst Fuhrmann, 'False Decretals', in *New Catholic Encyclopedia*, V, 822–23. For more recent literature, see Fuhrmann, 'Stand, Aufgaben und Perspektiven'.

[66] Manasses cited from the Old Testament, the Church Fathers (i.e., Leo I, Gregory I), and the Code of Justinian; cf. Williams, 'Archbishop Manasses I of Rheims', p. 818.

[67] Pseudo-Zephyrinus, in Hinschius, ep. 1. III–IV, p. 131; Cf. 74T, chap. 66.

an exorcist against an acolyte, a reader against an exorcist, or doorkeeper against a reader'.[68] Manasses could have ignored the accusations of his accusers on this condition alone. The assembling of adequate and competent witnesses was also required. Canon law decreed that a prelate could not be condemned without seventy-two witnesses; a cardinal-presbyter without forty-four; a cardinal-deacon of Rome without twenty-six; and a member of the lesser order (subdeacon, acolyte, exorcist, reader, doorkeeper) without seven. The False Decretals also stated the inevitable condemnation faced by those who dared to betray their teachers or leaders.[69] Members of the flock that dared to do so could be deemed infamous, and 'banished from the limits of the church until they have made satisfaction'.[70] The Church's spiritual concern in this matter was obvious, for 'if everything were to be judged in this world, there would be no room for divine judgements'.[71] The challenge posed to the ecclesiastical hierarchy is just as clear; a shepherd accused by his subjects was perceived as 'resisting the authority of him who set them over the subjects, for as the apostle says: "He who resists authority resists the ordinance of God"' (Romans 13. 2).[72]

There were, of course, some variations to the rule, and many interpretations; Manasses eventually fell victim to these legal allowances. Immediately following the Lyon council, Gregory confirmed the excommunication sentence passed by Hugh of Die, and again at his 1080 Lent synod,[73] validating the provost of Reims (Manasses) and Bruno (the canon of Reims) as the initial accusers. Yet before he was removed from his church, the Archbishop was given yet another opportunity to clear himself of the charges facing him. The conditions this time were far more specific than in the previous instance: Manasses was instructed to purge himself before Bishops Ursio of Soissons, Helinand of Laon, Gerard II of Cambrai, Roger of Châlons, and two others, to restore the seized property over which the complaints were made, and to retire to either the monastery of Cluny or Chaise-Dieu in order to 'live in a religious manner with one clerk and two laymen whose wages you shall pay'.[74] The ultimate objective of these conditions, as Gregory

[68] Pseudo-Silvester, in Hinschius, synodal decrees, chaps 2–4, p. 449; 74T, chap. 69.

[69] Pseudo-Anacletus, in Hinschius, ep. 3. XXXVIII–XXXIX, p. 85; cf. 74T, chap. 74.

[70] Pseudo-Alexander, in Hinschius, ep. 1. VI, p. 97; cf. 74T, chap. 76.

[71] Pseudo-Alexander, in Hinschius, ep. 1. VII, p. 98; cf. 74T, chap. 77.

[72] Pseudo-Fabian, in Hinschius, ep. 2. XXII–XXIII, pp. 165–66; cf. 74T, chap. 78.

[73] See *Reg.*, VII. 20.

[74] *Reg.*, VII., 20.

admitted to the clergy and people of Reims, was to test and to prove the extent of Manasses's obedience and humility.[75] In view of the Archbishop's persistent behaviour, the Pope's second ultimatum was overflowing with pastoral mildness and guidance.

It is hardly surprising that Manasses did not surrender to these explicit conditions. His disregard for papal and canonical authority up to this point had created little reason for such a response. Gregory's letter to the clergy and people of Reims reveals that the Archbishop had spurned the conditional terms; after the Pope had extended to him the olive branch, Manasses allegedly went so far as to further 'invade' the church of Reims and 'destroy it by shameless devastation [*impudenti devastatione*]'; he behaved as 'one who has not entered it through the door like a shepherd but by some other way as a thief and a most savage robber'. The extent of his actions — that is, his blatant disregard for the well-being of the see of Reims and the decrees of the Roman Church — were treated by the Pope as the ultimate act of disobedience; there could be no greater offence committed against the Roman Church. 'In truth', as the Pope concluded, 'the iniquity of his doings has so extended beyond measure that he is most deservedly subjected to condemnation and excommunication, so that in perpetuity he should entertain no hope of his restitution'. Further letters were issued to Count Ebolus of Roucy (nephew of Manasses, the provost of Reims), the bishops of the province of Reims, and King Philip I of France,[76] notifying them of, and seeking their assurance for, Manasses's excommunication and removal, as well as for promoting the free election of a suitable and worthy successor.

Pleading to the Count of Roucy was in this case an obvious political manoeuvre. Gregory was well acquainted with the powerful associations that the aristocratic Roucy family had long since maintained in the region of Reims, holding the title of viscount with the larger title of count. In the eleventh century, this local family dominated the see of Reims — being heavily involved with selecting archbishops — perhaps even being responsible for nominating Manasses to the see.[77] It has also been suggested that the Count was responsible for presenting the charges against Manasses directly in Rome, marking him as an opponent to Manasses and supporter of his nephew.[78] The Pope, therefore, pleaded to

[75] *Reg.*, VIII. 17.

[76] See *Reg.*, VIII. 18–20.

[77] Dunbabin, *France in the Making*, pp. 108, 166.

[78] Williams, 'Archbishop Manasses I of Rheims', p. 814. Ebolus's presence in Rome is verified by Manasses's letter to Gregory, cited in Hugh of Flavigny, p. 420.

Ebolus in respectful terms as 'nobilis et gloriosus' — the noble and glorious count — suggesting by the endearing language of his letter that the Count held some prior knowledge of the affair. Ebolus was entreated to withdraw himself from his 'pestiferous friendship' (pestifera amicitia) with Manasses and to make others do the same, all to acquire more favour with God and the blessed Peter. He was also asked to assist (*adiuvo*) the new archbishop that 'by wiser counsel the better part of the clergy shall elect for this see'.[79]

The papal appeal to the French king, by contrast, seems to be have been performed out of obligation. In this case, Gregory wrote to Philip I expressing a language of prepared forgiveness: to spare the King the faults of his youth if he would follow more closely the duty of his office as a preserver of mercy, defender of churches, and protector of the fatherless and widows.[80] The King was commanded not to bestow any further favour upon Manasses, to cut him off from his friendship, and to shun him by driving him from his sight. Gregory reminded the King of his duty to 'despise the counsels of the wicked and above all to abhor any association with excommunicates'.[81] The Pope also extended his inclination that Philip should in no way entangle himself in the election of a successor to the see of Reims. The election was to be carried out canonically; if any secular power attempted to intervene, Philip was charged with resisting them and extending his aid 'to him whom the more faithful and religious part shall elect'.[82] Arguably, Gregory still had his suspicions about the King's willingness to invest bishops within the kingdom of France. Elizabeth Hallam has interpreted the Pope's request for a free election as 'a measure of Philip's power'.[83] Indeed, contemporary writers showed the King to have taken 'a hard line against the church's attempts to diminish his control over it', and Manasses's ultimate excommunication at this council was only realised 'in the teeth of opposition from the king'.[84]

The motives for Gregory's pleas to the regional lay elite are relatively easy to understand. It was becoming customary for the Pope to ensure that his wishes could be met with as little resistance as possible. As Tellenbach aptly noted, popes had to consider seriously the affairs of the region and localities before they

[79] *Reg.*, VIII. 18.

[80] *Reg.*, VIII. 20.

[81] *Reg.*, VIII. 20.

[82] *Reg.*, VIII. 20.

[83] Hallam, *Capetian France*, p. 139.

[84] Hallam, *Capetian France*, p. 139.

intervened. In this particular case, to secure the Archbishop of Reims's deposition and the successful election and installation of his successor, Gregory had to 'assess soberly his relations with the ruler, with the neighbouring bishops, with the clergy of his diocese, especially those of the cathedral chapter, and with the inhabitants of the cathedral city, as well as weighing up his financial backing and the power of his relatives'.[85] Grasping the political realities prevalent in the diocese of Reims, Gregory naturally appealed to the good nature of Count Ebolus of Roucy and King Philip I of France, with mild apostolic threats and promises. In effect, the Pope needed and sought out influential lay allies. Whether Manasses was driven from his see with the support of these men is not absolutely clear, but his absence from the sources thereafter is certainly telling.[86] Twelfth-century sources note that he fled to the court of Emperor Henry IV, never to be heard of again after May 1081.[87]

Further recourse against simoniacal abuses in France was taken at Hugh of Die's Autun (1077), Poitiers (1078), Issoudun (1081) Toulouse (1081), and Meaux (1082) councils. Corroborative accounts in Gregory's *Register*, however, serve only to ratify the judgements for Hugh's council decisions, rarely going any further to explain or contextualize the allegations behind individual simoniacal charges. Forced to consider the wider political, social, and legal conditions in which simoniacal cases were surfacing, the challenges faced by the reformers in eradicating the abuse are quickly brought to light. For other than administrative means of letters and legates, the problem of simony in France was one of enforcement, an abuse 'met with differing degrees of success',[88] regardless of Hugh of Die's continuous and consistent legal activity.

Take for example the case of Archbishop Humbert of Lyon (*symoniacus*) who was deposed on the fifth day of the Autun (1077) council and replaced by Gebuin, the Archdeacon of Langres.[89] This matter receives close attention in Hugh of Flavigny's chronicle; the details of Gebuin's religiosity and competence in the

[85] Tellenbach, *The Church in Western Europe*, p. 186.

[86] *GC*, IX, col. 75; Tellenbach, *The Church in Western Europe*, p. 211. Manasses was succeeded by Bishop Helinand of Laon, one of his initial accusers.

[87] Guibert de Nogent, *De vita sua*, in PL, CLVI (1880), bk I, chap. 11, cols 853–56; Benzo of Alba, *Ad Heinricum IV imperatorem*, MGH, SS, 11 (1854), bk VI, p. 657.

[88] Cowdrey, *Pope Gregory VII*, p. 402.

[89] Hugh of Flavigny, p. 415; cf. Mansi, XX, col. 484.

church office, not to mention his fame and popularity with the people of Langres, are carefully mentioned. In fact, this is the only account by Hugh of Flavigny for Hugh of Die's lifetime that describes the conditions of a new election, and with such reverence. Details of the consecration performed by Hugh of Die on 15 October 1077 are also provided.[90] The account of Humbert's simony, however, is not so clearly spelled out. There is some mention that suspicion had arisen, in addition to Humbert's ensuing abdication from his episcopal office and subsequent retirement to a monastery, with the details of his death on the third ides of June 1076 following shortly thereafter.[91] The manner in which Gebuin ascended to the office, in turn, is not emphasized in any uncharacteristic fashion. Our only source for the event (Hugh of Flavigny) took pains to focus on Gebuin's campaign against *oblatrantes haeretici* — likely referring to simoniacs.

As this case illustrates, the fullest evidence of simoniacal cases comes from Hugh's Council of Autun in 1077. Furthermore, it was at that council that the long-standing dispute between Bishop Roger III (1066–93) of Châlons-sur-Marne (in the province of Reims) and the clerks of the church of Châlons was examined. The details of this case first appear in Gregory's letter to the Bishop, dated 17 March 1074, ordering Roger to present himself in Rome before the festival of All Saints (1 November) in order to settle the 'oft-repeated complaint of the church of Châlons'. Despite pressure from King Philip I of France, who was actively seeking Roger's absolution through means of letters and messengers, Gregory stuck to the rigour of canonical discipline. He chose to ignore the King's pursuit, recognizing the need for stronger proceedings ('multo gravius animadvertendum') yet wishing to act with apostolic mildness ('apostolica mansuetudine').[92]

A papal letter to Manasses of Reims in March 1075, in which account Roger's recalcitrance is explained more clearly, reveals the nature of the clerks' repeated complaint ('iterata proclamatio'). Gregory wrote that, after being summoned to a synod, Roger 'failed to come; when he received from our lips at first hand orders about the restitution of the clerks' benefices, he scorned to listen; then, when admonished by our letter, he again disdained to do the things that we enjoined'. Manasses was invoked to help 'restore to these clerks, wherever they shall wish to remain, the goods and the benefices that have been seized, having added and made

[90] Hugh of Flavigny, p. 416.

[91] *GC*, IV, col. 89.

[92] *Reg.*, II. 56.

good whatever they have lost of the use of their property'. This letter also reveals Roger's failure to visit Rome before the festival of All Saints as requested, resulting in his being 'deprived of his whole episcopal office'.[93] That he held this ecclesiastical office from 1066 to 1093 nevertheless implies his successful exoneration of the charges issued against him, presumably resulting from his restoring to the clerks what was rightfully theirs.

A similar dispute surrounded the abbey of Saint-Denis in Paris, where Abbot Ivo I (*c.* 1074–94) was accused of obtaining the abbacy simoniacally.[94] (The accusers remain anonymously described as *plures* and *quamplures*.) To 'give answer to the allegations', Gregory urged Ivo to present himself in front of his legates, should the opportunity arise, or in Rome before the feast of St Andrew (30 November).[95] The monks of Saint-Denis were likewise notified of the situation concerning their abbot. Having persisted since 1075, this allegation appears not to have been considered seriously until the Council of Autun, where the situation was resolved, clearing Ivo of all charges levelled against him.

It was also at this council that Bishop Radbod II of Noyon (1068–98) was accused of simony. A papal letter to Manasses of Reims (1075) reveals the complaint first brought forth before Pope Alexander II, whereby Bishop William of Utrecht had accused Radbod of un-canonically seizing a church of his in Brugge and selling it to 'some other clerk'.[96] Adhering to some unnamed ancient tradition extending back two hundred years, William claimed that the church was rightfully assigned to his see. Manasses had been charged with reprimanding Radbod if any wrongdoing could be discovered, and was further ordered to suspend him from episcopal office if this 'authoritative ruling' was disobeyed. It is uncertain whether any action was taken against the Bishop after 1075, but the situation was resolved at Hugh of Die's Autun council in 1077. While Cowdrey believes nothing further to be known of this matter, Hugh's letter to Gregory confirming the council decisions of Clermont and Autun, informs us that Radbod had admitted his simony and confessed his guilt before a public examination that included the Bishops of Laon and Langres, among other bishops.[97] Having promised to relinquish his claims to the church in Brugge, Radbod successfully maintained his episcopal office until 1098.

[93] *Reg.*, II. 56.

[94] *Reg.*, II. 65.

[95] *Reg.*, II. 64.

[96] *Reg.*, II. 58.

[97] Hugh of Die, letter 8, PL, CXLVIII, col. 744.

Other than these simoniacal accounts in the records for Autun, however, there exist only a handful of additional examples for Hugh's first legation. There is, for instance, a case in the records for the church of Saint-Eugene at Vieux (*Viancio*), regarding Hugh of Die's excommunication of Bishop Frotard of Albi at the Council of Toulouse in 1079.[98] The Bishop, it seems, had been reminded and called to the council but failed to attend or send a representative in his absence. According to the anonymous canon from the church of Saint-Eugene (who recorded this event), this canonical breach confirmed Frotard's guilt as a simoniac. The charges against him describe his bribing Bishop Froterius of Nîmes and his brother Bernard with fifteen horses in order to obtain the see of Albi. The account in the *Gallia Christiana* claims that Gregory VII had accused him previously of this very same crime.[99]

It is perhaps significant that the anonymous canon made no reference to Amatus of Oloron in his account. Existing evidence indicates the legate's presidency over this council, in a territory clearly within or bordering his legatine jurisdiction of Narbonne, Gascony, and Spain.[100] Why Hugh of Die is the only legate associated with Frotard's excommunication is indeed curious. It is known that Frotard did not relinquish his title to the office willingly but was overcome with a serious illness and, consistent with this account, accordingly died a miserable death.[101] Despite this seemingly rapid demotion, Frotard nevertheless managed to maintain his office until 1087, strongly implying his eventual cooperation with the edict pronounced against him.

One further and final simoniacal case can be gleaned from Hugh of Die's Council of Meaux in 1082.[102] Bishop Ursio of Soissons, who was deposed for

[98] *Notitia de ecclesia S. Eugenii de Viancio*, in *RHGF*, XIV, 49–52; cf. Baluze, VI, 431–38; *GC*, I, cols 11–12.

[99] *GC*, I, col. 11.

[100] Paul Ourliac, 'Le Concile de Toulouse de 1079', in *Mélanges offerts à Jean Dauvillier*, ed. by Mireille Castaing-Sicard and Germain Sicard (Toulouse: Centre d'histoire juridique méridionale, 1979), pp. 617–33 (p. 619).

[101] *Notitia*, p. 51.

[102] Similar to the earlier-held Council of Bordeaux (1079), the historiography surrounding Hugh of Die's Meaux council is confused, resulting in historians regularly treating it as two separate meetings. For the historical debate, see Labbe, X, cols 398, 401; Mansi, XX, cols 583–85; Schieffer, *Die päpstlichen Legaten*, pp. 130–32; Pontal, *Les Conciles de la France*, p. 186; P. R. Gaussin, 'Hugues de Die et l'épiscopat Franco-Bourguignon', *Cahiers d'histoire*, 13 (1968), 93–94; Goggin, 'Hugh Bishop of Die', pp. 128–31; and Fazy, 'Notice sur Amat', pp. 95 and 117.

having been appointed to his see by King Philip I, was replaced by Arnulf of Pamèle, the Abbot of Saint-Médard (Soissons).[103] Consecrated on 19 December 1081, Arnulf was unable to enter Soissons on account of Ursio's continual refusal to abandon his diocese.[104] The former figure was forced to take refuge at the Castle of Oulchy (Ulciaco), which Count Theobald of Blois had left provisionally to his disposition,[105] effectively helping to drive out a simoniac bishop and install the papacy's preferred candidate. How long Ursio had managed to occupy the see of Soissons, however, remains questionable. Michel Bur asserted that it was not until 1082 that both Ursio, and his already excommunicated metropolitan archbishop, Manasses I of Reims, were ultimately deposed.[106]

Clerical Unchastity

Like the struggle against simony, the Roman Church had been preoccupied with clerical chastity since as early as the fourth century. First pronounced at the councils of Elvira (early fourth century) and Nicaea (325), the prohibition of clerical marriage and concubinage emerged in the eleventh century as a primary reforming target in France as elsewhere. Condemnation of the abuse was made repeatedly at councils leading up to Gregory VII's pontificate, like those held at Rome in 1049, 1059, and 1060; Mainz in 1049; Coyaca in 1050; Compostella and Toulouse in 1056; Tours in 1063; and Gerona in 1068. Increasing concern for the sexual morality of the clergy saw the repudiation of wives and concubines, bringing with it the enforcement of clerical celibacy and purity to an unprecedented level.

Paralleled with the monastic models of purity given by Popes Leo IX (1049–54) and Nicholas II (1058–61), the dangers presented by clerical unchastity were just as obvious to Gregory VII. His spiritual basis clearly derived from the Book of Revelations in reference to an abhorred sect among whose many sins fornication was the greatest.[107] The derogatory connotation 'nicolaitan' or 'Nicolaite' —

[103] Labbe, X, col. 573.

[104] *Ex vita S. Arnulfi Suessionensis episcopi*, in *RHGF*, XIV (1806), 58.

[105] *Ex vita S. Arnulfi Suessionensis episcopi*, p. 58.

[106] Michel Bur, *La Formation du comté de Champagne, v.950–v.1150* (Nancy: L'Université de Nancy, 1977), p. 224. See Guibert of Nogent, *De vita sua*, bk I, chap. 11, cols 853–56.

[107] See Revelations 2. 6: 'Sed hoc habes quia odisti facta Nicolaitarum quae et ego odi', and 2. 14–15: 'Sed habeo adversus te pauca quia habes illic tenentes doctrinam Balaam, qui docebat

equating the sinfulness of clerical fornication with Nicholas, one of the seven deacons of the apostolic church[108] — was further imprinted on Gregory's mind after receiving a letter from Peter Damian sometime in 1059.[109] 'Clerks are called Nicolaites', Peter explained to the then archdeacon, 'when they have intercourse with women against the law of ecclesiastical chastity. Obviously, they become fornicators when they couple together in this foul commerce; they are rightly called Nicolaites when they defend their death-bringing plague as though by authority. For a vice is turned into a heresy when it is confirmed by the defense of misguided teaching.'[110] Damian was determined to clarify the prevailing misconceptions about the seriousness and offensiveness of the abuse, and Gregory appears to have followed with the same initiative after he became pope, but not necessarily with the same fervent attitude.

Although nicolaitism's meaning diversified and expanded, producing much opposition and debate, Gregory's understanding — according to its use in the *Register* — tended to adhere more closely to the biblical Revelation (apocalypse), equating the unclean act with the sin of fornication, choosing rather not to complicate its definition.[111] The absence of words like 'Nicolaite' in Gregory's *Register*, moreover, strongly suggests that despite his familiarity with the polemical writings of Damian (i.e., Book of Gemorrah, *Liber gratissimus*) and Humbert of Silva Candida (i.e., *Adversus simoniacos*), he 'preferred to campaign against clerical unchastity by using other arguments'.[112] These other methods treated chastity as

Balac mittere scandalum coram filiis Israhel, edere et fornicari, ita habes et tu tenentes doctrinam Nicholaitarum'; and Acts 6. 1–6.

[108] Acts 6. 5 'Et placuit sermo coram omni multitudine, et elegerunt Stephen virum plenum fide et Spiritu Sancto, et Phillipum et Prochorum, et Nicanorem et Timonem, et Parmenam et Nicolaum advenam Antiochenum'.

[109] For Damian's polemic on sexuality and the consequences of sexual activity among the episcopate, see *Die Briefe des Petrus Damiani*, ed. by Kurt Reindel, MGH, Briefe, 2 (1983), no. 61 (pp. 214–16).

[110] *Die Briefe des Petrus Damiani*, no. 65, pp. 230–31: 'Nicolaitae autem dicuntur clerici, qui contra castitatis aecclesiasticae regulam feminis admiscentur. Qui plane tunc fornicatores fiunt, cum fedi commertii copulas ineunt, tunc Nicolaitae iure vocantur, cum hanc loetiferam pestem velut ex auctoritate defendunt. Vitium quippe in heresim vertitur, cum perversi dogmatis assertione firmatur.'

[111] For an exception to this rule, see *Reg.*, II. 62. The word *Nicolaite* appears only once in Gregory's *Ep. vag.* (no. 16); cf. H. E. J. Cowdrey, 'Pope Gregory VII and the Chastity of the Clergy', in *Medieval Purity and Piety: Essays on Medieval Clerical Celibacy and Religious Reform*, ed. by Michael Frassetto (New York: Garland, 1998), pp. 269–302 (pp. 283–84).

[112] Cowdrey, 'Chastity of the Clergy', p. 283.

a distinctively superior virtue, reflecting more clearly the reformers' struggle to return the Holy Church to her former glory ('libera, casta, et catholica').[113]

The reformers' treatment of sexuality was far from original. Damian was merely one of many in this period who considered the act of sex to be filthy and impure.[114] To be sure, Damian's personal abhorrence of sex, viewing clerical marriage as heretical, did make a 'strong impression upon his contemporaries'.[115] But, as Cushing has argued, Gregory VII's notion of clerical unchastity stood in contrast to the ideas of contamination. Rather, the Pope 'tended to treat clerical marriage or concubinage as an issue of obedience'.[116] Like the issues of simony and lay investiture, therefore, the Pope's greatest challenge came with applying a uniform and condemnatory measure on the issue of nicolaitism, to ensure its dissemination and acceptance throughout Western Christendom.

The issues of whether married priests could engage in sexual intercourse with their wives after being ordained, whether priests or clerics who were married prior to ordination should dismiss their wives, and how the faithful were meant to receive the ministrations of married priests, all came to the forefront of much political and theological debate. For answers to these exact questions, however, it seems that canon law was already quite clear by the eleventh century: 'church councils, Carolingian capitularies, episcopal regulations [...] laid down precisely how those who were already married before they received higher orders should consort with their wives, and how close their relationship with women living in the same house might be'.[117] These regulations clearly existed, but were being ignored continually. The significance is that over the course of the eleventh century, and very much a result of the lack of cohesive law surrounding these

[113] See *Ep. vag.*, 54.

[114] James A. Brundage, *Law, Sex, and Christian Society in Medieval Europe* (Chicago: University of Chicago Press, 1987), p. 185; cf. Megan McLaughlin, 'The Bishop as Bridegroom: Marital Imagery and Clerical Celibacy in the Eleventh and Early Twelfth Centuries', in *Medieval Purity and Piety*, ed. by Frassetto, pp. 228–29 (pp. 209–35). For Burchard of Worms, see *Decretum*, XIX. 6, col. 977. For Honorius Augustodunensis, see *Offendiculum*, VIII, in *Libelli de lite imperatorum et pontificum saeculis XI. et XII. conscripti*, ed. by Ernst Dümmler and Ernst Sackur, MGH, Libelli, 3 (1897), chaps 8–13, pp. 40–41: 'De infamibus nuptiis', 'De uxore sacerdotis', 'De repudiata', 'De vidua', 'De virgine', and 'De sacrificio sacerdotum'. These writers, in addition to others like Gilbert de la Porée (*c.* 1080–*c.* 1156) and Abbot Guibert of Nogent (*c.* 1064–*c.* 1125), were too late to have influenced Gregory's ideology.

[115] James A. Brundage, *Law, Sex, and Christian Society*, p. 216.

[116] Cushing, *Reform and the Papacy*, p. 124.

[117] Tellenbach, *The Church in Western Europe*, p. 162.

complex issues, the validity of clerical marriage and thus the enforcement of celibacy intensified.[118] Before the First and Second Lateran Councils of 1123 and 1139, for instance, clerical marriage was tolerated legally. This reality did not deter eleventh-century church reformers, however, who continued to condemn clerical marriage.

Seeking to impress upon the clergy the importance of clerical chastity, Gregory VII began communicating the reformers' objectives in the first instance through increased papal correspondence. Writing to Patriarch Sigehard of Aquileia shortly after his 1074 Lenten synod, Gregory outlined the laity's expected role in promulgating the statutes and decrees of the holy fathers, previously decided with the assent and counsel of the whole Roman assembly.[119] Gregory resolutely decreed that 'if anyone in those orders which minister at the sacred altars, that is, priest, deacon, and subdeacon, has a wife or a concubine, unless they entirely put them away and perform appropriate penance, they should altogether abstain from ministering at the sacred altars, nor should they any longer obtain the benefice of any church or enjoy such as they have obtained'.[120]

Gregory's call for lay support in enforcing this celibacy policy was later circulated (February 1075) in three well-known letters to Archbishops Siegfried of Mainz, Werner of Magdeburg, and Bishop Otto of Constance.[121] These letters, as Cowdrey commented, 'are particularly noteworthy for Gregory's attempt to stimulate lay resistance to the ministrations of sinful clergy'.[122] That they were directed entirely to members of the clergy, however, suggests rather the imposing clerical role in ensuring that the Pope's 1074 synodal decrees against simony were 'inviolably observed' (inviolabiliter tenendum). Despite the fact that their audience was purely non-Gallic, they nonetheless testify that the Pope's overall objective for a celibate clergy formed a much greater, ideally universal concern. Combined with his attack on simony, Gregory felt 'enkindled by the duty' of his office to 'enforce the chastity of the clergy' for the purpose of driving out 'the foul defilement of polluting lust' (fedam libidinosae contagionis pollut-

[118] Brundage, *Law, Sex, and Christian Society*, pp. 217–20.

[119] *Reg.*, II. 62.

[120] *Reg.*, II. 62.

[121] *Ep. vag.*, 6–8. Added to these letters of 1075 is Gregory's urging of Dukes Rudolf of Swabia and Berthold of Carinthia to take action against the same abuses (*Reg.*, II. 45).

[122] H. E. J. Cowdrey, *The Cluniacs and the Gregorian Reform* (Oxford: Clarendon Press, 1970), pp. 14–15 n. *.

ionem).[123] Those who were found guilty of the crime of fornication were prohibited from celebrating Mass or ministering at the altar in lesser orders. If they chose to disobey the Pope's call to mend their ways, they were threatened with 'the shame of the world and the reproof of the people'. Yet whether these were adequate sanctions to enforce adherence to canons is entirely questionable.

It was not until November 1076 that Gregory referred specifically to the problem of clerical fornication in France. Writing to Countess Adela of Flanders, the reigning confusion among the faithful in comprehending the Roman decrees against nicolaitism becomes evident. 'It has come to our ears', wrote the Pope, 'that certain of your people are uncertain whether or not priests and deacons or others who minister the sacred altars and who persist in fornication should do duty at mass.'[124] Gregory attempted to clarify his position on the matter more precisely by declaring those clerics found guilty of fornication unable to perform sacred duties, and urged that they be 'driven outside the sanctuaries until they show fruits worthy of repentance'.

Gregory's concern for French clerics found guilty of this crime is again made clear in a similar letter to Count Robert I of Flanders (1076), which called on the Count to treat those obstructers of righteousness most severely as 'enemies of Christ' (inimici Christi).[125] The Count was likewise urged to resist unchaste priests and simoniacal bishops, while at once showing them no obedience. Both of these examples, addressing members of the lay elite who were noted for their influence in local and regional ecclesiastical matters, reflect a general confusion surrounding nicolaitism's meaning, and Gregory's efforts to clarify his intentions. In both letters, the Pope used active and pastoral language in an attempt to emphasize the seriousness of the abuse. He made it very clear to these lay members how those who resisted him would be punished, and how those who assisted him with his objectives would be rewarded.

By 1077, however, the papal message had not yet taken hold in every region of France. In March of that year, Bishop Josfred of Paris was urged to promote clerical chastity where it was misunderstood or — what is far more likely — where it was being ignored. The Pope's plea came shortly after the citizens of Cambrai had delivered a man named Ramihrdus to the flames because he had dared to utter that 'simoniacs and fornicating priests ought not to celebrate masses and that

[123] *Ep. vag.*, 6.

[124] *Reg.*, IV. 10.

[125] *Reg.*, IV. 11. For the furtherance of this case involving Bishop Hubert of Thérouanne, see *Ep. vag.*, 41.

their ministration ought in no way to be accepted'.[126] According in part to the Chronicle of St André de Castres, Ramihrdus had refused to take communion from the abbots or priests, and for this refusal the angered crowd 'denounced him as a heresiarch' before burning him.[127] Unwilling to believe, or incapable of understanding, this regional example, Gregory called for Josfred's assistance in spreading his 1074 Roman decrees with more clarity, illustrating his utter reliance on an obedient clergy for the proper instruction of the Christian faithful. It was up to Josfred, as Gregory noted, to 'everywhere forbid the whole people any longer to receive their [i.e., simoniacs] ministration, so that at least being put to confusion in this way they may be compelled to amendment of life and return to the chastity of religious continence'.[128] Reaching out to prominent and reform-friendly members of the clerical hierarchy, Gregory sought assistance wherever he could find it.

Thus before 1078, only three examples from the extant papal evidence depict Gregory's concern with clerical fornication in France. In concert, these cases expose the uncertainty amongst the Christian faithful in following closely the correct order of the Church, as Gregory understood and willed it. They also depict a laxity or moral apprehension amongst the French clergy in obeying Gregory's policies for a chaste clergy as defined by his 1074 and 1075 Lent synods. Most importantly, these letters illustrate the need for a vehicle to promote reform policy in the regions of France where it was least understood, and where its penetration was most urgent. The dearth of evidence on this matter, however, does not suggest that the problem of clerical unchastity was less rampant in France than in Italy or Germany. Gregory's *Register* is incomplete and should not be considered as incontestable evidence on this matter. The papacy's growing concern for this region certainly developed gradually, and its increasing intolerance for an unchaste clergy led to the Pope's heightened response in extending the legatine office for correcting the abuse.

Not until November 1078 did Gregory VII's campaign against nicolaitism find an audience among the episcopate; that is to say that this Roman meeting offers the first example of Gregory's promulgating legislation against this abuse.[129] The

[126] *Reg.*, IV. 20: 'symoniacos et presbyteros fornicatores missas non debere celebrare et, quod illorum officium minime suscipiendum foret'.

[127] *Chronico S. Andreae castri Cameracesii, 1001–1133*, in MGH, SS, 7 (1846), p. 540; cf. R. I. Moore, *The Birth of Popular Heresy* (London: Edward Arnold, 1975), pp. 24–25.

[128] *Reg.*, IV. 20.

[129] *Reg.*, VI. 5b (19 November 1078).

twelfth *capitulum* of this Roman synod concerned the chastity of the clergy, drawing distinct parallels with the ninth canon from Hugh of Die's earlier-held Council of Poitiers (January 1078), which decreed that 'no deacon, priest, or subdeacon should have a concubine or a woman living in his house in circumstances which might give rise to suspicion; anyone assisting at the Mass of a simoniac or unchaste priest shall be excommunicated'.[130] Thus it was not until Hugh's Poitiers council in 1078, as the evidence attests, that the full weight of Gregory's reforming initiative was received in France.[131]

The reverberations of this conciliar legislation are nevertheless called into question, especially failing any explicit evidence that clerical marriage, unchastity and concubinage did in fact pose a threat to the church in France. The only exception in this case comes from a letter to Bishop Hubert of Thérouanne, in which Gregory reproved the Bishop for 'consenting to fornication by the clergy'.[132] In addition, Hugh of Die's subsequent councils at Valence (1079), Bordeaux (1079), Toulouse (1079), Lyon (1080), Avignon (1080), Saintes (1081), Issoudun (1081), and Meaux (1082) make no reference to the abuse in either conciliar or legislative terms. With this lack of conciliar evidence develops a false sense that clerical marriage, concubinage, and fornication were negligible obstacles to the church in France at this time, and that the reformers' priorities lay foremost with tackling the abuses of simony and lay investiture. A glance at Orderic Vitalis's *Ecclesiastical History* (written *c.* 1114–41), however, draws out numerous examples denouncing this clerical abuse first in Normandy 'after the coming of the Normans',[133] and subsequently at the councils of Lisieux in 1064, Reims in 1064 and 1119, and Rouen in 1072, 1119, and 1128.[134] Given this fuller treatment in France, there is little reason for doubting Hugh of Die's promotion of clerical chastity throughout his legation. Still, there is no denying

[130] Mansi, XX, col. 498: 'Ut nullus diaconus, presbyter, vel subdiaconus concubinam habeat; sed nec aliam foeminam, unde mala suspicio habeatur, in una domo secum teneat, & quicumque huiusmodi sacerdotis, sive per pecuniam ordinate, missam scienter audierint, excommunicationi subjacere debeant.'

[131] Cowdrey, *Pope Gregory VII*, p. 363. For analysis of these canons, see Tillier, 'Les Conciles provinciaux', p. 566.

[132] *Ep. vag.*, 41.

[133] *The Ecclesiastical History of Orderic Vitalis*, ed. and trans. by Marjorie Chibnall, 6 vols (Oxford: Clarendon Press, 1969–80) (hereafter Orderic Vitalis), bk V, chap. 12, III, 120–22.

[134] Orderic Vitalis, bk IV, II, 200–01; bk V, chap. 12, III, 120–22 n. 4; bk XII, chap. 22, VI, 276–77; bk IV, II, 290–91; Orderic Vitalis, bk XII, chap. 25, VI, 290–92; bk XII, chap. 48, VI, 388–89.

that the abuse remained a matter of only marginal interest in the extant papal correspondence.

Lay Investiture

Compared to the reformers' campaigns against nicolaitism and simony, the question of lay investiture in late eleventh-century France appears almost non-existent.[135] Legislation against this abuse was first promulgated at the Peace Council of Bourges in 1031, which, as noted above in the case of simony, decreed that 'laymen should not place priests in the churches except through the bishop'.[136] One can assume that this council had some impact in shaping the Church's general outlook for the second half of the eleventh century. But for the most part the evidence for Gregory VII's pontificate points to only a few isolated cases of lay investiture or interference in France. That is not to suggest, however, that Gregory's intentions and efforts in this region were not influential in countering the abuse. The Pope's attitude, encompassing the concerned and sometimes hostile attention given by him in this matter, certainly developed alongside his other reforming ideas, reaching their zenith around 1077/78. Prior to that date, Gregory's position in dealing with the abuse in France had yet to be established, leaving the impression that the French king was active in investing only a limited number of sees; but for Philip I, the number of sees that he invested was presumably not as important as the principle of investiture, and the political importance attached to each individual see.[137]

Like many of his papal predecessors, Gregory believed that the episcopate ought to be freed of all secular cares, to allow the righteous pursuit of solely spiritual aims. The acceptance of a spiritual office or title by a bishop, abbot, or lesser member of the clergy from a member of the laity was thus interpreted as an infringement of canonical tradition — a transgression of two incompatible orders, contaminating the spiritual purity of a free election. The Pope's efforts to elimi-

[135] See especially Johann Englberger, 'Gregor VII. und die Bischofserhebungen in Frankreich: Zur Entstehung des ersten römischen Investiturdekrets vom Herbst 1078', in *Die früh- und hochmittelalterliche Bischofserhebung im europäischen Vergleich*, ed. by Franz-Reiner Erkens (Cologne: Böhlau, 1998), pp. 193–258; Augutin Fliche, 'Y'a-t-il eu en France et en Angleterre une querelle des investitures?', *Revue Benedictine*, 46 (1934), 283–95.

[136] Mansi, XIX, canon 22, col. 502.

[137] Bouchard, 'Kingdom of the Franks', p. 131.

nate the laity's role in the Church, particularly in implementing free episcopal and abbatial elections, in addition to the transferring of the ring and staff to a bishop-elect (a wholly symbolic act) represented the subordination of the spiritual to the temporal sphere. A bishop who received the gift of his bishopric (*donum episcopatus*) from the hands of a layman, or an abbot who received the equivalent promotion within his monastery or abbey, was then subverting, as Gregory saw it, the divine order of things. Eliminating this lay element was to ensure and preserve the sacred order of the Roman Church.

Yet at the beginning of his pontificate, Gregory appeared undecided on how to treat the subject of investiture. In 1073, when King Henry IV of Germany sought to invest two newly elected bishops from his imperial domain, Anselm II of Lucca and Hugh of Die, Gregory took a seemingly ambivalent approach to the matter. Neither case proves overly revealing in determining a marked attitude. Concerning the candidate for Lucca, the Pope appears to have approved the custom without too much deliberation, on the condition that the King absolve himself for his prior communion with an excommunicated person.[138] With the see of Lucca recognized as being in imperial territory, 'the real issue', as Cushing observed, 'was Henry's status following the Lenten synod of 1073, at which Alexander II excommunicated several of the king's advisers'.[139] For this reason alone Anselm's ordination was deferred until this absolution took place at Eastertide 1074 (at some point between 20 and 26 April).

The Pope's position in this matter was subject to Henry's making peace with the Church while adhering to the extant canon law, strengthening the argument that Gregory had — at this early stage of his pontificate — yet to adopt an opposing stance to lay investiture. There is certainly a sense that the Pope grasped the delicacy of the situation, and that he was not overly keen on bypassing or overruling Henry's role in investing bishops from within his territory. It has even been suggested that Gregory's countenancing of the royal claims to investiture were secondary to the Pope's approval of the bishop-elect.[140] As long as the latter was made known to him, Gregory could still maintain some element of political and administrative control over his bishops in distant provinces.

That Gregory ordained Hugh of Die in Rome on 16 March 1074 does not imply that Henry was deprived of his investiture privilege. It proves exceedingly

[138] *Reg.*, I. 21.

[139] Cushing, *Papacy and the Law*, p. 49.

[140] H. E. J. Cowdrey, 'Pope Gregory VII and the Bishoprics of Central Italy', *Studi medievali*, 34 (1993), 51–64 (p. 55).

difficult to read into a matter that evoked no objection from the German king — at least, no such evidence exists to this effect, rendering almost indecipherable Gregory's attitude towards Henry's involvement. It could be that he was testing the King's response and obedience to his investiture decrees, bearing in mind that the Investiture Controversy had yet to come to a head and that the decrees against this abuse were not promulgated until the following year at Gregory's 1075 Lent synod.[141] Furthermore, the kingdom of Burgundy, where the see of Die was located geographically, was ecclesiastically part of the kingdom of France. The metropolitan see of Lyon, and its four suffragan sees of Autun, Chalon, Langres, and Mâcon, were positioned outside of the boundaries of the German king, as was the ecclesiastical province of Vienne, suggesting that Hugh's consecration to the see of Die was of little interest to Henry.[142]

In all probability, Gregory's step to consecrate Hugh resulted from the Pope's political motivation to have him settle a dispute that had meanwhile arisen in that diocese.[143] Gregory's letter to Count William of Die (23 March 1074), notifying him of Hugh's appointment to this episcopal office, reveals a prevailing antagonism facing the church of Die due to the Count's despoiling of its property and the seizing of a certain clerk.[144] It was in Gregory's best interest to consecrate Hugh in Rome so that he could be dispatched immediately to Die in order to settle the affair in person — in effect, to reinstate order. In other words, the matter was perhaps not as complicated as one might assume, especially considering the Pope's vested interest in the provincial affairs of Die, and his underlying intentions for promoting Hugh to the legatine office later in 1075 (see above, Chapter 2).

[141] There are opposing historical views on whether Gregory first pronounced his decrees against lay investiture at his Roman synod of 1075 (for which no records exist), or his November synod of 1078. For the general thrust of this historical debate, see Rudolf Schieffer, *Die Entstehung des päpstlichen Investiturverbots für den deutschen König*, MGH, Schriften, 28 (1981), pp. 114–52, and Friedrich Kempf's review of this work in *Archivum historiae pontificae*, 20 (1982), 409–15. The primary evidence can be inferred from Hugh of Flavigny's chronicle (p. 412) and Arnulf of Milan's *Liber gestorum recentiorum*, ed. by Claudia Zey, MGH, SRG, 67 (1994), IV. 7, pp. 211–12; cf. *Reg.*, III. 10.

[142] See H. E. J. Cowdrey, 'The Structure of the Church, 1024–1073', in *NCMH*, IV, pt I (2004), 229–67 (p. 238).

[143] Cushing, *Papacy and the Law*, p. 51.

[144] *Reg.*, I. 69.

On the whole, the issue of lay investiture in eleventh-century France was not nearly as controversial as it was in Germany.[145] There is no record of any cases erupting on the scale of the invesiture controversy with King Henry IV, nor is there any evidence for any long-lasting cases that required the reformers repeated attention and care. Its elimination was not the foremost priority for reforming advocates in France, but it would be wrong to suggest that its opposition was not disseminated widely through Gregory's use of letters and legates. Supporting this claim is the election of Bishop Landeric of Mâcon in 1073 — one of the few recorded examples of investiture performed by the French king during Gregory's pontificate.[146] The nature of Philip's participation, however — that is, the true extent of his investing the bishop-elect — failed to cause any significant conflict with the Pope. And in dealing with this election, Gregory was more concerned that Philip should renounce simony, appearing to have had no difficulty in allowing him to invest the Bishop before consecration could take place.

Although at times closely related to the notion of simony, with the purchasing or granting of an ecclesiastical office, the extent of Philip I's intervention in the church was for the most part too insignificant for any true conflict ever to arise. Paradoxically, however, 'the strength of Gregory's general denunciations of lay investiture and their dissemination by his letters and legates, especially the energetic Hugh of Die, tell against any suggestion that, in his dealings with France and Burgundy, Gregory made it a matter of only marginal concern'.[147] The existing evidence, and particularly the active role exhibited by Hugh in the French council arena from 1075 to 1085, suggests that the Pope took the matter more seriously than initially assessed.

The height of the papacy's concern for lay investiture in France came in 1077, following Gerard II's election to the see of Cambrai — after his having received the *donum episcopatus* from the excommunicate German king Henry IV.[148] Upon learning of his un-canonical promotion, Gerard visited Gregory at Ficarolo, on the river Po, in order to confess that he had no prior knowledge of the King's excommunication, pleading a case of total ignorance.[149] For this unconditional

[145] See Augustin Fliche, 'La Primatie des Gaules depuis l'époque Carolingienne jusqu'à la fin de la querelle des investitures (876–1121)', *RH*, 173 (1934), 283–95.

[146] *Reg.*, I. 35.

[147] Cowdrey, *Pope Gregory VII*, p. 407.

[148] According to the decrees of Gregory's 1074 and 1076 Lenten synods (see *Reg.*, III. 10a), Henry was excommunicate and had been previously warned not to invest bishops (see *Reg.*, II. 52a).

[149] *Reg.*, IV. 22.

outburst of piety and forgiveness, Gregory was more than willing to exonerate the Bishop. Directing Hugh of Die on the desired settlement of this case, Gerard was to be given an opportunity at the legate's Autun council in September 1077 to plead his case in the latter's presence, in cooperation with Archbishop Manasses I of Reims (the metropolitan concerned) and his comprovincials. If the accused was willing to purge himself by an oath, and swear by oath what he had relayed to Gregory in Italy, then arrangements were to proceed for his official consecration into office.

Gregory himself referred to this judgement as an exercise of apostolic moderation (*apostolica moderatio*). It seems that the purpose of Hugh's Autun council was, first and foremost, to consider Gerard's case, not to punish him but rather to reset him on the path of righteousness. Gerard's behaviour and actions come across in this letter as honest and sincere, but it will never be known whether his ignorance of Henry IV's excommunication was intentional. There is nevertheless a sense that Gregory's display of mercy gave Gerard the benefit of the doubt, enabling him to occupy the see of Cambrai for nearly twenty-six years. The language of this letter also exhibits a certain diplomatic sensibility, including in the Pope's instructions to Hugh a policy that — although filled with stipulations — provided the legate with legal room to manoeuvre. Hugh could punish or forgive as was necessary, reflecting the papacy's increasing awareness in dealing with potentially volatile political and religious matters far from Rome.

In dealing with this case, Gregory had intended to 'placard' it throughout France 'with the utmost publicity and force'.[150] This intention presents a legitimate reason for summoning a council at Autun in the first place: the Pope was eager for Hugh of Die to parade the 1075 decrees (now lost) in a larger arena for the purpose of a more public and wide acclamation, ultimately hoping to broaden the awareness of the present French clergy as to the seriousness of, and criminal aspects associated with, lay investiture.[151] Renewing the twenty-second canon from the Fourth Council of Constantinople (869–70), Gregory reminded his bishops that laymen should play absolutely no role in the promotion of a bishop. Those clerics found guilty of assisting in lay investiture, he continued, would be 'tied and bound' by anathema.[152] From that point forward, anyone who might

[150] Cowdrey, *Pope Gregory VII*, p. 404.

[151] There is some dispute on whether the 1075 decrees in effect condemned lay investiture.

[152] *Reg.*, IV. 22. The decree pronounced at the Fourth Council of Constantinople reads: 'Quisquis autem saecularium principum et potentum vel alterius dignitatis laicus adversus communem ac consonantem atque canonicam electionem ecclesiastici ordinis agere tentaverit,

claim ignorance to the offence of lay investiture (as Gerard II of Cambrai had done), or who had previously received investiture through the hand of secular lords and powers, was obligated to visit Rome immediately and render his account.

One can assume, then, that this 1077 conciliar judgement applied also to Archbishop Ralph I of Tours, accused the following year at Hugh of Die's Poitiers council (January 1078) of receiving the *donum episcopatus* from Philip I. An additional accusation of simony surfaced when it was learned that Ralph had promised a wood (*silva*) to a knight in exchange for his help in promoting him to the see.[153] Ralph lashed out against these allegations and, accompanied by armed men, stormed the council proceedings, resulting in the near death of the monk and papal messenger/legate Teuzo. Hugh of Die described the whole affair as disorderly and chaotic, resulting in his suspending the Archbishop from sacerdotal office; but matters were not taken any further. Ralph was given the fair opportunity to purge himself of the simoniacal charges — reminiscent of the toleration extended to Gerard II of Cambrai — and the affair was relinquished to Gregory's judgement. The initial accusation of lay investiture, it should be noted, was ostensibly of less immediate concern to Gregory and Hugh, and is given no further mention in the sources.

A papal letter written sometime after 9 March 1078 reveals that Ralph was successful in recovering his episcopal and priestly office, yet reports concerning his simoniacal guilt continued to linger. As a result, Gregory was forced to send his legate Roger (subdeacon of the Roman Church) and an envoy to Hugh of Die to learn the 'plain and simple truth of this matter' (certam et meram veritatem huius rei).[154] Gregory's letter epitomizes his legal position on the case — opinions that were reiterated in a letter to the Archbishop a few months later (in the summer of 1078) — in which the Pope called for his unconditional adherence and obeisance to righteousness (*iustitia*).[155]

Ralph's unwillingness to settle this dispute immediately is interesting to note, especially considering the amicable nature of his relationship with Hugh during the first years of the legate's council activity (*c.* 1075–78); the Archbishop had received summonses to the prior legatine councils of Dijon (1076), Clermont

anathema sit, donec obediat et consentiat in hoc quod ecclesia de electione ac ordinatione proprii praesulis se velle monstraverit' (Mansi, XVI, cols 174–75).

[153] Hugh of Die, letter 7, PL, CLVII, col. 510; cf. Hugh Flavigny, p. 418.

[154] *Reg.*, V. 17.

[155] *Ep. vag.*, 23. See also *Ep. vag.*, 22 and 33.

(1076), and Autun (1077) for reasons that could have been associated only with canonical obligation and friendship — the former characteristic evidently having little to do with personal standing.[156] The years 1075–78 gave no obvious warning of this collaboration being threatened. Is it possible then to identify a turning point in their alliance?

This question is considered best in the political context of Ralph's association with King Philip I of France. One theory is that Ralph's outburst at Poitiers was 'orchestrated by the bishops of France because of the prohibition of investiture, first heard in France at Autun a few months before'.[157] Following this argument, Ralph's violent outburst was meant to 'discredit the legate'.[158] But what this hypothesis fails to explain is Ralph's sudden change of allegiance from an obvious reform advocate to a more royal, anti-reform attitude. Philip may indeed have resented the decrees against investiture given at Autun (1077), but the extent of his royal influence was weak; nor was Ralph a pawn in Philip's attempt to sabotage the French legates. Other than to gain royal favour, Ralph had little incentive to abandon the reform cause; he was quick to recover his ecclesiastical standing and again appeared in Hugh of Die's entourage by 1079/80.[159]

Furthermore, despite having acted in Philip's interest, Ralph is not generally depicted as being on good terms with the King. According to the *Narratio controversiae*, a source written sometime later by the anonymous author of Saint-Martin at Tours, Ralph's evident sympathy with the reforming legates Hugh of Die and Amatus of Oloron presented a threat to the French king.[160] Following the Council of Autun (1077), Philip had accused Ralph of favouring these legates to such a degree that he demanded a personal explanation in his court. Ralph refused to attend and, in defence of the sentences issued against him, launched his own campaign against the canons of Saint-Martin. This drawn-out scene between the King and the Archbishop lasted until 1082, the year that Ralph was deposed by Philip for a more favourable candidate — presumably someone with stronger royal sympathies. The reality of the situation makes it difficult to associate

[156] See Hugh of Die, letters 1–4, PL, CLVII, cols 507–09.

[157] Goggin, 'Hugh Bishop of Die', p. 272 — based on the evidence found in Manasses's letter to Gregory in *RHGF*, XIV, 611.

[158] Goggin, 'Hugh Bishop of Die', p. 277.

[159] For evidence of his reassuming the duties of his archiepiscopal office, see *Ep. vag.*, 33, 37; *Reg.*, VI. 35; VII. 15.

[160] *Narratio controversiae inter capitulum S. Martini Turonensis et Radulphum eiusdem urbis archiepiscopum*, in *RHGF*, XII, 460 (d).

Ralph's motivation for disrupting the Council of Poitiers with the notion of royal patronage.

On the one hand, King Philip I offered his protection and allegiance to the office of legation and directly to Hugh of Die. On the other hand he attempted to hinder the legate's progress in order to protect his royal right of investiture. Hugh's letter to the Pope, in which he clearly recognized the King's resistance to cooperate with the church, considered Philip as hostile to the Kingdom of Heaven ('quia contrarius erat regni coeli'). But Hugh was aware, despite the frequent dispatch of letters offering glory and honour to his legation while at the same time professing his cooperation and understanding, that the King was also sending letters to Duke William VIII of Aquitaine warning him not to allow 'conventicula' or 'quasi concilia' to be held in his territory of Poitiers. The King likewise warned the bishops in the Duke's jurisdiction that their attendance at this council would be considered an insult to his majesty (*majestas*) and a violation of loyalty (*fidelitas*).[161]

Doubtless, Ralph's outburst at the Poitiers council added insult and injury to Hugh's legation, but to what extent is entirely questionable. In his letter to Gregory, Hugh confided that his friends were as uncertain to him as his enemies. Yet based on his previous participation in council affairs, Ralph appears to have established some form of meaningful alliance with Hugh. There is no evident hostility in this relationship, but there are clear traces of amity and respect. Yet there is no escaping the fact that Ralph, somewhat out of character, barged in on the council proceedings at Poitiers. This might be interpreted as a desperate action by a man falsely or rightly accused of crimes against the Church, but there is no evidence suggesting a conspiracy attempt by the King and the Archbishop to undermine Hugh's (i.e., the reformers') authority. This point of view must be treated cautiously, especially when considering the authority and influence of the local and regional lay elite in matters of reform and law.

Similar to the campaigns for eliminating simony and nicolaitism in France, Hugh of Die orchestrated the dissemination of decrees against lay investiture and interference. At least, this is the impression left to us from the extant evidence. Although no canons survive to this effect, a letter from Archbishop Manasses I of Reims mentions that Hugh had in fact first announced the reformers' position on

[161] Hugh of Die, letter 7, PL, CLVII, cols 509–10; cf. Alfred Richard, *Histoire des comtes de Poitou, 778–1204*, 2 vols (Paris: Picard, 1903), I, 340.

lay investiture at his Autun council in September 1077. It was there that Bishop Ralph of Amiens and Ivo of Senlis were accused of having received the *donum episcopatus* from the French king,[162] and where Robert (son of Count William of Nevers) admitted to having received the bishopric of Auxerre before the canonical age of thirty — the age that Christ entered his ministry. The latter figure had not, like Ivo, accepted investiture from the King, but had obtained his see 'per familiares regis', which in Cowdrey's reading meant 'by currying favour at court'.[163] What these few cases suggest is that simony, more than lay investiture, was the reformers' principal concern.

More explicit action against lay investiture in France did come in 1079, however, when Gregory instructed Hugh to remove a certain unnamed invader from the church of Châlon. The legal term *intrare*, meaning 'to invade' or 'enter', was used here to signify this man's entrance to the church by means of temporal power, 'that is by royal investiture' (ab omni regimine).[164] Gregory reminded his legate to curb these 'lawless endeavours' (conatus illicitos), commissioning him with what appears to have been a new or at least enhanced legal power in seeking out and punishing those found guilty of committing this crime.

But Hugh presumably needed little instruction in punishing this abuse; his previous activity in the council arena often handled such matters. The first canon of his 1078 Poitiers council, for instance, echoed Gregory's view on investiture by declaring that 'no bishop, abbot, priest or clerk is to receive the gift of any bishopric, abbey or benefice from the hand of the king or the count or any laymen'.[165] The punishment of excommunication was threatened on any member of the laity who might stand 'in contempt of canon law' (decretis canonicis resistentes) by bestowing this privilege upon the clergy. Moreover, by this stage of his legatine career, Hugh was commissioned with enough authority to excom-

[162] For Ralph of Amiens see Manasses, *RHGF*, XIV, 611. For Ivo of Senlis, see Hugh of Die's report on the council proceedings of Autun (1077), letter 8, PL, CXLVIII, col. 744.

[163] Cowdrey, *Pope Gregory VII*, p. 362.

[164] *Ep. vag.*, 30.

[165] Mansi, XX, col. 498 (canon 1): 'Decrevit sancta synodus ut nullus episcopus, abbas, presbyter, vel quaelibet persona de clero accipiat de manu regis vel comitis, vel cuiuslibet laicae personae donum episcopatus, vel abbatiae, vel ecclesiae, vel aliquarum ecclesiasticarum rerum. Sed episcopus a suo metropolitano, abbas, presbyter, & caeterae inferiores personae a proprio episcopo, Si vero laici, decretis canonicis resistentes, ecclesias violenter tenere praesumpserint, ipsi excommunicentur; in ecclesis vero illis nullum divinum officium fiat, nullus ibi oret, lumen non ponatur, mortuus non sepeliatur, tantum baptismi gratia ibi non negetur, infirmis remedio poenitentiae & communionis non subveniatur.'

municate those who dared ignore the apostolic decrees enacted at Gregory's 1075 and 1078 councils, bearing a close resemblance to the eleventh canon from Pope Nicholas II's 1059 Lateran council.[166]

By 1080, a more resolute attitude towards lay investiture in France had been laid out. This was clearly the anticipated result after nearly five years of disseminating reforming measures to counter the abuse. Gregory had decreed previously at his 1078 November synod against any clergy receiving the investiture of a 'bishopric, abbey, or church from the hand of an emperor or king or any lay person, man or woman'.[167] Anyone found guilty of such a crime was to be rendered excommunicate, and their appointment to an ecclesiastical office considered null and void. This canon was reiterated at Gregory's 1080 Lent (Roman) synod, adding to this another canon directed more at the lay elite: emperors, kings, dukes, marquises, counts, and any secular powers whatsoever were warned henceforth that their investing of bishops or any other member of the ecclesiastical dignity, would earn them the same punishment of excommunication.[168] Citing from the book of Samuel (I Sam. 15. 23), and referring to the

[166] Mansi, XX, col. 876 (canon 11): 'Scimus quidem laicis ecclesias omnino non competere. Sed ubi illi ex toto auferri non possunt, saltem oblationes missarum et altarium laicis omnino prohibemus.'

[167] *Reg.* VI. 5b (Rome: 19 November 1078), canon 3: 'Quoniam investituras ecclesiarum contra statuta sanctorum patrum a laicis personis in multis partibus cognovimus fieri et ex eo plurimas perturbationes in ecclesia oriri, ex quibus christiana religio conculcatur, decernimus, ut nullus clericorum investituram episcopatus vel abbatie vel ecclesie de manu imperatoris vel regis vel alicuius laice persone viri vel femine, suscipiat. Quod si presumpserit, recognoscat investituram illam apostolica auctoritate irritam esse et se usque ad dignam satisfactionem excommunicationi subiacere.'

[168] *Reg.*, VII. 14a (Rome: 7 March 1080), canon 1: 'Sequentes statuta sanctorum patrum, sicut in prioribus conciliis, que Deo miserante celebravimus, de ordinatione ecclesiasticarum dignitatum statuimus, ita et nunc apostolica auctoritate decernimus ac confirmamus, ut, si quis deinceps episcopatum vel abbatiam de manu alicuius laice persone susceperit, nullatenus inter episcopos vel abbates habeatur nec ulla ei ut episcopo seu abbati audientia concedatur. Insuper etiam ei gratiam sancti Petri et introitum ecclesie interdicimus, quousque locum, quem sub crimine tam ambitionis quam inoboedientie, quod est scelus idolatriê, cepit, resipiscendo non deserit. Similiter etiam de inferioribus ecclesiasticis dignitatibus constituimus.' Canon 2: 'Item si quis imperatorum regum ducum marchionum comitum vel quilibet secularium potestatum aut personarum investituram episcopatuum vel alicuius ecclesiastice dignitatis dare presumpserit, eiusdem sententie vinculo se obstrictum esse sciat. Insuper etiam, nisi resipiscat et ecclesie propriam libertatem dimittat, divine animadversionis ultionem in hac presenti vita tam in corpore suo quam ceteris rebus suis sentiat, ut in adventu Domini spiritus salvus fiat.'

crime of disobedience, Gregory compared the abuse of lay investiture with the offence of idolatry. The seriousness, responsibility, and expectation to follow closely these Roman decrees had become a burden placed firmly upon both the lay and ecclesiastical communities — an onus which neither party in good conscience could choose to ignore.

The Laity's Role

Notwithstanding Hugh of Die's conciliar and legislative efforts at Autun (1077) and Poitiers (1078), the reformers' legal and moral success in the provinces relied on more than the skilful application of letters and legates — a characteristic of government that Gregory recognized early on in his pontificate. In addition to such commissioning, the Pope depended to a great extent on the French laity for implementing and disseminating his reforming policies and legislation. This support came in varying degrees: from those founding and upholding proprietary churches and monasteries, to those offering a safe environment in which legatine councils could be convened, where jurisprudence could be practised and implemented openly, and where reforming legislation could be disseminated more widely. In many instances, the local or regional presence of a legate facilitated this lay participation, bridging the gap between the provinces and the pope in Rome, making more accessible the recourse to law and reform.

Given this practical consideration, lay intervention could never be rooted out entirely, and it remains questionable whether this was ever the reformers' genuine intention. That is to say that in their efforts to transmit Roman legislation to northern France and Burgundy, church reformers like Hugh of Die benefited from the wilful assistance of like-minded political and reform-friendly figures. Permitting secular participation was a crucial ingredient for the effective governing of ecclesiastical business in the provinces, regardless of the reformers' previous efforts to stamp out their role in episcopal investiture and elections. The Council of Autun in 1077, for instance, would never have materialized in that region without arrangements having been made in advance with the local lay elite. Initially designed to be held in the vicinity of Cambrai, in the province of Reims — 'in partibus illis' — with the consent and counsel of King Philip I of France ('cum consensu et consilio'),[169] Gregory took additional measures with the church and the Bishop of Langres (in the province of Lyon) to secure a safe meeting place.

[169] *Reg.*, IV. 22.

And yet another possible location was arranged with Count Theobald I of Blois in case Philip dared oppose the commissioned legation.

The initial plan to hold a council in the ecclesiastical province of Reims was a very provocative move on Gregory's part. That the diocese of Cambrai was situated in the ecclesiastical province of Reims, yet belonged politically to the kingdom of Germany, leaves little wonder that Hugh of Die avoided convening there.[170] By 987, the county of Cambrésis had 'created a very weak political entity, into which imperial influences steadily percolated'.[171] Since this see's creation in the sixth century, the diocesan jurisdiction of Cambrai bordered with the empire and, until 1094, the see of Arras also fell under the Bishop's rule. Control of this diocese presented numerous possibilities for external interference in the council proceedings that would no doubt have rivalled Hugh's jurisdictional authority.

In view of Gregory's enacted decrees against lay investiture, King Philip I still garnered some support among those members of the French episcopate who were not submissive to a policy threatening the autonomy and established rights of their sees. For this reason, it would have proven disadvantageous for Hugh to convene a council in a region that might possibly rouse so much resistance. Yet Gregory specifically requested that a council be held there, suggesting that his intentions were to enforce his reform policy where it was opposed most strongly. And this he planned to do with the backing of canonical authority: his instructional letter to Hugh of Die quoted authoritatively canon 22 of the Fourth Council of Constantinople (869–70) on free elections without lay interference, in what marks the first time that such decrees were promulgated in France during his pontificate.[172]

The reasons for rejecting Langres and the county of Blois, it seems, were rather different. Bishop Rainald-Hugh of Langres (1065–85) had offered to be a helper (*adiutor*) and co-operator (*cooperator*) to the Roman Church and its legates, and Gregory placed great hope and confidence in his ability. Count Theobald I of Blois (1037–89) likewise offered to receive Gregory's legates with great devotion (*summa devotio*) and to furnish them with every facility for holding a council,

[170] See Lotte Kéry, *Die Errichtung des Bistums Arras 1093/1094*, Beihefte der Francia, 33 (Sigmaringen: Thorbecke, 1994), pp. 226–41.

[171] Dunbabin, *France in the Making*, p. 98.

[172] See *Reg.*, IV. 22; canon 22, in *The Oecumenical Councils: From Nicaea I (325) to Nicaea II (787)*, ed. by Giuseppe Alberigo and others, Corpus Christianorum Conciliorum Oecumenicorum et Generaliumque Decreta, 3rd edn (Turnhout: Brepols, 2006), pp. 182–83.

effectively providing them with the 'opportunity, advice, and aid in discharging ecclesiastical business'.[173]

The Count's support in this and other cases is treated as more than a matter of personal interest. Reputed for his piety and reform advocacy, Theobald had by this stage already established a precedent for support. In 1081 he offered Hugh of Die a nonpartisan environment in which to carry out the reformers' necessary ecclesiastical business, which assistance culminated into the legatine council of Issoudun. And though this council convened in lands so closely affecting the royal demesne, King Philip possessed no obvious reason(s) to oppose it. On the one hand the King 'was prepared to stand up for what he saw as his rights to exploit the lands and offices of the church',[174] reflecting a 'hard line against the church's attempts to diminish his control over it'.[175] But there is also evidence of Philip's religiosity: his generous grants to the Cluniac monasteries of Saint-Magloire, Saint-Benoît-sur-Loire, and Saint-Martin-des-Champs just to name a few, stood in sharp contrast to his 'uncompromising attitude to ecclesiastical reform',[176] especially over the abuses of simony and lay investiture.

Notwithstanding King Philip's seemingly twin-track position, Theobald's eagerness to assist reformers like Hugh of Die often set him against the French king. On account of Theobald's proximity to the royal demesne — at times threatening to encircle it with lands in Blois, Chartres, and Champagne — any domestic affair had 'immediate repercussions on crown interests'.[177] In 1077 the Count's offer to host what eventually became the Autun council effectively challenged Philip I's attempt to thwart its meeting. And although Theobald had adopted the new title of palatine count (*comes palatinus*)[178] under Philip in 1081, his ambition was to govern with the King, not to be governed by him. He was clearly 'linked to the king by ties of vassalage', as Hallam observed, 'but he nevertheless supported both the order of Cluny and the papal reformers against

[173] *Reg.*, IV. 22.

[174] Hallam, *Capetian France*, pp. 140–41.

[175] Hallam, *Capetian France*, p. 149.

[176] Hallam, *Capetian France*, p. 139.

[177] Dunbabin, *France in the Making*, p. 194. See also Jean Dunbabin, 'West Francia: The Kingdom', in *NCMH*, III (2000), 372–97 (p. 392).

[178] For examples of this title's sporadic use, see H. d'Arbois de Jubainville, *Histoire des ducs des comtes de Champagne depuis le VIe siècle jusqu'à la fin du XIe*, 8 vols (Paris: Durand, 1859–69), I, no. 58 (1081), 496–97; no. 59 (1083), 497–98.

royal interests'.[179] The Count's readiness in ecclesiastical affairs may have been influenced by the attitude of his father, Odo (Eudes) II, whose protection of the abbots of Marmoutier and various other church foundations showed a great appreciation for all things ecclesiastical.[180]

The charter evidence alone is insightful for disclosing Theobald's role in the founding of churches and monasteries, the approbation of elections, and other church-related business.[181] The fact that he considered himself as a useful reform ally, but that the papacy also recognized him as such, placed him among the ranks of invaluable defenders and protectors of St Peter. His founding of Coincy (in Picardy), for instance, a monastery constructed in gratitude to Abbot Hugh of Cluny for baptizing his son Odo, is often interpreted as sufficient evidence of his genuine favour for monasticism and monastic reform.[182] That he managed to obtain a reputation for piety by championing the reform cause to his own interest is also of great significance, especially considering that he stood a greater risk of injuring his power, as the reform movement aimed to reduce lay interference in the episcopacy. Tackling these obstacles straight on, Theobald emerged unscathed by the movement as reformers were — for the most part — 'more anxious to criticize their enemies than their friends'.[183]

Far from inexperienced in the ecclesiastical affairs of northern France, it was again Theobald's reforming allegiance that enabled Hugh of Die and Amatus of Oloron to convene a council at Meaux in 1082. Of particular interest here is the manner in which this meeting was organized; it was not convened, as is customary, at the Pope's request, but entirely at the Count's initiative. Wishing to settle a dispute between the monks of Montier-en-Der and Count Walter of Brienne († 1090), a surviving charter preserved in the monastery's cartulary tells us how Count Theobald I of Blois actively sought out Hugh of Die's intervention in this dispute.[184] The Count of Brienne stood accused of taking unlawful exactions from

[179] Hallam, *Capetian France*, p. 48.

[180] Bur, *La Formation*, pp. 222–25.

[181] For evidence of Theobald's involvement in ecclesiastical affairs of various sorts, see the charter evidence recorded in d'Arbois de Jubainville, *Histoire des ducs des comtes de Champagne* I, 475–504.

[182] Bur, *La Formation*, p. 224.

[183] Dunbabin, *France in the Making*, p. 194.

[184] *The Cartulary of Montier-en-Der, 666–1129*, ed. by Constance Brittain Bouchard (Toronto: University of Toronto Press, 2004), no. 68, pp. 175–77; cf. Hugh of Die, *RHGF*, XIV, letter 10, p. 787.

the monastery, for which action Theobald — heralded as 'magnus et magnificus vir' — had urged Hugh to excommunicate him. But Hugh approached this council with caution, exhibiting a degree of legal tolerance and patience before reaching a peaceful settlement over the customary dues owed to each party.[185]

The Count of Blois's initiative in actively seeking legatine assistance for a local dispute is a significant gesture, especially as there are no other such accounts for the entirety of Hugh of Die's legatine career, including his second term (1094–99) under Pope Urban II. Based on the existing evidence, it becomes clear that Theobald did not find it necessary to consult the Pope on a matter that likely would have been entirely unfamiliar to him. In other words, it was of local interest. His confidence in the legate's ability is a sure sign of Hugh's juristic status and presence. This confidence might be interpreted also as a quick legal manoeuvre undertaken by the Count, summoning assistance from an itinerant legate whose familiarity with the politics in the area of his jurisdiction would have far exceeded that of the Pope's, thus avoiding the lengthy appeal process to Rome. Whatever the case, Hugh of Die's legal role presented the Count with a viable option for immediate dispute settlement — a good example of demand for justice.

Theobald's initiative in this matter sheds further light on the importance of legates in carrying out the administrative and legal functions of ecclesiastical government, as well as revealing the independent authority that was commissioned to each legate. For the Count, already well acquainted with Hugh of Die through previous encounters at Autun (1077) and Issoudun (1081), this legate presented the perfect and willing candidate to answer his plea. That the Count contacted him directly implies that the 'origins of the transformation of the papal position in the world during the eleventh and twelfth centuries are to be found not in Rome but in the provinces'.[186]

The type of alliance established between Theobald and the reforming party is evidenced also in other regions. In south-western France, for example, the reformers' came to rely extensively on the assistance of Duke William VIII of Aquitaine (sixth count of Poitou), whose participation at Hugh of Die's 1078 Poitiers council greatly contributed to the transmission of reforming legislation in that region.[187] According to Bishop Ernaldus of Le Mans, as mentioned above, it was William's interest in preserving the decrees from this council that inevitably

[185] *Cartulary of Montier-en-Der*, ed. by Bouchard.

[186] Southern, *Making of the Middle Ages*, p. 145.

[187] For a firsthand account of his participation and cooperation with the reformers, see *Reg.*, II. 24.

led to their inclusion in local contemporary canonical collections like the *Collectio Tarraconensis* and the *Collectio Burdegalensis*.[188] His refusal to obey the King of France, as well as his efforts to promote the decrees to the regions of his care, evoke a genuine interest and concern that fell in line with Gregory's reforming ideology.

William's participation at Hugh of Die's 1078 Poitiers council, and his efforts to ensure its success, are also good indications of his authority in that region. The Duke's careful attention to these decrees — ensuring their dissemination to an even larger arena — could also have been used to protect the monastery to which, since the time of Duke William the Great (995–1030), the dukes of Aquitaine had attached a great religious value. It was William VIII's sympathetic position toward reform, and his regional power, that presumably led to the council being held in Poitiers to begin with. It was, moreover, the monastery of Saint-Hilaire that housed the council proceedings after the initial disturbances caused by Archbishop Ralph I of Tours, and it was due to the Duke's will and consent that the assembly was able to continue relatively undisturbed on the council's sixth day.[189]

Revealing a reforming mentality closely aligned with Gregory, the papal *Register* portrays a trusting alliance that by this point in 1078 was clearly established with Duke William. The level of his cooperation with the Roman Church — evident as early as 1074 for ending his uncanonical marriage to

[188] Mansi, XX, col. 499: 'Ernaldus Cenomanensis episcopus, et Guandalbertus Fulconi decano salutem. Abbas majoris monasterii, et monachi eius conquesti sunt de me apud Lugdunensem primatem, et caeteros primores Pictavensis concilii, quod eorum oratoriam capellam apud Sablolium aedificare prohibemus. At illi rationem ostendentes, quod id fieri non deberet, rogaverunt, ut eis aedificandi licentiam tribuerem. Quorum auctoritati non obedire inreligiosum ducens, quod petebant benigne concessi. Mandamus itaque tibi et ex nostra auctoritate jubemus, ut cum domno Hilberto S. Martini monacho, per quem episcopalem aquam et altare et crucem ferream misimus, Sablolium usque pergas, et in loco quem ostenderit aquam spargas, et crucem figas. Vale.' This account, which is also found in Baluze's *Miscellanea*, VI, 565, fails to cite its original source. Confirming further these canons as products of Hugh of Die's 1078 Poitiers council is a letter from William to the canons of Saint-Hilaire (Mansi, XX, col. 500): 'Si autem aliquis ex istis, scilicet ex clericorum filiis, vel caeteris spuriis, antequam edictum Domini papae Gregorii VII. quod de illis promulgatum est in concilio Pictavensi a Domino Hugone Diensium episcopo, et sedit apostolicae legato esset recitatum, factus est in illa canonicus sicut ille utique permisit, ut ita permaneat, permittimus.'

[189] *La Chronique de Saint-Maixent*, p. 145: 'Anno MLXXVIIII Hugo episcopus Lugdunensis, et legatus romane Ecclesie, tenuit concilium Pictavis, primo die apud Sanctum Petrum et alio die ad Sanctum Hilarium.' See also Hugh of Die, letter 7, PL, CLVII, cols 509–10.

Hildegard of Anjou, and his willingness to join Gregory's expedition (*expeditio*) to Constantinople[190] — illustrates how lay intervention of this sort was conducive to the workings of Gregory's reforming government. In dealing with the iniquities of King Philip I of France, and other disobedient prelates and clerics in south-western France, William's role is made especially clear. His compliance in assisting Gregory's legates in discharging ecclesiastical affairs placed him at the service of St Peter ('ad servitium sancti PETRI'), and his personal investment in the ecclesiastical possessions and business of his jurisdiction greatly contributes to this favourable disposition.[191]

Gregory is often seen petitioning William's support in matters concerning the Roman Church. From 1074, the Pope's letters begin to show a confidence in the Duke's ability to help secure the aims of the reform movement. Acting as 'one who sincerely loves St Peter and ourself',[192] Gregory called upon William to confront the French king Philip I in order to 'restrain his hand from the destruction of churches'. The Duke was petitioned here as an intermediary between the papal and royal courts, instructed to act in concord with the Roman Church in bringing Philip's 'iniquities home to him'. But William did not give in under this pressure. He managed to stay on the Pope's good side, remaining a faithful advocate to the reform movement throughout his life, while at the same time staying faithful to the French king. To the latter he proved his fidelity, but never — it must be said — in military terms. He had accumulated enough wealth, territory, and power to be considered the King's equal, and this position allowed for room to manoeuvre when handling ecclesiastical matters.

William assumed a role in ecclesiastical affairs for the implementation of justice (*iustitiam tractandam*).[193] This appreciation is most evident from the transgressions of Bishop Isembert II of Poitiers, a case that occupied the Duke's attention for nearly five years before the Bishop successfully cleared himself of all charges.[194] A papal letter to the Duke in April 1079 suggests that lay involvement in Aquitaine was customary and expected, and that Gregory, knowing full well the extent of William's faithfulness to St Peter, was prepared to exploit his assistance

[190] *Reg.*, II. 3; I. 46.

[191] *Reg.*, II. 3.

[192] *Reg.*, II. 18.

[193] *Reg.*, II. 24.

[194] See *Reg.*, II. 2–4, 23–24.

to reach a desired resolution.[195] In one sense, it was due in large part to efforts such as these that papal influence and reform doctrines could be implemented effectively in distant regions beyond Rome. Hugh of Die's legatine council efforts were by far the most effective and reliable means for the dissemination of papal policy, but William's initiative ensured that the decrees would be administered properly to networks beyond the scope of the council arena.

Duke William VIII's interest in conciliar affairs fits with a history of comital governing in Aquitaine. Upon offering his support to Hugh of Die in 1078, it is possible that William was thinking of his predecessor William V (990–1029), whose Council of Poitiers in 1010 attracted churchmen from the whole duchy, including the territory comprising the ecclesiastical provinces of Aquitaine, Bourges, and Bordeaux.[196] The history of ecclesiastical and peace synods in this duchy (at Le Puy in 975 and 994, at Charroux in 989 and 1028, Narbonne in 990, Limoges in 1031, Poitiers in 1000 or 1011–14 and 1038) suggests that ecclesiastical affairs were a familiar part of ducal government, thus weakening any possibility — however slight — that William's interest in the council was simply self-aggrandizing. As Jane Martindale observed, 'even when conciliar deliberations are portrayed as almost exclusively ecclesiastical', the dukes' participation in the tenth and early eleventh century was often demanded by the council fathers.[197] In light of their willingness to participate in church matters, lay intervention need not be viewed merely in terms of interference.[198]

On the contrary, the defence of church property, rights, and revenues — in the name of reform or the preservation of customs and tradition — depended to a great extent on the success of secular leadership and assistance in ecclesiastical affairs. The dukes of Burgundy offer further testimony to this working lay relationship with the church, standing as authoritative political figures and staunch supporters of the reform movement; they dominated their region (comprising Nevers, Mâcon, Beaune, Dijon, Langres, Auxerre, and Troyes) 'by chivalry, by friendship and by cooperation',[199] in addition to the buildup of economic

[195] *Reg.*, VI. 32.

[196] Martindale, 'Peace and War', p. 157. Duke William V also convened the Council of Limoges in 994, and attended the councils of Charroux II (1027), Poitiers II (1029/31), and Limoges IV (1031).

[197] Martindale, 'Peace and War', p. 158.

[198] See François de Fontette, 'Évêques de Limoges et comtes de Poitou au XIe siècle', in *Études d'histoire du droit canonique*, 2 vols (Paris: Sirey, 1965), I, 553–58.

[199] Dunbabin, *France in the Making*, p. 184.

resources. This prosperity had come only gradually, however, following a struggle to regain and assert their committal control following the disintegration of the old Carolingian administrative pattern. The dukes eventually prospered not through the acclamation of new lands or titles, but through the promotion of these new and powerful relationships with local castellans, independent counts and bishops, and episodic visits to the royal court.

Recognized by Orderic Vitalis as a man of 'outstanding justice' (iusticia insignis),[200] Duke Hugh I of Burgundy (r. 1075–78) ranks high among the reform-friendly members of the French lay elite. His efforts at increasing peace through assemblies at Bèze and Palleau serves to strengthen this honest reputation, which activity earned him the respect of Burgundian nobility like the Counts of Mâcon, Nevers, and Chalon.[201] By far the most extensive evidence exhibiting the Duke's reform partisanship, however, comes from his participation at Hugh of Die's 1077 Autun council. According to this council's subscription list, the Duke's name appears first before any reference is made to the ecclesiastical participants, suggesting not only the extent but also the importance of his contribution to the council proceedings. The exact details of his participation, however, are as unclear as the identities of the 'illustrious men' (multi illustres viri) who accompanied him. But there is little doubt as to the Duke's interest in the ecclesiastical affairs of this region. That he provided the opportunity and means for reforming decrees to be pronounced at Autun is interpreted from a letter written by Archbishop Manasses of Reims to Gregory VII.[202]

Referring to the consecration of Bishop Ralph of Amiens 'contra auctoritatem et canones' by two of his own suffragan bishops,[203] Manasses attempted to exculpate himself by denying knowledge of what he recognized as a blatant violation of Gregory's 1074 and 1075 Roman decrees. It is particularly his familiarity with this reforming legislation, and his acknowledgement of its circulation, that serves to confirm Hugh's efforts in promulgating them at his legatine councils.[204] For the first time, Hugh's efforts in transmitting and disseminating reform principles were proven by means other than enacted punishments and conciliar sentences.

[200] From Orderic Vitalis, bk XIII, VI, 430–31.

[201] Guy II (1065–78), William I († 1098), and Hugh II († 1078) respectively; cf. Dunbabin, *France in the Making*, p. 182; Jean Richard, *Les Ducs de Bourgogne et la formation du duché du XIe au XIVe siècle* (Paris: Les Belles Lettres, 1954), p. 24.

[202] Manasses, *RHGF*, XIV, 611.

[203] Helinand of Laon and Theobald of Soissons.

[204] Manasses, *RHGF*, XIV, 611.

The extant canon law, and the new religious and moral climate created by reformers since the 1050s, meant that everyone in the ecclesiastical realm was subject to the same legal conditions. From this point onward, and as Gregory presumably envisioned it, no one could hide behind the notion of ignorance to the reformers' objectives; that is, there was really no use in pleading custom.

Like the Aquitanian dukes of this period, Hugh of Burgundy's interest in ecclesiastical affairs fits with his role for administering justice to the territories of his jurisdiction. Taking into account the favourable political climate in late eleventh-century Burgundy, there is no reason to treat Hugh I's intervention at the Council of Autun as anything more than serving ecclesiastical interests, in effect acting as the Church's protector and defender. His concern for justice and his preceding reputation in ecclesiastical affairs, are all legitimate reasons for his interest in overseeing the council proceedings. And if his religious convictions were in fact as strong as Orderic Vitalis has suggested, then a reason other than religious devotion is not necessary to explain the extent of his conciliar participation.

The Duke's high regard for the Church's spiritual life is evidenced further by his unexpected entry into the monastery of Cluny in 1078. With this action comes a better sense of just how highly Hugh of Burgundy's assistance was regarded by the papacy and the Christian subjects in his realm. Writing to Abbot Hugh of Cluny on 2 January 1079, Gregory reproved the Abbot for having received the Duke into his cloister without first consulting him on the matter.[205] As a result, in what he considered a careless manoeuvre, the Pope lamented over the hundred thousand Christians being left without a guardian ('centum milia christianorum careant custode'). Gregory's grievance in this matter is interesting to note as it expresses his views that good princes who fear and love God were scarcely found in the entire West. The reformers' loss of a protector and defender was an understandably sensitive issue, especially when accompanied by the fear that his successor in government would not be as willing to cooperate in matters affecting the Roman Church.

As these few examples illustrate, the reformers' efforts to eliminate lay investiture and interference in France are seldom evidenced through conflict or clashes of interest. Despite the fact that many of the problems facing the Roman Church were linked to its ties with the local aristocracy, it remained extremely common

[205] See *Reg.*, VI. 17.

in parts of France (as elsewhere) for the laity to assume a leading role in matters of church administration — which is not to say that it took the form of investiture or meddling in ecclesiastical appointments. In view of the existing evidence, it is not out of the question to suggest the reformers' initiative in seeking out lay interference for achieving mutual objectives, calling on the laity's assistance in the name of reform while channelling their intervention towards positive ends.

Following the death of Archbishop Wilfred of Narbonne (*c.* 1019–79), for example, a council was convened at Toulouse under Amatus of Oloron and Hugh of Die to validate a successor to that see. Gregory promoted his own nominee by the name of Dalmatius (1081–96), Abbot of La Grasse, while Bishop Peter of Rodez (1046–90) was promoted in opposition by the local lay power Viscount Aymeric of Narbonne (*c.* 1080–1105/06).[206] Because it was common in southern France for the lay elite to take a leading role in matters of church administration, Aymeric's attempt to install his own nominee to the see of Narbonne fell in line with his predecessor's right of jurisdiction. Only after church reform began taking hold in the Narbonnais region was lay intervention no longer considered a temporal right or privilege.

Lay response to what could amount to a loss of status was of course varied, but there are more than a few examples citing on the whole a positive regional attitude towards reform. The viscount of the city of Toulouse (Adhémar), for example, acted as a great protector and advocate over the monastery of St Sernin, reaping also the financial rewards from the income produced at the monastery's allods at Grisolles and Baniols. This one variation suggests that Aymeric's relentlessness in opposing the papacy might present an isolated and indeed personal case.

The grandiloquent language of Gregory's letter projects desperation in keeping the laity in the region of Toulouse under papal control. The fact that Peter of Rodez was successful in occupying the see of Narbonne for two years (until 1081) is an indication of his authority and support in that region. Gregory appeared conscious of the potential dangers, relying on his only available means of papal legates, letters, and canon law, effectively threatening to confirm Aymeric's excommunication. Gregory was offering the Viscount a chance to save his soul, but his motives carried obvious political undertones, ultimately trying to ensure that his archbishop-elect (Dalmatius) was the decisive successor to the see of Narbonne. For this to become possible, the Pope called upon Counts Raymond IV and Bertrand II of Saint-Gilles (Raymond's son, Count of Provence) to bring

[206] On Gregory's support for Dalmatius, see *Reg.*, VIII. 16.

'prompt help to the church of Narbonne which now for a long time has been invaded by members of the devil'.[207] And by petitioning for their aid in resisting the Viscount (*pervasor*) by any able means, Gregory was enticing the counts with the promise of 'prosperity and honour in the next life'.

As for Peter, he was never found guilty of any wrongdoing and maintained his office as the Bishop of Rodez until 1090. Although his unlawful possession of the archdiocese of Narbonne was tantamount to simony, it appears that the greatest opposition to the papacy rested entirely with the viscount's interference in ecclesiastical matters, which lay role the papacy took great pains to temper.

Given the reformers' treatment of this case, there is a growing sense that the question of lay investiture in France was predominantly one of temporal interference, which could be tolerated to some extent, as long as it benefited the reformers' broader objectives. The enactment of Roman legislation in a council setting was a natural starting point for disseminating the papacy's stringent views on the issue, but the practical steps towards eradicating this abuse — as the evidence admits — were assessed often in an entirely local setting, on an individual case-by-case basis. This is where the role of the legate and laity often intersected. In this way, adopting a judicious approach to the abuse at hand, the reformers' were able to evaluate the seriousness of each accusation and punish the guilty offenders when it suited their more immediate needs and interests. Looking beyond the theoretical models for extirpating simony, nicolaitism, and lay investiture, it was this local and regional application of reform and law that provided the greatest possible means for transformation in late eleventh-century France.

Dispute Settlement and Other Business

More time consuming than the abuses of simony, nicolaitism, and lay investiture, and equally as rooted in local custom and tradition, were the numerous and ongoing disputes in France on matters of ecclesiastical rights, privileges, and properties. Yet while it was common in this period for legatine councils to settle disputes between religious houses, this could be a separate matter entirely from why the council initially met. In such cases, which for the most part were concluded swiftly, both parties — along with a few other religious men — were summoned canonically for the express purpose of making their case legally known;

[207] *Reg.*, VIII. 16.

both sides of the case were heard, testimony was given if necessary, a decision was pronounced, and the matter was resolved. More specific quarrels, on the other hand, such as those necessitating the legate's presence, were more often than not the result of a long and arduous conflict. Disputes such as these usually evoked active correspondence between the religious house and the pope, lodging complaint after complaint to Rome, adhering to ancient written and often-unwritten canonical rules. Such complaints were commonly referred to a legate by the pope, who was seldom acquainted nor had the time or care to be with the true state of affairs.[208]

The significance of this trivial business comes primarily from the papal response. After all, even the most trifling ecclesiastical affairs, however local or regional in their interests, did (in theory) implicate Gregory's reforming church. Presenting cases seldom concerned with the main tenets of church reform (as examined above), the reformers were accountable nevertheless for each individual appeal and/or complaint made to Rome. Writing to Hugh of Die in 1082–03 concerning a dispute over the monastery of Saint-Symphorien (Saint-Benoît-sur-Loire), for example, Gregory was forced to admit his inability in even recalling the dispute, as well as his failure to find a letter in his *Register* referring to it.[209] For reasons such as these, it becomes easy to see how the legate developed as a conciliatory adjudicator in order to implement justice (*iustitia*) and law (*ius*) more effectively on the pope's behalf. A great majority of legatine activity under Gregory VII dealt with such trivial (to some) and time-consuming matters, alleviating and assuming the Pope's burden of responsibility, thereby fulfilling the obligations of his (i.e., the legate's) office.

Of the thirteen legatine councils convened by Hugh of Die between 1075 and 1085, in fact, most were concerned with dispute settlement or other ecclesiastical business. Given our earlier assessment on the varied roles of the legatine office (see above, Chapter 3), the legal adjudication offered in these ecclesiastical assemblies was no less important. Indeed, legatine councils, though often summoned in response to a local initiative, were always called at the Pope's incentive, demonstrating yet again the many ways for Gregory to extend his reach into the various Christian provinces. This supervisional condition implies that, regardless of Gregory's personal knowledge of individual cases, legatine intervention was always encouraged and determined by the Pope's will. Not only did he fashion the

[208] See *Reg.*, IX. 33 for a good example of Gregory's difficulties in dealing with disputes far from Rome.

[209] *Reg.*, IX. 32.

council agenda by committing legates to predetermined cases, but he also commissioned them with the fullest representative authority to date, thereby enhancing their legal privilege in the ecclesiastical courtroom.

The more capable and legally endowed the representative agent, the more authoritative, intimidating, and useful their presence in the council arena. Offering an exceptional example of this outlook, Hugh of Die's translation from the bishopric of Die to the archdiocese of Lyon in 1082 was arguably another such political manoeuvre to endow him with regional authority, while also acting to clear up some of the confusion and conflict of authorities that had existed between the jurisdictions governed by Hugh (Gallia) and Amatus of Oloron (Narbonne, Gascony, and northern Spain). After that date, Hugh could add primatial authority to his already extensive territorial jurisdiction of northern France and Burgundy. It is entirely possible that, as Gregory's use of the legatine office gained momentum, he was more willing to invest in his agents a greater part in the *plenitudo potestatis* than previously imagined.

Nowhere is this papal initiative more apparent in the sources than for the collaborative activity of Hugh of Die and Amatus of Oloron at the councils of Bordeaux (1079), Toulouse (1079), Saintes (1081), Issoudun (1081), and Meaux (1082). In October of 1079, for example, Gregory charged both legates to settle a lingering dispute between Abbot Arnald of Saint-Sever (diocese of Aire, in Gascony) and Abbot Trencardus of Sainte-Croix (Bordeaux) over the church of Sainte-Marie at Soulac.[210] Upon dispatching his legates, Gregory attached his ruling to restore to the abbey of Saint-Croix whatever was in dispute. It is interesting to note the measures exacted by the Pope to ensure that his legal ruling would be carried out in full. Amatus and Hugh were encouraged to use any lawful means to remove the Abbot of Saint-Sever; if he remained obstinate in his possession of the church, he was to be barred from celebrating communion. The Pope also notified Abbot Arnald firsthand of the actions being taken against him, instructing him in the meantime — before Gregory's legates could reach him — to restore the church of Sainte-Marie to Sainte-Croix of his own free will.[211] Gregory's firsthand knowledge of the case ensured that the reformers' desired outcome would prevail.

[210] *Reg.*, VI. 24; cf. Amatus of Oloron, *Epistolae*, in *RHGF*, XIV (1806), 762–76 (hereafter cited as Amatus of Oloron) (letter 1, p. 763). There is no evidence of this dispute in the cartulary of Saint-Sever.

[211] *Reg.*, VI. 25.

The issue at hand, as Archbishop Gozelin of Bordeaux reminded the Pope, had been settled previously in 1074 after the Abbot of Saint-Sever failed to attend a council held by Gregory's then legate in France, Cardinal-bishop Gerald of Ostia.[212] The injustice effected by the Abbot's ignoring of canonical authority in either providing a suitable excuse or sending representatives on his behalf was interpreted as proof of his guilt. His contempt for authority cost him the rights and possessions of the church of Sainte-Marie, which the Pope ordered to be restored to the monastery of Sainte-Croix. In accordance with canon law, Arnald was encouraged to visit Rome before the feast of All Saints (1 November) if he felt slighted by the decree and wished to make a formal appeal. Whether Arnald observed Gregory's offer is not clear, but the fact that this case required further attention five years later at Bordeaux (1079) is proof that he either ignored the papal ruling entirely, or that his appeal — if registered — warranted a further enquiry into the dispute.

A privilege drawn up by Amatus of Oloron provides us with a more detailed explanation of the council events. According to this account, the Abbot of Sainte-Croix had been summoned to and attended Bordeaux (1079) with six unnamed monks in order to defend the rights of the church of Sainte-Marie.[213] Here we discover that Arnald's predecessor, Abbot Gregory of Saint-Sever, had previously given the rights of the disputed church to Pope Alexander II; the Pope then immediately transferred the church to Abbot Trencardus of Sainte-Croix's possession. Upon hearing this decisive testimony, the council members reaffirmed Gregory VII's earlier decision that the possession rights of Sainte-Croix were to remain 'firma et illibata'. In this particular case, as with most cases involving a dispute between two monasteries, Gregory appealed to canon law 'as the determining factor'.[214] His policy of consistently and continually doing so illustrates his 'respect for the *privilegia* of all churches', and again emphasizes his concern for the 'preservation and recovery of ecclesiastical rights as much as possible'.[215]

While the cartulary of La Sauve-Majeure (Bordeaux) provides a full and rare subscription list of the council attendees,[216] the records for Amatus of Oloron's

[212] *Reg.*, I. 51.

[213] Amatus of Oloron, letter 1, p. 764. Bouquet's account is an extract from the cartulary of Sainte-Croix, Bordeaux.

[214] Gilchrist, 'Economic Policy of Gregory VII', p. 389.

[215] Gilchrist, 'Economic Policy of Gregory VII', p. 395.

[216] These were Archbishops Gozelin of Bordeaux, William of Auch, Ralph I of Tours, and Bishops Boso of Saintes, Ademar of Angoulême, William of Périgueux, Raymond of Bazas, Hugh

conciliar role are more helpful for corroborating Hugh of Die's legatine activity. The former legate was certainly present at Issoudun in 1081,[217] in what represents the largest council for Hugh of Die's legation in terms of attendance. Cowdrey is quick to point out Issoudun's location 'in the north of the county of Marche', thus falling under Amatus's legatine jurisdiction, but conceding that 'little of the agenda concerned Aquitaine'.[218] This consideration, along with the floating jurisdiction often attributed to Hugh of Die, might serve to explain his presidence in a council that lay outside his assigned territory of northern France and Burgundy. In addition to settling a dispute between the canons of Saint-Hilary (Poitiers) and the bishops and monks of Bourges over the rights of a church at Vouzailles (Poitiers),[219] this council, and the events following, centred on the excommunication of Bishop Gosfred of Chartres.[220]

Similar considerations joined the efforts of these two legates again in 1082, at the Council of Meaux, which convened to settle a dispute between the monks of Montier-en-Der and Count Walter of Brienne,[221] as well as for electing a new bishop to the see of Meaux.[222] The latter account, which saw Abbot Robert of Rebais ordained following the death of Bishop Walter I on 19 November 1082,[223] was spearheaded by Gregory's incentive and approval. Hugh of Die's role was essential to confirming the Abbot's succession. Reinforcing the validity of this new appointment, Gregory related how the election had followed closely the newly prescribed canon 6 of his 1080 Roman council.[224] His reasons for doing so

of Bigorre, Donald of Agen, with their suffragan co-bishops, abbots, religious clergy, and laity (see *Grande cartulaire de la Sauve Majeure*, ed. by Charles Higounet and Arlette Higounet-Nadal (Bordeaux: Fédération historique du Sud-Ouest, 1996), no. 2, pp. 34–35; cf. Mansi, XX, col. 529; Jean Mabillon, *De re diplomatica*, VI, 586–87). Added to this were four anonymous abbots, and Duke William VIII of Aquitaine and his leading men (Amatus of Oloron, letter 1, p. 765).

[217] In the diocese of Bourges, in the county of Marche. See Mansi, XX, col. 579.

[218] Cowdrey, *Pope Gregory VII*, p. 368.

[219] Amatus of Oloron, letter 5, p. 768.

[220] For a history of this case, see *Reg.*, IX. 15–16; IX. 32.

[221] Mansi, XX, cols 583–85; cf. Clarius, *Chronicon Sancti Petri*, year 1082, pp. 134–35; *Cartulary of Montier-en-Der*, no. 68, pp. 175–77.

[222] Clarius, *Chronicon Sancti Petri*, year 1082, pp. 134–35; cf. Mansi, XX, col. 583. For Robert's own words on his election, see Mansi, XX, cols 586–88.

[223] Clarius, *Chronicon Sancti Petri*, year 1083; cf. *Ex Chronico Turonensi*, in *RHGF*, XII (1877), 461–78 (p. 464); cf. Mansi, XX, col. 583.

[224] *Reg.*, VII. 14a (Rome: 7 March 1080): 'Quotiens defuncto pastore alicuius ecclesie alius est ei canonice subrogandus, instantia visitatoris episcopi, qui ei ab apostolica vel metropolitana sede

are reflected in the ensuing events which saw the metropolitan over Meaux, Archbishop Richerius of Sens, not so willing to accept an election accomplished without his approval or consent.

Feeling his authority to be thwarted, Richerius and his supporters immediately excommunicated the bishop-elect, but they were not entirely justified in doing so.[225] A glance at this canon 6 shows that an election could be carried out legally with the 'consent of the apostolic see or of its metropolitan' (in deliberatione sedis apostolice sive metropolitani sui). Gregory obviously opted for the former condition. Ignoring Gregory's synodal legislation, and disregarding entirely the apostolic authority held by Amatus and Hugh in overseeing episcopal elections, Richerius ordained his own bishop on 4 November by the name of Walter II (1082–1102). Due however to Robert's immediate and untimely death, there was little more to be contested, and Richerius's persistence eventually paid off — Walter occupied the see for a further twenty years.[226]

The contemporary cartulary of Montier-en-Der provides more details of the council proceedings at Meaux, recording Count Warin of Rosnay's[227] donating the church of St Margerie (north-west of Montier-en-Der) to the monastery of Cluny.[228] Having recognized that this property rightfully belonged to Montier-en-Der,[229] the Count handed over to that Burgundian monastery the allodial property of Rozerières, Mussey, and Jonchery.[230] Hugh of Die confirmed this charter, which legal account can be used also as evidence for confirming the subscription list provided in his council summary.[231]

directus est, clerus et populus remota omni seculari ambitione timore atque gratia apostolice sedis vel metropolitani sui consensu pastorem sibi secundum Deum eligat. Quod si corruptus aliquo vitio aliter agere presumpserit, electionis perperam facte omni fructu carebit et de cetero nullam electionis potestatem habebit, electionis vero potestas omnis in deliberatione sedis apostolice sive metropolitani sui consistat. Si enim his, ad quem consecratio pertinet, non rite consecrando teste beato Leone gratiam benedictionis amittit, consequenter is, qui ad pravam electionem declinaverit, eligendi potestate privatur.'

[225] Clarius, *Chronicon Sancti Petri*, year 1082; cf. Mansi, XX, col. 583.

[226] *GC*, VIII, cols 1608–09.

[227] Rosnay was twenty kilometres south-west of Montier-en-Der.

[228] *Cartulary of Montier-en-Der*, no. 67, pp. 172–74. See also Count Garin of Rosnay's letter describing the donation, Mansi, XX, col. 585.

[229] *Cartulary of Montier-en-Der*, no. 67, p. 173.

[230] *Cartulary of Montier-en-Der*, no. 67, p. 173.

[231] *Cartulary of Montier-en-Der*, no. 67, can be consulted to trace the history of this donation.

The final case at Meaux examined the excommunication of Bishop Lambert of Thérouanne,[232] whose false actions against that church are depicted in Gregory's letters *c.* 1082–83.[233] The course of events exacted at this council is understood best by illustrating the severity of the charges brought against the Bishop, thereby exemplifying his violent opposition to the church of Thérouanne. Lambert, as Gregory noted,

> afflicted with the harshest capacity five clerks wishing to go to a Roman synod and to make a complaint against his malice, and because to evade canonical discipline he has without licence made off as a fugitive from his own church. In this state of excommunication, he has by heretical depravity had himself consecrated, or rather desecrated, deacon, priest, and bishop by bishops who have been suspended from their office. Thereafter, with Count Robert [of Flanders] accompanying him with an army, he has gone to the city itself as an enemy and with an armed band, and with a hatchet and an axe and other means of violence he has hacked and broken down the doors of the church which the clergy and people had barred against him. Also he has in so devilish a manner carried away the cross and image of the Saviour of a man who was making to offer to him with his right hand before those same closed doors a deed of repudiation and who was as with his own voice forbidding him entry into the church that — a thing that we have never read or heard of as having been done before — he has torn off from him his right hand. And in this way the thief and robber, breaking in with lances and swords [i.e., of his followers] unsheathed, has wounded some of the clerks and has put others to fight half-alive, and he has ravaged and rent asunder the houses of all who would not have communion with him. Indeed, he has so far led astray the count himself that he has driven out of his entire land all clerks who would not obey him, depriving them of all their goods, and he has so proudly rejected two epistles of our own that he has uttered to those who brought them words which were insulting and highly unworthy of so great a prince.[234]

In the mid-eleventh century, the Viscount of Rosnay, Tescelin, and his wife gave the church of Margerie (diocese of Troyes) to the monks at Montier-en-Der, securing for themselves a proper burial ground for their own bodies (*Cartulary of Montier-en-Der*, no. 35, pp. 123–24). Their rights to this church are nowhere mentioned. Count Warin and his wife Adelaide, however, had at some point during Alexander II's pontificate — between 1061 and 1073 — given this same property to Cluny, seeking for themselves, their ancestors and successors, the remedy of souls, and confirming it with their sons Gibuin and Walter (*Recueil des chartes de l'Abbaye de Cluny* (Paris: Imprimerie Nationale, 1888), nos 3377, 3378). Then, in 1074, Bishop Hugh I of Troyes (1059–75) granted the church to Abbot Bruno of Montier-en-Der (*Cartulary of Montier-en-Der*, no. 63, pp. 164–65).

[232] In the province of Reims. For a history of Gregory VII's dealings with the bishops of Thérouanne, see A. Giry, 'Grégoire VII et les évêques de Térouane', *RH*, (1876), 387–409.

[233] See *Reg.*, IX. 13, 31, 33–36, and *Ep. vag.*, 47 respectively.

[234] *Reg.*, IX. 35 (1083).

The reasons for Lambert's excommunication illustrate some serious offences against the church, though not the worst kind imaginable. From this above-cited letter comes a sense of the papacy's vulnerability to offer assistance, epitomized by Gregory's plea to the laymen and bishops of Flanders, and even further exhibited in his letter urging Count Robert of Flanders to restore the church of Thérouanne, for which condition he was partly at fault.[235] The Count was guilty of stripping Archdeacon Arnulf, Abbot 'M', and Ingelrannus of their possessions and casting them out because — obeying apostolic command — 'they would have nothing to do with one Lambert'.[236] Robert had been implored to cease supporting the heretic Lambert (*haereticus*) on account of his deposition and excommunication, and to 'free the captive church from his tyranny and oppression'.[237] But the clerks of Thérouanne continued to complain to Rome about Robert's failure to comply with these conditions, and Gregory confessed that he was becoming weary from the complaints.

The aftermath of Meaux is difficult to piece together.[238] Gregory's letter to Hugh of Die in 1083 shows that Lambert had denied any knowledge of the excommunication charge passed against him at this council.[239] He even denied that he had ever been summoned to attend a council concerning this matter. It seems that Lambert hoped to evade canonical discipline, as Gregory had earlier recognized, by simply pleading ignorance to the procedure of legal authority. This is where matters become confusing on account of the scanty evidence. Presumably sympathizing with the Bishop, Gregory went ahead and absolved him before realizing the full extent of the charges prescribed by Hugh's letter (now lost). The papacy here seems to have been left in the dark — the likely result of Hugh's failure to report what had been decided at the council. After hearing only Lambert's side of the story, Gregory was forced to act accordingly. Once the true charges against Lambert had come to light, however, Gregory quickly ordered Hugh of Die and Abbot Hugh of Cluny to hold a council in order to 'more fruitfully and effectively deal with this business'.[240] No such collaborative council ever materialized.

[235] Gregory urged Robert to return from exile the provost E. (unknown), the dean S. (unknown), and the deacon Ingelrannus, whom he had deprived of property.

[236] *Reg.*, IX. 35.

[237] *Ep. vag.*, 47 (1082–83).

[238] Cowdrey, in *Ep. vag.*, p. 114 n. *.

[239] *Reg.*, IX. 33 (1083).

[240] *Reg.*, IX. 33 (1083).

This particular case illustrates the potential pitfalls facing the papacy in enforcing the council decisions of its legates. In spite of Gregory's hardening stance on the main tenets of reform, there were still ways for the accused to avoid immediate canonical discipline. Disputing the authority of a legate, denying knowledge of a sentence, pleading directly to Rome: these were all means by which a case could be dragged out over an extended period of time, quite often forgotten, or the charges might be dropped entirely. But the problem was not just tangled up in the complexities of correctly interpreting and enforcing the extant canon law; it also surrounded the system of appeal, which required the papacy to consider the numerous cases brought to Rome. The office of legation, as stressed throughout this study, was developing *ad hoc* to lighten this load. This was arguably Count Theobald of Blois's reasoning for soliciting Hugh of Die's assistance in settling the dispute involving Count Walter of Brienne. It was a common occurrence for the papacy to be either ill acquainted with the disputations of each case, or unable to recall the sometimes-prevailing disputes that might have originated under previous pontificates. Two of Gregory's letters, for example, describe the Pope's unfamiliarity with Lambert's case, admitting to no recollection of the actions that had previously been taken in this matter; a record of this dispute could not even be found in Gregory's *Register*.[241] Examples such as these make it is easier to understand why the sentences passed at Meaux — or at any other council for that matter — were not immediate, and why many conciliar cases were often left open or unresolved.

To illustrate this point more clearly, let us consider the evidence for the Council of Saintes (8 January 1081), summoned to settle the long-standing dispute over the metropolitan status of Tours, which the clergy of Dol (north-east Brittany) refused to acknowledge.[242] The origins of this dispute resurfaced in 1076 following the election of Evenus (Abbot of Saint-Melaine, Rennes) to the see of Dol.[243] Gregory, who had heard parts of the case at an earlier synod in either 1076 or 1077, was already well versed in the matter.[244] But his greatest and most immediate concern, it seems, rested with securing Evenus's position among the local clergy and lay elite. At that time, King William I of England was involved in a siege of Dol following the rebellion of his Breton follower Ralph de Gael.

[241] See *Reg.*, IX. 32 and 33.

[242] For the dating of this council, see Amatus of Oloron, letter 3, p. 767; cf. *La Chronique de Saint-Maixent*, p. 147.

[243] See *Reg.*, V. 5 and 22–23; *Ep. vag.*, 16.

[244] Mansi, XX, cols 572–73.

Refusing to appoint the candidate sent to Rome by these rebels (a man by the name of Juhel), Gregory sought to conciliate William by selecting what he considered to be a 'politically neutral figure'[245] — and one that might obviously 'assist his own political schemes'.[246]

It took nearly five years from Evenus's ordination in 1076 before this conflict over metropolitan status came to a head at the Council of Saintes (1081). The noticeable shift in the papacy's hardening attitude is not easy to identify. In denying the rights of Tours over Brittany, the see of Dol was effectively claiming metropolitan status for itself. It follows that the papacy could not ignore such a display of disobedience, to what the Pope no doubt regarded as a direct challenge to his supreme authority. Complaints had been filtering into Rome from Archbishop Ralph I of Tours, who naturally felt that this election had caused a great injustice to his own see.[247] Yet Gregory tried to settle the dispute by merely pleading with the Archbishop to be more content with the 'considered thought'[248] that had been pronounced in 1076 — that is, his granting of the *pallium* to the see of Dol until further legal reasoning might prove in favour of the see of Tours.[249] But this appeasement did little to reconcile Ralph's concerns.

In a letter to the bishops of Brittany and to the clergy and people living in the ecclesiastical province of Tours (1080), Gregory acknowledged the potentially disastrous effects of this controversy, and how much trouble it had caused his 1080 Lenten synod. Ralph's complaints were used as evidence that the church of Tours had lost its rights and that Brittany owed 'subjection and reverence to the church of Tours as its spiritual mother and metropolis'.[250] According to Gregory, Bishop Evenus of Dol had not only failed to produce authority for the Pope's consideration, 'but even his own words put forward in defence seemed to be backed by no authenticity to which credence might be given'. The papacy had presumably discovered that, despite the church of Dol's persistence since the ninth century in winning papal approval, no metropolitan status had ever actually been conferred on a Breton bishop.

[245] Cowdrey, 'Anglo-Norman Church and Kingdom', p. 101.

[246] Julia M. H. Smith, 'The Archbishopric of Dol and the Ecclesiastical Politics of Ninth-Century Brittany', *Studies in Church History*, 18 (1982), 59–70 (p. 60).

[247] See *Reg.*, IV. 13. See also *Reg.*, IV. 17.

[248] *Reg.*, IV. 13.

[249] *Reg.*, IV. 5.

[250] *Reg.*, VII. 15.

Gregory nevertheless deemed it necessary to send Amatus of Oloron and Hugh of Die to Saintes for further legal consideration. In so doing, the Pope sought to clarify this matter in legal terms, appealing to the ancient custom of sees as far back as could be traced, yet having ostensibly decided the outcome beforehand. Gregory stipulated that if his legates could

> recognise that the Bretons have authentic authority of the apostolic see, that is, of such pontiffs whose coming to office and way of life were worthy and lawful, by which they could withdraw themselves from subjection to the said church of Tours, they should henceforth remain undisturbed in their liberty. But if it shall emerge that they cannot have the defence of such authority as we have just mentioned, then, with all controversy being silenced henceforth and for ever, they should recognize the church of Tours as their mother and metropolis, and they should show to your archbishop the subjection and obedience that is proper for a metropolitan, reserving to the bishop of Dol the use of the *pallium*, on condition, however, that none of his successors at any time should aspire to this dignity; but, as we have said above, both they — that is, those who will be appointed to the church of Dol, and also the other bishops of Brittany should remain subject in perpetuity to the jurisdiction of the archbishop of Tours.[251]

This case entailed a lengthy discussion before a settlement was finally reached in favour of Tours.[252] It was decreed at this council, for all succeeding bishops of Brittany, that the monks of Dol should show obedience to the Archbishop of Tours *in perpetuum*.[253] But the dispute was not so easily or quickly laid to rest, carrying on well into Urban II's pontificate and not fully settled until Pope Innocent III's ruling in favour of Tours in 1199.[254] Writing to Archbishop Ralph II of Tours in 1094, Pope Urban II reconfirmed the legatine sentence passed at the Council of Saintes,[255] ratifying this primacy in a letter addressed to all the bishops in Brittany (11 April 1094).[256] One suspects that the hardening papal stance on this issue was occasioned primarily by the inconvenience that it had caused the Roman synod in 1080. Prior to that year, Gregory had only to deal with the matter through letters of complaint, which could be and often were ignored. His familiarity with the legal intricacies of this case remains difficult to assess, as does his genuine concern for the privileges of this metropolitan see before 1080.

[251] *Reg.*, VII. 15.

[252] Mansi, XX, col. 573.

[253] Mansi, XX, col. 574.

[254] Smith, 'Archbishopric of Dol', p. 60.

[255] Pope Urban II, letter 30, *RHGF*, XIV, 708; cf. JL, 5519.

[256] Pope Urban II, letter 31, *RHGF*, XIV, 709–10; cf. JL, 5520.

Admittedly, a settlement between Tours and Dol might not have been so easily reached had it not been for the absence from this council of the Norman bishops and abbots. Their failure to attend earned them episcopal suspensions by Hugh's hand, with exception being granted to the Archbishop of Rouen and the Abbot of la Couture.[257] And as has been examined already, it was at this council that Hugh of Die excommunicated the many knights who failed to surrender tithes — a synodal judgement that was later rescinded by Gregory's intervention, and for which legal action Hugh was admonished by the Pope.

Another dispute raised at this Saintes council concerned the monasteries of Sainte-Croix and Sainte-Radegonde (Poitiers) and their respective rights.[258] The real quarrel surrounded the election of a new deacon to the church of Sainte-Radegonde by the name of Hugh, and his faltering obedience to the abbess. Gregory's letter to the deacon and the other clerks of Sainte-Radegonde (1082) shows that the privileges of this monastery 'anciently granted to the monastery of Sainte-Croix' were being infringed; the clerical duties bound to Sainte-Croix were not being performed, and the church of Sainte-Radegonde was being held 'with its offices without the abbess's licence and authority'.[259] It seems that Hugh the deacon was responsible for diminishing the rights of the church of Sainte-Croix; Amatus of Oloron and Hugh of Die were called in to examine more closely the contents of these privileges.

It was declared at this council that the deacon Hugh was under strict obligation to 'render proper service [*competens servitium*] to both churches'. 'Thus you are in no way to diminish the rights of the church of Sainte-Croix', Gregory added, 'while the abbess may not compel you to do anything which you can refuse by canonical authority.' In order that neither party might overthrow this papal ruling, and so that no further complaints on this issue would ever reach Rome, Gregory threatened a graver censure (*gravior censura*) upon anyone who might 'violate the authority of the rightful privileges of the apostolic see'. Commissioning his legates, while simultaneously dispatching letters of warning, Gregory served to alleviate the Curia in Rome of many regional and local disputes. It proved easier for him to rely on the authority of his agents in matters of local significance, and particularly in matters that could not be given his personal

[257] *Reg.*, IX. 5. Archbishop William of Rouen and the Abbot of la Couture were restored from their suspension.

[258] See Amatus of Oloron, letter 4, p. 767.

[259] *Ep. vag.*, 49.

attention. This was an administrative action upon which Gregory was gradually coming to depend.[260]

According to Amatus of Oloron, however, the primary reason for convening at Saintes was to resolve a quarrel between the monastery of Regula (St Peter de La Réole)[261] — formerly called Squirs — and Bishop Raymond II of Bazas (1057–84).[262] After the church of Saint Benedict of Fleury (Orléans) had held the monastery for sixty years without any dispute, Raymond began complaining that the rights of the monastery were rightfully his by donation charter. How this claim first came into effect is difficult to surmise. It has been suggested (perhaps falsely) that the monastery of Fleury had acquired the monastery as far back as 778, after its foundation by Charlemagne.[263] Unfortunately for the Bishop, there was not enough evidence — 'nec bonam, nec malam' — to support his case. The accusations were thus quickly put to rest, the contemporary charter was confirmed in the presence of Duke William VIII of Aquitaine, and peace and concord were restored to the monastery. Offering testimony to the legislative function, legal authority, and efficiency of the legatine council, this case reached a quick and decisive settlement.[264]

Similar to the role exhibited at Hugh's 1078 Poitevin council, William of Aquitaine's participation can be assessed by his political role in administering justice to the regions under his jurisdiction. Taking advantage of the council (thus legal) arena to confirm this donation charter,[265] William's role at this council again suggests his close ties with the papacy as a patron and benefactor of monastic houses. Since William the Great, the counts of Poitou had established 'un atelier monetaire' at Saintes.[266] The region of Saintonge provided wealthy revenue for the Poitevin counts, and their interest in the ecclesiastical affairs of this region is evident from the surviving council evidence bearing the title *dux Aquitanorum*.[267]

[260] *Ep. vag.*, 49.

[261] Near the Garonne River, in the diocese of Bazas (province of Eauze).

[262] Amatus of Oloron, letter 2, p. 765; cf. Mansi, XX, col. 571.

[263] See *Dictionnaire d'histoire et de géographie ecclésiastiques*, ed. by Luc Courtois and Eddy Louchez, 29 vols to date (Paris: Letouzey et Ané, 1912–), VII, col. 69.

[264] Amatus of Oloron, letter 2, p. 765.

[265] Amatus of Oloron, letter 3, p. 766; cf. Alfred Richard, *Histoire des comtes de Poitou, 778–1204*, 2 vols (Paris: Picard, 1903), I, 350–51.

[266] Richard, *Histoire des comtes de Poitou*, I, 286–87.

[267] See *Cartulaires inédits de la Saintonge: Cartulaire de l'Abbaye Royale de Notre-Dame de Saintes*, ed. by Abbé T. Grasilier, 2 vols (Niort: Clouzot, 1871).

The justice exercised by the Poitevin rulers in this district, both inside and outside of the city of Saintes, was of great importance to settling disputes, demonstrating also the extension of their political power.

Cases such as these show that the summoning of collaborative councils served more than an administrative purpose. Dual representation provided the reformers with a necessary legal satisfaction, offering the papacy more thorough consideration of ongoing and/or contested legal cases, avoiding accusations of prejudice, enhancing their ability to reach appropriate and decisive settlement, while bringing to bear the assistance of apostolic consolation and authority. At times a seemingly superfluous measure, commissioning multiple legates was not an altogether irregular action. A prescribed legal and administrative reasoning presumably existed behind such commissioning — though no established method exists for assessing the effectiveness of such a legal alliance as it benefited the eleventh-century machinery of reform.

With the exception of Saintes,[268] which council gave rise to the excommunication and suspension of all the Norman bishops and abbots who failed to attend, the decisions reached by Hugh and Amatus in conciliar setting can be seen as following closely the reformers' agenda. Determining the legal and administrative necessity for uniting two legates, on the other hand, requires a closer look at Gregory's motivations in summoning councils of this sort. These contributing factors — political as well as religious — are illustrated best through the Pope's attempted collaboration of Hugh of Die with his namesake, the esteemed Abbot of Cluny — meetings which, though planned, never actually materialized in the council arena.

Concerning the excommunication of Bishop Lambert of Thérouanne in 1083, an affair that Gregory considered most weighty (*grandis*) and in need of more searching investigation (*diligens inquisitio*), the Pope commissioned Hugh of Die to assemble together a council of bishops, abbots, and other religious men in association with Abbot Hugh of Cluny (1024–1109).[269] With Hugh regarded as suspect (*suspectus*) to both Lambert and his supporter Count Robert I of Flanders, the Abbot was commissioned alongside Gregory's leading legate in Gallia to deal more fruitfully and effectively with ecclesiastical disputes.[270] This general suspicion — indicating, in Roman legal terms, that he was likely consid-

[268] *Reg.*, IX. 5.

[269] See *Reg.*, IX. 33, 35.

[270] *Reg.* IX. 34 (1083).

ered prejudicial[271] — only intensifies and elucidates Gregory's need for mobilizing a secondary representative agent.

The machinations of King Philip I of France can be credited with fomenting this corrupted disposition. Hugh of Die's history of holding councils in regions deemed undesirable by the King (while securing the support of local counts such as Theobald I of Blois),[272] sentencing high members of the clergy belonging to the *regnum Francorum* (i.e., Archbishops Manasses of Reims, Richerius of Sens, among others),[273] and pronouncing decrees which challenged Philip's role in ecclesiastical matters (i.e., lay investiture at Autun in 1077, simony and clerical unchastity at Poitiers in 1078),[274] had seriously strained their existing relationship. Given such considerations, it becomes increasingly evident that in this and other matters alike, Gregory petitioned for Abbot Hugh of Cluny's assistance so that the suspicion of Hugh of Die's conduct would in no way 'impede the order of things usefully to be done' (ordinem rerum utiliter gerendarum inpediat).[275] Acknowledging the King's suspicions, and the similar mistrust of Hugh's behaviour exhibited by the Count of Flanders and the Bishop of Thérouanne, Gregory took precautionary measures to ensure that this mistrust would not thwart existing relationships and alliances. He did not, it should be noted, ever consider dismissing or replacing his legate but chose rather to balance his judgement with the appointment of a skilled assistant.

Hugh of Cluny's assistance, therefore, was elicited as a 'moderating influence'.[276] Because Hugh of Die's methods for extending and implementing papal reform policy were often viewed by his contemporaries as severe, uncompromising, and

[271] On the legal (Roman) terminology of this right of refusal, not formally adopted into canon law until the later twelfth century (despite its existence in Roman law and later reproduction in the early eleventh century by Burchard of Worms in his *Decretum*, bk I, chap. 63, col. 565: 'Similiter si aliquis episcoporum metropolitanum suspectum habuerit, apud primatem dioceseos, aut apud hanc apostolicam sedem audiatur'), see Linda Fowler, '*Recusatio Iudicis* in Civilian and Canonistic Thought', *Studia Gratiana*, 15 (1972), 718–85 (p. 735).

[272] For Count Theobald's support, see *Reg.*, IV. 22. That the Count of Blois confided in the assistance of Gregory's legates, see particularly Hugh of Die, *RHGF*, XIV, letter 10, 787–88; Mansi, XX, col. 583.

[273] For this account, see *Reg.*, V. 17.

[274] For the Council of Autun, see *Reg.*, IV. 22 and Manasses, *RHGF*, XIV, 611; for the Council of Poitiers, see Hugh of Die, letter 7, PL, CLVII, col. 511, Hugh of Flavigny, p. 419, and Mansi, XX, col. 498.

[275] *Reg.*, IX. 34.

[276] Cowdrey, *Pope Gregory VII*, p. 369.

partisan, the Abbot's role in exercising tolerance and patience is commonly viewed as an attempt to curb the legate's reforming enthusiasm — a characteristic that seemed wholly set on eliminating simony, nicolaitism, and lay investiture. More specifically, Gregory employed the Abbot 'to counter-balance the bishop's severity as he went about the pope's business in France'.[277] As Cowdrey has argued, he was greatly valued as a 'salutary check upon Hugh of Die/Lyons, both as a man of sober judgement who carried authority in French affairs, and as a man of mercy and reconciliation whose characteristic style of action was no less necessary than Hugh of Die/Lyon's zeal and rigour'.[278]

It does well to remember, however, that the Abbot was a legatine assistant, thus never assuming the permanent status of legates like Hugh of Die, Amatus of Oloron, Anselm II of Lucca, and Altmann I of Passau. Theodor Schieffer interpreted these suggested collaborative councils as a papal attempt to divide and share Hugh of Die's legatine authority, but no formal mandate was ever issued to the Abbot that might have legitimized his elevated status to that of a permanent legate.[279] His position falls more accurately among the ancillary ranks of representatives like Hugh Candidus, the monk Teuzo, and the Roman subdeacon Hubert, all of whom were employed under Gregory for assisting as judges in specific, short-term ecclesiastical matters — their powers were delegated and consequently restricted. The Abbot's legal capacity in the case involving the Bishop of Thérouanne, then, was more as 'that of a judge-delegate in a specific case than as a partner in the legatine authority'[280] of Hugh of Die. This point rings even truer when we consider that judges-delegate worked in small teams, 'invested with papal authority for the occasion'.[281] Referring to Hugh of Cluny as quasi-legatine risks exaggerating the true extent of his authority. The prevailing legate-abbot relationship suggests an evident superiority in the former's ability to command in matters of church law.

An earlier example from 1078, involving a list of complaints that had been brought to Gregory's attention by Archbishop Manasses I of Reims, alludes to the Abbot's assistance as a legal formality. The specific details of these cases — which were essentially accusations brought against Archbishop Warmund of Vienne,

[277] Cowdrey, *Pope Gregory VII*, p. 369.

[278] Cowdrey, *Pope Gregory VII*, p. 371.

[279] See *Reg.*, IV. 22.

[280] Schmutz, 'Foundations', p. 228.

[281] Southern, *Making of the Middle Ages*, p. 146.

Bishops Helinand of Laon, Theobald of Soissons, and the provost of Reims — are not as relevant here as Gregory's proposed actions for resolving them. Deigned to act charitably, 'so that the oppressed may find you to be wise defenders, while oppressors may acknowledge you as lovers of righteousness',[282] the Pope again summoned Hugh of Die and Hugh of Cluny's assistance. This approach, as Gregory presumably envisioned, was to evoke a careful and desired balancing of canon law and Christian tolerance. As one can well imagine, attempting to please both the accusers and the accused in matters of litigation was in reality a somewhat impractical expectation. But as Gregory saw it, adhering to the authority of the canons could yield no other result in justice and law than the absolute truth that bound all Christians.

Gregory's letter likewise sheds some light on his understanding of the limits or framework of legatine authority *c.* 1078. Legates, as his March memorandum of that year emphasized, were reminded to exercise charity and mildness in council affairs: 'to bear with some things and even to disregard some things'.[283] They were considered as defenders of the oppressed and protectors against oppression. It becomes evident that Hugh of Cluny's role in conciliar affairs followed closely along these more pastoral lines. The Abbot was a defender of righteousness; the oppressed of the Church could find in him a rational and knowledgeable man willing to defend their well-being, a man who would not pass sentences before seriously considering every angle of a case. This character impression stands very much in contrast to Hugh of Die, who frequently exhibited a swift and decisive temper, yet all the while claiming his close adherence to canonical rigour. As such, he was irrefutably an active agent against oppressors of the Church. His interpretation of canon law, according to Gregory, at times left much to be desired. His method and temperament is described best by the French historian, Augustin Fliche, who reflected on how Hugh of Die considered all procrastination as a weakness, and remained convinced that the best way to provoke returns (*retours*) and conversions to the true Christian faith as dictated by canon law was to hit the episcopate hard (*frapper durement*).[284] The measures necessary to bring about these *retours* were for Hugh a matter of little consideration in relation to the results yielded.

[282] *Reg.*, VI. 3.

[283] *Reg.*, V. 17.

[284] Fliche, *La Réforme Grégorienne*, III, 206.

In considering the papal motives for joining the efforts of both men, one question remains: did Hugh of Die perhaps skilfully avoid collaboration with his Cluniac namesake? Cowdrey argues that he did, chalking Hugh of Die's failure or inability to implement Gregory's requests down to 'differences of temperament and outlook, and also the ancient differences between the Burgundian bishops and the abbots of Cluny about Cluny's liberty'. These conditions, he goes on to argue, 'may have resulted in Hugh of Die's already showing something of the antipathy towards the abbot which became publicly manifest in the sequel to Gregory's death'.[285] Whatever the case, all remaining legatine councils presided over by Hugh between 1078 and 1080 show him to be quite capable and not always unwilling to act with another ecclesiastic in holding councils. One example in particular from 1075[286] might serve to eliminate the possibility of avoidance altogether.

In that year, according to the anonymous author of the vita of Count Simon of Crépy, Hugh of Die and Hugh of Cluny were active in settling a dispute between the Count and King Philip I of France over the lands of Simon's father (Ralph of Valois).[287] The two Hughs were entreated by Gregory to assist and advise the Count on reaching a peaceful settlement with the King in order that the former might rightfully regain his father's lands, which had been attacked and plundered after his death. Hugh of Die's participation in this affair had to be undertaken with the legatine title (*legatus apostolicae sedis*) because his episcopal office would not have extended to ecclesiastical matters of such importance. There is also a point to be made in the fact that Hugh of Die was acting far from his home territory, exceeding his episcopal jurisdiction and falling more comfortably under his legatine jurisdiction. It is entirely possible that this collaborative experience between Hugh of Die and Hugh of Cluny in 1075 created and fostered some ill relations. It could very well be the case that Hugh of Die's experience in dealing with the Abbot was somehow compromised, resulting in the possible thwarting of any further collaborative efforts. Whatever the case, no further meetings were ever recorded between these two men, but this did not prevent Hugh of Die from actively continuing to pursue the reform objectives set out by Gregory and his predecessors.

[285] Cowdrey, *Pope Gregory VII*, p. 371.

[286] For the exact date of this event, see *Chronica Albrici monachi Trium Fontium*, ed. by G. H. Pertz, MGH, SS, 23 (1874), p. 797.

[287] See *Ex vita B. Simonis comitis Crispeiensis*, *RHGF*, XIV (1806), nos i–iv, 37–38.

The legal influence of collaborative councils under Gregory VII can thus be seen as developing alongside the legatine office. Yet among the number of agents at his disposal in the late 1070s and early 1080s, only a select handful of ecclesiastics can be credited with legitimately forging new legal and administrative boundaries. Just as there is no quantitative method for distinguishing the overall legal efficiency created by councils of this genre, very little evidence exists for substantiating Gregory's preferred use of certain legates — other than connections of personal friendship, which are difficult to substantiate from the piecemeal and often one-sided evidence. Many collaborative legatine efforts outside the council arena were assigned to members of the Roman Church (see Appendix 3); Cardinal-bishop Peter of Albano teamed up with Bishop Ulrich of Padua, Cardinal-bishop Hubert of Palestrina with Cardinal-bishop Gerald of Ostia, and Peter (Cardinal-priest of S. Grisogono and librarian of the Holy Roman Church) with John Minutus (Cardinal-priest of S. Maria in Trastavere). The alliance of Hugh of Die with Amatus of Oloron overshadows the infrequent commissioning of legates like Cardinal-bishop Gerald of Ostia with the Roman subdeacon Rainbald, and Abbot Bernard of Saint-Victor (at Marseille) with Cardinal-deacon Bernard, emphasizing Gregory's reliance on — and preference for — those endowed with more permanent status.

Of course, not all collaborative legatine efforts culminated in the holding of a council. Failing to secure safe passage through Germany from either Henry IV or Rudolf of Swabia (1077), as mentioned above, Gregory called on the assistance of his legates Cardinal-deacon Bernard and Abbot Bernard of Marseille.[288] Forced to seek refuge in Lombardy, the Pope confirmed the authority granted to his legates in clearing a path for his safe journey towards his intended destination, in order to settle the ongoing kingship dispute. Gregory took care to note that if either king prevented his legates from fulfilling this task, they were to 'resist him by all means and with all your powers to death if need be, while likewise forbidding him the government of the whole kingdom'. In a pastoral letter addressed to all the faithful in Germany, Gregory attempted to make known the obedience that must be exhibited to his legates, confirming penalties against those who might get in their way.[289] This contemporary example helps contextualize the potential struggles of legates perambulating in a foreign province, and Gregory's

[288] See *Reg.*, IV. 23.

[289] *Reg.*, IV. 24.

challenge in enforcing their legal precedence outside of Rome — through individual or collaborative commissioning.

In light of these considerations, very little evidence exists for linking collaborative councils of this period with an increase in legatine efficiency and/or administration. At least, the available sources are not so precise as to admit the benefits that possibly coincide with employing two legates in the council arena. There is nothing to convince us that the cases under discussion were receiving more thorough legal and moral consideration as a result of this enhanced papal representation, though this is surely in part what Gregory intended. Nor is there any evidence to suggest that a council's legal authority was enhanced through the presidence of multiple agents. We can only assume that this was the case: it seems that there would have been little reason for summoning councils of this sort without these administrative and legal objectives in mind. And Gregory's providing his agents with greater authority and independence in juristic matters was surely not intended to weaken or disassociate his interest with the provincial affairs filtering into Rome. On the contrary, the legatine office transformed under Gregory's care to suit the reformers' immediate legal and administrative needs.

Summoning collaborative councils was thus a further extension of this papal concern for upholding righteousness, influenced by Gregory's care for the extant political and spiritual climate. Dual representation was, as the above examples have shown, a perfectly viable measure for reaching these desired objectives. Instilling his legates with a procedural competence in the holding of councils, and educating them with the effective application of law in the council arena, Gregory created a willing body of government in tune with his desired reforming policies. The success of these alliances, on the other hand, was determined as much by the reformer's objectives as by the merits and competency of those undertaking the legatine office. Again, as these examples illustrate, the legal cognisance of individual figures like Hugh of Die was tantamount to ensuring the successful application of law and reform in the regions of his jurisdiction and beyond.

Of course, collaboration was not essential to ensuring the penetration of reform at local levels. The historical narrative for Hugh of Die's Council of Valence (May 1079),[290] for example, which convened to deal with the contested abbacy of Déols (also known as Bourg-Dieu),[291] illustrates this point clearly. The Cluniac monk, Warmund of Vienne, had been appointed abbot to this monastery

[290] In the ecclesiastical province of Vienne, approximately seventy-two kilometres south of Lyon.

[291] Located close to Châteauroux, in the diocese of Bourges.

in 1074, and remained in this office until his death *c.* 1081, even after his election to the archbishopric of Vienne in 1076.[292] The monks of Déols, however, raised up their own candidate by the name of Walter, ignoring entirely the excommunication issued at Gregory's 1079 Lenten synod.[293] It would seem that Warmund's perpetual absences from the abbey, due in most part presumably to his archiepiscopal duties, had led the monks to install a replacement abbot of their own accord.[294] In his efforts to secure obedience and devotion for Warmund (the papacy's preferred choice), Gregory ordered the monks to present themselves at Valence on the first Sunday after Pentecost (18 May) to await Hugh of Die's judgement on the matter.[295] Ostensibly, their ignoring of the canons caused Gregory the greatest offence, for there was hardly a more serious threat to the Roman Church than disobedience, which was tantamount to heresy.

In a similar letter, eight lay magnates[296] in the region of Bourges were accused of rejecting Warmund and invading the abbey of Déols 'against what is right and against an apostolic excommunication'.[297] The Pope threatened these aristocratic men with excommunication so that they would cease interfering in local ecclesiastical affairs and so that his preferred abbot might ultimately receive due obedience. Like the monks of Déols before them, the lay magnates' presence was requested in Valence to hear Hugh of Die's judgement.[298] The Pope's delegation to his legate of matters involving local and regional lay elite is a good example of his reliance on Hugh's knowledge of local affairs. It might be suggested further that Hugh's prior associations with this region — as both a son to the abbey of Romans (Saint-Bernard, diocese of Vienne)[299] and Bishop of Die — would have enhanced his social and legal standing among the concerned parties. This was, after all, one considered reason for appointing ultramontane (*ultramontanus*)

[292] D. N. Huyghebaert, 'Un Légat de Grégoire VII en France: Warmond de Vienne', *RHE*, 40 (1944/45), 187–200 (especially p. 188).

[293] *Reg.*, VI. 27.

[294] Huyghebaert, 'Un Légat de Grégoire VII', p. 190.

[295] *Reg.*, VI. 27.

[296] Lords Ralph of Châteauroux, Oddo of Issoudun, Eppo of Charenton and la Châtre, Humbald of Vierzon and Mehun, Everard of Argenton, Boso of Cluis, Girald of Linières, and Adelard of Chateaumeillant.

[297] *Reg.*, VI. 28.

[298] *Reg.*, VI. 28.

[299] See *Reg.*, II. 59.

legates in the first instance: as a means for settling matters in the localities where they first came to light.

Both of Gregory's letters give the impression that neither the monks of Déols nor the lay magnates were really opposed to Warmund's appointment. Because the excommunicated abbot, Walter, had been the monks' preferred choice, his deposition had caused a deeper and perhaps more personal rift among the ecclesiastical and secular community. The succession of abbots had presumably for long rested within the nobility of local lay families in this region. Indeed, the selection of bishops and abbots leading up to the eleventh-century reform was almost always influenced by such secular factors, and this was hardly a custom that ended with the turn of the century.

In order for this case to have been considered at Valence as Gregory outlined in his letter, the attendance of all concerned parties was essential. Gregory's position on this matter can be interpreted from a letter to Archbishop Gozelin of Bordeaux written in 1074, citing Pseudo-Isidore to the effect that 'canonical authority does not support an accusation in writing when the persons concerned are absent, nor does it admit cases without an examination of the parties which is well established by scrutiny'.[300] For the dispute not to have been settled might suggest that the monks of Déols, as well as the eight aforementioned members of the local aristocracy, remained stubborn in their disobedience. The fact that there are no records for their excommunication, that Warmund was soon after promoted to the abbacy of Déols, and that no further record of this case can be found in the papal *Register*, strongly suggests that his installation took place, and could only have taken place, in the presence of the aforementioned men in a formal council setting under Hugh of Die's supervision and presidency.

In terms of its influence for further promoting Gregory's reforming objectives, the Council of Valence appears to have contributed very little. Hugh of Die only ever considered the one case discussed here, and this single affair was only awarded papal-legatine attention because of the Pope's vested interest in the concerned monastery of Déols. Complaints launched by the monks of this abbey against Warmund of Vienne had presumably been filtering into Rome since as early as 1074, the year that this monastery first came under the Pope's care: when Warmund was appointed to the abbacy. The possible attention given to this matter by the Curia between 1074 and 1079 — though our knowledge is limited

[300] *Reg.*, II. 4. See Pseudo-Calixtus II, in Hinschius, chap. 17, p. 141, and Pseudo-Stephanus, in Hinschius, chap. 8, p. 185.

by a sheer lack of evidence — serves once again to explain why Gregory's *Register* is the only source for determining the course of events for this council.

The evidence *ex silentio*, however, does not imply the unimportance of this council meeting. Rather, it brings to light many questions concerning the Pope's motivation in seeking clarification and judgement in a matter far from Rome. The simple fact that Hugh of Die was active in this region is evidence enough that the Council of Valence carried more weight than a local or diocesan council. There remains, of course, a possibility that Hugh's presence in that region of Vienne was nothing more than the papacy's attempt at power control, in effect extending the reformers' legal and moral influence through the charismatic leadership of this agent of reform. It would be inaccurate, however, to suggest outright the legate's presence as a direct means to assert papal primacy. There is simply not enough evidence to support this claim.

Bearing the council's outcome in mind, the Pope's incentive for organizing this assembly does not appear disingenuous. The Council of Valence was certainly not convened to disseminate reforming policies outright — it was simply too small and local of a meeting. From an entirely historical perspective, the general purpose for convening this council was dispute settlement. Other than the Gregory's personal interest in safeguarding the rights of Déols, there is no evidence of his attempt to assert a reforming agenda of any sort. Hugh of Die's earlier-held councils at Autun (1077) and Poitiers (1078), by comparison, were much more aligned with this greater papal objective, intended to issue decrees and sentences which might resonate to the very borders of Christendom.

Other legatine councils, like those held in 1079 by Hugh of Die at Bordeaux, Toulouse, and Valence, were clearly of less significance than those just mentioned. They were convened to deal with individual and specific cases, to settle drawn-out disputes that had been gestating in the localities for varied lengths of time, and often, cases about which the Pope was not well informed, nor had the time or care to be. Their overall importance does not rival the Autun or Poitiers councils, whose outcomes echoed more closely the spiritual, moral, and legal sentiment of Gregory's 1074/75/76/78 Roman councils, and the efforts begun by his papal predecessors. But for all participants, especially the plaintiff(s) and the accused, regional and local legatine councils offered the only objective means for dispute settlement. Through the legal medium of a legate and his council, the Pope's ultimate review would prevail, eliminating any lingering or interfering elements of local power politics, particularly those emanating from the temporal sphere.

At Valence in 1079, the eight lay magnates opposing Warmund's promotion to the abbacy of Déols were ultimately threatened and removed from the picture, though Gregory still relied on their cooperation for enforcing Hugh's conciliar decision. For the monks of Déols, being summoned to a legatine council forced them to accept what they had long resisted: to pay due reverence and obedience to the papal-selected Cluniac monk, Warmund of Vienne. Finally, for the papacy, the Council of Valence fulfilled its primary function(s) for settling a long-held dispute, upholding the rights of its ecclesiastical properties and appointments in a distant region, all the time asserting its overlordship over the local church and lay elite. Significantly, the roots of church reform were held strong by obedience and justice in the localities. Continuous efforts by reformers like Hugh of Die were crucial to safeguarding the papacy's struggle to maintain spiritual, moral, and legal dominance throughout Western Christendom.

To emphasize this point, consider the further and final example of Hugh of Die's 1080 Lyonnais council, at which meeting the legate examined the strife between Archbishop Gebuin of Lyon (1077–82) and Abbot Hugh of Cluny, stemming from a property dispute between the Abbot and Bishop Landeric of Mâcon (1074–96).[301] After hearing complaints about the Cluniac abbot's invasion of the church of Mâcon's temporal rights,[302] Gregory requested that the dispute be settled out of court, placing the Abbot in charge of the negotiations. If the complaints laid by Landeric were deemed false, then the rights of the church were to be retained. If, however, there was any truth in the complaints against him, the rights were to be returned 'without a disturbance' or for a 'suitable exchange'.[303] If no settlement could be reached, which one can easily imagine might be the case when the stake is personal, then the matter was to be brought before Hugh of Die and Abbot Bernard of Saint-Victor (at Marseille) for settlement. Significantly, Hugh of Cluny was charged with the authority to negotiate a settlement that entirely affected his own interests — in a case in which he was a concerned party; Gregory's role was that of mediator. It is little wonder then that the discussion either broke down, or was perhaps never even initiated, ultimately bringing the case before Hugh of Die in a formal council setting.

That Hugh of Die was already familiar with this dispute is certain, having been urged by the Pope in 1079 to consider the affair at his next legatine council. In this letter, Gregory expressed his distress over the contention between these two great religious men. 'In truth', he wrote, 'just as concord between them could and

[301] This crisis likely originated *c.* 1074, the year that Landeric succeeded Drogo to the see of Mâcon. See Cowdrey, *Cluniacs*, p. 52.

[302] Cowdrey, in *Ep. vag.*, p. 77 n. 5.

[303] *Reg.*, VI. 33.

would benefit many, so there is no doubt that serious harm may and will arise to very many people from their disagreement.'[304] The fact that Gregory found it necessary to inform his legate about the nature of the dispute, before the Abbot was given sufficient time to resolve it of his own accord, suggests to me two things: the Abbot's potential unwillingness to return the rights to the church of Mâcon, and Gregory's personal interest in settling the dispute once and for all. Because both letters were issued simultaneously, it is plausible to suggest that Gregory had anticipated the Abbot's refusal for dispute settlement.

Whatever the Pope's true intentions, there is a sense here that Hugh of Cluny was in unlawful possession of the property rights.[305] By the time that the Council of Lyon met, nine or ten months after the dispatching of this letter, the quarrel between the Abbot and the clerks of Mâcon had yet to be settled. Gregory's forewarning to the Abbot evidently had very little effect, and his trust that the matter might be resolved out of court went unrewarded. The final resolution of this dispute is nowhere directly mentioned in the existing sources, and it remains impossible to verify whether Hugh of Cluny was even in attendance at Lyon. His personal interest in the property rights of the church would certainly have benefited from his absence; in prolonging the dispute, the Abbot could have held on to the property rights for a delayed period of time. Based on the evidence *ex silentio*, however, we are left assuming that the case was settled at some point during Hugh of Die's Lyonnais council. No further complaints from the clerks of Mâcon are found in the papal *Register*, which suggests that Hugh of Cluny did eventually accede to Gregory's demands. This being the case, credit can surely be given to Gregory's effective use of papal legation, threatening more thorough investigation of a case that he clearly intended to be resolved locally.

Existing records for this council, particularly Gregory's letter to Hugh of Die (1079), offer an interesting template for understanding the agent-principal relationship between pope and legate. The cases at Lyon are prime examples of the resistance facing church reformers in the early 1080s, in what can be treated as serious challenges to their reforming objectives in France. In dealing with both *causae maiores et minores*, Hugh was given specific instructions on the manner in which individual cases ought to be settled. The dispute between Cluny and Mâcon is but one example of the Pope's dependence on the office of legation for settling regional matters. For the most part, these cases were unfamiliar or of little

[304] *Ep. vag.*, 30.

[305] *Ep. vag.*, 70.

interest or concern to the Holy See. In delegating authority to his legate in France, Gregory was continually shaping the parameters of legatine authority, consequently limiting the level of supervision required in administering ecclesiastical matters in distant regions. The office of legation was being transformed consciously by Gregory to meet the administrative and legal needs of his government, but also to compensate for the papacy's inadequacy in dealing with matters far from Rome. It seems to me that these elements are not mutually exclusive: both played an important role in disseminating reforming principles to the various provinces of Western Christendom.

Chapter 7

Conclusion

The final years of Hugh of Die's first legation, from 1082 to 1085, were sporadic as a consequence of Gregory VII's political decline in Rome. As a direct consequence, the efficiency with which this legate was able to carry out the terms of his office was greatly diminished. To what extent Hugh's role in Gregory's reform programme to France was tied up with the politics of Rome, however, remains to be assessed; it is this latter consideration that forms the basis of this conclusion. For on the whole, the years 1082 to 1085 held much opportunity for Hugh of Die to maintain a foothold in the council arena. The existing political circumstances north of the Alps, and the ongoing abuses being carried out against the church in France, provided this legate with ample opportunity for continuing in his quest for a pure and chaste episcopate, through the continued implementation of righteousness, justice (*iustitia*), and law (*ius*). Hugh's reforming campaign over the course of these years depended heavily upon external papal factors of authority, supervision, and instruction, not to mention lay support in the regions where councils were being held — features that are commonly overlooked in the existing scholarship of this period, or at the very least taken for granted.

After successive legatine councils at Lyon (January/February 1080), Avignon (February 1080), Saintes (8 January 1081), Issoudun (18 March 1081), and Meaux (26 October 1082), Hugh of Die convened a council at Lyon late in 1082 to deal with Count Fulk IV 'le Réchin' of Anjou (1043–1109), whose cruel treatment of the church of Tours was discovered. Among those in attendance at this council were Bishops Agano of Autun, Robert of Langres, Walter of Cavaillon, Landeric of Mâcon (vice-primate of the church of Lyon), with all the clerics, bishops, abbots, clerks, and monks from the province of Tours. As far as numbers go, this was a well-attended gathering of mostly suffragan bishops to

Lyon, with the exception of Cavaillon, which see was subordinate to the Pope alone. Significantly, however, Hugh of Die's participation at this council is under question. A description in the conciliar evidence of Landeric of Mâcon as 'vice primatis curam gerentes ecclesiae Lugdunensis'[1] suggests this prelate's role as provincial representative in Hugh's absence. One suspects that Hugh, at the time of the council, was likely on his way to Rome to receive the *pallium* for his recent translation to the archdiocese of Lyon.[2] There is also reference in the papal sources to a sentence issued against the canons of Saint-Martin by 'our legates'[3] — which offers an intriguing contradiction. Although vague in its Latin description, this reference implies the presidency of Hugh of Die and Amatus of Oloron — the only legates active in France during this period. The absence of any further descriptive evidence associating Hugh with the council proceedings, however, makes it difficult to prove that Lyon was anything more than a diocesan or provincial council — the more likely scenario.

Complicating matters further is Hugh of Flavigny's account, which fails to mention this council. In fact, this chronicle fails to record any conciliar activity following Hugh of Die's Council of Avignon in 1080. It is worth asking here whether this silence is enough to discount the legate's conciliar participation outright? The councils of Saintes (1081), Issoudun (1081), and Meaux (1082) were all councils held in conjunction with Amatus of Oloron, and all convened beyond the borders of Hugh's assigned legatine jurisdiction of northern France and Burgundy, yet they do not merit any attention in Hugh of Flavigny's *Chronicon*. And even more disparagingly for the council historian, the records for the 1082 Lyonnais council are not so descriptive as to mention exactly who presided. It is primarily our inability to locate Hugh of Die's whereabouts following the Council of Meaux that makes his participation at Lyon impossible to verify. Even though his position as Archbishop of Lyon would certainly have merited his presence there, it would be futile to speculate further.

What this evidence suggests is that from 1082 onwards, Hugh of Die's role in the ecclesiastical affairs of France loses its intensity. From 1075 to 1082, as this study has shown, Hugh's presence in the council arena remained constant; the number of councils being held has proved the only variable figure. But following the Council of Avignon in 1080, Hugh's name begins to slowly disappear from

[1] Mansi, XX, col. 588.

[2] *Reg.*, VI. 34–35, and Pope Urban II's letter (no. 165, PL, CLI, cols 438–39) to Hugh of Die.

[3] *Ep. vag.*, 52.

the primary sources. And indeed, following the Council of Meaux in 1082, his name disappears altogether until 1085. Needless to say, this historiographical gap poses a large problem for the historian of this period. Yet this inactivity is more a hindsight interpretation of Gregory's pontificate, considered in relation to the strong imperial resistance from King Henry IV of Germany and his supporters. At the time, following the Council of Meaux in 1082, there were no indications that Hugh's reforming efforts were about to experience a period of recession of any sort. His translation to the archdiocese of Lyon later that year would have suggested quite the opposite, if anything foreshadowing an even more active career with the possession of two important ecclesiastical offices. Whatever the reasons, Hugh's zeal and confidence once exhibited in preceding councils seems to have been hindered severely. The question remains to what, if anything, can this apparent decline be attributed?

To suggest hostility, a deterioration, or collapse in the papal-legatine relationship is entirely unfounded and should be dismissed immediately. Despite his receiving a papal warning in March 1078 for his actions at the councils of Autun (1077) and Poitiers (1078),[4] and again following his Council of Saintes in 1081,[5] there is no reason to suggest a decline in Hugh of Die's enthusiasm for implementing reform in the regions of Gallia. In both cases just mentioned, Gregory was acting in accordance with canonical rigor (*rigor canonicus*) while Hugh ostensibly struggled to adopt the Pope's theoretical notion of canonical tolerance and restraint of discretion (*discretionis temperantiam*). It likewise proves impossible to blame the declining number of legatine councils during these final years of Gregory's pontificate on the sparse evidence. The records for this period are certainly wanting — particularly in the papal *Register* — leaving significant gaps in the historiography, but there is a sense that the root of Hugh's council inactivity goes much deeper than this. External political and administrative factors in Rome surely played a much greater part than the evidence admits.

Very few theories, in fact, can be drawn from existing conciliar records *c.* 1082–85. After more than two years of council inactivity, reflected by a silence in the sources following his 1082 Lyonnais council, Hugh of Die convened a council at Brioude (in the Auvergne) in 1085 to settle a dispute between Archbishop Ralph I of Tours and the monastery of Marmoutier. Hugh presided over this meeting with special assistance from Bishops William of Auxerre and

[4] *Reg.*, V. 17.

[5] *Reg.*, IX. 5.

Dalmatius of Narbonne, in addition to other bishops and abbots from various provinces. One further consideration is that Amatus of Oloron assisted at this council in the legal capacity of co-presider, but this conjecture comes only from the records of a later meeting in Dol (also in 1085), where the charges against the Archbishop of Tours were confirmed.[6]

The neglect of this council in contemporary sources questions the purpose and legitimacy of its meeting. It is worthwhile, perhaps, to speculate on whether Brioude should be considered a legatine *concilium* at all, in the strict contemporary sense of the word. In terms of its importance to Hugh of Die's reforming efforts, it seems at first glance insignificant, yet Hugh's presence there was nonetheless mandatory. There seems to be more to this dispute than the evidence admits, especially when considering the grave matter of excommunicating a metropolitan archbishop. That the Archbishop of Tours shared a long-standing friendship with Hugh since 1075 is worth iterating in this regard, demonstrating a relationship complete with council summonses on the one hand, and accusations for clerical misconduct on the other.

The potential significance of meeting at Brioude, however, is reflected best in the evidence for Dol, a colloquium held shortly afterwards confirming the decisions promulgated at Brioude, in effect making the charges known to a wider audience.[7] But some ambiguities still remain: Mansi, for instance, does not reveal the sources for his record of either meeting, but his account of Brioude was ostensibly taken verbatim from a record of Marmoutier.[8] The majority of council participants listed in this short account, indeed those who were present to confirm Ralph's excommunication charge, were from among the episcopate.[9] There is also a vague reference to 'many other bishops and abbots'. But from this evidence comes a sense that this dispute was of a very local or regional interest, despite the outcome of excommunication.[10]

[6] *De tribulationibus [...]* [*Tabula of Marmoutier*], in *RHGF*, XIV (1806), 95; cf. Mansi, XX, col. 798.

[7] Mansi, XX, col. 799.

[8] *Tabula of Marmoutier*, *RHGF*, XIV, 95, is the only known source for this council. Cited by Mansi (XX, cols 797–800), this excerpt is extracted from the work of Laurent Bouchel (1588–1629) ('ex editione Laurentii Bochelli') — taken from his 1619 edition of Gregory of Tours *in-octavo*, and later incorporated by Bouquet (1806). The true source of this commentary is unknown.

[9] These were the *praesuli* (i.e., bishops) of Le Mans and Poitiers, with the assistance of the lord abbot, Prior Bernard, and many brothers from the congregation of Marmoutier.

[10] Mansi, XX, cols 799–800.

Resulting primarily from the nominal conciliar evidence, the exact date of Brioude also remains in dispute. Mansi, most likely using Labbe and Mabillon as his guides, provides the inaccurate date of 1094, placing the council during Urban II's (1088–99) pontificate.[11] Jean Liron, on the other hand, in *Singularités historiques et littéraires*, argued that this meeting took place in 1085, before the death of Pope Victor III (1087) and quite ostensibly during the lifetime of Archbishop Ralph I of Tours († 1086), who was of course the figure under investigation.[12] Carefully weighing but ultimately rejecting the evidence provided by Mabillon (whose work also relied on the record of Marmoutier), while pointing out the many dating faults in that monastery's record, Liron's argument is by far the most convincing.[13] Supported most recently by Odette Pontal (1995),[14] this line of reasoning seems the most persuasive, especially when taking into account Urban II's church dedication to the monastery of La Sauve Majeure (Silva Major — near Bordeaux) in 1095/96, which later record places the council approximately ten years prior (1085).[15]

The scanty evidence for the Council of Brioude nevertheless fails to render a complete account of its importance, but perhaps this should not be our primary interest. It seems to me more fruitful to consider this council in the wider context of Hugh of Die's reforming efforts under Gregory VII. It should not be forgotten that following this meeting, Hugh's legatine activity came to a precipitous halt after an active and intensive ten-year period in office — expiring only with Gregory's death in May 1085. Hugh's initiative leading up to this point, from 1080 to 1085, exhibited some noticeable changes in momentum, but this does not suggest a marked decline in the need for reform or in his ability to disseminate legislation to the various regions of France. His legation was influenced by external political factors confronting the papacy in Italy. Explaining the extent to which Hugh's own reforming objectives were tied up with the politics of Rome, however, is not a simple task. It is debatable whether the papacy's ability

[11] Mansi, XX, cols 799–800. Mansi erroneously indicates the date MCXIV, clearly inverting the X and C, to mean 1094 and not 1114.

[12] Jean Liron, *Singularités historiques et littéraire*, 12 vols (Paris: Didot, 1738–40), IV (1740) 454–94.

[13] Liron, *Singularités historiques et littéraire*, IV, 466 passim.

[14] Pontal, *Les Conciles de la France*, p. 187.

[15] See the *Tabula of Marmoutier*, *RHGF*, XIV, 95 n. '(b)': 'Tandem pacis et concordiae gratia inter nos et Turonenses B. Mauricii canonicos, jam tunc decennio nos persequi non cessantes, faciendae, monasterio nostro ab eodem visitato.'

to implement reform in the provinces could be severed completely without direct representation. The deterioration of the agent-principal relationship as a result of this political and administrative decline was imminent, but there were factors on the demand side impelling this development.

To make sense of the evidence *ex silentio*, Hugh of Die's inactivity in the council arena is considered best in view of the political conditions facing Gregory's pontificate *c.* 1082-85.[16] The Pope's declining political power in Rome caused by King Henry IV's military campaigns to Italy in 1080–81 and 1081–82, the Emperor's capture of Rome in 1083–84, the strengthening Guibertine factions in Germany and northern Italy (including Rome), and Gregory's eventual exile to Salerno under the leadership of Robert Guiscard and the Normans (June 1084) — all had damaging effects on his ability to administer and lead the Roman Church and its administration as pope. But to what degree did Gregory's being distant from Rome affect the legatine action that was by definition remote from Rome? It would prove mere speculation to blame the evident decrease in Hugh's council activity on a lack of reforming initiative. The abuses of the French clergy were certainly far from being fully eradicated, leaving little reason for Hugh's deteriorating or lacking incentive. Furthermore, Hugh would have continued to administer his archiepiscopal office despite the prevailing conditions in Rome, and his energy in promulgating and implementing reform, as demonstrated by his second legation under Urban II from *c.* 1094 to 1099 was far from being extinguished.

The consequences of weakened papal supervision are thus manifest: as the Pope lost his grip on the eternal city, so too did he lose his ability to govern Christendom and administer the provinces. For the early 1080s, as Cowdrey aptly noted, 'when Gregory was hard-pressed at Rome by Henry IV of Germany, it was more difficult than ever for him to keep track of events in France'.[17] But to what extent did Hugh rely on papal instructions for the governing of his office? A glance back at the ten years of Hugh's first legation clearly shows the developing character of an independent and self-assured administrator and arbitrator. With increasing experience in the council arena, Hugh had come to expect a level of papal interference. By 1082 he had certainly shown himself competent enough to handle the ecclesiastical matters in France under his own initiative, despite the occasional papal warning for the severity of his actions. Why, then, are we con-

[16] For a summary of the events that unfolded between Gregory VII and Henry IV, see Cowdrey, *Pope Gregory VII*, pp. 199–231, and Blumenthal, *Investiture Controversy*, pp. 113–34.

[17] Cowdrey, *Pope Gregory VII*, p. 365.

fronted with this conciliar silence for the final years of Gregory's pontificate? To what degree is our interpretation of this period limited by the extant evidence?

It seems unlikely that the political, moral, and religious climate of Hugh's jurisdiction did not warrant the convening of councils between 1082 and 1085. Offering some comparison, only four other church councils were held in France over these years: at Charroux (11 November 1082), Saintes (1083), Compiègne (1085), and Oissel (5 September 1082), Châlons-sur-Marne (1084)[18] — an evident decline in activity for Latin Christendom. It is most certainly the case that the papal chancery was not so systematic as to include every matter of business in the *Register* during these turbulent years of Gregory's pontificate. Whatever the case, the essential point is that without papal consent and instruction, the legatine privilege, authority, and jurisdiction to convene councils was rendered null and void.

This condition calls to mind the well-known theoretical concept of papal supremacy (Matthew 16. 18), which legal and administrative maxim is represented also in Gregory's *Dictatus papae* (*c.* 1075).[19] In practice, however, theories of papal command were seldom recognized in practice, especially in the *ad hoc* and sometimes hostile environment of the council arena. Yet in light of all the transformations that the legatine office experienced as it became more formalized under Gregory VII, the basis of legatine authority still derived theoretically from papal delegation and jurisdiction.[20] And originating at the Pope's commission, powers in practice and legitimization of office were authorities that could be revoked just as easily. This means that no matter how detached a legate might be from Rome — either politically or geographically — he was influenced inevitably by the prevailing political climate and circumstances affecting the Pope. Given this practical reality, the declining political situation in Rome must surely be regarded as the key influence in bringing Hugh's reforming initiative to a standstill.

Considering the close legal ties binding pope and legate, particularly in matters of authority and jurisdiction, the effects of a waning papal administration become increasingly prevalent. The importance of maintaining communications with the pope makes it plausible to suggest that without frequent correspondence, and without instruction on specific legal cases, Hugh of Die would have possessed

[18] See Mansi, XX, cols 579–82 (Oissel); col. 581 (Charroux); col. 589 (Saintes); col. 610 (Châlons-sur-Marne); col. 610 (Compiègne).

[19] See *Reg.*, II. 55a.

[20] Figueira, *Plenitude of Power*, p. 74.

little reason or incentive to hold a legatine council. For this reason, it seems slightly out of place for a council to have convened at Brioude in 1085. With Gregory having already been exiled to Salerno, it is unlikely that Hugh took the unprecedented measure of convening a council of his own accord, effectively abusing the Pope's fullness of power. Believing that he did would provide a wholly unsatisfying end to Hugh's first legatine term; it would have been an uncharacteristic move on his part, and acting entirely against the authority of his office.

But other than a pressing need to settle the dispute between Archbishop Ralph I of Tours and the monks of Marmoutier, what other suitable explanation can be offered? It seems far more likely, despite the possible presence and participation of his fellow legate Amatus of Oloron, that Brioude was nothing more than a provincial council, convened under the auspices of Hugh's title of primate over the ecclesiastical provinces of Lyon, Tours, Sens, and Rouen. This would certainly justify his holding a council without papal approval, offering perhaps the only viable explanation for convening at this location. If this is indeed the case, it could be argued that Hugh's conciliar activity as legate — and possibly even his legatine activity outright — ceased to function after 1082.

A wider consideration of legatine activity in the early to mid-1080s serves to confirm this suspicion. Sent by the Pope to selected regions of France in 1084 for (amongst other duties) the collection of papal revenues (Peter's Pence),[21] Cardinal-bishop Peter of Albano ('legati nostrae apostolicae sedis') and Prince Gisulf of Salerno were commissioned to publicize Gregory's renewed excommunication of Henry IV and the anti-pope Clement III (Guibert of Ravenna) — a sentence issued at the Council of Salerno shortly after the Pope's arrival there in July 1084. In the same year, Peter of Albano was dispatched to Germany with Cardinal-bishop Odo of Ostia for a similar cause.[22] In 1085, as Bernold of Constance informs us, Odo convened a council at Quedlinburg (Quitelineburg) from 20 to 26 April under the title *legatus domni apostolici*, the outcome of which saw Guibert of Ravenna (and not Henry IV) anathematized as a heresiarch, apostate, and invader of the apostolic see.[23] From these three cases, particular attention should be given to Gregory's choice of legates; it is certainly curious, for instance, that neither Hugh of Die nor Amatus of Oloron were selected as his preferred messengers to France. That Gregory entrusted this dissemination to

[21] *Reg.*, VIII. 23; see also *Ep. vag.*, 54.

[22] Bernold of Constance, *Chronicon*, year 1084, p. 445.

[23] Bernold of Constance, *Chronicon*, year 1085, pp. 448–52; cf. Becker, *Papst Urban II*, pp. 71–75.

less-experienced and temporary papal legates serves to illustrate just how varied his use of legates could be, implying also that Hugh and Amatus were likely absent from his court at Salerno.

In view of this changing political climate, the reformers' campaign in France can be judged as being only partially successful. But this does not mean that Gregory and Hugh's initiative in this region should go entirely unnoticed, regardless of the Pope's legislation having only a marginal effect on later canonical collections. Over the course of his twelve-year pontificate, with particular emphasis on the first four years of his reign (1073–77), the consolidation of Gregory's reforming programme brought the papacy one step closer to transforming reforming objectives into reality. By the end of 1078, the entire *societas Christiana* had been notified of this papal policy in some shape or form, and to the seriousness with which matters of clerical chastity, simony, and lay investiture were being treated henceforth. But unlike many of his predecessors, Gregory had managed to disseminate Roman decrees more successfully into regions beyond Italy with the help of a developing machinery of legation and law, and particularly — as this study has shown — through the legatine work of Hugh of Die.

But soon after the contested election of his papal successor Victor III (1086–87), 'the expedients which had been adventurous in the days of Gregory VII became antiquated'.[24] Successive popes gradually ceased viewing native, permanent legates as essential instruments for administering the various provinces, at least not to the same extent as that exhibited by Gregory VII's administration. Neither was the legal function of reforming legates entirely abolished with Gregory's passing, although their ability to operate throughout Western Christendom was decreased noticeably in the late 1080s and 1090s.

Despite Ivo of Chartres's success in having Hugh of Die promoted to the legatine office under Pope Urban II *c.* 1093/94,[25] the conciliar activity carried out during this second legation pales in comparison to the years 1075–85. The itinerant nature of Urban's pontificate, moreover, and the numerous councils convened by this pope in France, must have unsettled the intensity of legatine activity in the 1090s. Finally, Ivo's attempt to extend Hugh's legation for a third term under Paschal II (1099–1118) did not come to fruition. Hugh, perhaps not

[24] Southern, *Making of the Middle Ages*, p. 146.

[25] See Rony, 'La Légation d'Hugues', p. 129; Ivo of Chartres, letter 24, PL, CLXII, cols 35–36: 'Sed hanc meam laetitiam postea pertubavit quod mihi dictum est te in tanta pertubatione humerum (tuum v.c.) hunc oneri nolle supponere.' See also Ivo of Chartres, *Correspondance*, letters 24, 54, 55, 59, 60, 62, 65, 68.

reluctantly, lived out the rest of his years as primate and archbishop of Lyon, until his death at Susa (near Turin) in 1106.[26] From this gradual decline in ecclesiastical responsibility comes a sense that the papacy no longer desired or needed Hugh's ecclesiastical services in personal, legislative, or administrative terms.

A glance at the fifty or so years following Gregory's death strongly supports this conclusion. For France in the late eleventh and twelfth centuries, the scope of legation was narrowing perceptively, placing this administrative office as it existed in the eleventh century into more specific context. Against the hundred or so legatine councils held in this region between 1050 and 1140, no more than fifteen councils were held over the remaining part of the twelfth century — a considerable decline from Gregory's pontificate.[27] Such a pattern can be attributed to the reforming papacy's more immediate need for permanent legation, which administrative office gradually diminished in usefulness as other church institutions became more structured and formalized in the twelfth and thirteenth centuries. It was particularly the papacy's growing ability to handle legal matters autonomously, with the help of newer ecclesiastical offices like judge-delegate, and the more readily available church courts and bodies of consolidated canon law, that diminished the need for legatine support, to the extent of eliminating permanent native legation altogether. After Gregory VII, as Southern convincingly argued, 'new mechanisms had to be devised to bridge the gap between Rome and the provinces',[28] and the available eleventh-century machinery was seemingly ill-adapted to meet twelfth-century needs.

Yet without the support of willing and able legislative and administrative agents like Hugh of Die, it seems unlikely that Gregory VII's reform initiative would have penetrated the regions of France to the degree that it did. Gregory's use of legates, but also the way(s) in which Hugh of Die exercised, honed, and developed the skills and powers of his office, enabled future developments in the field of papal and legal representation — through greater experience and use — to create a more efficient model and machinery of papal government. It was the work of future popes to shape this legal foundation according to their respective governmental, political, religious, and social needs and expectations.

[26] See Ivo of Chartres, *Epistolae*, letter 109, in *RHGF*, XV (1878), 70–177 (p. 118).

[27] Hiestand, 'Les Légats pontificaux en France', pp. 61, 78.

[28] Southern, *Making of the Middle Ages*, p. 146.

Appendix 1

HUGH OF DIE'S LEGATINE COUNCILS

Under Pope Gregory VII (1073–85)		
1	Anse	1075
2	Dijon	1076
3	Clermont	1076
4	Autun	1077
5	Poitiers	1078
6	Bordeaux	1079
7	Valence	1079
8	Toulouse	1079
9	Avignon	1080
10	Lyon	1080
11	Issoudun	1081
12	Saintes	1081
13	Meaux	1082
Under Pope Urban II (1088–99)		
14	Autun	1094
15	Portus Ansillae	1099

Appendix 2

Hugh of Die's Correspondence

The following correspondence is arranged by chronological order; the sources are listed by letter number, followed by the column or page number in parentheses.

Ref.	Date	Sender	Recipient	Subject	Source
1	1075	Hugh of Die	Archbishop Ralph I of Tours	Invitation to the Council of Anse (1075)	PL, CLVII, 1 (507)
2	1076	Hugh of Die	Archbishop Ralph I of Tours	Invitation to the Council of Dijon (1076)	PL, CLVII, 2 (507–08)
3	1077	Hugh of Die	Archbishop Ralph I of Tours	Invitation to the Council of Clermont (1076)	PL, CLVII, 3 (508)
4	1077	Hugh of Die	Archbishop Ralph I of Tours	Invitation to the Council of Autun (1077)	PL, CLVII, 4 (508–09)
5	?	Hugh of Die	N/A	Donation charter giving the church of the Holy Faith of Castellitum and the church of Saint-Victor to Abbot Bego and the holy faithful of Conches	PL, CLVII, 5 (509)
6	1077	Hugh of Die	Pope Gregory VII	Concerning the Autun Council (1077)	PL, CXLVIII, 8 (744–45); cf. *RHGF*, XIV, 79 (613–14)
7	12 May 1077	Pope Gregory VII	Hugh of Die	Directions concerning the election of Gerard II to the see of Cambrai	*Reg.*, IV. 22

Ref.	Date	Sender	Recipient	Subject	Source
8	Late 1077	Pope Gregory VII	Hugh of Die	Instructs Hugh about the episcopal election at Chartres	*Reg.*, V. 11
9	1078	Hugh of Die	Pope Gregory VII	Concerning the Council of Poitiers (1078)	PL, CLVII, 7 (509–11); cf. *RHGF*, XIV, 80 (615–16)
10	22 Aug. 1078	Pope Gregory VII	Hugh of Die and Hugh of Cluny	Instructs the two Hughs about matters raised in Rome by Archbishop Manasses I of Reims	*Reg.*, VI. 3
11	25 Nov. 1078	Pope Gregory VII	Hugh of Die	Instructs Hugh to investigate the excommunication of Count Robert I of Flanders	*Reg.*, VI. 7
12	1079, April–May	Pope Gregory VII	Hugh of Die	Instructs Hugh on various matters	*Ep. vag.*, 30
13	1079, summer	Pope Gregory VII	Hugh of Die	Instructs Hugh to settle a dispute between Bishop Landeric of Mâcon and Abbot Hugh of Cluny	*Ep. vag.*, 70
14	1080	Archbishop Manasses I of Reims	Hugh of Die	Reasons why Manasses could not attend the Lyonnais council (1080)	*RHGF*, XIV, 9 (781–86)
15	1081	Hugh of Die	All faithful of the Holy Church	Concerning the Council of Meaux (1082)	*RHGF*, XIV, 10 (787–88)
16	1081	Pope Gregory VII	Hugh of Die and Amatus of Oloron	Instructs them to act with restraint in business affecting King William I of England	*Reg.*, IX. 5
17	4 Dec. 1081	Pope Gregory VII	Hugh of Die	Calls on Hugh to account for a judgement passed on Bishop Gosfred of Chartres	*Reg.*, IX. 15
18	24 Oct. 1081–82	Pope Gregory VII	Hugh of Die	Instructs Hugh to expedite an election to Lyon	*Reg.*, IX. 18

Ref.	Date	Sender	Recipient	Subject	Source
19	1081–82	Pope Gregory VII	Hugh of Die and Abbot Richard of Marseille	Instructions to settle a dispute between the clergy of Dax and their opponents	*Ep. vag.*, 44
20	1082–83	Pope Gregory VII	Hugh of Die	Condemns the imprisonment of Bishop Odo of Bayeux by the English king	*Ep. vag.*, 53
21	1082–83	Pope Gregory VII	Hugh of Die	Dispute over the monastery of Saint-Symphorien at Autun	*Reg.*, IX. 32
22	1083	Pope Gregory VII	Hugh of Die	Commits the case of Bishop Lambert of Thérouanne for further investigation	*Reg.*, IX. 33
23	1087	Hugh of Die	Countess Matilda of Tuscany	Concerning the election, promotion, and consecration of Abbot Desiderius of Montecassino as Pope Victor III	PL, CLVII, 8 (511–14)
24	1088	Hugh of Die	Countess Matilda of Tuscany	Ibid.	PL, CLVII, 9 (514–16)
25	1088	Hugh of Die	Archbishop Hugh of Besançon	Dispute between the Archbishop and the monks of Saint-Bénigne, Dijon	PL, CLVII, 10 (516)
26	1094	Hugh of Die	Bishop Lambert of Arras	Invitation to the Council of Autun (1094)	PL, CLVII, 11 (516–17)
27	1094	Hugh of Die	Count Robert of Flanders	Commends Robert's help in restoring Lambert to the see of Arras	PL, CLVII, 12 (517)
28	1094	Hugh of Die	Archbishops, bishops, abbots, and all other faithful of the Church	Absolution of Count Fulk IV (le Réchin) of Anjou	PL, CLVII, 13 (517–18)

Ref.	Date	Sender	Recipient	Subject	Source
29	1094	Hugh of Die	Hugh of Cluny	Donation charter giving the church of Saint-Desiderius (in Brescia) to the Abbot of Cluny	PL, CLVII, 14 (518–19)
30	17 June 1094	Pope Urban II	Hugh of Die	Concerning a dispute between the Archbishop of Vienne and the Bishop of Grenoble	PL, CLI, 116 (389)
31	1095	Hugh of Die	Bishop Lambert of Arras	Informing Lambert about the death of a holy woman from the church of Arras by the name of Emma	PL, CLVII, 15 (519)
32	1095	Hugh of Die	Bishop Lambert of Arras	Instructs Lambert to reconsider a case heard in his court between the Bishop of Amiens and Archdeacon Fulk	PL, CLVII, 16 (519–20)
33	Dec. 1095	Pope Urban II	Hugh of Die	Concerning the primacy of Lyon	PL, CLI, 165 (438–39)
34	1096	Hugh of Die	Bishop Ivo of Chartres	Pleading with Ivo to punish Ursio, the King's *dapifer*, for his capture of a priest by the name of Rotger	PL, CLVII, 17 (520)
35	1096	Hugh of Die	Bishop Agano of Autun	Concerning Hugh of Flavigny's promotion to the abbacy at Saint-Bénigne at Dijon	*RHGF*, XIV, 15 (792)
36	*c.* 1096	Hugh of Die	Abbey of Savigny	Donation charter giving the chapel of Saint-Peter of Compostela and the church of Saint Laurence to Saint-Martin of Savigny	*RHGF*, XIV, 30 (528)
37	1097	Hugh of Die	Bishop Ivo of Chartres	Chastises the Bishop for his part in the election of a new archbishop of Sens, without first seeking his legatine approval	PL, CLVII, 18 (520–22)

Ref.	Date	Sender	Recipient	Subject	Source
38	1097	Hugh of Die	Pope Urban II	Concerning Abbot Robert of Saint-Rémi, Reims	*RHGF*, XIV, 18 (793–94)
39	1097	Pope Urban II	Hugh of Die	Concerning Hugh's involvement in choosing a successor to the see of Die	PL, CLI, 216 (488–89)
40	1097–98	Hugh of Die	Abbot Robert of Molesme	Concerning the beginnings of the Cistercian order	PL, CLVII, 22 (523)
41	1097–98	Hugh of Die	Bishop Robert of Langres	Ibid.	PL, CLVII, 23 (523–24)
42	1097–98	Hugh of Die	Pope Paschal II	Commends the messengers of Alberic and the Cistercian abbot	PL, CLVII, 24 (525)
43	1097–99	Pope Urban II	Hugh of Die	Concerning the adultery of King Philip I of France	PL, CLI, 280 (538)
44	1099	Hugh of Die	Archbishop Daimbert of Sens	Concerning the abbey of Saint-Peter of le Vif (Sens)	PL, CLVII, 19 (522–23)
45	May 1099	Pope Urban II	Hugh of Die	Concerning Archbishop Daimbert of Sens	PL, CLI, 292 (543–44)
46	1099	Pope Urban II	Hugh of Die	Concerning Abbot Robert of the Cistercians	PL, CLI, 295 (545)
47	*c.* 1100	Hugh of Die	Bishop Ismeon of Die	Concerning a dispute over a church in *vallum Guzantium* (Goussainville?) between the monks of Cruas and Bordeaux	Cartulary of Savigny, 870
48	*c.* 1100	Hugh of Die	Abbey of Savigny	Donation charter giving the church of Saint John of Brulliolois to Saint-Martin of Savigny	PL, CLVII, 29 (527–28)
49	*c.* 1100	Hugh of Die	Abbey of Savigny	Donation charter giving the church of Bessenay to Saint-Martin of Savigny	PL, CLVII, 31 (528)

Ref.	Date	Sender	Recipient	Subject	Source
50	1103	Hugh of Die	Archbishop Anselm of Canterbury	Concerning Hugh's safe return from Jerusalem, and Anselm's persecution by the English king	*RHGF*, XIV, 25 (795–96)
51	1103	Hugh of Die	Bishops of Le Puy, Langres, and Cabillon	Invitation to come help Bishop Berard of Mâcon, against the monks of Cluny	*RHGF*, XIV, 26 (796)
52	1106	Hugh of Cluny	Hugh of Die	Donation charter for the church of Saint-Germain	PL, CLVII, 27 (525–26)
53	31 May 1106	Hugh of Die	Charter	Settlement between the monks of Saint-Bénigne, Dijon, and the clerks of Besançon	PL, CLVII, 28 (526–27)
54	1106	Hugh of Die	Archbishop Hugh of Besançon	Concerning the abbey of Saint- Bénigne, Dijon	*RHGF*, XIV, 27 (796–97)
55	*c.* 1093/94	Ivo of Chartres	Hugh of Die	Concerning the state of the church in France	PL, CLXII, 24 (35–36); see trans. by Leclercq
56	*c.* 1094	Ivo of Chartres	Hugh of Die	Concerning the disputed succession to the see of Orléans	PL, CLXII, 54 (65–66)
57	*c.* 1094	Ivo of Chartres	Hugh of Die	Concerning the churches of Beauvais and Nîmes	PL, CLXII, 55 (66–67)
58	?	Ivo of Chartres	Hugh of Die	Challenging Hugh's authority to consecrate elections	PL, CLXII, 59 (69–70)
59	*c.* 1098/99	Ivo of Chartres	Hugh of Die	Concerning the recognition of primacy by the Archbishop of Sens	PL, CLXII, 60 (70–75)
60	?	Ivo of Chartres	Hugh of Die	Concerning the consecration of the Bishop of Nevers	PL, CLXII, 61 (75–76)

Ref.	Date	Sender	Recipient	Subject	Source
61	?	Ivo of Chartres	Hugh of Die	Again, concerning the disputed see of Orléans	PL, CLXII, 66 (82–85)
62	?	Ivo of Chartres	Hugh of Die	Ibid.	PL, CLXII, 68 (87–88)

Appendix 3

REFORMING 'GREGORIAN' LEGATES

The details here are inferred from Gregory's *Register* and *Epistolae vagantes*, and the work of Grosse, Schieffer, Schmutz, Robinson, Goggin, and Cowdrey. It should be noted that the legations noted here cannot always be assigned a specific date or dates. The duration of legatine appointments, as has been seen, was dependent entirely on Pope Gregory VII's purpose in first commissioning them.

The following is based primarily on accounts from the papal *Register* and therefore rarely instructs the legate as to the exact length of his legation. Some legates were dispatched for independent cases, while others served as papal representatives on a more permanent basis. The information in the Source column is divided into collaborative and independent commissioning, but does not provide the precise details (i.e., exact date, region, or duration) of where each legation took place.

Legate(s)	Active in/Appointed	Date	Source
Cardinal-bishop Gerald of Ostia	France, Germany, and Spain	1073–77	*Reg.*, II. 2, 12, 23, 25, 29–30, 51; III. 10; V. 7 ——— With the Roman subdeacon Rainbald: *Reg.*, I. 6, 16, 63, 64 ——— With Cardinal-bishop Hubert of Palestrina: *Ep. vag.*, 14
Hubert (Roman subdeacon)	France and England	1073, 1076–80	*Reg.*, I. 8; III. 10a; IV. 10, 17; V. 19, 22; VI. 7; VII. 1, 16, 23, 25–26; *Ep. vag.*, 23, 34

Legate(s)	Active in/Appointed	Date	Source
Albert (Roman deacon)	France and/or England	1073	*Reg.*, I. 8 (together with Hubert)
Cardinal-deacon Gregory	Bohemia and Italy	1073–74 1077	With Cardinal-deacon Bernard: *Reg.*, I. 17, 38, 44–45 ——— *Reg.*, IV, 26–27
Cardinal-deacon Bernard	Bohemia and Germany	1073–74 1077–78	With Cardinal-deacon Gregory: *Reg.*, I. 17, 38, 44–45 ——— With Abbot Bernard of Marseille: *Reg.*, IV. 23–24; V. 7, 16
Hugh Candidus (Cardinal-priest of San Clemente)	France	1073, 1078?	*Reg.*, I, 6–7; V. 14a
Rainbald (Roman subdeacon)	France and Spain	1073–74	*Reg.*, I, 6, 16, 63, 64 (all with Cardinal-bishop Gerald of Ostia)
Cardinal-bishop Hubert of Palestrina	Germany	1074–75	*Reg.*, II. 25, 29–30, 51; III. 10; *Ep. vag.*, 14 (all with Cardinal-bishop Gerald of Ostia)
John Minutus (Cardinal-priest of S. Maria in Trastavere)	England	Spring 1074	*Reg.*, I. 70 (with Peter)
Peter (Cardinal-priest of S. Grisogono and librarian of the Holy Roman Church)	England	Spring 1074	*Reg.*, I. 70 (with John Minutus)
Archbishop Gerald of Siponto	Serbian Kingdom	1074	*Reg.*, I. 65
Bishop Hugh of Die/Archbishop of Lyon	Northern France and Burgundy	1075–85	See Appendix 2

Legate(s)	Active in/Appointed	Date	Source
Abbot Gepizo of Saint-Bonifazio (Rome) and Abbot Maurus of S. Saba (Rome)	Italy (March of Fermo)	1075	*Reg.*, II. 40, 46, 48
Two unidentified legates	Poland and Russia	1075	*Reg.*, II. 73, and *Reg.*, II. 74
Bishop Amatus of Oloron/Archbishop of Bordeaux	Gascony, Narbonne, and Spain	1074–85	With Abbot Bernard of Saint-Victor: *Reg.*, II. 2; IV. 28; VI. 20 ——— With Hugh of Die: *Reg.*, VI. 24–25; IX. 5, 24, 35 ——— *Reg.*, VII. 10, 20; *Ep. vag.*, 21, 40, 44, 47, 49, 52, 71
Bishop Landulf of Pisa	Corsica	1077–78	*Reg.*, V. 4; VI. 12
Abbot Bernard of Saint-Victor (at Marseille)	Germany	1077–78	With Cardinal-deacon Bernard: *Reg.*, IV. 23–24; V. 7, 16; VI. 15–16 ——— With Bishop Amatus of Oloron: *Reg.*, VI. 20 ——— *Ep. vag.*, 27
Teuzo (monk)	France	1077– *c.* 1079	*Reg.*, IV. 17; V. 22; VII. 1
Cardinal-priest (later abbot) Richard of Saint-Victor (at Marseille)	Spain and France	1078–82?	*Reg.*, V. 21; VIII. 2, 4; IX. 23; *Ep. vag.* 42, 50 ——— With Hugh of Die: *Ep. vag.*, 44
Roger (Roman subdeacon)	France	Spring 1078	*Reg.*, V, 20; *Ep. vag.*, 22 (meant to be carried out with Hugh of Die and Hugh of Cluny; no such meeting ever materialized)

Legate(s)	Active in/Appointed	Date	Source
Peter (unidentified papal legate)	Serbian kingdom	1078	*Reg.*, II. 17; V. 12
Unidentified legate (possibly a papal *nuncio*)	Germany	1078	*Reg.*, V. 15
Cardinal-bishop Peter of Albano	Aquileia, Germany, and France	1078–80	With Ulrich of Padua: *Reg.*, VI. 38 and VII. 3; *Ep. vag.*, 25, 27, 31 ——— *Reg.*, VII. 12; *Ep. vag.*, 38
Bishop Altmann of Passau	Germany	1079–80	*Reg.*, IX. 3, 10; *Ep. vag.*, 26
Abbot Hugh of Cluny	France	1077–78	*Reg.*, IV. 22; V. 20, 22; VI. 2–3; VII. 12, 20; IX. 31, 33–34; *Ep.vag.*, 23, 37–38, 70
Bishop Ulrich of Padua	Aquileia and Germany	1079	With Cardinal-bishop Peter of Albano: *Reg.*, VI. 38; VII. 3; *Ep. vag.*, 27, 31
Bishop Anselm II of Lucca	Lombardy	1080	No evidence in Gregory's correspondence (see *Vita Anselmi*, *Vita Mathildis*, and *De thesauro canusinae*)
Prince Gisulf of Salerno	France	1084	With Cardinal-bishop Peter of Albano: *Reg.*, VIII. 23 ——— *Ep. vag.*, 54
Cardinal-bishop Odo of Ostia	Germany	1084	*Ep. vag.*, 54

BIBLIOGRAPHY

Primary Sources

Acta pontificum Romanorum inedita, ed. by J. Pflugk-Harttung, 2 vols (Tübingen: Fuess, 1880–88)

Amatus of Oloron, *Epistolae*, in *RHGF*, XIV (1806), 762–76

Anselm of Canterbury, *Epistolae*, in PL, CLVIII–CLIX (1903)

——, *The Letters of Saint Anselm of Canterbury*, trans. by Walter Fröhlich, 3 vols (Kalamazoo: Cistercian, 1993)

Baluze, Étienne, *Miscellanea*, 5 vols (Paris: Per Bibliopolarum Societatem, 1678–1715)

Bernard of Clairvaux, *Opera omnia*, PL, CLXXXII (1879)

Bernold of Constance, *Apologeticus super decreta, quae venerabilis papa Gregorius eiusdem nominis septimus in Romana synodo promulgavit contra symoniacos et incontinentes altaris ministros*, in *Libelli de lite imperatorum et pontificum saeculis XI. et XII. conscripti*, ed. by Ernst Dümmler, Friedrich Thaner, and Ernst Sackur, MGH, Libelli, 2 (1892), 60–88

——, *Chronicon*, in *Die Chroniken Bertholds von Reichenau und Bernolds von Konstanz, 1054–1100*, ed. by Ian S. Robinson, MGH, SRG, 14 (2003)

Berthold of Reichenau, *Chronicon*, ed. by Robinson, in MGH, SRG, 14 (2003)

Bonizo of Sutri, *Liber ad amicum*, in *Papal Reform of the Eleventh Century*, trans. by Robinson, pp. 158–261

Briefsammlungen der Zeit Heinrichs IV., ed. by Carl Erdmann and Norbert Fickermann, MGH, Briefe, 5 (1977)

Bruno of Segni, 'The Sermon of the Venerable Bishop Bruno Concerning Simoniacs,' in *Papal Reform of the Eleventh Century*, trans. by Robinson, pp. 377–90

Bullaire de l'Abbaye de Saint-Gilles, ed. by M. l'Abbé Goiffon (Nîmes: Jouve, 1882)

Burchard of Worms, *Decretum*, in PL, CXL (1880), cols 537–1057

Cartulaire de Brioude, ed. by M. Henry Doniol (Clermont: Thibaud, 1863)

Cartulaire de Cormery (791–1505), ed. by M. L'abbé J.-J. Bourassé (Paris: Dumoulin, 1861)

Cartulaire de l'Abbaye de Saint-André-le-Bas de Vienne, in *Collection de cartulaires dauphinois*, ed. by Chevalier (1869), I, 3–207

Cartulaire de Saint-Sernin de Toulouse, ed. by C. Douais (Paris: Picard, 1887)

Cartulaires inédits de la Saintonge: Cartulaire de l'Abbaye Royale de Notre-Dame de Saintes, ed. by Abbé T. Grasilier, 2 vols (Niort: Clouzot, 1871)

The Cartulary of Flavigny, 717–1113, ed. by Constance Brittain Bouchard (Cambridge, MA: Medieval Academy of America, 1991)

The Cartulary of Montier-en-Der, 666–1129, ed. by Constance Brittain Bouchard (Toronto: University of Toronto Press, 2004)

Chartarum viennensis diocesis ineditarum, in *Collection de cartulaires dauphinois*, ed. by Chevalier, (1869), I, 211–316

Chartes et documents de Saint-Bénigne de Dijon, ed. by Maurice Chaume and Georges Chevrier, 2 vols (Dijon: Société des Annales de Bourgogne, 1943)

Chartularium Saviniacense, in *Collection de documents inédits sur l'histoire de France: Cartulaire de l'Abbaye de Savigny* (Paris: Imprimerie impériale, 1853)

Chevalier, Ulysse, ed., *Collection de cartulaires dauphinois*, 10 vols (Lyon: Schevring, 1869–1912)

Chronica Albrici monachi Trium Fontium, ed. by G. H. Pertz, MGH, SS, 23 (1874)

Chronico S. Andreae castri Cameracesii, 1001–1133, ed. by Ludwig Bethmann, in MGH, SS, 7 (1846), pp. 526–50

Chronico S. Benigni Divionensis, in *RHGF*, XII (1877), 310–11

Clarius, *Chronicon Sancti Petri Vivi Senonensis (Chronique de Saint-Pierre-le-Vif de Sens)*, ed. by Robert-Henri Bautier and Monique Gilles (Paris: Éditions du Centre national de la recherche scientifique, 1979)

The Collection in Seventy-four Titles: A Canon Law Manual of the Gregorian Reform, ed. and trans. by John Gilchrist (Toronto: Pontifical Institute of Mediaeval Studies, 1980)

Decretales Pseudo-Isidorianae et capitula Angilramni, ed. by P. Hinschius (Leipzig: Tauchnitz, 1863; repr. Aalen: Scientia, 1963)

De tribulationibus, et angustiis, et persecutionibus Majori-monasterio injuste illatis ab archiepiscopis et clericis S. Mauricii Turonensis; et de adquisitione et renovatione privilegii et libertatis eiusdem ecclesiae [*Tabula of Marmoutier*], in *RHGF*, XIV (1806), 95

Die Briefe des Petrus Damiani, ed. by Kurt Reindel, MGH, Briefe, 2 (1983)

Die Konzilsordines des Früh- und Hochmittelalters, ed. by Herbert Schneider, MGH, Ordines de celebrando concilio (1996)

Dionysius Exiguus, *Collectio prima Decretorum pontificum romanorum*, in PL, LXVII (1863), cols 229–316

Diversorum patrum sententie sive Collectio in LXXIV titulos digesta, ed. by John Gilchrist (Vatican City: Biblioteca Apostolica Vaticana, 1973)

Eadmeri monachi Cantuariensis vita Sancti Anselmi archiepiscopi Cantuariensis (The Life of St Anselm, Archbishop of Canterbury by Eadmer), trans. by R. W. Southern, 2 vols (London: Nelson, 1962)

The Ecclesiastical History of Orderic Vitalis, ed. and trans. by Marjorie Chibnall, 6 vols (Oxford: Clarendon Press, 1969–80)

The 'Epistolae vagantes' of Pope Gregory VII, trans. by H. E. J. Cowdrey (Oxford: Clarendon Press, 1972)

Ex chronico Turonensi, in *RHGF*, XII (1877), 461–78

Gallia Christiana, 16 vols (Paris: Palmé, 1715–1865)

Gesta episcoporum Cameracensium, ed. by Ludwig Bethmann, in MGH, SS, 7 (1846)

Grande cartulaire de la Sauve Majeure, ed. by Charles Higounet and Arlette Higounet-Nadal (Bordeaux: Fédération historique du Sud-Ouest, 1996)

Gregory I, Pope, *Registrum epistularum*, ed. by Dag Norberg, Corpus Christianorum Series Latina, 140 (1982)

Gregory VII, Pope, *Das Register Gregors VII*, ed. by Erich Caspar, MGH, Epistolae Selectae, 2, 2 vols (1920–23)

——, *Epistolae et diplomata pontificia*, PL, CXLVIII (1844)

——, *The Register of Pope Gregory VII*, trans. by H. E. J. Cowdrey (Oxford: Clarendon Press, 2002)

Gregory IX, Pope, *Corpus iuris canonici*, 2 vols, ed. by E. Friedberg (Leipzig: Edelmann, 1878–81; Graz: Akademische Druck- und Verlagsanstalt, 1955)

Hugh of Die, *Epistolae et privilegia*, in PL, CLVII (1898), cols 507–28

——, *Epistolae Hugonis Diensis episcopi*, in *RHGF*, XIV (1806), 776–96

Hugh of Flavigny, *Chronicon Hugonis monachi virdunensis et divionensis abbatis Flaviacensis*, ed. by G. H. Pertz, MGH, SS, 8 (1848), pp. 280–503

Ivo of Chartres, *Epistolae*, in *RHGF*, XV (1878), 70–177

——, *Epistolae*, in *Sancti Ivonis Carnotensis Episcopi opera omnia*, PL, CLXII (1854), cols 1–287

—— (Yves de Chartres), *Correspondance*, ed. by J. Leclercq, Les Classiques de l'histoire de France au Moyen Âge, 22, 2 vols (Paris: Les Belles Lettres, 1949)

Labbe, Philippe, *Sacrosancta concilia ad regiam editionem exacta*, 16 vols (Paris: Societatis typographicae librorum ecclesiasticorum jussu regis constitutae, 1671–72)

La Chronique de Saint-Maixent, ed. by Jean Verdon (Paris: Les Belles Lettres, 1979)

Lanfranc of Canterbury, *De corpore et sanguine domini adversus Berengarium Turonensem*, in PL, CL (1880), cols 407–42

Leo I, Pope, *Sancti Leonis Magni Romani pontificis opera omnia*, PL, LIV (1846)

Mansi, Johannes D., ed., *Sacrorum conciliorum nova et amplissima collectio*, 31 vols (Florence: Apud Antonium Zatta, 1759–98)

Narratio controversiae inter capitulum S. Martini Turonensis et Radulphum eiusdem urbis archiepiscopum, in *RHGF*, XII (1877), 460

Obituarium Lugdunensis ecclesiae, ed. by M.-C. Guigue (Lyon: Scheuring, 1867)

The Oecumenical Councils: From Nicaea I (325) to Nicaea II (787), ed. by Giuseppe Alberigo and others, Corpus Christianorum Conciliorum Oecumenicorum Generalium Decreta, 1, 3rd edn (Turnhout: Brepols, 2006)

Paschal II, Pope, *Epistolae*, in PL, CLXIII (1854), cols 31–470

Patrologia cursus completus [...] series Latina, ed. by Jacques-Paul Migne, 221 vols (Paris: Garnier, 1844–1902)

Paul of Bernried, *Life of Pope Gregory VII*, in *Papal Reform of the Eleventh Century*, trans. by Robinson, pp. 262–364

Peter the Deacon, *Chronicle of Montecassino*, ed. by Hartmut Hoffman, MGH, SS, 34 (1980)

Recueil des actes de Philippe Ier, roi de France (1059–1108), ed. by M. Prou, Chartes et diplômes relatifs à l'histoire de France (Paris: Imprimerie nationale, 1908)

Recueil des historiens des Gaules et de la France, ed. by M. Bouquet, 24 vols (Paris: Palmé, 1738–1904)

Regesta pontificum Romanorum, ed. by P. Jaffé, 2nd edn ed. by W. Wattenbach and others, 2 vols (Leipzig: Veit, 1885–88)

Rodulfi Glabri historiarum libri quinque, ed. by John France (Oxford: Clarendon Press, 1989)

Simonis gesta abbatum S. Bertini Sithiensium, ed. by O. Holder-Egger, MGH, SS, 13 (1881)

Urban II, Pope, *Beati Urbani II Pontificis Romani epistolae et privilegia*, PL, CLI (1844), cols 283–560

——, *Epistolae*, in *RHGF*, XIV (1806), 688–737

Vogel, Cyrille, and Reinhard Elze, *Le pontificale romano-germanique du dixième siècle*, 3 vols (Vatican City: Biblioteca Apostolica Vaticana, 1963)

Secondary Sources

Austin, Greta, 'Authority and the Canons in Burchard's *Decretum* and Ivo's *Decretum*', in *Readers, Texts and Compilers*, ed. by Brett and Cushing, pp. 35–58

——, *Shaping Church Law Around the Year 1000: The 'Decretum' of Burchard of Worms* (Aldershot: Ashgate, 2009)

Autenrieth, Johanne, 'Bernold von Konstanz und die erweiterte 74-Titelsammlung', *DA*, 14 (1958), 375–94

Bachmann, Johannes, *Die päpstlichen Legaten in Deutschland und Skandinavien (1125–1159)*, Historische Studien, 115 (Berlin: Ebering, 1913)

Bachrach, Bernard S., 'A Study in Feudal Politics: Relations between Fulk Nerra and William the Great, 995–1030', *Viator*, 7 (1976), 111–22

——, 'Towards a Reappraisal of William the Great, Duke of Aquitaine (995–1030)', *Journal of Medieval History*, 5 (1979), 11–21

Barstow, Anne Llewellyn, *Married Priests and the Reforming Papacy: The Eleventh-Century Debates*, Texts and Studies in Religion, 12 (New York: Edwin Mellen, 1982)

Becker, Alfons, *Papst Urban II (1088–1099)*, MGH, Schriften, 19. 1 (1964)

——, *Studien zum Investiturproblem in Frankreich: Papsttum, Königtum und Episkopat im Zeitalter der gregorianischen Kirchenreform (1049–1119)*, Schriften der Universität des Saarlandes (Saarbrücken: West-Ost, 1955)

Bendix, Reinhard, *Max Weber: An Intellectual Portrait* (Berkeley and Los Angeles: University of California Press, 1966)

Benson, Robert L., *The Bishop-Elect: A Study on Medieval Ecclesiastical Office* (Princeton: Princeton University Press, 1968)

Benz, Karl Josef, 'Die Regula Benedictini in den Briefen Papst Gregors VII', in *Itinera Domini: Gesammelte Aufsätze aus Liturgie und Mönchtum*, ed. by Emmanuel von Severus (Münster: Aschendorff, 1988), pp. 263–79

Bienvenu, Jean-Marc, 'Les Caractères originaux de la réforme grégorienne dans le diocèse d'Angers', *Bulletin philologique et historique du comité des travaux historiques et scientifiques*, 2 (1968), 545–60

Bligny, Bernard, *L'Église et les ordres religieux dans le royaume de Bourgogne aux XIe et XIIe siècles* (Paris: Persée, 1960)

Blumenthal, Uta-Renate, 'Codex Guarnerius 203: A Manuscript of the *Collection in 74 Titles*', *Bulletin of Medieval Canon Law*, 5 (1975), 11–33

——, 'Conciliar Canons and Manuscripts: The Implications of their Transmission in the Eleventh Century', *Proceedings of the Ninth International Congress of Medieval Canon Law*, ed. by Peter Landau and Joers Mueller (Vatican City: Biblioteca Apostolica Vaticana, 1997), pp. 357–79

——, *Gregor VII. Papst zwischen Canossa und Kirchenreform* (Darmstadt: Primus, 2001)

——, 'Hugh of Die and Lyons, Primate and Papal Legate', in *Lateinische Biographie von der Antike bis in die Gegenwart. Scripturus vitam. Festgabe für Walter Berschin zum 65. Geburtstag*, ed. by Dorothea Walz (Heidelberg: Mattes, 2002), pp. 487–93

——, *The Investiture Controversy: Church and Monarchy from the Ninth to the Twelfth Century* (Philadelphia: University of Pennsylvania Press, 1988)

——, 'The Papacy, 1024–1122', in *NCMH*, IV, pt II (2004), 8–37

——, 'Poitevin Manuscripts, the Abbey of Saint-Ruf, and Ecclesiastical Reform in the Eleventh Century', in *Readers, Texts and Compilers*, ed. by Brett and Cushing, pp. 87–100

——, 'Pope Gregory VII and the Prohibition of Nicolaitism', in *Medieval Purity and Piety*, ed. by Frassetto, pp. 239–67

Blumenthal, Uta-Renate, and Detlev Jasper, '*Licet nova consuetudo* — Gregor VII. und die Liturgie', in *Bishops, Texts*, ed. by Brasington and Cushing, pp. 45–68

Bollenot, Gilles, 'Un Légat pontifical au 11ème siècle: Hugues évêque de Die (1073–1082), Primat des Gaules (1082–1106)' (unpublished doctoral dissertation, Université de Lyon, 1973)

Bouchard, Constance Brittain, 'Burgundy and Provence, 879–1032', in *NCMH*, III (2000), 328–45

——, 'The Geographical, Social and Ecclesiastical Origins of the Bishops of Auxerre and Sens in the Central Middle Ages', *Church History*, 46 (1977), 277–95

——, 'The Kingdom of the Franks to 1108', in *NCMH*, IV, pt II (2004), 120–53

——, 'Laymen and Church Reform around the Year 1000: The Case of Otto-William, Count of Burgundy', *Journal of Medieval History*, 5 (1979), 1–10

——, 'The Origins of the French Nobility: A Reassessment', *American Historical Review*, 86 (1981), 501–32

——, *Sword, Miter, and Cloister: Nobility and the Church in Burgundy, 980–1198* (Ithaca: Cornell University Press, 1987)

Bowman, Steven B., and Blanche E. Cody, eds, *In iure veritas: Studies in Canon Law in Memory of Schafer Williams* (Cincinnati: University of Cincinnati, College of Law, 1991)

Brasington, Bruce C., and Kathleen G. Cushing, eds, *Bishops, Texts and the Use of Canon Law around 1100: Essays in Honour of Martin Brett* (Aldershot: Ashgate, 2008)

Brett, Martin, 'Canon Law and Litigation: The Century before Gratian', in *Medieval Ecclesiastical Studies: In Honour of Dorothy M. Owen* (Woodbridge: Boydell, 1995), pp. 21–40

Brett, Martin, and Kathleen G. Cushing, eds, *Readers, Texts and Compilers in the Earlier Middle Ages: Studies in Medieval Canon Law in Honour of Linda Fowler-Magerl* (Aldershot: Ashgate, 2009)

Brooke, C. N. L., 'Gregorian Reform in Action: Clerical Marriage in England, 1050–1200', *Cambridge Historical Journal*, 12 (1956), 1–21

Brooke, Z. N., 'Pope Gregory VII's Demand for Fealty from William the Conqueror', *English Historical Review*, 26 (1911), 225–38

Brundage, James A., *Law, Sex, and Christian Society in Medieval Europe* (Chicago: University of Chicago Press, 1987)

——, *Medieval Canon Law* (London: Longman, 1995)

——, 'Sexuality, Marriage, and the Reform of Christian Society in the Thought of Gregory VII', *SG*, 14 (1991), 69–73

Bull, Marcus, ed., *France in the Central Middle Ages, 900–1200* (Oxford: Oxford University Press, 2002)

Bur, Michel, *La Formation du comté de Champagne, v.950–v.1150* (Nancy: L'Université de Nancy, 1977)

Cam, Helen M., 'Mediaeval Representation in Theory and Practice', *Speculum*, 29 (1954), 347–55

Cheney, Christopher, 'The Deaths of Popes and the Expiry of Legations in Twelfth-Century England', *RDC*, 28 (1978), 84–96

Chevallier, Jules, *Essai historique sur l'église et la ville de Die*, 8 vols (Montélimar: Bourron, 1888–1909)

Corbet, Patrick, *Autour de Burchard de Worms: L'Église allemande et les interdits de parenté (IXème–XIIème siècle)* (Frankfurt: Klostermann, 2001)

Cowdrey, H. E. J., *The Age of Abbot Desiderius: Montecassino, the Papacy, and the Normans in the Eleventh and Early Twelfth Centuries* (Oxford: Clarendon Press, 1983)

——, 'Cardinal Peter of Albano's Legatine Journey to Cluny', *Journal of Theological Studies*, 24 (1973), 481–91

——, *The Cluniacs and the Gregorian Reform* (Oxford: Clarendon Press, 1970)

——, 'Death-bed Testaments', in *Fälschungen im Mittelalter*, MGH, Schriften, 33, 6 vols (1988), IV, 703–24

——, 'The Gregorian Reform in the Anglo-Norman Lands and in Scandinavia', *SG*, 13 (1989), 321–52

——, 'The Papacy, the Patarenes and the Church of Milan', *Transactions of the Royal Historical Society*, 18 (1968), 25–48

——, 'The Peace and the Truce of God in the Eleventh Century', *Past and Present*, 46 (1970), 42–67

——, *Pope Gregory VII* (Oxford: Clarendon Press, 1998)

——, 'Pope Gregory VII and the Anglo-Norman Church and Kingdom', *SG*, 9 (1972), 79–114

——, 'Pope Gregory VII and the Bishoprics of Central Italy', *Studi medievali*, 34 (1993), 51–64

——, 'Pope Gregory VII and the Chastity of the Clergy', in *Medieval Purity and Piety*, ed. by Frassetto, pp. 269–302

——, *Popes, Monks and Crusaders* (London: Hambledon, 1984)

——, 'Simon Magus in South Italy', *Anglo-Norman Studies*, 15 (1993), 77–90

——, 'The Spirituality of Pope Gregory VII', in *The Mystical Tradition and the Carthusians*, ed. by James Hogg, Analecta cartusiana, 1 (Salzburg: Institut für Anglistik und Amerikanistik Universität Salzburg, 1995), pp. 1–22

——, 'The Structure of the Church, 1024–1073', in *NCMH*, IV, pt I (2004), 229–67

Crozet, René, 'Le Voyage d'Urbain II et ses négociations avec le clergé de France (1095–1096)', *RH*, 179 (1937), 271–310

Cushing, Kathleen G., *Papacy and the Law in the Gregorian Revolution: The Canonistic Work of Anselm of Lucca* (Oxford: Oxford University Press, 1998)

——, *Reform and the Papacy in the Eleventh Century* (Manchester: Manchester University Press, 2005)

d'Arbois de Jubainville, H., *Histoire des ducs des comtes de Champagne depuis le VIe siècle jusqu'à la fin du XIe*, 8 vols (Paris: Durand, 1859–69)

Dauphin, Hubert, 'L'Abbaye Saint-Vanne de Verdun et la querelle des investitures', *SG*, 1 (1947), 237–61

——, *Le Bienheureux Richard, Abbé de Saint-Vanne de Verdun* (Paris: de Brouwer, 1946)

Debord, A., *La Société laïque dans les pays de la Charente, X[e]–XIIe s.* (Paris: Picard, 1984)

De Fontette, François, 'Évêques de Limoges et comtes de Poitou au XIe siècle,' in *Études d'histoire du droit canonique*, 2 vols (Paris: Sirey, 1965), I, 553–58

Degert, A., 'Un ouvrier de la réforme du XIème siècle, Amat d'Oloron', *RQH*, 84 (1908), 33–84

Des Chapelles, M. Grillon, *Notice sur l'Abbaye de Déols* (Paris: Chaix, 1857)

Devailly, Guy, 'Les Restitutions de paroisses au temps de la réforme grégorienne: Bretagne et Berry; Étude comparée', *Bulletin philologique et historique du comité des travaux historiques et scientifiques* (1968), 583–97

——, 'Une Enquête en cours: L'Application de la réforme grégorienne en Bretagne', *Annales de Bretagne*, 75 (1968), 293–316

Dictionnaire d'histoire et de géographie ecclésiastiques, ed. by Luc Courtois and Eddy Louchez, 29 vols to date (Paris: Letouzey et Ané, 1912–)

Dictionnaire du droit canonique, 7 vols (Paris: Letouzey et Ané, 1935–65)

Drioux, Georges, 'Un Diocèse de France à la veille de la réforme gregorienne: Le Pape Léon IX et les évêques de Langres Hugues et Hardoin,' *SG*, 2 (1947), 31–41

Duggan, Charles, 'Papal Judges Delegate and the Making of the "New Law" in the Twelfth Century', in *Lordship, Status, and Process in Twelfth-Century Europe*, ed. by Thomas N. Bisson (Philadelphia: University of Pennsylvania Press, 1995), pp. 172–99

Dunbabin, Jean, *France in the Making, 843–1180* (Oxford: Oxford University Press, 1985)

——, 'West Francia: The Kingdom', in *NCMH*, III (2000), 372–97

Dunken, Gerhard, *Die politische Wirksamkeit der päpstlichen Legaten in der Zeit des Kampfes zwischen Kaisertum und Papsttum in Oberitalien unter Friedrich I*, Historische Studien, 209 (Berlin: Ebering, 1931)

Englberger, Johann, 'Berthold con der Reichenau und die Investiturfrage: Zum Problem eines Investiturverbots der Fastensynode von 1078', *DA*, 53 (1997), 81–117

——, 'Gregor VII. und die Bischofserhebungen in Frankreich: Zur Entstehung des ersten römischen Investiturdekrets vom Herbst 1078', in *Die früh- und hochmittelalterliche Bischoferhebung im europäischen Vergleich*, ed. by Franz-Reiner Erkens (Cologne: Böhlau, 1998), pp. 193–258

Fawtier, Robert, *The Capetian Kings of France: Monarchy and Nation (987–1328)*, trans. by Lionel Butler and R. J. Adam (London: Macmillan, 1960)

Fazy, Max, 'Notice sur Amat, évêque d'Oloron, archevêque de Bordeaux et légat du Saint-Siège', *Bulletin de la faculté des lettres*, 34 (1908), 77–142

Figueira, Robert C., 'The Canon Law of Medieval Papal Legation' (unpublished doctoral dissertation, Cornell University, 1980)

——, 'The Classification of Medieval Papal Legates in the *Liber Extra*', *Archivum historiae pontificiae*, 21 (1983), 211–28

——, 'Decretalists, Medieval Papal Legation, and the Roman Law of Offices and Jurisdiction', *Res publica litterarum*, 9 (1986), 119–35

——, '*Legatus apostolice sedis*: The Pope's "Alter Ego" According to Thirteenth-Century Canon Law', *Studi medievali*, 27 (1986), 527–74

——, 'The Medieval Papal Legate and his Province: Geographical Limits of Jurisdiction', *Apollinaris*, 61 (1988), 817–60 (repr. in *Plenitude of Power: The Doctrines and Exercise of Authority in the Middle Ages; Essays in Memory of Robert Louis Benson*, ed. by Robert C. Figueira (Aldershot: Ashgate, 2006), pp. 73–105)

——, 'Papal Reserved Powers and the Limitations on Legatine Authority', in *Popes, Teachers, and Canon Law in the Middle Ages*, ed. by James R. Sweeney and Stanley Chodorow (Ithaca: Cornell University Press, 1989), pp. 191–211

——, 'Subdelegation by Papal Legates in Thirteenth-Century Canon Law: Powers and Limitations', in *In iure veritas*, ed. by Bowman and Cody, pp. 56–79

Fliche, Augustin, *Histoire de l'église*, VIII: *La réforme grégorienne et la reconquête chrétienne (1057–1123)* (Paris: Bloud & Gay, 1946)

——, 'La Primatie des Gaules depuis l'époque Carolingienne jusqu'à la fin de la querelle des investitures (876–1121)', *RH*, 173 (1934), 329–42

——, *La Réforme Grégorienne*, Spicilegium sacrum Lovaniense, 6, 9, 16, 3 vols (Paris: Bloud & Gay, 1924–37)

——, 'Le Cardinal Humbert de Moyenmoutier: Étude sur les origines de la réforme grégorienne', *RH*, 119 (1915), 41–76

——, 'Le Pontificat de Victor III', *RHE*, 20 (1924), 387–412

——, *Le Règne de Philippe Ier, roi de France (1060–1108)* (Paris: Société française d'imprimerie et de librairie, 1912)

——, 'Y'a-t-il eu en France et en Angleterre une querelle des investitures?', *Revue Benedictine*, 46 (1934), 283–95

Fliche, Augustin, and Victor Martin, *Histoire de l'Église*, 21 vols (Paris: Bloud & Gay, 1945–62)

Fouracre, Paul, and others, eds, *The New Cambridge Medieval History*, 7 vols in 8 books (Cambridge: Cambridge University Press, 1995–2004)

Fournier, Paul, 'Étude sur les Fausses Décrétales', *RHE*, 8 (1907), 19–56

——, 'Le Décret de Burchard de Worms: Ses caractères, son influence', *RHE*, 12 (1911), 670–94 (repr. in *Mélanges de droit canonique*, ed. by Kölzer, I, 393–448)

——, '*Le Liber Tarraconensis*: Étude sur une collection canonique du XIe siècle', in *Mélanges de droit canonique*, ed. by Kölzer, I, 259–81

——, 'Le Premier manuel canonique de la réforme du XI siècle', *Mélanges d'archéologie et d'histoire de l'école française de Rome*, 14 (1894), 147–223

——, 'Les Collections canoniques romaines de l'époque de Grégoire VII', *Mémoires de l'Institut national de France: Académie des inscriptions et belles-lettres*, 41 (1920), 271–397 (repr. in *Mélanges de droit canonique*, ed. by Kölzer, II, 425–550)

Fournier, Paul, and Gabriel Le Bras, *Histoire des collections canoniques en occident depuis les Fauses Décrétales jusqu'au Décret de Gratien*, 2 vols (Paris: Sirey, 1931–32)

Fowler, Linda, '*Recusatio Iudicis* in Civilian and Canonist Thought', *Studia Gratiana*, 15 (1972), 718–85

Fowler-Magerl, Linda, *Clavis canonum: Selected Canon Law Collections Before 1140*, MGH, Hilfsmittel, 21 (2005)

——, 'The Collection and Transmission of Canon Law along the Northern Section of the *Via Francigena* in the Eleventh and Twelfth Centuries,' in *Bishops, Texts*, ed. by Brasington and Cushing, pp. 129–40

——, 'Fine Distinctions and the Transmission of Texts', *ZRG, kan. Abt.*, 83 (1997), 146–86

——, 'The Relationship between Seemingly Unspectacular Pre-Gratian Collections in the Manuscripts Paris, Bibliothèque Nationale, Lat.3858C and Florence, Biblioteca Medicea Laurenziana, Ashburnham 1554', in *Scientia veritatis*, ed. by Münsch and Zotz, pp. 241–60

——, 'Vier franzöisische und spanische vorgratianische Kanonessammlungen', in *Ius commune*, Festgabe für Helmut Coing, 17 (1983), pp. 123–46

Fransen, Gérard, 'Autour de la collection en 74 titres', *RDC*, 25 (1975), 61–73

Frassetto, Michael, ed., *Medieval Purity and Piety: Essays on Medieval Clerical Celibacy and Religious Reform* (New York: Garland, 1998)

Friedlaender, Ina, *Die päpstlichen Legaten in Deutschland und Italien am Ende des XII. Jahrhunderts (1181–1198)*, Historische Studien, 177 (Berlin: Ebering, 1928)

Fuhrmann, Horst, 'Die 74-Titel-Sammlung (*Diversorum patrum sententiae*)', in *Einfluß und Verbreitung der pseudoisidorischen Fälschungen*, 3 vols (Stuttgart: Hiersemann, 1972–74), II, 486–509

——, 'False Decretals', in *The New Catholic Encyclopedia*, V (2003), 822–23

——, 'Papst Gregor VII. und das Kirchenrecht zum Problem des *Dictatus Papae*', *SG*, 13 (1989), 123–49

——, 'Stand, Aufgaben und Perspektiven der Pseudoisidorforschung', in *Fortschritt durch Fälschungen? Ursprung, Gestalt und Wirkungen der pseudoisidorischen Fälschungen*, ed. by Wilfried Hartmann and Gerhard Schmitz (Hannover: Hahn, 2002), pp. 227–62

——, 'Über den Reformgeist der 74-Titel Sammlung (*Diversorum patrum sententiae*),' in *Festchrift für Hermann Heimpel zum 70. Geburtstag*, 3 vols (Göttingen: Vandenhoeck & Ruprecht, 1971–72), II, 1101–20

Galliou, Patrick, and Michael Jones, *The Bretons* (Oxford: Blackwell, 1991)

Gaudemet, Jean, 'Grégoire VII et la France', *SG*, 13 (1989), 213–40

——, 'Regards sur l'histoire du droit canonique antérieurement au Décret de Gratien', *Studia et documenta historiae et iuris*, 51 (1985), 73–130

Gaussin, P. R., *L'Abbaye de la Chaise-Dieu (1043–1518)* (Paris: Cujas, 1962)

——, 'Hugues de Die et l'épiscopat Franco-Bourguignon', *Cahiers d'histoire*, 13 (1968), 77–98

——, *Le Rayonnement de la Chaise-Dieu* (Brioude: Watel, 1981)

Gilchrist, John, 'Canon Law Aspects of the Eleventh-Century Reform Programme', *JEH*, 13 (1962), 21–38

——, *Canon Law in the Age of Reform, 11th–12th Centuries* (Aldershot: Ashgate, 1993)

——, 'Changing the Structure of a Canonical Collection: The *Collection in Seventy-four Titles*, Four Books, and the Pseudo-Isidorian Decretals', in *In iure veritas*, ed. by Bowman and Cody, pp. 93–117

——, 'Eleventh and Early Twelfth Century Canonical Collections and the Economic Policy of Gregory VII', *SG*, 9 (1972), 377–417

——, 'Gregory VII and the Juristic Sources of his Ideology', *Studia Gratiana*, 12 (1967), 3–37

——, 'The Reception of Pope Gregory VII into the Canon Law (1073–1141)', *ZRG, kan. Abt.*, 59 (1973), 35–82

——, 'The Reception of Pope Gregory VII into the Canon Law (1073–1141), Part II', *ZRG, kan. Abt.*, 66 (1980), 192–229

——, '"Simoniaca Haeresis" and the Problem of Orders from Leo IX to Gratian', *Proceedings of the Second International Congress of Medieval Canon Law* (Vatican City: S. Congregatio de seminariis et studiorum universitatibus, 1965), pp. 209–36

——, 'Was there a Gregorian Reform Movement in the Eleventh Century?,' *Canadian Catholic Historical Association*, 37 (1970), 1–10

Giry, A., 'Grégoire VII et les évêques de Térouane', *RH*, 1 (1876), 387–409

Goggin, Hazel, 'Hugh Bishop of Die and Archbishop of Lyons (1073–1106): An Agent of Papal Reform in France' (unpublished doctoral dissertation, Trinity College, Dublin, 1995)

Grosse, Albert, *Der Romanus Legatus nach der Auffassung Gregors VII* (Halle: Kaemmerer, 1901)

Grosse, Rolf, ed., *L'Église de France et la papauté (X^e–XIIIe siècle)* (Bonn: Bouvier, 1993)

Guillot, Olivier, 'Administration et gouvernement dans les États du comté d'Anjou au milieu du XI siècle', in *Histoire comparée de l'administration (IVe–XVIIIe siècles)*, ed. by Werner Paravicini and Karl Ferdinand Werner (Munich: Artemis, 1980), pp. 311–32

——, *Le Comte d'Anjou et son entourage au XIe siècle*, 2 vols (Paris: Picard, 1972)

Guyotjeannin, Olivier, 'L'Influence Pontificale sur les actes épiscopaux français (Provinces écclesiastiques de Reims, Sens et Rouen, XIe–XIIe siècles)', in *L'Église de France et la papauté*, ed. by Grosse, pp. 83–102

Hallam, Elizabeth M., *Capetian France, 987–1328* (London: Longman, 1980)

——, 'The King and the Princes in Eleventh-Century France', *Bulletin of the Institute of Historical Research*, 53 (1980), 143–56

Haller, Johannes, 'Pseudoisidors erstes Auftreten im deutschen Investiturstreit', *SG*, 2 (1947), 91–101

Halphen, Louis, *Le Comté Anjou au XI siècle* (Paris: Picard, 1906)

Hartmann, Wilfried, ed., *Bischof Burchard von Worms, 1000–1025* (Mainz: Selbstverlag der Gesellschaft für Mittelrheinische Kirchengeschicht, 2000)

——, 'Burchards Dekret: Stand der Forschung und offene Fragen', in *Bischof Burchard von Worms*, ed. by Hartmann, pp. 161–66

Healy, Patrick, *The Chronicle of Hugh of Flavigny: Reform and the Investiture Contest in the Late Eleventh Century* (Aldershot: Ashgate, 2006)

——, 'Hugh of Flavigny and Canon Law as Polemic in the Investiture Contest', *ZRG, kan. Abt.*, 91 (2005), 17–58

Hefele, Charles Joseph, and H. Leclercq, *Histoire des conciles*, 12 vols (Paris: Letouzey, 1907–52)

Hiestand, Rudolf, 'Les Légats pontificaux en France du milieu du XIe à la fin du XIIe siècle', in *L'Église de France et la papauté*, ed. by Grosse, pp. 54–80

Hoffmann, Hartmut, and Rudolf Pokorny, *Das Decret des Bischofs Burchard von Worms*, MGH, Hilfsmittel, 12 (1991)

Humbert of Silva-Candida, *Humberti cardinalis libri III. adversus simoniacos*, ed. by F. Thaner, in *Libelli de lite imperatorum et pontificum saeculis XI. et XII. conscripti*, ed. by Ernst Dümmler, Lothar von Heinemann, and Friedrich Thaner, MGH, Libelli, 1 (1891), pp. 95–253

Hunt, Noreen, *Cluny under Saint Hugh* (London: Edward Arnold, 1967)

Huyghebaert, D. Nicolas, 'Un Légat de Grégoire VII en France: Warmond de Vienne', *RHE*, 40 (1944–45), 187–200

Imbart de la Tour, P., *Les Élections épiscopales dans l'église de France du IXème au XIIème siècle: Étude sur la décadence du principe électif* (Paris: Hachette, 1891; repr. Geneva : Slatkine-Megariotis Reprints, 1974)

Janssen, Wilhelm, 'Die päpstlichen Legaten in Frankreich', *Kölner Historische Abhandlungen*, 6 (1961), 1–206

Jasper, Detlev, 'Burchards Dekret in der Sicht der Gregorianer', in *Bischof Burchard von Worms*, ed. by Hartmann, pp. 167–98

——, '*Inveni in canonibus apostolorum* ... Zu einer mittelalterlichen Fälschung auf Papst Clemens I', in *Papsttum, Kirche und Recht im Mittelalter: Festschrift für Horst Fuhrmann zum 65. Geburstag*, ed. by Hubert Mordek (Tübingen: Niemeyer, 1991), pp. 201–13

Jasper, Detlev, and Horst Fuhrmann, *Papal Letters in the Early Middle Ages* (Washington, DC: Catholic University of America Press, 2001)

Kempf, Friedrich, 'Die päpstliche Gewalt in der mittelalterlichen Welt: Eine Auseinandersetzung mit Walter Ullmann', *Miscellanea historiae pontificiae* 21 (1959), 117–69

——, 'Ein zweiter *Dictatus Papae*? Ein Beitrag zum Depositionsanspruch Gregors VII.', *Archivum historiae pontificiae*, 13 (1975), 119–39

Kempf, Friedrich, and others, eds, *Handbook of Church History*, III: *The Church in the Age of Feudalism*, trans. by Anselm Biggs (London: Burn and Oates, 1969)

Kéry, Lotte, *Canonical Collections of the Early Middle Ages (ca.400–1140): A Bibliographical Guide to the Manuscripts and Literature* (Washington, DC: Catholic University of America Press, 1999)

——, *Die Errichtung des Bistums Arras 1093/1094*, Beihefte der Francia, 33 (Sigmaringen: Thorbecke, 1994)

Knox, Ronald, 'Finding the Law: Developments in Canon Law during the Gregorian Reform', *SG*, 9 (1972), 421–66

Kohnle, Armin, *Abt Hugo von Cluny (1049–1109)* (Sigmaringen: Thorbecke, 1993)

Kölzer, Theo, ed., *Mélanges de droit canonique*, 2 vols (Aalen: Scientia, 1983)

Kuttner, Stephan, '*Liber canonicus*: A Note on the *Dictatus papae* c. 17', *SG*, 2 (1947), 387–401

Lackner, Bede K., *The Eleventh-Century Background of Cîteaux* (Washington, DC: Cistercian Publications, 1972)

Ladner, Gerhart B., 'The Concepts of "Ecclesia" and "Christianitas" and their Relation to the Idea of Papal "Plenitudo potestatis" from Gregory VII to Boniface VIII', *Miscellanea historiae pontificiae*, 18 (1954), 49–77

——, 'Gregory the Great and Gregory VII: A Comparison of their Concepts of Renewal', *Viator*, 4 (1973), 3–31

——, 'Two Gregorian Letters: On the Sources and Nature of Gregory VII's Reform Ideology', *SG*, 5 (1956), 221–42

Landau, Peter, 'Burchard de Worms et Gratien: À propos des sources immédiates de Gratien', *RDC*, 48 (1998), 233–45

——, 'Neue Forschungen zu vorgratianischen Kanonessammlungen und den Quellen des gratianischen Dekrets', *Ius Commune*, 11 (1984), 1–29

——, 'Vorgratianische Kanonessammlungen bei Dekretisten und in frühen Dekretalen-Sammlungen', in *Proceedings of the Eighth International Congress of Medieval Canon Law, San Diego, 1988*, ed. by Stanley Chodorow (Vatican City: Biblioteca Apostolica Vaticana, 1992), pp. 94–116

Laurent, M.-H., 'Chanoines et réforme à Aix-en-Provence au XIe siècle', *SG*, 4 (1952), 171–90

Le Bras, Gabriel, 'L'Activité canonique à Poitiers pendant la réforme grégorienne (1049–1099)', in *Mélanges offerts à René Crozet*, ed. by Pierre Gallais and Yves-Jean Riou (Poitiers: Société d'études médiévales, 1966), I, 237–39

——, 'Le Droit romain au service de la domination pontificale', *RHDFE*, 27 (1949), 377–98

Leclercq, J., 'La Collection des lettres d'Yves de Chartres', *Revue Bénédictine*, 56 (1946), 108–25

——, 'Simoniaca Heresis', *SG*, 1 (1947), 523–30

Lexikon des Mittelalters, 9 vols (Munich: Deutscher Taschenbuch, 2003)

Leyser, Karl, *Communications and Power in Medieval Europe: The Gregorian Revolution and Beyond*, ed. by Timothy Reuter (London: Hambledon, 1994)

——, *Medieval Germany and its Neighbours, 900–1250* (London: Hambledon, 1982)

——, 'The Polemics of the Papal Revolution', in *Medieval Germany and its Neighbours, 900–1250* (London: Hambledon, 1982), pp. 138–60

Liebermann, Felix, 'Anselm von Canterbury und Hugo von Lyon', in *Historische Aufsätze dem Andenken an Georg Waitz gewidmet*, ed. by Georg Waitz (Hannover: Hahn, 1886), pp. 156–203

Liron, Jean, *Singularités historiques et litteraires*, 12 vols (Paris: Didot, 1738–40)

Loud, G. A., 'Abbot Desiderius of Montecassino and the Gregorian Papacy', *JEH*, 30 (1979), 305–26

Lühe, Wilhelm, *Hugo von Die und Lyon: Legat von Gallien* (Breslau: Jungfer, 1898)

Magnou-Nortier, Elisabeth, *L'Introduction de la réforme grégorienne a Toulouse (fin XIe–début XII siècle)* (Toulouse: Centre régional de documentation pédagogique, 1958)

——, *La Société laïque et l'église dans la province ecclésiastique de Narbonne (zone cispyrénéene) de la fin du VIIIe a la fin du XIe siècle* (Toulouse: Association des publications de l'Université de Toulouse-Le Mirail, 1974)

Manitius, Max, *Geschichte der lateinischen Literatur des Mittelalters*, 3 vols (Munich: Beck, 1911–31)

Martindale, Jane, '"His Special Friend"? The Settlement of Disputes and Political Power in the Kingdom of the French (Tenth to Mid-Twelfth Century)', *Transactions of the Royal Historical Society*, 5 (1995), 21–58

——, 'Peace and War in Early Eleventh-Century Aquitaine', in *The Ideals and Practice of Medieval Knighthood*, ed. by C. Harper-Bill and R. Harvey (Woodbridge: Boydell, 1992), pp. 147–76

McKeon, Peter R., 'Gregory VII and the Primacy of Archbishop Gebuin of Lyons', *Church History*, 38 (1969), 3–8

McLaughlin, Megan, 'The Bishop as Bridegroom: Marital Imagery and Clerical Celibacy in the Eleventh and Early Twelfth Centuries', in *Medieval Purity and Piety*, ed. by Frassetto, pp. 209–35

Meyer, Otto, 'Reims und Rom unter Gregor VII', *ZRG, kan. Abt.*, 28 (1939), 418–52

Michel, Anton, *Die Sentenzen des Kardinals Humbert, das erste Rechtsbuch der papstlichen Reform*, MGH, Schriften, 7 (1943)

Moore, R. I., *The Birth of Popular Heresy* (London: Edward Arnold, 1975)

——, 'Family, Community and Cult on the Eve of the Gregorian Reform', *Transactions of the Royal Historical Society*, 30 (1980), 49–69

——, *The First European Revolution, c. 970–1215* (Oxford: Blackwell, 2000)

Mor, C. G., 'Le Droit romain dans les collections canoniques des Xe et XIe siècles', *RHDFE*, 6 (1927), 512–24

Mordek, Hubert, '*Proprie auctoritates apostolice sedis*: Ein zweiter *Dictatus papae* Gregors VII.?', *DA*, 28 (1972), 105–32

Mundy, John Hine, *Liberty and Political Power in Toulouse, 1050–1230* (New York: Columbia University Press, 1954)

Münsch, Oliver, and Thomas Zotz, eds, *Scientia veritatis: Festschrift für Hubert Mordek zum 65. Geburstag* (Ostfildern: Thorbecke, 2004)

Murray, Alexander, 'Pope Gregory VII and his Letters', *Traditio*, 22 (1966), 149–201

New Catholic Encyclopedia, 19 vols (Washington, DC: Catholic University of America Press, 1967–95)

Ohnsorge, Werner, *Päpstliche und gegenpäpstliche Legaten in Deutschland und Skandinavien 1159–1181*, Historische Studien, 175 (Berlin: Ebering, 1928)

Ourliac, Paul, 'Le Concile de Toulouse de 1079', in *Mélanges offerts à Jean Dauvillier*, ed. by Mireille Castaing-Sicard and Germain Sicard (Toulouse: Centre d'histoire juridique méridionale, 1979), pp. 617–33

Pacaut, Marcel, 'Les Légats d'Alexandre III (1159–1181)', *RHE*, 50 (1955), 821–38

Pelster, F., 'Das Dekret Burkhards von Worms in einer Redaktion aus dem Beginn der gregorianischen Reform', *SG*, 1 (1947), 321–51

Perrin, John W., '"Legatus" in Medieval Roman Law', *Traditio*, 29 (1973), 357–78

——, 'Legatus, the Lawyers and the Terminology of Power in Roman Law', *Studia Gratiana*, 11 (1967), 461–90

Petersmann, Johanna, 'Die kanonistische Uberlieferung des Constitutum Constantini bis zum Dekret Gratians', *DA*, 30 (1974), 356–449

Pontal, Odette, 'Les Caractères et l'évolution des conciles de la France capétienne du Xe siècle jusqu'à 1215', *Annuarium historiae conciliorum*, 30 (1998), 185–95

—, *Les Conciles de la France capétienne jusqu'en 1215* (Paris: Cerf, 1995)

—, *Les Statuts Synodaux*, Typologie des Sources du Moyen Âge Occidental, 11 (Turnhout: Brepols, 1975)

Rennie, Kriston R., 'The Application of Reform in Eleventh-Century France: The Conciliar Activity of Hugh, Bishop of Die (1073–82), Archbishop of Lyons (1082–1106), and Legate to Gregory VII (1075–85)' (unpublished doctoral dissertation, King's College, London, 2005)

—, 'The *Collectio Burdegalensis*: A Poitevin Collection?', in *Proceedings of the Thirteenth International Congress of Medieval Canon Law, Esztergom, Hungary, 3–9 August 2008* (Vatican City: Biblioteca Apostolica Vaticana, forthcoming)

—, 'The *Collectio Burdegalensis* and the Transmission of Canonical Texts to Bordeaux *c.* 1079', *ZRG, kan. Abt.*, 94 (2008), 1–20

—, 'The Council of Poitiers (1078) and Some Legal Considerations', *Bulletin of Medieval Canon Law*, 27 (2008), 1–20

—, 'Extending Gregory VII's "Friendship Network": Social Contact in Late Eleventh-Century France', *History*, 93 (2008), 475–96

—, 'Hugh of Die and the Legatine Office under Gregory VII: On the Effects of a Waning Administration', *RHE*, 103 (2008), 27–49

—, '*Imbutus divinis dogmatibus*: Some Remarks on the Legal Training of Gregorian Legates', *RHDFE*, 85 (2007), 301–13

—, 'Reform in the Localities: The Council of Valence (May 1079)', *Annuarium historiae conciliorum*, 37 (2005), 43–55

—, '"Uproot and Destroy, Build and Plant": Legatine Authority Under Pope Gregory VII (1073–85)', *Journal of Medieval History*, 33 (2007), 166–80

Reuter, Timothy, 'Gifts and Simony', in *Medieval Transformations: Texts, Power, and Gifts in Context*, ed. by Esther Cohen and Mayke B. De Jong (Leiden: Brill, 2001), pp. 157–68

Reynolds, Roger E., 'The Liturgy of Rome in the Eleventh Century: Past Research and Future Opportunities', in *Scientia veritatis*, ed. by Munsch and Zotz, pp. 227–39

—, 'The Turin Collection in Seven Books: A Poitevin Canonical Collection', *Traditio*, 25 (1969), 508–14

Richard, Alfred, *Histoire des comtes de Poitou, 778–1204*, 2 vols (Paris: Picard, 1903)

Richard, Jean, *Les Ducs de Bourgogne et la formation du duché du XIe au XIVe siècle* (Paris: Les Belles Lettres, 1954)

Robinson, I. S., *Authority and Resistance in the Investiture Contest* (Manchester: Manchester University Press, 1978)

—, 'Church and Papacy', in *The Cambridge History of Medieval Political Thought, c. 350–c. 1450*, ed. by J. H. Burns (Cambridge: Cambridge University Press, 1988), pp. 252–305

—, 'The Dissemination of Letters of Pope Gregory VII during the Investiture Contest', *JEH*, 34 (1983), 175–93

—, 'The Friendship Network of Gregory VII', *History*, 63 (1978), 1–22

—, 'Gregory VII and the Soldiers of Christ', *History*, 58 (1973), 169–92

——, 'The Institutions of the Church, 1073–1216', in *NCMH*, IV, pt I (2004), 368–460

——, *The Papacy 1073–1198: Continuity and Innovation* (Cambridge: Cambridge University Press, 1990)

——, ed. and trans., *The Papal Reform of the Eleventh Century: Lives of Pope Leo IX and Pope Gregory VII* (Manchester: Manchester University Press, 2004)

——, '*Periculoso Homo*: Pope Gregory VII and Episcopal Authority', *Viator*, 9 (1978), 103–31

——, 'Pope Gregory VII (1073–1085): Bibliographical Surveys II', *JEH*, 36 (1985), 439–83

——, 'Pope Gregory VII, the Princes and the Pactum 1077–1080', *English Historical Review*, 94 (1979), 721–56

——, 'Reform and the Church, 1073–1122', in *NCMH*, IV, pt I (2004), 268–334

Rolker, Christof, *Canon Law and the Letters of Ivo of Chartres* (Cambridge: Cambridge University Press, 2010)

——, 'The *Collection in Seventy-four Titles*: A Monastic Canon Law Collection from Eleventh-Century France', in *Readers, Texts and Compilers*, ed. by Brett and Cushing, pp. 59–72

Rony, Abbé, 'Élection de Victor II: Conflit entre le nouveau pape et Hugues, archevêque de Lyon', *RHEF*, 14 (1928), 145–60

——, 'Hugues de Romans: Légat Pontifical (1073–1106)', *RQH*, 107 (1927), 287–303

——, 'La Légation d'Hugues, archevêque de Lyon, sous le pontificat d'Urbain II (1088–1099)', *RQH*, 112 (1930), 124–46

——, 'La Politique française de Grégoire VII: Conflit entre le pape et son légat', *RQH*, 108 (1928), 5–34

Ryan, J. Joseph, *Saint Peter Damiani and his Canonical Sources: A Preliminary Study in the Antecedents of the Gregorian Reform* (Toronto: Pontifical Institute of Mediaeval Studies, 1956)

Sayers, Jane E., *Papal Judges Delegate in the Province of Canterbury, 1198–1254* (Oxford: Oxford University Press, 1971)

Schieffer, Rudolf, *Die Entsehung des päpstlichen Investiturverbots für den deutschen König*, MGH, Schriften, 28 (1981)

Schieffer, Theodor, *Die päpstlichen Legaten in Frankreich vom Vertrage von Meersen (870) bis zum Schisma von 1130*, Historische Studien, 263 (Berlin: Ebering, 1935)

Schmutz, Richard Antone, 'The Foundations of Medieval Papal Representation' (unpublished doctoral dissertation, University of Southern California, 1966)

——, 'Medieval Papal Representatives: Legates, Nuncios, and Judges-Delegate', *Studia Gratiana*, 15 (1972), 441–63

Smith, Julia M. H., 'The "Archbishopric" of Dol and the Ecclesiastical Politics of Ninth-Century Brittany', *Studies in Church History*, 18 (1982), 59–70

Smith, L. M., 'Cluny and Gregory VII', *English Historical Review*, 26 (1911), 20–33

Somerville, Robert, 'Cardinal Stephan of St Grisogono: Some Remarks on Legates and Legatine Councils in the Eleventh Century', in *Law, Church and Society: Essays in Honor of Stephan Kuttner*, ed. by Kenneth Pennington and Robert Somerville (Philadelphia: University of Pennsylvania Press, 1977), pp. 157–66

——, 'The Councils of Gregory VII', *SG*, 13 (1989), 33–54

——, 'The French Councils of Pope Urban II: Some Basic Considerations', *Annuarium historiae conciliorum*, 2 (1970), 56–65

——, *Papacy, Councils and Canon Law in the 11th–12th Centuries* (Aldershot: Ashgate, 1989)

Somerville, Robert, and Bruce Brasington, *Prefaces to Canon Law Books in Latin Christianity: Selected Translations, 500–1245* (New Haven: Yale University Press, 1998)

Southern, Richard W., *The Making of the Middle Ages* (London: Hutchinson, 1953)

——, *Western Society and the Church in the Middle Ages* (Harmondsworth: Penguin, 1970)

Sweeney, James Ross, 'Gregory VII, the Reform Program, and the Hungarian Church at the End of the Eleventh Century', *SG*, 14 (1991), 265–75

Tardif, Joseph, 'Une Collection canonique poitevine', *RHDFE*, 21 (1897), 149–216

Tellenbach, Gerd, *The Church in Western Europe from the Tenth to the Early Twelfth Century*, trans. by Timothy Reuter (Cambridge: Cambridge University Press, 1993)

——, *Church, State and Christian Society at the Time of the Investiture Contest*, trans. by R. F. Bennett (Oxford: Blackwell, 1940; repr. 1959)

Tillier, Jean-Claude, 'Les Conciles provinciaux de la province ecclésiastique de Bordeaux au temps de la réforme grégorienne (1073–1100)', *Bulletin philologique et historique du comité des travaux historiques et scientifiques*, 2 (1968), 561–81

Ullmann, Walter, *The Growth of Papal Government in the Middle Ages* (London: Methuen, 1955)

——, *A History of Political Thought in the Middle Ages* (Harmondsworth: Penguin, 1965)

——, *Medieval Papalism: The Political Theories of the Medieval Canonists* (London: Methuen, 1949)

——, *Principles of Government and Politics in the Middle Ages* (New York: Barnes and Noble, 1961)

——, '*Romanus Pontifex indubitanter efficitur sanctus*: *Dictatus papae* 23 in Retrospect and Prospect', *SG*, 6 (1959–61), 229–64

Vones-Liebenstein, U., 'Der Verband der Regularkanoniker von Saint-Ruf: Entstehung, Struktur und normative Grundlagen', in *Regula Sancti Augustini: Normative Grundlage differenter Verbände im Mittelalter*, ed. by Gerd Melville and Anne Müller, Publikationen der Akademie der Augustiner-Chorherren von Windesheim, 3 (Paring: Augustiner-Chorherren, 2002), pp. 49–103

——, 'Les Débuts de l'abbaye de Saint-Ruf à Avignon au XIe siècle: Contexte politique et religieux', in *Crises et réformes dans l'église de la réforme grégorienne a la préréforme* (Paris: CTHS, 1991), pp. 9–25

Weber, Max, *Economy and Society*, ed. by Guenther Roth and Claus Wittich, 2 vols (Berkeley and Los Angeles: University of California Press, 1978)

Weigand, Rudolf, 'Mittelalterliche Texte: Gregor I., Burchard und Gratian', *ZRG kan. Abt.*, 84 (1998), 330–44

Weiss, Stefan, *Die Urkunden der päpstlichen Legaten von Leo IX. bis Coelestin III. (1049–1198)* (Cologne: Böhlau, 1995)

Williams, John R., 'Archbishop Manasses I of Rheims and Pope Gregory VII', *American Historical Review*, 54 (1949), 804–24

Wojtowytsch, Myron, '*Proprie auctoritates apostolice sedis*: Bemerkungen zu einer bisher unbeachteten Überlieferung', *DA*, 40 (1984), 612–21

Zema, D. B., 'Economic Reorganization of the Roman See during the Gregorian Reform', *SG*, 1 (1947), 137–68

——, 'Reform Legislation in the Eleventh Century and its Economic Import', *Catholic Historical Review*, 27 (1941), 16–38

Index

Medieval Church Studies

All volumes in this series are evaluated by an Editorial Board, strictly on academic grounds, based on reports prepared by referees who have been commissioned by virtue of their specialism in the appropriate field. The Board ensures that the screening is done independently and without conflicts of interest. The definitive texts supplied by authors are also subject to review by the Board before being approved for publication. Further, the volumes are copyedited to conform to the publisher's stylebook and to the best international academic standards in the field.

Titles in Series

Megan Cassidy-Welch, *Monastic Spaces and their Meanings: Thirteenth-Century English Cistercian Monasteries* (2001)

Elizabeth Freeman, *Narratives of a New Order: Cistercian Historical Writing in England, 1150–1220* (2002)

The Study of the Bible in the Carolingian Era, ed. by Celia Chazelle and Burton Van Name Edwards (2003)

Perspectives for an Architecture of Solitude: Essays on Cistercians, Art, and Architecture in Honour of Peter Fergusson, ed. by Terryl N. Kinder (2004)

The Voice of Silence: Women's Literacy in a Men's Church, ed. by T. de Hemptinne and M. E. Góngora Diaz (2004)

Emilia Jamroziak, *Rievaulx Abbey and its Social Context, 1132–1300: Memory, Loyalty, and Networks* (2005)

Saints, Scholars, and Politicians: Gender as a Tool in Medieval Studies, ed. by Mathilde van Dijk and Renée Nip (2005)

Text and Controversy from Wyclif to Bale: Essays in Honour of Anne Hudson, ed. by Helen Barr and Ann M. Hutchison (2005)

Alison I. Beach, *Manuscripts and Monastic Culture: Reform and Renewal in Twelfth-Century Germany* (2007)

Lena Roos, *'God Wants It!' The Ideology of Martyrdom in the Hebrew Crusade Chronicles and its Jewish and Christian Background* (2007)

Weaving, Veiling, and Dressing: Textiles and their Metaphors in the Late Middle Ages, ed. by Kathryn M. Rudy and Barbara Baert (2007)

James J. Boyce, *Carmelite Liturgy and Spiritual Identity: The Choir Books of Kraków* (2009)

Studies in Carthusian Monasticism in the Late Middle Ages, ed. by Julian M. Luxford (2009)

In Preparation

Gunilla Iversen, *Laus angelica: Poetry in the Medieval Mass*, ed. by Jane Flynn, trans. by William Flynn

Kevin J. Alban, *The Teaching and Impact of the 'Doctrinale' of Thomas Netter of Walden (c. 1374– 1430)*